NORWAY MEETS AMERICA

The Story of My Parents

by Margrethe Hoff

Edited by Dr Bradley James Elliott

ISBN: 979-8332-8564-8-8

Cover spread design by: John Huber
Interior Layout and Design: Blake Arensen

Written in loving memory of
my mother,
Jeanne Rood Hoff,
and
my father,
Ørnulf "Ernie" Hoff,
especially for all their adored grandchildren:
Lucia, Sara
Mishawn, Jack
Mikael, Joshua, Matthew, Benjamin, Hannah
Brent Jr, Seth, Ian
Esther, Ruth, TJ, Luke
…and their children

"Honor thy father and mother…"

PREFACE

When my mother passed away in January 2003, it deeply grieved me that my daughter, my nieces, and my nephews would not have their grandmother to influence and love them. I wanted them all to know her well so I began this book about Mom for them.

Writing out my own memories has also been therapy for my wounded, grieving heart, having "lost" Mom to Alzheimer's years before she left us physically.

Over the years I had gathered Ma's old letters to her Aunt Esther and from her Grandpa Travis. I reviewed my own journals, too, where I had collected letters and emails. I looked at photos, reviewed Ma's journals, and interviewed some of Ma's friends and my father. Dad was not a big talker, and especially about the war years. The most effective method for the loosening of the tongue was asking questions nonchalantly after pumping him with a glass of Cabernet Sauvignon. I wrote on and off over the years, *"as the Spirit moved me,"* as Ma used to say. When Dad passed on at the end of 2017, I knew I wanted to honor him as well and wished I knew more of his story.

In January 2023, I broke my right distal radius, and could do almost nothing: no piano, no guitar, no writing, no driving. I decided to research more about my father's story on-line and, much to my amazement, found several resources including people in Norway, Sweden and on the Isle of Man who kindly sent me documents. All of this shed a bright light on Dad's escape to Sweden on skis and his top-secret transfer to London. It also cast a bright light on my grandfather's imprisonment by the Nazis.

My dad's sister in Norway, Tante Gerd, shared her memories, too. Even now it is the highlight of every week, the day my husband

and I call "Pancake Thursday (*Pann'kak' torsdag*) when we eat blueberry pancakes (in memory of my Norwegian grandmother, Farmor) and then call Tante Gerd. So much laughter. Such a delight she is, sharp as a tack. Her insights have been invaluable and we call her "The Oracle."

In October 2023 my husband James and I went to visit my cousins in Trondheim (where Dad grew up) and to Larvik to see Tante Gerd and more cousins, and then to Røros and Stugudalen to meet with new friends and learn more about the time and the area Dad skied to freedom. So many kind Norwegians helped us! In fact, each time we go to Norway, we fall a little more deeply in love with the country and the people, just like my American mother did.

As you read this book you will see some common threads running throughout, for example, words relating to music, song, singing or melody appear well over six hundred times! Clearly our family breathes music in and out as deeply as fresh air itself.

This book contains *my* memories of my dear parents and our American Norwegian family in addition to information from the various sources mentioned. Living away from my parents for so many years in Luxembourg brought me closer to them in some ways. I tried to make up for the distance by writing and calling often, so correspondence between us brought us nearer and gave me treasured recollections of my parents.

This book is not an exhaustive biography but it does capture some of the key interesting stories, alongside my best memories of my parents.

Memories do not read like a slide under a microscope but they are chiseled into our minds and taken out for review over time, cherished and put back in place. I do not claim to have recorded them with the precision of an analytical chemist but I have written them as accurately as I recall, as I heard, as I experienced.

May these memories be a blessing to you, too.

"Whatever things are true, whatever things are noble...whatever things are lovely, whatever things are of good report, if there is any virtue... anything praiseworthy – think on <u>these</u> things."

Hoff Family Tree

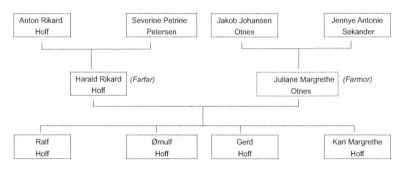

| Anton Rikard Hoff | Severine Petrine Petersen | Jakob Johansen Otnes | Jennye Antonie Sekander |

| Harald Rikard Hoff *(Farfar)* | Juliane Margrethe Otnes *(Farmor)* |

| Ralf Hoff | Ørnulf Hoff | Gerd Hoff | Kari Margrethe Hoff |

Rood Family Tree

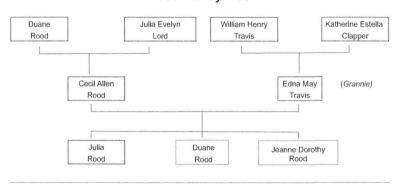

| Duane Rood | Julia Evelyn Lord | William Henry Travis | Katherine Estella Clapper |

| Cecil Allen Rood | Edna May Travis *(Grannie)* |

| Julia Rood | Duane Rood | Jeanne Dorothy Rood |

Our Family Tree

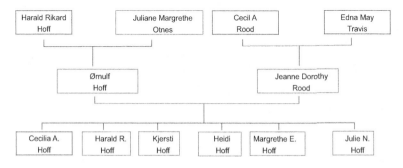

| Harald Rikard Hoff | Juliane Margrethe Otnes | Cecil A Rood | Edna May Travis |

| Ørnulf Hoff | Jeanne Dorothy Rood |

| Cecilia A. Hoff | Harald R. Hoff | Kjersti Hoff | Heidi Hoff | Margrethe E. Hoff | Julie N. Hoff |

CONTENTS

CHILDHOOD MEMORIES OF AN AMERICAN - NORWEGIAN FAMILY

I knew we were close to home when the yellow school bus descended the mountain, curving around winding River Road. The tailwind of our passing made dandelions, daisies and brown-eyed Susans sway in a gentle dance. The bus entered a tunnel of trees, protective branches intertwined above, forming a leafy canopy. The world briefly turned a warm, pale golden green. Coming back into the light, we passed our neighbors, the Thomas', house.

A smile spread across my five-year old face as Bill, bus driver and owner of "Bill's Meat Market" in our small town of Deposit, New York, stopped at Box 7 to let me off at "Chestnut Grove". It was a fine day, full of the promise of late spring. Sunshine warmed my fair head as I carefully crossed the country road. I ran down the sidewalk, jumping every crack of the large square rocks embedded side by side. I hopped up the two massive stone slab steps between the enormous pillars of the front porch. The front door was open, and passing through the screen door I called out, "Maa-aa, I'm HOO-OME!"

O, the lovely "safe" feeling, knowing Mom would always be there, waiting for me with a hug and a ready smile! Her presence smoothed over the days' events gone awry.

I sniffed the delightful smell that greeted me. Mmmmmm, something chocolate baking in the oven. I turned the hallway corner and looked across the dining room. There she was in the kitchen, standing at the sink by the window looking out on a purple lilac bush. She had an apron 'round her waist, and she turned towards me, her large brown eyes twinkling, "How was school today, Mags?" She wiped her hands on a faded dish towel, and put her arms around me. I gave her a big hug, and told her about my day. What a treat to have her to myself for a few hours those afternoons! Kindergarten only lasted half-days then. I was the last child of five at that point, and the others wouldn't be home for a while.

Some days I had to share Ma with Gretel, a 3-year-old Norwegian girl Ma babysat. This gave Ma the chance to exercise her favorite language, Norwegian, and to earn some extra money. Ma's love of Norway and Norwegians meant she was always seeking them out, including Gretel's parents. Ma had lived and worked in Norway, and spoke impeccable Norwegian. I didn't speak Norwegian then but kids always manage to communicate somehow. I taught Gretel "jump-the-dandelions," a game I'd invented, out in the tall grass of the field beside our house. I showed her all the wonders of nature: fascinating spitballs on weed stalks, how to make a blade of grass sing holding it between your two thumbs sideways and blowing hard, snapping open "touch-me-nots" by tapping under the hanging bloated lobes, and checking if she liked butter by holding a small buttercup under her chin.

One cool day, Gretel and I were playing out in the field. Ma came out with our Norwegian sweaters so we wouldn't get cold. Ma handed me my sweater, made by my Norwegian grandmother, and she helped Gretel get into hers. I was jealous of the attention Ma gave this little interloper, and I looked on with disdain, clutching my sweater in clenched fists.

Ma looked at me and understood at once.

"Here, let me help you with those clasps."

My icy glare melted in the warmth of her tone. She hugged me and went back inside. There Ma would be busy washing, folding clothes and cleaning. "A woman's work is never done," she said. Especially true for a woman with five children.

Jeanne Dorothy Rood of upstate New York, and Ørnulf "Ernie" Hoff of Trondheim, Norway met in Oslo, Norway and married in a grand cathedral, Nidaros Domkirke in Trondheim, when she was 28 years old. Oddly enough, they did not seem to be able to have children at first. They married rather late compared to the norm for the 1950s: Ma was already *ancient* for childbearing back then. Hence, everyone assumed they would have children straight away after marriage, but, as she said, "It didn't work out that way. It wasn't that we were trying to avoid it, it just didn't happen."

Sadly, her first pregnancy ended in a miscarriage, after about 2 months. Then in December 1955, three years after they had tied the knot, when Ma was 32, their first child was born. She was a sweet girl with curly blond hair. "We named her Cecilia, after my father Cecil," she said. He had recently passed away.

Harald, Ma's favorite (only) son was born less than 2 years later. He was named after Dad's father, Harald Rikard Hoff. Celia called him Beau, supposedly since she couldn't say *boy*, which is what Dad was hoping for again the next time around. Regarding procreation, Ma used to say, "Once I got started, it just didn't stop." She had only wanted 2 kids. "I had a girl and a boy and I thought that was enough, but your *father...*" On that score, children numbers 3 through 6 (all girls) are glad for the paternal influence.

Somehow Ma managed to maintain her sanity, although it was often at risk. At one point she had three children under the age of 4 years old, and my parents weren't even Catholic. She used to say, "I'm worse than the old lady who lived in a shoe, she had so many children, she didn't know what to do." The chaos of small kids meant she often had to wash clothes and bake in the evenings since there was no time for such activity during the day.

Beyond the great workload, her little ones brought much joy and many a smile to her face. There were stories about each of us, which Ma told us many times over the years. Once Ma noticed little Cecilia looking up at the sky. "Whatchya doin,' Ce?" Ma asked her. "I'm sick 'n tired 'n I'm goin' up," came back the small voice. Ma smiled, recognizing a line from one of her many relatives, who had answered Celia's question as to why an elderly lady had died.

Brother Beau was an imaginative child, but his creativity

sometimes bore disastrous results. When he was in his "Superman" phase, he dove through a window Ma had just cleaned, thinking the glass was not yet back in place. Luckily, neither he nor his Superman costume were hurt.

Kjersti, the beautiful strawberry blond, who we call Kjer (pronounced Cher), was born after Beau in December 1958. Regarding her birth, she always used to remind us that 1) she was the only child for whose birth Daddy was present and 2) she was born on a Sunday, and according to the old nursery rhyme, "Sunday's child is bonny, blithe, and gay". (My mother hated the fact that the original meaning of that word had changed. "It was such a nice word and now you can't even use it hardly without things being confused.")

Kjersti was a child who wanted things to be "just so," and Ma used to call her "The Duchess." At a birth weight of "only" 8 pounds, she was the smallest of Ma's babies (the scrawny runt, we'd affectionately called her years later). Kjer complained about being short, as the rest of us were tall. Ma used to tell her in that sing-song voice, "Remember, good things come in small packages." Beau used to say they'd actually *found* Kjer under a skunk cabbage, those strange round plants that grew down by the river, and stunk to high heaven when you kicked them (and then ran like the devil).

Heidi came next, a lovely girl with Ma's brown hair and deep brown eyes, born in November 1960. Her delivery was not one of the easiest, and the doctor had to use forceps. Before Heidi was born, Ma told her friend Alice Fish about a dream she'd had.

"Alice, I had a dream that I had a big baby girl, and she was dressed in a lovely yellow dress!"

"Another girl?" said Alice.

"Well, yes."

After Heidi's birth, Alice came in to visit. She threw the yellow dress on the hospital bed and said, "Well you've got the baby girl and here's the yellow dress to go with her!" Ma told this story many times. (There is a bit of confusion over *which* baby girl was involved. My sisters may argue on that point. I think it was for Heidi's birth).

The Hoff family of 7 in 1963

Where was Daddy, each time the stork arrived? According to Ma, he was usually on the golf course. In those days, fathers were not expected to participate.

I was supposed to be the last, born in early May 1963, an adorable, modest little blondie with blue eyes. Ma was pushing 40. She used to tell me that I was her Mother's Day present. My brother Beau, who had wanted a brother, asked if they couldn't call me "Margrethe Edna *Harald* Hoff." They dropped the Harald, fortunately for me, and so I was the namesake of both my grandmothers minus my brother. (Ma's mother, our beloved Grannie, was named Edna May Rood. Dad's mother was Margrethe Hoff, our dear Farmor.)

Ma wrote me once:

> Well, I remember when you were born. I was staying in Grannie's apartment - - she was up in Endwell with Ernie and the other kids. My nephew Tony took me to the hospital. Had Mother's Day in the hospital so we got carnations on our tray.
>
> You were born between 4 and 5:30 pm so Dr. Dungan (who was in reserve officers) had to go to his drill group. He said anytime he got through before 6 he had to go. I think it was on a Thursday.
>
> So much for that. Rev. Fear said, 'She looks just like Mr. Hoff!' Guess that is true too. You two think a lot alike too.

I was born at the Read Memorial Hospital in Hancock, delivered by Dr. C. E. Dungan. I weighed 11 pounds, 13 ½ ounces. I was baptized by Rev. Fear in the Methodist church in

Hancock when I was 2 months old. I know these details because Ma, God bless her, actually managed to put together a baby book for me, even for poor old child number 5. There are a total of 6 photos in it, like the six years I enjoyed being spoiled as the baby of the family.

In 1966, we moved from Endwell, New York as my parents had bought the beautiful 15-room colonial-style house known as Chestnut Grove, with a property sprawled out over 4 acres on River Road, one mile outside of Deposit, NY. The house was built in 1847 by a wealthy man named Alvin Devereux. It was a perfect place to raise a large family. It was not a house, it was a mansion. Besides innumerable bedrooms and two large living rooms, there were back rooms, and two bathrooms.

Living in such a populous family, I longed for solitude at times. My bedroom had a working sink above a shiny white cupboard which was perfect when you needed to disappear. There were closets which bore hidden corners and shelves big enough for a small child to climb upon, to create secret spaces for reading. Off the pantry, by the kitchen, there was a dark, musty old closet, which had potential as a great hiding place, but was a shade too spooky for me. Daddy's super long fishing boots hung there and ancient pickle jars lined the shelves. I swear, there were other miscellaneous items in there dating back to the original owners.

A narrow second set of stairs descended into a back room, by which you could easily sneak into the playroom to escape an unwanted encounter. Otherwise, you could stop in the small square space between two doors, to peer through the keyhole into the playroom, spying presence unbeknownst to others. This was important when playing "Sherlock Hemlock" with my friend Julie Feehan, who also came from a large family. We dressed up like male detectives and carried a tiny notebook, carefully writing down what we observed happening in the house. It was a splendid house to live and play within.

Outside, there was a delightful side porch looking down into the valley, where a gentle breeze blew on hot summer days, a wonderful place for reading, or just "sittin' and visitin.'" The porch was sheltered under the outstretched arms of the great oaks. My mother adored the big old oak and maple trees surrounding our home. One of her favorite poems was "I think that I shall never see / A poem lovely as a tree" (Kilmer). The largest oak tree, where Dad hung the wooden swing by thick ropes, was 18 feet around in September 2023 and is hundreds of years old. That immensely huge and ancient oak felt like a familiar old friend. It took the steady passing of years and wrapped them around itself like a shawl of stability: "What's gone is behind, what's before is according to Plan, take your place in the stream of life, little one. I' seen it all, I'm still here, unmoved, waiting for the unfolding."

I wish I could have seen the grove of great American chestnut trees which had surrounded the house and given its name. They died off from a fungal blight in the early 1900s. They were more than 100 feet tall with fat trunks like our largest oak. Their nuts were eaten by man and creatures, the tree's tannin was used for making leather and their wood was resistant to rot and easy to work with. It is likely that our old house was made in part from chestnut wood.

Our oak and maple trees lost a lot of leaves in the fall, leaving many musty-colored heaps. We would help Ma and Daddy clean up the yard each autumn. Two of us would place our feet on opposite corners holding down an old sheet as Ma raked the leaves up into it. We sometimes made faces at one another while waiting for the sheet to be filled. Then we carried the load between us and dumped the leaves down the bank towards the river, with great gusto. Ma never seemed to mind much our messing around as we worked. Sometimes we cleared winding paths in the middle of the brightly colored leaves making a kind of maze. Then we'd chase one another around, careful to remain within the paths, and laugh like fools until Ma called us to take away the next heap.

A tree is truly a thing of beauty. We all loved those enormous oak and maple trees surrounding the house. Some of their branches seemed longer than the trees were tall, and they spread out interminably overhead. When Ma wasn't looking, we'd climb on them and watch the squirrels and chipmunks below. Those tree trunks also served as lovely hiding places.

Our thin frames could also easily disappear behind the large white pillars which crowned the front porch of the majestic house. The "seeker" took her place half-way up the sidewalk, her back to us as we each hid behind a different pillar. When the counting was done, she'd turn, and make a guess: "I think Heidi is behind Pillar number 2. Number 2: show yourself". If Heidi was behind Pillar number 2, she was then "it".

Besides those grand pillars, there are several bay windows. In one living room is the lovely bay window which was added on for the owner's daughter's wedding. "George W. Stockley of Ohio married Oct.15, 1874 at the home of Alvin Devereux, Chestnut Grove, Deposit, NY, by Rev. Edward Taylor to Olivia Devereux of Deposit." In a mid-October more than 100 years later, Roger King of Ohio married my sister Julie Hoff of Deposit, in the very same place.

With the house came impressive furnishings, including a mahogany bookcase, a massive bed made of 2 kinds of walnut, and an accompanying dresser. A similar bed and bureau is found in the Blair House, in Washington D.C., also known as "The President's Guest House."

The house has a breath-taking view of the valley, through which the Delaware River flows. It is an amazing house, situated not far from Rood's Creek, where Ma grew up. She remembered driving by "the Devereux house" as a child, and wishing that one day she might live there. In a letter Ma wrote to a journalist in January 1967 she said, "One thing that interests me personally is that Mr. Devereux bought the land from my Great-Great Grandfather Rood. We have only 4 acres with the house but the original farm was huge and was located on both sides of the river."

I had just turned 3 when we moved in. Walking down the driveway, I held my mother's hand. Perhaps I was little, but I'd already learned the importance of staking your claim quickly when negotiating rights in a family of seven. As we walked past the white and purple lilacs, I looked up at the second-floor windows above the kitchen. It seemed to me a room with a lot of windows, a big space for making fun.

"Can I have <u>that</u> room up there?" I asked, pointing at an upstairs window.

"We'll see."

At the time I didn't recognize the typical response to avoid conflict with a small, rather spoiled child. (When my own daughter was young, it became familiar, useful vocabulary.) Being the baby of the family, I ended up with the bedroom closest to Ma and Daddy's, and the room above the kitchen became Beau's.

However, we did not move into the house straight away, but briefly stayed in the red summer cottage on the property. The cottage, nestled in the woods below, overlooked the Delaware River. I remember cramming in besides my mother and another sibling on the couch, which opened into a bed, in the big room off the kitchenette. Others were in the bedroom, the only other room besides the screened-in back porch. (From that terrible height, it was a scary place to stand, by the back porch screen. You felt that the whole building might just topple over down the bank into the river.)

Then we moved into the spacious old house, which my mother filled with her many beloved family antiques and heirlooms, including her ancient perfume bottle collection. Some bottles dated back to her great-grandmother Jane Chandler Clapper. Mom loved all her antiques!

She greatly enjoyed the history associated with our house. It had been a "safe house" for runaway slaves during those terrible years of the Civil War. The "Slave Cellar" was a secret room where fugitive slaves hid before being transported further North to freedom via the Underground Railroad. The "Slave Cellar" is reached by moving some rugs and boards in the floor of one of the back rooms, which Daddy used as his workshop. How it fascinated us kids! What were the original owners of my home like, those brave people who had risked their lives to hide fugitive slaves, years ago? It made me proud to be living in such a place.

We weren't often allowed down in that slave cellar, but I remember once climbing down there with 2 of my sisters and my brother. My heart beat rapidly as we descended into darkness. It was just a musty, damp place with a dirt floor but it conjured up images of courageous men and women, slaves who had crouched there more than a century before. "Look!" my brother exclaimed, pointing the flashlight at one of the walls. My heart dropped to my feet. I turned, expecting to see a skeleton. "Doesn't that wall look as if it had been quickly bricked up!? Maybe it was a doorway there...yeah...and maybe there was once a tunnel that went under the river." He always had the best imagination and we believed along with him.

Ma researched whatever background information could be found and kept copies of records and articles associated with the house. One stated: "Alvin Devereux November 1847 bought land of Ira Rude. He built a saw mill and in 1848 built a tannery, manufacturing leather for 30 yrs. The saw mill ended when hemlock bark was exhausted. During that time, they made 425,000 sides of leather and used 90,000 cords of bark. In 1847 he cleared several hundred acres of land on the banks of the river and although the soil was very poor, he developed scientifically the land into very rich farming land. Paul Devereux, his son, continued farming and had a dairy of pure-bred Jersey cattle. It was known as "Chestnut Grove Farm."

Ma also told us that a President, Grover Cleveland, once slept in our house. There are other important things to know about Grover Cleveland, besides that nocturnal stay at Chestnut Grove. He was the only president to be married in the White House, and the only President to win two non-consecutive terms. Besides that, his daughter Ruth had a chocolate candy bar named after her. Now *there's* a claim to fame.

In the spring of 1968 several important family events took place:

1. I celebrated my fifth birthday
2. I went to the movies for the first time to see "The Jungle Book" (accompanied by my 13-year-old sister Cecilia) and
3. My musical career was launched – Grannie gave me my first guitar (toy. I also loved the Slinky but not as much as the guitar).

4. My Norwegian grandparents came to visit us from Trondheim on May 8, 1965 (exactly 20 years after the end of World War 2 in Europe).

Our Norwegian grandparents' visit was significant for our family. Although they spoke not a word of English, we felt their love and affection. The photos from those days reveal a great tenderness towards us: Kjersti, sitting on Farmor's lap with Farmor's arms holding her close, Cecilia, seated beside Farfar, their hands entwined, Heidi, sitting on Farmor's lap, Heidi and Kjersti, each one seated on one of Farfar's legs with his arms around each one, Farmor's arm around Beau, me, squished into a lawn chair with Farmor, her arms about me. Clearly, they were fond of us.

Their presence also underscored the reality of our Norwegian heritage. Upon arrival in JFK airport in New York City, my grandparents went through the standard border customs inspection but were pulled aside because of a strange, white powdery stuff they had with them. The customs people did not know what it was and were perhaps worried about drugs. Having survived Nazi-occupied Norway, our grandfather was *not* about to give up the stuff to the customs officers. He stood firm and insisted (in Norwegian) that it was nothing to be alarmed

Farmor, Farfar, Dad and Hoff kids

about. Of course, they understood not a word and finally Dad was allowed back into customs and explained that it was only *lefse*, potato pastry, which has a powdery, floury surface. Despite the US customs challenge, my grandfather was determined he was not giving up that precious lefse and was going to bring it to his son, come what may. This, for sure, is a good kind of stubbornness that comes with being from Trondheim.

Our grandfather, "Farfar," or literally, "father's father" was actually a gentle, unassuming man. One felt comfortable in his company. Farfar loved watching birds, careful to identify each one. My Norwegian cousin Ingunn remembers visiting at his house. Each time he got out the beloved bird book and they looked at all the birds, enjoying together the wonder of each one's unique beauty. He also loved to take in the golden moments of sunset, sitting quietly watching the sun's descent.

While visiting us Farfar recorded the days' events in his little brown notebook in an extremely difficult to decipher Norwegian handwriting. It is full of family events and his grandchildren, meals and games, a birthday, mothers' day and more (my translation):

Farfar's Notebook Entries:
Thursday May 9
Margrethe's birthday...great rejoicing over all the gifts, a toy guitar from Grannie, from her parents and siblings - a toy (Slinky) and from us two, Mother's handmade Little Red Riding Hood picture, 3$ and a cake...After dinner, TV together with the children and at 8 pm the children go to bed. The older children can stay up for a bit in their pajamas, lying on the floor in the play room, watching TV. For the grownups, coffee in the living room and liqueur and chatting about family and friends in Norway until long into the small hours of the night.

Stillness descended upon the house and soon all slept the sleep of the righteous in their lovely bedrooms in a good bed.

(Stilllhet senket seg over huset og snart sov alle mann de rettferdiger sovn i prektige soverom og en god seng)
Saturday May 11

Weather is still grey. The whole family went to the library and then shopping for Mother's day. The children were all so intent on buying the gifts, there were eager discussions on what to buy.

Sunday May 12 Mother's Day

Big day with presentation of gifts for Mother and both grandmothers. All the children came in to us and presented a beautiful porcelain figurine of a woman and a card. Great joy on both sides. Farmor went to the Methodist church where Cecilia and Kjersti sang in the choir. They both have lovely voices.

Tuesday May 14

Yes, today it is 8 days since we arrived here. Time passes so quickly and we are enjoying ourselves and feel at home in the family life here…Mother and I are in great shape and could stay longer. Cecilia says every day we should stay until her birthday in December.

Our grandparents played jump rope with us, Farfar holding

Farmor, Dad & Farfar behind our house 1968

one end of the rope and Farmor at the other end, turning it round and round while we jumped. I got it into my head that my Farfar just *had* to learn to play American baseball while he was in the USA. We headed out to stand underneath the arms of the old oak tree, where we children often played sports. I had him take the baseball bat up to his shoulder and stand ready to swing and explained by words and gestures what it takes to play the game. My parents got quite a kick out of that. (I probably would have included Farmor but she always wore a classy dress so I must have figured that wasn't going to work. However, it did not prevent her from driving Dad's Wheelhorse tractor around the field! Farfar had fun with that, too).

The folks took my grandparents shopping and sightseeing in Binghamton, Niagara Falls, Washington D.C. and of course Daddy took us all to the golf course to show them the passion of his life. My mother must have been exhausted by it all but she was a good sport and always enjoyed conversation in her favorite language, Norwegian. Farmor helped with cooking, making Norwegian Cream Cake (*bløtkake*) and other goodies. She helped to prepare the school lunch bags for the kids. There were meals outside and many visits from friends -even little Gretel came and met them. They stayed for a month and must have cherished every moment with us who lived so far away. It would be the only time I met my gentle grandfather. It was a great blessing to our whole family having them with us, and we were sad when they left to return home to Trondheim, Norway.

Around this time, when Ma was in her mid-40s she started to go into menopause prematurely, like one of her grandmothers had done before her. The problem was, when she did get her period, she hemorrhaged heavily and kept getting anemic. The family doctor at the time was Dr. Nicola Muia. This thin gentle Italian man, who probably *was* Catholic, prescribed Estrogen hormone since Ma was "much too young for menopause." The estrogen was an effective cure. Shortly after, Ma found out she was pregnant, and she cried (not for joy).

After I was born, she had tried every possible contraception method available, aside from the pill, which she didn't think was good for women. "It's just not natural," she said. At the time she got pregnant, she'd been using some kind of barrier, anti-spermicidal cream promised to be "highly effective" and all the rage in the late '60s. Three of our neighbors, Freida Carlson, Shirley Davis, and Charlene Eardmann had been using it too. All three ended up pregnant.

I can almost envision the little pre-Julie egg after fertilization by a persistent, Viking sperm, which beat all odds, laughing its way through the cream barrier. Upon contact, the tiny zygote gleefully descended the tube, snuggling into that warm, nourishing womb, waiting to be launched into the rest of life's adventures with zeal. But for the moment, she paused for about a 40-week holiday, in preparation mode.

I was six years old. It was a hot summer day in July 1969. I was on the stone steps behind the back hut, doing flips around the metal bar, which normally served as a hand railing, not an acrobatic device. It is a wonder I never cracked my head open on the stone, flipping around like that.

Such efforts made me thirsty, so I decided to go inside for something cold. I headed for the freezer, remembering that I'd miraculously convinced Ma to buy popsicles the previous day. I passed Heidi who was sticking a round, blue Chiquita banana sticker on the edge of the back kitchen door, adding to our collection. I stepped over a sleepy Vesla, our Saint Bernard, who wagged her tail in a friendly greeting. I strode into the pantry, where the refrigerator was and ironing board was set up.

Ma was there ironing, dressed in a bright yellow summer dress (yellow was her favorite color). I looked up at her, stopped, and then looked again. Suddenly, I realized that my mother was taking on enormous dimensions. She was "as big as a barn."

With childlike tact I said, "Mommy, I think you're getting awfully *fat*."

"Well, no," she said with a half a smile and little enthusiasm, "there's a baby in here."

When the *surprise* child came along on Sunday afternoon, July 27, Ma named her Julie Nicoletta. Julie, after her sister Julia and Nicoletta, a variation on the Doctor's name. I thought *I* was a big baby, but Julie was the whopper, weighing in at almost 13 pounds.

When Ma was still in the hospital, I used the typewriter to write her a special message. Ma must have gotten a kick out of it, for she kept it for all those decades.

```
Dear Mommy,
I am glad that you had the baby and I'm
real glad that we now have six kids.
And I wish that you would come home
and if you come home, you will have a
great big surprise. I will give you two
presents and would you let me go to
Gloria's ? Mommy? Get well fast and you
will have a real, real, big surprise.
COME HOME SOON.

       Love Maggie

  P.S. Ican count for you on the
  typewriter fr om 2 to 10.
  234567890- 234567890 ¼½@¢?:;.,,and
I wish that you would give me a cat.
Vesla and Princy are fine.and I wish that
someday you would let me wash the dishes
and Kjersti and Heidi dry
  them. Maggie


       The end, MOTHER.
              S
               I
                G
                 N
                  E
                   D

     a      e
       g  i
     M    G


                    (MAGGIE HOFF)
```

In preparation for the new baby, Beau, my sweet and hopeful brother, who still longed for a brother, had made a kind of baby bed from part of an old doll carriage. He painted it a beautiful deep blue. But the infant meant to be a "he" turned out to be a "she," and besides, only one plump leg of the Viking babe would fit in that small bed of dashed hopes.

My mother brought the baby home, coming into the living room, an action, which in and of itself signaled the significance of the occasion. The living rooms were mostly "off limits" to us kids, since Ma wanted to keep them nice for whenever company came. Also, they were full of family antiques, which she did not want accidentally ruined by "rambunctious" kids. Ma sat down on the loveseat, which she had bought "for a song" from Nettie Axtel. It was upholstered in a rich, green velvet material, which was smooth under your palm if you rubbed it in one direction, but rough and spikey if you rubbed it the wrong way. I sat down by Ma and seized the moment to run my hand over the green material. *Carpe diem* for a 6-year-old.

Kjer came over and looked at the baby, who's skin seemed darkish, and whose brown hair stuck up in tufts. She was

*Ma w/ Julie
on the green
loveseat*

immediately struck by the sight and thought to herself, "Why, she looks like an *Indian*." She felt fascinated and slightly flabbergasted. "An Indian baby in our family!?" I didn't know quite what to think, but to me, the most important thing was that it was a <u>girl</u>, so I was glad. As she grew, she turned out looking like the rest of us, American-Norwegians, not quite so exotic after all.

Julie was the last of the clan, and probably the one with whom Ma shared the most adventures and conspiracies. Ma was nearly forty-six years old when her last child was born, now *that* was a geriatric pregnancy! Talk about ending up with a bang, Julie was (and still is) *major* high energy. Ma said she was "a whirling dervish – has to be doing something every minute." Julie was an adorable toddler, her big brown eyes framed by a head full of curls. She was always smiling and laughing, and often into mischief. She'd have been a handful for <u>any</u> mother, but imagine being a 46-year-old mother, caring for Julie besides having five other children, a husband and various pets needing your attention!

It is critical for every family to have an "outside" support system. Ma had a priceless mother, our dear Grannie, who helped her navigate the challenges of marriage and raising a large family. Grannie was not only a listener, a quiet counselor and helper: she had raised my mom to be who she was. How thankful I am, that Ma had such a great mother.

Grannie had retired from teaching in 1959 and began to really enjoy her grandchildren. To us grandkids who lived a town away, in Deposit, the greatest joy of life was to spend a weekend one-on-one with Grannie at her apartment at 17 East Main Street, Hancock at the old Rood home. She would spoil us with her attention and wonderful treats. To this day, the sound of a passing train gives me a warm, safe feeling, reminding me of the trains we'd hear in Hancock, at Grannie's home.

It was also a delight for us when Grannie came up to Deposit to spend the weekend. We used to argue about who would get to sleep with her. We ended up having to pick numbers out of a hat. It wasn't that she read us stories in bed, or gave us candy or anything like that: we simply wanted to be near her as much as possible. She had an amazingly calm, loving manner about her. I don't ever remember her raising her voice, yet she managed to keep us all in line. This was helpful for Ma who had her hands full with us kids.

Ma wasn't really the type of mother to "fuss" over her kids unnecessarily. She gave us a lot of freedom growing up in the country (or maybe she was just plain too busy with endless cotton diapers and keeping house to be overly supervisory). Anyhow, we were always off playing games outside, like softball, kickball, "Kick the Can" or pretending to be Indians walking noiselessly through the woods, or swinging down the river bank we called "Blindman's Bluff," hanging onto the branch of a small tree and jumping wildly towards the great Delaware. My brother Beau and my sister Kjer once created names for all the paths we made in the woods, and Beau made little artistic signs for each walkway.

At dusk we sometimes ran around in circles around the tall pine trees which led down to the cottage. The ground was good for running since there wasn't much grass growing there. We'd run and laugh until we were out of breath and dizzy with the irrepressible energy of youth. What pleasure did we derive from such frenzied motion? Well, it was, like, it was... just being together, enjoying life in common, feeling like part of Creation or something. I dunno really. (At this point, I can hear one of my nephews saying, "But were my aunts and my mother partially brain-damaged in their early years? Was life really so boring you had to run around trees for kicks?" OK, I'll admit, sounds stupid. Life was maybe simpler then. No Nintendo or Gameboys to keep us nailed to a fixed spot and we weren't allowed to constantly breastfeed off the mindless Boob tube either.)

When it just got to be dark enough in summer, we'd catch fireflies, those wonders shining with mysterious light. Sometimes, if I found a glass jar with a lid, I'd put a small twig and some grass in with a few fireflies and bring them into my bedroom to watch the glory, later, as I lay in bed.

On late summer nights we played Flashlight Hide and Seek, which was terribly scary to me. I avoided the old barn, for fear of swooping barn swallows and bats. Sometimes we'd play "Old

Grey Wolf" a game handed down from generation to generation. It involved more running around the house in the dark. Utter insanity. One person would be the wolf, and go hide somewhere in the perimeter of the house. The rest of us would then try to run all the way around the house, back to "home base," the old Oak tree, without the wolf catching us. Whoever the wolf touched had to then hide together with the wolf while those who had escaped counted, while the growing pack of wolves hid themselves. The running around the house continued, until there was one poor sucker left by himself to try to run around the house without anyone touching him. I always let myself be caught long before then, so I'd not be left by myself running around in the dark. I was no fool.

In daytime we were often climbing trees, even reading books up in the two-level tree house which Beau had built. It had a great leaf-speckled view of the river. We might sit for a while on the huge stone we had named "Plymouth Rock" or skip pebbles on the river. In those earliest days the river was even clean enough to swim in. (I remember Ma's eternal bright-red one-piece bathing suit. She wore it all through my entire childhood. It was just one color, and kind of quilted, with a white lining. It never wore out. I'm sure it's still in the house somewhere. They don't make clothes like that anymore. If they did, stores would go out of business.)

Ma would say to Daddy at the dinner table, "The river's awfully low." The breaking news of the day. Once, when the river was down, Kjer, Heidi and I ventured out in it, jumping the rocks which just broke the surface. They were slippery and we navigated with both the joy of being out in the river and the fear of falling in. We saw masses of elongated fish swimming around us looking like snakes moving in for the attack. Our screaming got the attention of the twin boys who lived on the other side of the river, and they came over to investigate, telling us with cool courage that they were only harmless eels. That heroic act explains why I agreed to go to the Prom with one of them, years later in high school, though I hardly knew him.

My sisters and I sometimes played Bank, using the special

accounting pads of paper Dad brought us. We loved to play veterinarian, too: someone would be the secretary, taking appointments down in a small book on a card table set up under a maple tree. Then the others would come with various sick stuffed animals, and whoever was vet would fix things up, accounts were paid and the next client arrived. How I loved that grown-up feeling, carrying Monopoly money in one of Ma's old purses, then paying for the visit and receiving my change. (Those days Ma wished she had a few *less* bills to pay.)

We had a long driveway beside the house, shaped like a big circle, and we called the lawn in the middle "the island." Sometimes we played kickball there. We'd ride our bikes around the driveway for fun too, stopping to "do errands" along the way. The island had quite a few maple trees, plus the lilac bushes, and one big stump which was our pirates' ship. We put up a stick, with a skull and cross bones flag, and climbed up to sail foreign seas, a rebel's heart pushing us to venture off, attacking any ship we'd meet. In that stump, pieces of wood could be pulled out, and we hid messages of great importance underneath them.

Sometimes, we'd feel an archeological urge and would sneak out and dig in the river bank which descended behind the big old barn, an area which our predecessors of the late 1800s used as a garbage pit. We'd find old-fashioned bottles; odd perfume and ink bottles, with bubbles in the glass, so you knew they were really old.

We'd also sneak down to play restaurant in the old red cottage, although Ma never wanted us to go in there (I don't really know why. Maybe she, too, feared it might fall down into the river). There was a small square screen/vent thingy between the kitchen and the bedroom, and one of us stood on the bed, avoiding tiny mice turds, and placed an order to the waitress standing on the other side of the wall, on a chair in the kitchenette, who wrote it all down and prepared it for imaginary serving.

(Wait a minute, did I just write "square screen/vent *thingy*"? Lord, I sound like Ma. She'd say things like, "Can you hand me that thing on the thing over there?" "Which thing?" "*That* thing.")

Each day, around 5 or 5:30 p.m., my mother would round us up for the evening meal, which was always shared together. Each one sat around the dining room table at his or her appointed place, which remained a fixed position and no one ever thought to take anyone else's place. I sat just to Dad's right, by the kitchen. Celia sat just to Ma's right.

If we were out in the woods or down by the river playing, Ma would call us in by ringing the big old hand bell which signaled it was time to come for dinner. When we heard that bell ringing, we dropped whatever we were doing and ran up to the house, mainly because by dinner time we were all "starving." At the table, we would talk over the day's events, as often as not laughing and poking fun at one another. My sister Kjersti and I have exchanged some emails about those family meals. She wrote, "I sure do miss being home and at the dinner table. It was always so nice and warm and everyone gabbing, etc." Those meals together somehow gave us a sense of security, and most of us have tried to continue this tradition in our own families, as much as possible.

I can't imagine having to cook every day for 8 people and have it all be warm at the same time. Ma didn't really enjoy cooking and she wasn't the most gifted cook. Occasionally, a meal might burn if she got distracted "doing 6 things at once." Daddy jokingly called her "The Great Cooker." My stomach turns when I think of the fish she used to make. Daddy loved fish but you couldn't get fresh fish in the store back then. Those so-called fish must've been frozen for months, and the terrible fishy taste and smell was accentuated by the fact that she *boiled* it to death, then poured melted butter on top. Gives me the shivers to this day.

Ma's most infamous meal was the terrible J.D. (Jeanne Dorothy) Meatloaf – it went beyond description. There was many an evening of boiled hotdogs and potatoes, or tuna fish casserole and potatoes, or hamburgers and more potatoes. Daddy, who refused "that Chinese white stuff" (rice), always wanted potatoes, being a true Norwegian. I used to love it on the occasional evening when we had "Free For All", which meant you could eat whatever you found in the fridge.

We laugh at Ma's cooking abilities, but her roast beef and gravy was good, and she did manage to prepare a lovely 20-pound-plus turkey dinner for us every Thanksgiving. There was always an air of excitement, and sometimes Ma got a little nervous during preparation time. "Wouldja move it!?" she'd say if you got in her way in the kitchen. It was a place to avoid. Ma, her mother Grannie, and Aunt Julie would be in the kitchen preparing the big tasty meal. Tasty but not salty: Ma never used a lot of it, since she said, "Salt's a slow poison," a line she heard many times from some relative (now, one of my sisters reading this says to herself, "Wasn't it her grandfather said that?" How could I possibly keep track of which relative said what? Heck, I was little, and Ma had so many canned lines like that one I don't remember anymore who said what!)

Anyhow, with so many people present for Thanksgiving, we were often too many to fit around the dining room table, so we had card tables set up nearby. Ma would put out the old Native American salt and pepper shakers and other quaint items to dress up the table for the festivities. Often, she'd put out her best hand embroidered tablecloth (and threaten to "string up" whoever spilled gravy on it).

Ma's sister, Aunt Julie (otherwise known as "Dip," God knows why) and husband, Uncle Emile, would occasionally come up from Washington with their kids, so with Grannie, we were often 14-15 people. It was madness trying to get everyone together to sit down, "Who's sitting where?" and trying to appease all the children who wanted to sit next to Grannie, of course. Thanksgiving was a time for family, and what a blessing it was to gather around that table, holding hands as Daddy got one of us girls to say a blessing on the meal. After that moment of peace, mayhem broke out.

"Pass the corn, please."

"Quit sittin' on the rolls, Celia!"

"Can I have the gravy, please?"

Ma would go back into the kitchen to refill dishes as they emptied.

(One year, when I was around 6, I got up from the table to do some "big business". I forgot to close the bathroom door, and sitting there a long while, sang to myself like usual. I was always singing to myself much to my sisters' chagrin. I sang as I dressed. I sang as I ran. I sang on the pot. This time was no different, only I forgot to close the door.)

"OOOOOVer the River and THROOOOOOUGH the woods to Grandmother's house we GOOOO," I sang as I pushed to finish quickly and get back to my food. Apparently, they all heard me and died laughing. It was a story I was to live through many a Thanksgiving after, much to my dismay.)

Oh, the wonderful food, and for once, seemingly endless! There was corn, tender turkey, cranberry sauce, "smashed" potatoes, gravy, stuffing, rolls you could slather in butter, and for sure delicious desserts Ma had prepared in advance.

Ma was *great* at baking cookies, cakes, pies and typical Norwegian goodies (*gorukake, fyrstekake, krumkake, bløtkake*). She made apple pie, rhubarb pie (I never touched the stuff) sugar cookies, chocolate cake, chocolate chip cookies, and other delights. There was, however, one cookie press she had (I use it now, it was in almost perfect condition when she gave it to me as an adult), which I remember her struggling with, which she couldn't get to work right most of the time ("this damn thing..... Ooh, pardon my French").

She did instill a love of baking in her daughters. She passed on to us the famous "Double Chocolate Delight" recipe for cake, which was usually requested for Birthday menus (the one day each year you could choose the evening menu). Believe me, I never asked for boiled hotdogs OR potatoes. Ma had made up her own chocolate drop cookies recipe which was great to eat raw (she'd dip her finger in to taste it and say, "Cook's privilege"). How wonderful it was to slather her freshly baked cinnamon buns in butter and savor every bite.

One tip she taught us about baking is when you make pie dough, "...it's best to use a large, wide-tined fork to mix it together." To this day I do just that and every time, I think of her. She taught us how to make Norwegian Prince's Cake (*fyrstekake*), which is made from ground almonds. "Make sure you get whole aylmonds *with* the skin and grind them up yourself," she advised. She always pronounced almonds like "aylmonds".

Usually, everything was made from scratch but sometimes we'd get pre-prepared mixes. When Julie and I were the last two kids left at home, we would sometimes bake a batch of brownie mix and eat *the entire pan* between the two of us, all in secret when Ma was out. We then carefully burnt some toast to cover up the smell so we'd not be found out.

"For cryin' out loud!" She cried, "Who's been burnin' toast!?" All beings faded into the woodwork. She was so mad, because the entire house smelt of carbonized toast, and that night she was having the ladies over for "Book Circle."

"Book Circle" was a monthly ladies' club where they read books and wrote a critique, sharing their thoughts about the books in one another's homes. As my parents both loved books, our home was filled with them. I can hardly remember a room in the house which didn't have books in it (except the bathrooms!). In the living room there were several bookshelves, filled with books in English and in Norwegian. There were titles by Kierkegaard and by Norwegian politicians or diplomats Ma had met or worked for.

We were somewhat interested in those books. We sometimes would sneakily turn the key of the glass cupboard and look at the scantily clad people in the paintings depicted on the smooth pages of the Heritage series of books. Kjersti, Heidi, and I once found a small book on the bookshelf by the piano which was to learn to speak Italian. Kjersti insisted we learn some of the phrases. I remember laughing hysterically at how to say, "You're welcome," which sounded to us like the slang for someone expecting a baby ("Prego").

Ma had wanted to be a librarian and her love of books endured as long as she lived. She liked all kinds of books, and especially enjoyed historical novels and biographies. As she said, "Sometimes, the truth is stranger than fiction." In Study Club, she wrote, "The authenticity of a biography depends on who wrote it, how well they researched the material and what diaries they had access to. Some biographies aren't accurate because they choose to omit facts thus not revealing some of the subject's true character. *George Washington: Man and Monument* by Marcus Cunliffe, who did extensive research in order to discover the real Washington, concluded that George Washington 'derived satisfaction from doing his duty and from being widely admired for it.' He was an exceptional figure." Another biography she enjoyed was by Catherine Drinker Bowen, *John Adams and the American Revolution*. She enjoyed Robert James Waller and once sent me an article he wrote about a cat, "A Canticle for Roadcat." She also enjoyed the Diana Garibaldi books, one of which reminded her of a song from her youth, and she wrote, "It's interesting what you learn sometimes. In 6th 7th and 8th grade music we had some old hardcover song books we used to sing from – one song was "Charlie Is My Darling." I never knew until I read her first book that it was a song in favor of Charles Stuart when they were trying to put him on the throne in Scotland." (What a memory Ma had! A song from her youth never forgotten.)

Another time she wrote, "I finally finished reading the Sigrid Undset biography that Dad got for me in Norway. Being a serious biography, it took a while to digest because it went into detail about her methods of writing and Middle Ages research. I always loved the Middle Ages. I still have my 5th grade history book on the subject. And of course, Nidaros Domkirken *(Cathedral)* is from the Middle Ages."

Ma served on the Library Board for some years, as she was always a big supporter of the Deposit Free Library, where both Cecilia and I worked as librarian's assistant during our high school years. (I *loved* working there: the quiet and handling all those books and checking out the new titles. I used to stick my nose in a book whenever Mrs. Clearwater (the ancient librarian Kjersti renamed Mrs. "Murkywater") shuffled into the bathroom and locked herself in for a smoke. Smoking wasn't allowed in the library and she always came out exceptionally kind and accommodating, a breath mint in her mouth.)

One time Ma wrote me about a book she was reading

(870 pages!) which was "so interesting and breathtaking, her descriptions, plot, etc is so interesting." She always had her nose in a book, too. She often bought books as gifts for us and later for her grandchildren. As a kid, there was a stretch of a few years we didn't have a television. I don't think I missed it at all, and many an evening was spent with all the family side by side in the living room, each one reading his or her book. *(Yes, we were indeed a strange bunch).*

Mom and Dad managed to give us a wonderful home; not an easy job to achieve in any day or age. As I think of my family, I realize that we were incredibly blessed to have a mother like we did. She taught us so many things, just by the way she lived, by being herself. Her love of life and positive outlook transformed our house into a home.

It was, indeed, a wonderful home to grow up in.

Music filled our home since both my parents loved it. Ma had taken piano and clarinet lessons in her youth. I loved to hear her play "September in the Rain" on the piano (she had memorized it). She encouraged us to learn an instrument in school, and once even arranged for me to take a few piano lessons from dear old Evelyn Azalia Campbell (since they didn't teach piano at school).

Ma was always humming or singing some song or another from her youth. She'd motion with her arms and wiggle her hips as she sang "Chattanooga Choo-choo" or "He's the boogie woogie bugle boy of Company B, They made him blow a bugle for his Uncle Sam". We laughed when she sang the old "Cocaine Bill and Morphine Sue strolling down the avenue…Oh, honey have a sniff, have a sniff on me, O honey have a sniff on me" (WHAT in tarnation?!!) or "Flat Foot Floogie," a jazz song from the Depression era when she was a kid.

She taught us girls to sing together at an early age, as she accompanied us on the piano. It was hard work learning all the harmonies. Often Kjersti, Heidi and I were in training under Commander Mrs. Hoff as she put us through the works to get the parts right. Not only that, she made us memorize all the words so we were never holding sheet music when we sang. The exhilaration of singing in tight harmony with my sisters was like moving in another dimension to me, I loved it. Learning to sing before an audience at an early age took away the fear of being in front of people for talks or presentations later in life. (Thanks, Mom!)

We sang in church and in the annual 4-H talent show. One year the show was held in the Delaware County Infirmary, and we won 1st prize. "The gold seal for act of the day was presented to the Hoff Sisters of Deposit, for a melody of songs in three parts," said the newspaper clipping which Ma kept in her drawer. I was 9 or 10 years old. We beat out a gymnastic exhibition, a piano solo, baton twirling, a skit, and other musical attempts. Unfortunately, no one from Nashville was there, so we didn't get signed up to make a record. (That was back when CD's weren't yet invented.)

In one of our songs, there was a line from the 23rd Psalm, "... goodness and mercy all my days, will *surely* follow me". I told my sisters the "surely" part made me think of a girl from school, Shirley, who I imagined was always copying me. Ma said, "Well, that's the highest form of a compliment, Maggie." I didn't see it that way. While singing this song together at some competition, we came to the line, "Will *Shirley* follow me?" and the 3 of us cracked up laughing right there, in front of all those people. But I do not remember Ma being mad.

Ma's favorite concert was one she reminisced about for years afterwards. Julie was in 4th grade, and she and our neighbor Christine were trying to learn to play the violin, Suzuki method, like Kjersti and I had learned, from Mrs. Phyllis Baker, our music teacher. Julie and Christine were good friends, and for their first concert, they played the simplest songs all beginners were obliged to learn. The parents should've been paid for sitting through those ear-breaking "melodies".

Now, Christine was plagued with loud hiccups whenever she got nervous. The children filed out onto the stage into the lights. By woeful error, Mrs. Baker had allowed Julie and Christine to stand side by side. Standing there, in front of the large audience, Christine's nervousness soon became evident. She got started gulping, her diaphragm spasms fostering uncontrollable giggles from Julie, and soon they both laughed out of control, the movement of their bouncing shoulders further adding to the terrible violins' cries. Suppressed laughter is always the worst fuel for multiplied mirth. They just couldn't stop during that short concert as they pulled the bows over the screeching strings. It was a real comedy. They gave up learning the violin shortly after that, but the concert was *inoubliable*.

Whenever we participated in school concerts, Ma and Daddy would come to listen. We were in orchestras, bands, choruses, and musicals. I was lucky to have had one teacher, Mr. Gary Watson, who wrote musicals and designed roles specifically made for the actors/actresses he had at his disposal. It was great fun. Ma loved it when I sang in those musicals in high school. In later years she often said, "I still remember you singing "What I did for Love" in that green gown you never gave back to Mr. Watson's teacher girlfriend." I wonder, is it still hanging there in my bedroom closet?

In addition to her love of music, my mother loved animals which meant we were allowed to have pets. As if 5 kids weren't

VESLA AND FAMILY—Vesla, the Hoffs' playful Saint Bernard, reigns over the household. Julie, left, in a Norwegian knit; Kjersti, in her Hardanger costume, and Margrethe in a costume from Trondelag, sometimes find her an armful.

Kjersti, Julie and Margrethe with VESLA
"The Evening Press"
2/4/1971 Photo:
John Williams

enough to take care of, my parents got a purebred Saint Bernard in 1966, a huge dog they named "Vesla," which means "little one" in Norwegian. Vesla fit perfectly into the family community. Even the brown color of her soft coat seemed to match the brown panels of our house. Her soft muzzle seemed nearly elastic between my small palms, as I squished her jowls back and forth. She patiently accepted the affectionate hugs and caresses we showered upon her, wagging her long tail in delight.

How wonderful it was for us, growing up with Vesla! She would sit and watch TV with us, her front legs on the floor, her rump up on the couch between us kids. Vesla had such a sweet personality, she never seemed to mind our shenanigans. When we were still small enough, we tried to ride on her broad back. She'd play with us in the yard, sometimes dragging me around by a long Bard-Parker (surgical) tube held in her mouth, my skinny arms grasping the other end, as I laughed like a fool. Vesla was a gentle soul, sleeping peacefully in front of the old apple tree, while little white Pansy the rabbit crawled over her or slept beside her.

Vesla often slept on the kitchen floor or the pantry room floor. I was always fascinated to watch her dreaming. Her legs would move a bit, her tail flopped up and down, you heard her whimpering slightly, and you wondered what dogs' dreams were made of. It couldn't have been chasing other animals, not our gentle Vesla.

She did have some "enemies": the Davis' boys' two German Shepherd dogs. Shirley and Dick Davis had four boys, and they kept their 2 dogs tied up pretty much since they were rather mean brutes or so they seemed to us. (The boys were fine, we used to play a lot of softball with them. It was the fastest the kitchen ever got cleaned up, Ma used to say, on nights we had an agreement with the Davis's to play ball.) If ever their dogs got loose, and roamed over in our direction, Vesla went mad and chased after them. I was proud of her, especially since I was terrified of those wicked beasts myself. Vesla was our great defender, despite her gentle nature.

Vesla rarely roamed the neighborhood, she almost always

stayed on our property. She was clever that way. So we'd let her out to do her "business" and Ma would whistle that familiar Vesla whistle to call her back inside. Ma kept Vesla in the house whenever she was "in heat." Nevertheless, she once ended up pregnant. How excited we were, to think of cutie-pie baby St. Bernards in the house! But when they arrived, they were all tragically stillborn but one, who was utterly adorable, but we weren't allowed to keep him and he was given away.

Of course, having a St Bernard meant a lot of work for Ma, as sometimes the dog would end up "puddlin'" on the kitchen floor. But the worst must have been cleaning up all that fur and slobber (St. Bernards shed fur and drool terribly.) We'd be in the playroom hanging out, when someone would notice an enormously long dribble of slobber hanging from her mouth. "OH NO!" someone exclaimed, and eyeing the potential danger we all sprang up hurriedly. She turned her head from one kid to the next, as if sensing our excitement. "AAAAAHHHH, watch out, she's gunna SWING!!!!!" someone yelled, just before she shook her head vigorously, like she did her fur coat after a swim in the river. Almost in slow motion, the unwanted bodily liquid would spray across the room, targeting an unlucky victim in the line of motion, as we all grossed out. Other times we'd all be in the playroom, when Vesla'd let out what seemed to be a deadly, poisonous gas, which also cleared the room in record time.

Like most mothers, Ma ended up caring for most of the miscellaneous pets we accumulated over the years. Besides Vesla, there was a whole line-up. Once our elderly neighbor, Robin Thomas, asked Ma if he could give me his talking myna bird, Jake. At first, I loved that bird and thought he was ultra cool: he laughed and talked and swore JUST like Robin. "Hi, Jake," he said over and over as he cocked his head ridiculously and hopped from side to side in the cage. Mynas are black and white birds, terribly clever at repeating words and sounds. He seemed at first an infinitely amusing pet, but with time, I started to neglect him. I ended up hating to clean the poop-covered newspapers lining the bottom of his cage, and trying to put a bowl of water inside his cage for his weekly bath without him nipping me. He ended up "in a better place" after just a few years, and I think Ma was as relieved as I was, but probably didn't feel as guilty.

My mother got Heidi a boy tiger cat named Johan who turned out to be a Johanna. Before that, Kjersti had a white cat named Princy, who used to nap with me on the playroom couch. We inherited a nervous long-haired Afghan hound named Tara from an "interesting" couple, adopted friends of dear old Norwegian Astrid who lived in Pennsylvania. Tara's long, silky hair was a lovely thing to see when she ran through the sunlit field behind the house. But her frail frame always struck me as sickeningly thin. Tara's claim to fame was that one Sunday afternoon she pulled the rest of the unfinished turkey (or was it a ham?) off of the kitchen table in a sly, quiet manner, and devoured it quickly while we ate dessert unaware in the nearby dining room (perhaps she wasn't as dumb as she looked).

Pansy, Vesla's unlikely companion, was one of several white rabbits we kept for a while. They lived outside, first in cages we kept on the red cottage porch, but then free under the cottage, having innumerable babies that had babies which gradually became wild, until their lineage slowly diminished, the last ones either relocating to the nearby forest or perhaps eaten by local wild animals (my mother's theory). Kjer's rabbit, Pansy, lived the longest; mine was called Clover. I would hold Clover in my arms as long as I dared, sensing her longing to return to earth, where her bright white fur contrasted with the lush green grass in the yard in front of the cottage. Her nose was such a delicate pink, her fur soft as silk between my fingers. Eventually, I let her down as her spastic struggles and sharp claws convinced me time was up. My sisters and I would stretch out on the grass as we watched the rabbits eating purple and white clover, and we would search for 4-leaf clovers which Kjersti said would bring us luck. How sad I was when Clover disappeared one day, never to return.

The most mysterious pet disappearance, however, was that of Heidi's turtle, which she eventually found in her room from the noxious fumes escaping out from the far corner under her bed. His corpse was promptly buried in the backyard where the other extinguished pets rested in peace. That was the end of the turtle era. Once we had fish too, the aquarium displayed in the playroom bay window between Ma's Christmas cactus and other plants she carefully nurtured there. "FISH" was the first word my little sister Julie said, which Beau taught her and had her tell to us, as he crouched down beside her proudly.

Our Vesla lived to be something like 12 years old, and gently fell asleep. We buried her out back by the barn and missed her sorely. In her late teens, Julie managed to convince my parents to let her acquire another St. Bernard, years after the sorrow of Vesla's death had subsided. There was a big dog house for him in the back yard, and Julie would put her arm around the dog's neck in an affectionate hug, oblivious to the slobbery face and transfer of multiple fur hairs to whatever she was wearing. That dog didn't last long and I don't even remember his name. Of course, I was off getting my degree at that time anyway.

Besides the pets, there were often wild animals passing through the yard or field to drink from the river behind the house, or inhabiting the many trees: grey squirrels, red squirrels, adorable nervous chipmunks with that sassy black stripe down their back, red foxes, and even black bears. Many times, in the winter snow, we would find the tracks of the menagerie of our neighborhood. Animals were a normal part of life in the country, and they even invaded my dreams. I'll never forgot one time I dreamt I could fly. I flew up above our house, and saw a huge Noah's ark descending the driveway to our home. Maybe I was in hopes for even more animals. Ma said, "Lord forbid!" when I told her. Ma always told us her dreams, and had an old book which was supposed to tell the meanings, so I'll have to look that one up some day.

Pets really are good for children, although of course they don't grow up at the same rate. The animals we had were good company and the object of many small hearts' ample affection. We adored them all, and were lucky to have a mother who found room in our already full house, for all sorts of creatures. Mom's care of and love for animals was an example to us.

My mother always adored cows. Perhaps she inherited it from

her Grampa Travis on the farm, where he called out to each one by name, or maybe it grew in her heart as she helped her Grampa round them up to come back to the barn. Our house was situated across from a big sloping field, where our neighbor, everyone's "Uncle Al," kept several black and white milking cows. In the early morning hours, you could hear the gentle tinkle of the bells tied around their necks, and the splashing sound of spraying yellow or brown streams, tails lifted to the sky.

In the house, Ma had a collection of cows that overflowed from the kitchen into the pantry room. One of the bedroom walls in the house holds a picture of a little blonde girl picking flowers in the middle of a field full of cows: it had been my mother's when she was a child. There were cow pictures, cow knickknacks, cow towels, and a cow cookie jar that "mooed" when you opened it.

When I was in high school, a stray black cat from the neighborhood chose our front porch under which to have her kittens. It had been a long stretch since we'd had animals. How did that creature know Ma had such a soft spot in her heart for cats? That mama cat became a part of the household and Ma affectionately named her "Babbins" or sometimes "Babs". She lived beyond 20 years, and was spoiled rotten by my mother. When Ma and Dad were alone, after all the kids had flown the coop, they would sit on the couch watching the nightly news as usual, with Babbins curled up at one end sleeping. Ma told me, her voice full of delight, how Babbins would sometimes get up, slowly stretch, and walk right over Dad's lap with seeming disdain in order to get to Ma's lap, to snuggle down there beneath endless caresses.

By her example Ma also taught us to care for the elderly and the handicapped. Her love and respect for them was obvious all throughout her life. As a young mother, she and Grannie often visited a very old lady who was a distant cousin named Evelyn Gerard, in Hancock. There's a photo of me holding Ma's hand just outside of Evelyn Gerard's house. I remember her since I was a bit frightened of her loud voice (she was partially deaf) and she was imposingly tall. Kjersti remembers Evelyn Gerard telling her once, "Why don't you girls *do* something with your hair, looks like a horse's tail." I suppose she didn't like our long hair up in a ponytail.

In my school years I remember Ma often visiting and playing cards with a rather eccentric ancient lady called "Billie" Bower who lived down our road. She was a brittle old woman, terribly thin, and she used to walk to town with her head wrapped in a white scarf: she must have been somewhere between 80 and 100. She lived alone in a fine trailer down River Road, wore big earrings, and reminded me of a gypsy waif. I thought she was kind of cool, even if she seemed distant: she didn't give a hoot about what people thought of her, or so it seemed to me.

Ma loved to stop and visit with Delos Axtell, exchanging ideas and opinions on various topics. Delos, who was handicapped and wheelchair bound, had a brilliant mind. His quick wit matched my mother's. He wrote articles for the local paper. I believe he lived with his sister, Ruth. He would tease me to make me smile, trying to set me at ease. I think he sensed my fear of his enlarged head and my impatience waiting for them to finish: he and Ma could go on chatting for what seemed an eternity to me.

Ma also visited with the sweet old couple, Vene and Walt Boyer. Vene had been handicapped by polio and was often in a wheelchair. (She and Walt gave us the best candy at Halloween, *after* Uncle Al, of course.) Another elderly friend of Ma's was the kind and gentle Evelyn Azalia Campell. Ma said "Evelyn used to cart me around when I was a kid." Before Ma got her driver's license, she even braved the rides to town to buy groceries with Evelyn, who lived further down our road. I often accompanied Ma on those trips, in hopes of getting a chocolate bar or some other goodie, although that was extremely rare. Ma would put on her bright red lipstick and pull the loops of her purse over her wrist calling out, "Maggie, Evelyn's here!"

Evelyn's ancient car stood waiting at the side of the street up by the mailbox. We climbed in, Ma in front, me in back, and her huge, old blue Chrysler began to float back and forth over the entire surface of the curving River Road. She gripped and ungripped the steering wheel, the greater the frequency, the greater her nervousness, as she looked over to her passenger, Ma, chatting away in oblivion. My mother, unaware of the current danger, focused all her attention on Evelyn, catching up on the latest neighborhood news, and sharing any tidbits she had for the occasion. I, however, in the backseat, prayed silently under my breath. *O GOD, please let me see the morning light alive, in one piece.*

I walked alongside my mother as she did her grocery shopping. The town supermarket, the "A&P" had 5 short aisles and we'd pass through each one slowly, as Ma calculated down to the last penny to get the most for the food budget she'd planned, to keep us within our means. Rare was the day when she could give me a dime for a candy bar. She used coupons she had clipped out of newspapers and magazines, and was very careful with spending, out of necessity. Having enough for a family of eight was not easy.

We also moved slowly since Ma would always meet someone she knew. She often chatted with the butcher, Harland McFettric, who was from Hancock. No matter where she was, whether at home in Deposit or visiting in another state or country, she could strike up a conversation and find something in common with just about anyone. Her simple way of making people feel at ease, her strong curiosity, and her kind interest in others made conversation a natural talent. Somehow, seeing her in action, I felt the world was, in fact, really a small place, that everyone is perhaps distantly related somehow. (Of course, Deposit *was* a small place, having more cows than people.)

I was learning a lot from my mother, although I was not aware of it at the time.

Whenever she went into town to go grocery shopping, or any where's else, Ma *always* had to have her bright red lipstick on. "Without it, I don't feel dressed," she'd say. Ma was *usually* nicely dressed. When she was in her "glory days" living in Washington and in Norway, she always "dressed to the nines," as she said. The photos show she was not exaggerating. In my teen years, however, the colors she picked to wear were something of a shock to me (bright pink, checkered pantsuit, etc.).

Regarding clothing, or the lack thereof, my mother was not the kind of person to feel inhibited in any way. After bathing, she would run down the hallway from the bathroom to their bedroom, smelling of "Jean Naté" perfume, singing as she went, and stark naked, much to Kjer's and my embarrassment.

I think I could count on my fingers the number of times Ma and Daddy went out in the evening, leaving us with a babysitter. I hated it, in any event, if it was the kind but wide and elderly Mrs. Cipes, (Beau called her affectionately "Ole Lady Cipes"). She wore thick stockings, which were rolled up over her knees. Once when we were playing kickball on the Island, Kjer's hand-me-down pants split from back to front, and Mrs.Cipes sewed them up nicely for her, before Ma got home. Mrs. Cipes was a nice person, but I didn't like the oldish smell of her, and I hated having to kiss her cheek. When she kissed you, it was the slobbery kind, not so appealing for a small child.

Occasionally, we had Marsha as sitter, the eldest of the Vandermark clan down the road, and she was a pleasure, although I barely remember what we did. It seems that shortly after she arrived, alas, it was time for me to go to bed. We had strict hours for bedtime during the school year, and the hour for bed depended on the age you were at. Being one of the youngest, I usually missed out on the most fun times at night. In early June, before school was out, it stayed light so long, it was sheer drudgery lying in bed in nearly broad daylight at 8 o'clock, hearing the sound of robins' song and the motor of Dad's red riding tractor as he finished mowing the field before sundown.

It was better on weekends, when we could stay up later. Sometimes, we had people over for dinner. It was always exciting for us kids when Ma planned an evening of bridge at home with several other couples. She would get dressed up all snazzy, her hair freshly permed, her jewelry and shoes matching the outfit perfectly, her lips shimmering with red lipstick. For us, it meant leftover treats we rarely got: potato chips, Coca-Cola, etc. While my parents and their friends were playing cards, moving from table to table in the living room, we'd quietly sneak downstairs and into the kitchen to see whatever goodies might be found. How odd it was to smell the lingering wafts of the guests' smoking but fun to hear them all laughing companionably.

We were not allowed in with the bridge night guests, except to say goodnight before bed. I remember Mr. and Mrs. McGranaghan from Hancock, she with her long hair piled up on her head, her big eyes blinking behind enormous glasses, and her drawn out way of talking, he with his quiet manner, gentle smile and smelly pipe. I'll never forget Dr. Mangus, one of the other bridge men, a big man quick to smile, who tried to impress us by taking out his false teeth.

It didn't matter how late they'd stayed up; Ma was always the first one up in the next morning. I'd find her down in the kitchen cleaning up, or drinking a cup of coffee, and eating a piece of leftover "*fyrstekake*" (Norwegian almond cake) for breakfast as she listened to the news on the radio kept on the kitchen window sill.

She was definitely a morning person, truly *matinale*. She woke up very early every day. None of us kids used alarm clocks on school days, as we didn't need to. Ma would make the rounds waking us up to get ready. She'd open my door, poke her head in and say in a sing-song voice, "Time to get up and hear the birdies singin,' Maggie Dooty".

Even with caring for all of us and that huge old house, she rarely gave the impression that she was tired, and seemed so full of life and energy.

And that's just how she was as a child, too.

"LITTLE LIGHTNING"- MOM'S EARLY YEARS

Little Lightning, as Jeanne Dorothy was referred to by her father Cecil, ran rather than walked through life. With unlimited energy she skipped across the farmyard, as often as not chased by her pet hen. She sat still, for now, her big brown eyes fixed on Cecil's animated face as he told one of his famous bear cub stories to his three children:

"Then what happened, Pop?" asked her older brother Duane, sometimes called "Sonny."

Cecil turned and gave him a one-armed squeeze. "Now, as usual," he continued, "the hired hand was coming into the milk house carrying two big jugs he had *just* filled up with milk. Now who do you think was right there in front of him?"

"I know!" cried Jeanne, her mischievous brown eyes twinkling with excitement.

"You shush," said Julia, the eldest of the three. "Let Pa tell it."

"Well," he said, winking at Jeanne, "that darned little bear cub got right underfoot and before you know it, the hired man tripped over the little cub, and spilled the milk a-a-a-a-ll over the floor!"

The children laughed as they imagined the scene. Cecil got up from the bed. "You kids get to bed now, ya hear?"

"Please, Dad, just *one* more of your bear cub stories, please?" pleaded Jeanne, clutching her favorite Growly Bear. "I think I've made up enough stories for one night," he answered. "Get to sleep now," he said kissing each one goodnight, and heading for the door.

Jeanne arranged her bear amidst the many small "friends" which comprised her teddy bear collection. She often held conversations between them, using different voices, talking out of the side of her mouth.

"Sonny," she said, now addressing her brother, as she wiggled her two rather large big toes, "you wanna' play bears with me tomorrow?" Duane, a gentle boy who adored his little sister, agreed.

"Hey, I've got an idea," put in Julia, surprising them both. "Let's play wheelbarrow tomorrow!"

They would blindfold one person, covered with a blanket so he could not peek, and take him around in the wheelbarrow, weaving all over the farm. Then they would stop, and the blindfolded person would have to guess exactly where they were.

"Alright!" they agreed, and Jeanne said, "But I'm 'IT' first." There was a moment of silence, then she said, "Sonny, we might play cards after that, if you want."

"OK," he responded, "But no cheats and pullouts, ya' hear? Now get to sleep."

Sleep gently covered the three children, like a soft and cozy blanket.

Cecil Allen Rood and Edna May Travis had three children: Julia, (born in 1919), Duane, (born in 1921), and Jeanne. Jeanne was born on a Thursday, October 4, 1923 ("Thursday's child has far to go." Ma used to quote this from an old English nursery rhyme from the 1800s). She was the last baby and the fourth generation to be born and raised in the old Travis Homestead in Roods Creek, near Hale Eddy, NY. Her maternal grandparents, William Henry Travis and Katherine Clapper Travis lived in the other half of the huge, rambling house. They had had eight children, 5 boys and 3 girls. (Many of these, my mother's aunts and uncles, came often to visit them.) Living in proximity to these loving grandparents and other relatives fostered cherished and enduring relationships which impacted all three children positively.

The blessing of growing up on a farm gave my mother a love and respect for animals and appreciation for the peace of a rural lifestyle, living close to Creation. For example, Mom enjoyed the cows: they held a special place in her heart ever after. Sometimes, the children would help their grandpa round up the cows from the upper fields to bring them down to the lower fields, avoiding the damp edges where the forget-me-nots grew profusely, and then back to the barn at night. One time, she wasn't paying attention to where she put her feet and suddenly, she heard the clear sound of a horse's whinny in the distance. She stopped to listen and then looked down: she had nearly stepped on a rattlesnake! She felt sure that the Lord had protected her through that horse's voice. Besides the cows and horses there were cats, dogs and chickens on the farm including a grey cat called "Little Babes." There was also the beloved Curly the dog and her own little pet hen that followed her around. Perhaps it was her Grandpa Travis who inspired in her a deep love of farm animals.

Grandpa Travis had a blue stone business at Roods Creek. Bluestone, a type of sandstone, is a sedimentary rock with a warm, blue/gray hue. Grandpa Travis bought the stone from the quarry men and sold it to businesses in New York City and other places. (The New York City Hall features a 20 foot by 20 foot slab of bluestone from the Hancock bluestone quarry). Ma had lots of photos of the stone dock. But by the early 1900s, the bluestone business had declined due to the increased use of concrete so running the farm became his primary occupation.

By some strange quirk of providence, the Travis property where her mother grew up had originally belonged to her father Cecil's ancestors, the Rood family, from which the area and creek took its name. The original Rood had been given a land grant long before the American Revolutionary War. As my mother once proudly wrote, "You can see how deep my roots were."

When Edna May Travis married Cecil Rood, the young couple moved into the other half of the large Travis family homestead. It was a wonderful place for children to grow up: the house was full of books, it was surrounded by rich fields and forest, nearby was a small creek, and all kinds of flowers and berries grew in the vicinity. (Also, Ma wrote once that mounds of a mysterious Native American burial ground were not far away and that her grampa tended to them faithfully.)

Edna, (known to us as Grannie) was a loving, patient mother. She was capable and calm, a good balance for Cecil's sometimes volatile personality. She was a beautiful seamstress, making lovely clothes for her 3 children. She was also a well-loved schoolteacher in a one-room schoolhouse. She loved to read and together with her mother, Grandma Kate, they instilled in Jeanne a great love of reading, starting quite early.

As Ma told us often, her childhood was so happy, you can hardly believe that she grew up in the aftermath of the Great Depression. The US Stock market which had boomed in the 1920s, crashed terribly in October 1929, when Ma was just six years old. Terrible unemployment and financial distress impacted many people. When poor folks came to their farm, as they passed through the area, they would ask to chop wood in exchange for a meal, which was kindly accepted by Ma's family. In this way the person in need was not simply given a handout, they were given respect as well as a little help.

In general, the impact of the financial crisis, failing banks and widespread unemployment was more visible in the cities than in the rural agricultural communities of New York State. However, Ma's grandparents on both sides lost large sums of money in the crash, as their savings were in the Nichols Bank in Hancock which collapsed. Folks had to find a way to make do with a lot less, and gradually pull themselves together financially, looking *forward* to a better future rather than crying over losses. This is just what the Rood and Travis families did.

During the Depression, it was mainly Grannie's substitute teaching which helped keep the family afloat. In addition, Grannie's generous sister, Aunt Esther, who was also a teacher, came through with financial help on many occasions. Aunt Esther never married and had no children of her own, so, she spoiled her nieces and nephews.

Besides being a good storyteller, Ma's father, Cecil, was a man of many trades. He was a carpenter, a mail carrier and at times worked in the stone quarry, with his father-in-law, Grandpa Travis. As mentioned before, Cecil was known, on occasion, to have a fiery temper (Daddy called it "the famous 'Rood' Temper"). Knowing Grannie's gentle way, I can imagine that she "kept the peace" in moments of Cecil's difficult behavior. But

Cecil was a good man, and Ma loved her father dearly, always defending him. He had been an outstanding baseball player in his high school days. Ma said it had been frustratingly hard when his dreams of pitching in major league baseball were crushed one summer: his index and middle fingers were partly cut off on a slicing machine while working as a butcher's assistant: "What a shock and what a sad thing for him!" (From then on, he was affectionately known to friends as "Knubby." How subtle.) Still, his great love of baseball lasted all his life. Since the early 1900s baseball was probably the most popular sport in the USA - the World Series began in 1903. Daddy told me that Cecil knew every baseball player along with their number of homeruns, etc. He also managed many a local team back in the day.

In addition to his love of baseball, Cecil was a passionate man who would really give it his all when he got involved in working for a cause. This trait was passed on to his fiery daughter Jeanne. He could also cuss like a sailor (NOT if he was around his wife) but still, he was a man of Christian faith. Whenever one of the children did something naughty, Cecil would say, "The ole' devil's just *rubbin'* his hands in glee!"

Grannie's mother, Katherine Estella Clapper Travis (the beloved Grandma Kate, or "Gram," (1868 - 1938) took care of Ma while Grannie was teaching. She was a spirited and fun-loving person. A photo of her with three of her grandchildren on the farm shows her spunk: she holds a massive double-bit axe and the back of the photos says, "Coming to Fight the Germans – World War I." Jeanne's head is poking up out from Grandma Kate's right hand.

"I was very close to my Grandma Travis." Ma wrote. "She was always special. Since my mother taught school, Grandma took care of me: taught me my numbers and how to read (when I was 4 years old)." Ma told us that once there was a person nearby, reading the newspaper. "I can read, too," she told him, but the man didn't believe that a four-year-old could read. She promptly took the newspaper and read it aloud. "That really shut him up fast," she said.

Grannie was also Ma's teacher in the one-room school house

Gram Kate with an axe

*Ma, 4 years old with
Curly and Grandma Kate 1927*

where all ages were taught together. Ma said, "She never showed any favoritism and I had to call her Mrs. Rood in the classroom." Grannie always told her not to show her report card to anyone. Ma got very good marks, which she earned, but Grannie didn't want anyone thinking otherwise.

Ma always remembered the poems they read in her early years of schooling. "We always had lots of poetry in elementary school," Ma said. "One of my favorites was 'October's Bright Blue Weather,' maybe because I was born in October but mostly because I loved the golden rod and all the pretty colored leaves on the trees… I'm glad I grew up in the country close to all the flowers and woods and nature."

October's Bright Blue Weather

O suns and skies and clouds of June
And flowers of June together,
Ye cannot rival for one hour
October's bright blue weather.

When loud the bumble-bee makes haste,
  Belated, thriftless vagrant,
And golden-rod is dying fast,
  And lanes with grapes are fragrant...
                    - By Helen Hunt Jackson (1830-1885)

Ma and the other kids in the Roods Creek one room school house loved climbing trees and picking flowers in the surrounding woods, pasture lands and fields. There were pink and white lady slippers, dutchman's breeches, stars of Bethlehem, and jack rabbit flowers, to name a few. My mother always loved flowers. She wrote, "The most wonderful flower of all was the trailing arbutus which appeared in April. My Dad always went out the 3rd or 4th week to get a bouquet. They were the sweetest smelling flowers: a very fragrant, faint, pleasant scent. We were always very careful not to uproot the whole vine. We picked lots of forget-me-nots and white daisies for Mom and Gram – sometimes we made daisy chains...we didn't pick the clover – we thought the rabbits needed them..."

"Growing up in the Travis family homestead... was a very special experience. It was wonderful to roam the woods and pasture land, be close to nature and flowers and always feeling the presence of God and appreciating nature."

There at the homestead, many relatives influenced Ma in a marked way as she grew up. The context of a large, extended family made for a secure and solid place of both belonging and identity. She often spoke to us of her grandparents, of Uncle Walt, Uncle Vern, Aunt Hat, Aunt Flossie, etc. She was very close to Aunt Esther, Grannie's younger sister, affectionately known to her as "A-nut," a funny misspelling of Aunt. (As a child, I called Aunt Esther "the Other Grandmother," since she always came to visit us together with Grannie when we lived in Endwell, NY. They were often bearing gifts for us kids.)

Ma always spoke warmly of her early years growing up in a home rich in love and interesting people. Many of the useful expressions she passed on to us came from this context. Some that I remember are as follows:

"Honesty's the best policy."
"You've made your bed, now you gotta' lie in it."
"Salt's a slow poison."
"Everything in moderation."
"Well, you'll eat a peck o' dirt in your life."
"Cold hands, warm heart."
"That dog 'If'"
"Better days are comin'."
"This, too, shall pass."

There were many intellectual discussions there on the farm. Referring to her family's love of debate, Ma wrote once in a letter written in the 1940s, "...at the farm, they didn't talk war, they fought it." Ma and all her cousins (they were 10 altogether, five boys and five girls) would spend each summer together at the homestead. There was "always room for one more" and the homestead freely expanded to embrace whoever visited.

At the farm, the carefree years of youth passed at that lovely, unhurried childhood-pace. Days were full of adventure, learning and laughter. Life sped up when Ma turned eleven and the family moved into the "big" town of Hancock. Her father Cecil got a job working for a man named Harry Craft who built houses and had a lumber company in town. The family lived at the Rood home at 17 East Main Street, then referred to occasionally as "Back Street." The house had been built by Chester Rood, Ma's great-grandfather. There was a large, two-story barn next door, which had been used as a kind of workshop where wagons and buggies were made.

Hancock is located at the junction of the east and west branches of the Delaware River. It is named after a founding father of the USA, John Hancock, who signed the Declaration of Independence with unmistakably large hand-writing. (Was he a man full of himself, or did he just have poor eyesight or was there some other reason? He was important enough that there are some twenty towns called Hancock in the USA in various states.)

Living in Hanock meant access to lots of other kids, and to the much-appreciated movie theatre, which was located on Front Street, not far from the town pharmacy. Different kinds of adventures began and Ma, who loved to write even from an early age, began to record them. Over the years, she kept several diaries or notebooks – she liked to write down her experiences. At the end of 1935, when she was 12 years old, Ma kept a diary pretty-darn-faithfully through to the end of 1936. It was a small, pocketsize diary given to her for Christmas. It is a testimony to her fun-filled, happy youth.

She was then in the eighth grade, and loving life. It was that carefree time when everyone that you love is immortal and Time itself is a kind, smiling friend. She was always playing something and "messing around." Her days were full of family and friends, games, movies, radio, clarinet and piano and cats. Two of her dearest school friends at the time were Edith Wheelock (later Martin), who lived nearby (her father ran the Wheelock family pharmacy), and Charlotte Elizabeth Cooper (later Parmley), who lived outside of town at French Woods. Charlotte and Ma were born 5 days apart. Ma's mother (Grannie) was substitute teaching quite often. In the back of the diary, Ma wrote that her height was 5 ft 1 inch, weight 85 lbs, her eyes were brown, as was her hair. She was a (short-lived) member of Camp Fire Girls club, wore shoe size 6, hosiery: 9 ½, hat size 22, dress size 14 (years).

Ma's words from the diary are found below indented, with her own spelling. I reviewed the entries with Ma's good friend, Edith Wheelock in 2003, who gave clarifying background information.

Memories from a 12-Year-Old Eighth Grader's Diary

Christmas 1935

Had a swell time, had a big dinner at 1 o'clock, had the tree after dinner. Received many nice presents. Skirt, ski pants, ski shoes, Shirley Temple hat pocket book set. Socks, material for pajamas, garters, $2.00, and towel/washcloth, many other things. Begeals came down...

Went down to Edith (Edie)Wheelock's (E.W.) & played ping-pong. Bobby Bonnefond (B.B.) came over, played Ping pong with him - Thrill! Thrill! ...went up to L.W. (Louise Williams) and rode down hill. Went to Edith's at 7:30 played anagrams w/ Bobby, E.W. and B.W. Bed at 10:30.

Got up at 9:00 went to Edith's played anagrams. Came to

Grandma Travis. Did not do much after supper just sat around longed to be at home in Hancock as I felt sickish.

Saturday – Wrote to Charlotte Cooper. Played cards. Played piano (I do every day for that matter). Washed windows. Rode down hill. Went to Deposit around 4 o'clock. Uncle Nelson *(Grannie's youngest brother)* made fudge.

At last got Curly (our dog) to come in the house. Little Babe's black and white kitten found dead yesterday.

Monday – Played cards in the morning and messed around. In the afternoon went to Deposit. Aunt Esther bought me a pair of rubbers. Rode down hill and skied. Can ski from top of the pasture hill.

Aunt Esther, Grannie's red-headed younger sister, really spoiled my mother. She was described by someone that knew her as "a highly successful schoolteacher" in Hastings, NY, not far from New York City. She was very generous, Ma's favorite Aunt, and the one she spoke of the most. When Ma lived in Norway, she wrote several letters to Esther, all of which her aunt kept. Esther got tuberculosis at some point in her life, and had a long and difficult recovery, during which she learned to make jewelry, some of which I still have.

Dec 31
Helped Grandma can meat. Cleaned Grandma's window seat and found anything from a 5-cent piece to sheet music of "Bells of St Mary's." Came down to Hancock at 5 o'clock. Douglas and Aunt Hat were here. Took Doug to the show, had ice cream, popcorn. Bed at 12:00. Old year out.

Jan 1, 1936
Rode down hill at Edith's...lot of fun. Played anagrams and Ping Pong. Did the dishes after supper. Went to the show with E.W. Got home and read. Went to bed. Little Babes was there too.

Jan 2, 1936
Rode down hill with E.W. and B.W. Had a swell time. Went home washed breakfast and lunch dishes and went to the Post Office. We coasted in the afternoon too. Played cops and robbers on sleds. Made some fudge. Went down to Edith's and stayed all night.

Jan 3, 1936

Went to take my music lesson, came home, messed around. Had lunch, slipped on the ice. Went down to E.W. played make-up. Went to the store.

Cut some rug rags.

NOTE: Rug rags are strips of cloth cut or ripped by hand. You tie them together at the ends, and then roll up into a ball. You use a crochet hook to work the strips into a rug of many colors. Ma taught me this when I was a kid.

Went to a party had a swell time. Learned 3 new card tricks.

Sunday—Went to Sunday School at the Methodist Church. Came home read Nancy Drew I mean Judy Bolten mystery story. They certainly are swell books. Went down to Edie's and listened to the Jack Benny program on the radio (30 minutes of comedy).

Monday – I helped R.B. in arithmetic class. Fooled with R.B. in vocational Guidance class. Came home and played anagrams. Went down 3 (kids) on a sled after school.

Thursday – Fooled around in Arithmetic class. Charlotte (Elizabeth Cooper, C.C. or C.E.C.) came out (from French Woods) and stayed all night. We rode downhill after school…went to the show, "Little Miss Marker." We had popcorn and ice cream.

Friday Jan 10, 1936 - Music lesson was O.K. Got a new book. Fooled in Arithmetic class again. To-day is Mom's birthday. Hope I see B.B. after supper. Grandma Travis, Nelson, Grandpa and Anna and Roy came down, we had a swell time. We went to bed at 12:30.

Ma loved her Grandma and Grampa Travis. He remained close to her all his years, writing back and forth to her when she left home and was off to college.

Saturday – Helped Mom. Rode down hill. We had a snowball fight. Went to Bob Bonnefond (Bobby B.) and played parchese. Thrill, Thrill. We went to Grandma Rood's to supper.

Ma's Grandma Julia E. Rood lived nearby. She had a fabulous

English flower garden. She was quite spry, and Ma found her once when she was 85 years old, standing on top of her dining room table, cleaning the chandelier! (Eventually, she went senile or something - it was said that she had fallen down the stairs). One time, Ma and Duane were supposed to be keeping an eye on her but they got distracted playing something. Then, when they realized she was nowhere to be seen, they went down the road looking for her. When they caught up with her, she said to them, with a mischievous look in her eye, "I went just as fast as I could, didn't I?"

Sunday – Went to Sunday School. Bob B. went too. I had to play the piano thanks to Louise Williams. Darn her.

Louis Williams, referred to as "L.W.", was another girl from Hancock, who was very prim and proper, a strait-laced girl. When she brought her flute to church, Jeanne was obliged to accompany her.

Made fudge, went to a movie. Oh dear I can't stop thinking about Bobby. I must be getting very silly.

Tuesday – Fooled all Arithmetic period, Voc. Guidance class. I'll never forget that day. Had band practice after school. I have a lame hand trying to reach so far on the piano. Am going to orchestra practice after supper. Bob B is going to the show. I hope I see him there.

Had clarinet lesson… Fooled again in class. After the dishes were done went to Edith's. There are only 2 more Arith. Classes oh dear How I'll miss those classes.

Edith played the clarinet, too – they were in band together. Before Ma's family moved in to the village of Hancock, whenever there was some band event Ma would stay all weekend at Edie's house so she could participate. One time, Ma participated in an all-county or all-state orchestra. During the final concert, the conductor dropped dead of a heart attack. They had been playing, "A Royal Welcome Home" and they just kept on playing! Years later, she had her clarinet made into a *lamp* (of all things), and displayed it proudly on a round table in one of the living rooms.

> *Jan 17, Friday* – Went to Edie's birthday party. Yesterday, she took a lot of us girls to the show. Won a prize. Had a lot of fun. Gave Bobby his penny. I wonder if he really likes me. I wish I knew.

> *Saturday* – Started saving for a dog I want to buy one. I rode down hill with C.E.P. and E.W.

> *Monday* – Had Home Ec and History test. Had English and Silent reading. I wish Aunt Louise would hurry and come back. It snowed all day yesterday. It was awful deep. Mom substituted. Ate lunch at school. I went to Edith's and studied. I got an awful cold. Nothing much else. Well-well.

Aunt Louise was Bobby Bonnefond's great aunt, and Edith Wheelock's step-grandmother. She lived across the street from Edith's house, and Jeanne greatly appreciated her dry humor, as she often teased her.

> *Wed.* – I am hoarse and bark like a dog. Had regents (test) in Arithmetic. I passed Home Ec and Silent reading. My cold is worse. I am very horse. Boo Boo.

> *Sat.* – I went to the store. Went to the show … "Air Hawks." It was swell. I am listening to the "Hit Parade." Sure is swell. "Round and Round" is 1st.

Hit Parade was the young peoples' favorite radio program. It played the Top Ten most popular songs one after the other, in order, each Saturday night.

> *Sunday* – Went to Sun. School. I got out a book, a Judy Bolten. It was a swell book. I read that in the afternoon till dinner then I went to church in the afternoon. I listened to Major Bowes' Amateur Hour and went to bed.

Major Bowes' Amateur Hour was something like the "GONG Show" of the 1970s and 1980s: people sang or performed and if they were not any good, he would "gong" them off the program.

Monday – Oh dear no more Arithmetic classes. I have a new subject which is Civics. I went to "In Person" with Ginger Rogers in it. E.W. and I went. It was swell.

They have a new Social Studies teacher, Mrs. Mac. She is very funny. She talks very fast and is very strict. You can hardly keep from laughing in her classes.

Edie told me how this teacher used to get all excited sometimes, and say, "Now listen up people, this is important history we're talking about!"

Bobby and I fooled in Voc. Guidance class. I went to Shirley Temple in "The Littlest Rebel." It was a swell picture. I named my dog Bobby the 2nd.

Thursday – Bobby sits next to me in music class. I don't like L.W. so good she is too snoopy.

Miss Wells got mad at me in music class cause I wouldn't sing. Band practice after school. Orchestra after supper.

Miss Wells was a very young, gentle and polite teacher. "The kind eighth graders eat alive," Edie said. She and Miss Ward were the 2 young attractive teachers of the school and they were both after the one eligible bachelor teacher. Jeanne, Charlotte, and Edie used to keep a close eye on the on-going saga. In the end, he didn't marry either of them so all bets came to no avail.

Wed – Went to the show, "China Seas" with Jean Harlow. I saw R.B. there. I wish he would sit with me in the show sometime soon. I went to Camp Fire Girls meeting after supper. I am secretary.

Camp Fire Girls did not last long – it quickly died out for some reason. They didn't really mind, Edie said, since there was *plenty* else to do for fun as long as Jeanne was around.

Feb 7 Friday ...music lesson this morning. Saw Bobby and "flirted." I don't know if that is the right word or not but I love him.

Sunday – I have been reading. Melody Lane Mystery. I went to Sunday School.

Tuesday – Charlotte came. We rode down hill after band practice. Saw Bobby for a short time. We had a lot of fun. Charlotte and I rode down hill after supper. Hope I see Bobby.

Edie and Jeanne were also in the Hancock Town Band, and Louis William's father was the director. One time, Mr. Williams couldn't show up for practice for some reason, so someone went to get Miss Wells, since she lived nearby the Fire House where they practiced on the upstairs floor. One of the males in the band got all huffy, quickly put away his instrument and left, saying, "*I ain't* having any woman directing *me*!"

Feb 12 – Lincoln's Birthday. We had a lot of fun. Went up to Mrs. Moran's took a heart-shaped valentine to her. We went to the show… "A Tale of 2 Cities" It was good. Went to bed at 20 of 10. Did lessons in bed.

Thursday – Charlotte went home today.

What's this!? Her friend Charlotte stayed overnight at Ma's *during the school week*? And not only that, stayed for *two* nights! This was unheard of when we were growing up, never on a week night, and almost never 2 nights in a row. Grannie must have been some cool mother, either that, or Ma was a majorly good finagler.

I got a valentine from Mrs. Lerpoy. Camp Fire Girls meeting. We made cookies to sell. Little Babes went to bed with me.

Friday Feb 14 - Valentine's Day. Bobby my boyfriend gave me a Valentine. Boy I like him. I gave him one too. Mom had Mr. & Mrs E and Mr. And Mrs R over to play cards. Started an igloo.

Saturday – Built an igloo. Played out of doors all day. Saw Bobby a lot. Played with Edith, Ramona and Billy. Started to build a snow fort. I changed my mind and tore it down. Went to the show with E.W. after supper. It was swell. "Shanghai."

Ramona Cook was a neighbor girl, younger than Ma and Billy, with whom they sometimes played.

Tuesday – Had gym to-day. Saw Bobby. Wonder when he's going finish the snow house. Had band and orchestra practice. Didn't see Bobby after supper. Made up a poem about meself and Bobby. Weather is colder.

Wednesday – Had clarinet lesson. Saw Bobby. Fooled in Voc. Gui. Class. Made a poem about Bobby. He kept. Mom and I went to the show "Mutiny on the Bounty." It was good.

Thursday – Sang popular songs in music class again. There was Camp Fire Girls also. We have decided on our names. Mine is Fawn-Moosquin Indian. The weather is still cold.
Had my piano lesson. Fooled in Gui. Class. Bobby gave me a poem he wrote about me. He came up after supper, we had a lot of fun.

Sat. – Feb 22 Washington's birthday. Rode down hill with Bobby, Sonny, Edie and Bill *(Edie's brother, who later grew up and took over the family pharmacy in Hancock)*. I made a cake. Billy took me to the show this afternoon.

Sun – Didn't go to Sunday school today. Traded stamps with Sonny and worked jig saw puzzles. Listened to Eddie Cantor and Major Bowes.

Mon. –Had a test in Voc. Gui. so we had no time to fool…went with E.W to A Night at the Opera. It was awful good. We are reading the play Nathan Hale in English.

Wed. –Fooled in Guidance Class. I guess I am very silly, but I like Bobby. I may get over this silly spell but I will always have a strong friendly feeling towards Bobby. Went to the show w/ Edith. It was Annie Oakley.

Fri. – Had music lesson. Mom substitute taught, I had lunch over to school. The band played in assembly. I went up to Grandpa's. I rode up with Miss Watress.

I couldn't believe this when I read it, this is incredible. Miss Evelyn Watress, later Mrs. Evelyn Campbell, used to drive *me* around when I was a kid! I had no idea that she was so very ancient.

Saturday – Helped Grandma with the dishes. Explored overhead in the pigpen. Found different things. Put jigsaw puzzles together...I tried to climb up in the attic but was not successful.

Ma had the liberty of exploring all over the farm. When I read this diary entry of farm adventures to Ma's friend Edie, she laughed at the line about trying to climb into the attic and said, "If Jeanne couldn't get there, nobody could!"

Edie remembered Grandpa Travis as "a very kind, nice man, always very polite to me whenever I stayed the weekend with Jeanne at the farm." Grandpa Travis made it a point to take his grandchildren to Sunday school. He also gave them a love of books and even taught them to carve things from wood.

A diary entry from a few weeks later shows Jeanne's love of her Grandpa:

Grandpa sold all his cows: except Dar 3. He hated to see Suky Jane go. I wish we could give that cow to him for his birthday.

Helped with the dishes, sewed quilt blocks. Saw three books Grandpa had when he was small. Carved a man out of spools.

MARCH

I wish Bobby could come up to-night but he can't get out of his house because he and Sonny got into some trouble. Had ice cream for supper. Listened to the radio.

Miss Wells blamed me and Louise for not singing. We WERE singing. She is always picking on us. I played "Easy Money," a board game like Monopoly, with Sonny.

I stayed over to the cafeteria for lunch. We had lots of fun. In Voc. Gui. Bobby and I fooled not as much as usual but we had a good time. We played Easy Money. Bed at 11:30.

Being at the cafeteria was a big deal to Ma and Edie: it didn't happen all that often, and it meant getting to pick out whatever you wanted to eat. After the meal, they had permission to go to the library, pick out books and read, which they loved to do.

Sat. – Helped Mom some. I bought a pair of roller skates I roller skated with Edith. Saw Bob, he was skating too.

Sun. – Skated before and after Sun. School. About seven we played Easy Money: Bobby, me, Sonny and Dad. We listened to Major Bowes on the radio.

Mon. – Bobby and I fooled in class. Mr. Hockmer, the school principal, gave a supper for the band, it was good. We had to play before the board of Education.

Tues – In gym class we are tap dancing. I roller skated with Bobby after school. After supper I did the dishes. I went outdoors and skated with Bobby. Bobby danced with me on roller skates. We had loads of fun. Julia skated too.

Wed. – I don't like Miss Ward. I saw and fooled with Bobby in Voc Gui class. He gave me some marbles last night.

Can you believe how often Ma was fooling around in class and not paying attention!? On this, Edie's comment was the following: "She always seemed to get away with it, somehow, she always came up 'sunny side up.' Maybe it was that sweet smile, that innocent look, and those big brown eyes."

Tues. – I am making a Washington monument in art club. I went to Senior dance with Edith. We had a lot of fun. Julia sang over the microphone. She did good. I went to bed at 11.

Wed. – Had clarinet lesson this a.m. but Miss Wells didn't get there till 8:30. There weren't very many people at school on account of flood. *(The East Branch of the Delaware River had flooded).*

Sat. March 21 – Roller skated. Bob Sands let me ride his bicycle.

Bob Sands was a rather "glamorous" character living on Main Street in Hancock. He came in and out of their lives over the years, as his father worked in Brazil, was rather well off, and they wanted their son to have a good education, so he was often sent back and forth to the States.

Played with Edith in the morning. Went to the show in the afternoon. Aunt Lura (Cecil's sister) and Uncle Clarence came up. Mom and I went down to Grandma's after supper.

Sun. –Went to Sunday School. Read the funnies (*comic strips*). Rode Matt's bike in the afternoon. After supper we played Hide and Seek.

Monday March 23 – My daffodils are beginning to come out.

She already had a garden!

I had Band after school. We have to play at the festival Friday night. Marion Baxter and I went bike riding. We had a swell time and are going again some time.

Marion was the daughter of one of Grannie's teacher colleagues who lived across the river.

Grace Barbara Busfield was down to supper. I had orchestra after supper. I wore my overalls to supper. ...I have been staying at the cafeteria all week (*Grannie substitute taught*). We had the first part of the art test today. It was quite easy but more or less hard.

Friday – Grace Barbara set my hair after school. The festival was to-night. I wore my evening dress for the first time. It was lots of fun. Nelson and Grandpa were there.

Aunt Esther often bought Ma beautiful long gowns when there was an important formal dance to attend.

Sat. – Helped Mom with the washing. Went downtown and got cloth for a dress. I went to Edith's. We read. We fooled around and sang songs. Listened to part of the Hit Parade.

Sun. – Got up about 10 o'clock. Didn't go to S.S. After dinner fooled around. I went down to Grandma Rood's and took her some daffodils.

Mon. – Miss Ward sent me out in the hall from Home Ec. I didn't do a thing but breathe hard. She is worse than anything. Tests started. So far I got 88 in science. I got 89 in History – I left out a whole question or I would have gotten more. I guess my class average will bring it up.

APRIL
Sat. – I helped mom with the washing. I put up about a million clothes lines. (Hanging the clothes up to dry outside). I went to

Deposit with E.W. I climbed tree in back yard. Sewed on skirt blouse.
Mon. – We raised the duce in Home Ec. (not our fault. Charlotte
Cooper was so funny tapping under the table). Haha. Ate at cafeteria.
Got 90 in English, 96 in Civics.

Ramona Cook and I got Little Babe's kitten out from under Sand's
porch. It took us about all morning. Nelson came down in the
afternoon. Aunt Esther came too. I went up to Grandma's with
Nelson. We are going to churn Saturday.

Fri. – Aunt Esther bought me 2 new dresses. One is blue the other is
brown and yellow. I wrote to C.E.C. Sent an Easter card. I sent away
for a cat and dog cross-stitch pillow.

Ma learned different kinds of handwork, like sewing, cross
stitch, and embroidery. When she was 13, she cross-stitched
a picture of a house beneath which was written, "Be it Ever
so Humble, There's no place like home - 1936." When I was
grown, she embroidered me a lovely bird tablecloth and made
many other such things for each of her children. She once made
us blankets which were square pieces cut from old wool coats,
crocheted around with variegated yarn and sewn together. I still
have mine, it's my favorite color, green, too.

Sat. - AT GRANDMA TRAVIS'S EASTER VACATION Week

JOY! The whole week spent at the farm with Grandma and
Grandpa Travis. She's too busy having fun to write in her diary.
She keeps growing taller:

Fri. – Aunt Esther came down for my music lesson. I wore one of my
new dresses boy they are too short. Julia was supposed to come home
but she stayed at Aunt Florence's in Washington.

Aunt Esther knew that music was important to her niece. She
had bought my mother a lovely new clarinet for her birthday,
which was hugely appreciated.

Sun. – Helped churn…Oh, fish hooks, school to-morrow. Aunt
Esther went back to Hastings'. Of course I went home. Little Babe's
kittens are doing nicely.

Mon. – In Home Ec we have started making dresses. Had orchestra. C.E.C. stayed all night with me. We went to the Country Doctor. It was a good picture. We did lessons after we got home.

Tues. ...same old rigamoroll. In gym we practiced stunts. After school practiced the piano. Julia came home from Washington. She brought me a dog pin and a blouse.

Wed. – Had clarinet lesson. In orchestra we practiced the old times waltz boy is that a piece or is that a piece. When us clarinets get able to play that we ought to be able to go on Major Bowes Ametuer Hours. I passed all of my tests thank goodness. We played baseball.

Fri. – Had my music lesson. Gee in Science I just hate it.

Cecil managed a Town baseball team on the side for a few summers. This love of baseball stuck with Ma:

Sat. – Played baseball 'bout all morning. Helped Mom some. Went down to Grandma Rood's for supper. Had chicken boy was it good.

Sun. – Messed around, read the funnies. Played baseball. All of us kids quarreled about all day. Had ice cream, did my lessons, listened to the radio.

Wed. – Clarinet lesson I just hate to get up so early unless I wake up real early. We have been practicing the Skater's Waltz for the Exhibition. Slide, hop, step, step.

Thur. – Gym again. I will be glad when school is out. My I will be glad when the exhibition is over. I got my Little Blacknose "The Story of a Pioneer" book. Boy am I glad to get that. I will keep it always if I can. Grandma and Nelson came down.

MAY
Fri. – I hope it is nice over the week-end. I am going out to Charlotte's...Could hardly wait for school to get out so that we could be on our way. We had fun on the bus. Louise is awful funny. Went to bed and talked. (We always do).

Sat. – Went over to Margarite's. Had a lot of fun. Louis is awful funny. He is Aunt Louise's twin brother.
(Aunt Louise was Edie's step-grandmother).

Sun. – Played baseball. Made candy. Had a SWELL time.

Mon. – We had to make the darn old beds as usual in Home Ec. Miss Ward is getting worse every day. Had orchestra. Practiced the "Skater's Waltz" after school. Edith and I are partners. Slide, Hop, Step, Step. Little Babes has 2 new grey kittens: Itsy and Bitsy.

Every year there was a special exhibition in gym class. The year they did the "Skater's Waltz," they wore their snow suits for the show. When I spoke with Edie in 2003 she swore they had practiced so much that she "...could still do that Waltz today, if asked."

Sat. – Went to Grandma's...did dishes for Grandma, helped churn. Played croquet.

She spent a lot of time with her Grandma Travis, both helping her with chores and learning fun things like how to make fried cakes and how to quilt. Ma said, "I always picked black-eyed Susan flowers for Gram because that's what she called me, "my black-eyed Susan." Her Gram fascinated her with interesting tales about her own childhood, growing up in Hungry Hollow. Her father, Sylvester L. Clapper, born November 3, 1840, had pioneered at Hungry Hollow. He went there with his bride, Jane Chandler Clapper, (born June 2, 1848), and built a log cabin. He set about clearing the land to make a lovely farm and eventually built a house. Grandma Kate was born in the log cabin but her sisters were born in the house. Sylvester Clapper shipped 60-pound tubs of butter to New York City. He had rigged up a type of turnstile so a horse could be hitched up to do the churning. Occasionally, Grandma Kate would take my mother back to see the old home in delightfully rural Hungry Hollow. "The small, winding road follows a brook and before you have gone very far into the Hollow, you feel a million miles from the noise and confusion of civilization," Ma described it with love.

Tues. – Played Bat Ball in Gym...lots of fun. Mrs. Mack is still just as funny as ever. We had the usual row in music class. C.C. (Charlotte Cooper) and I have a way of getting each other's attention by clearing our throats.

Wed. – Home Ec. Miss Ward is going to lose her reputation if she don't watch out. Went to the show. Al Jolson in "Singing Kid." It was good.

"The Singing Kid" was a musical film released in April 1936. Amazing that it was available already within one month in little Hancock, NY!

Thurs. – Played Bat Ball. Had the usual row in music class. I wish Bobby would slap Miss Well.
Went to the show, "Charlie Chan at the Circus" boy it was good.

Fri. – Sent for my Ginger Rogers slacks. I hope they come soon. *(Edie had the same pants. "We thought we were such hot stuff in those slacks," Edie said.)*

Sat. –Decoration Day. *(Memorial Day)* Played bat ball with Edie most all morning. Marched in the Parade at 1:00. Went to the show, "The Life of Louis Pasteur," it was good. Went to the tin house, had to wait on table. Had 3 dishes of ice cream. Had a swell time.

Ma and Edie did all kinds of other things besides going to the movies. Young Jeanne, always ready for an adventure, once convinced Edie to stage a cat fight between their two tom cats. Their cats were both good fighters, and they set them face to face for a major confrontation. In the fracas which ensued, both girls got scratched, and the cats took off "lickety-split" in opposite directions.

Sun. – Slept late. Read most all morning. ...did dishes. Went down to E.W. and played baseball and "Annie, Annie over." Had a swell time...did my lessons and went to bed.

These were the days when kids played games *outside*. "Annie, Annie Over" is a ball game with two teams, one on each side of a shed. There is a lot of throwing the ball, yelling, trying to catch the ball, tagging the opposition, and running around. When one team has all the players, the game is over. It's basically a great way to have your kids expend all their energy, running around like mad.

JUNE 1936

Wed. – Had clarinet lesson. We have to play a trio for commencement. Took an awful fall in the corridor and hurt my arm. Edith and I went up to Grandma's.

Thurs. – Our last gym class for this year, boy was I glad… at 5:00 we started for Davidsons cottage at Sommerset Lake near French Woods on our orchestra party. We went swimming and had a lot of fun. I got home about 10:30. Aunt Florence and cousin Donald Surine came up from Washington.

Friday – Had my piano lessons. Called up Granpa and him and Nelson and Donald and Aunt Florence came down. I went back with them. They have a swell car. Ginger Rogers slacks came.

Sat. – At Grandma's. Helped with churning. Went to Deposit. Got the kittens out there are two of them, one is black the other is white. My it was hot. After supper we came down to Hancock. I didn't feel good and had to take some medicine. Had a swell time riding back. I just love to ride at night.

Sun. – We had muffins for breakfast. I at last got Donald and Sonny to play baseball. We also played croquet. I went to church. We had chicken for dinner.

June 9 – Passed all my tests. Am now to go in 9th grade! First year high school. Julie graduated from High School. Aunt Esther bought me a new dress and play suit.

JULY - WASHINGTON TRIP

This was Ma's first trip to the big city – a month long vacation at her Aunt Flossy (Grannie's older sister) and Uncle Frank Albert Surine's house. Two years after this trip, Ma and her Uncle Frank began a "battle" by poems on cats. Letters went back and forth for over a year, in discussion of the value of those feline creatures and revealing Uncle Frank's strong sense of humor. Uncle Frank was a tall, lanky, quiet man, who worked for the Department of Justice. Quite gentle of nature, he was perhaps somewhat dominated by his wife's Florence's stronger personality, Dad said, "She had a strong character."

Florence Jane (better known as Flossy) and Frank Surine

had a daughter Louise, and two sons, Don and Bob. Flossy was nice, a very active person, plump, with a round face and reddish hair. She trained at Teacher's college, like Grannie, graduating in 1909 in the 3-year "Professional Course" at Cortland, New York. There were 174 in the class. My cousin Lana remembers Aunt Florence taking her family all over Washington, D.C. sightseeing, when Lana was a child. Sadly, Flossy died of either uterine or ovarian cancer in 1955. Ma became quite close with her cousin Louise Surine and their friendship lasted a lifetime.

July 5 – Well, well, we got up quite early and started for Washington about 8:15. Uncle Frank, Louise, Aunt Florence…lots of fun on the way down. Elmer *(Louise's boyfriend)* came up.

Monday – We went over to Silver Springs got Post cards to send. Played Pinochle with Wayne Eddie…We went to the store 3 times. Louise and I went to the movie.

Wed. – Aunt Florence and I went downtown around 10 o'clock. Rode on trolley, bus, exculator, elevater. Went to the Fox theatre and saw Ossie Nelson on the stage. Went to Rock Creek park.

Rock Creek Park is a large National Park right in Washington, D.C. One of the older National Parks, it has several forts from the Civil War.

Wed July 15 – (Wayne's birthday) Louise, Elmer and I went out to Glen Echo. We went swimming and I had my first ride on a roller coaster. BOY! Was I scared. We played cards with Wayne.

Sat. – Helped Louise clean up the house. Aunt F, Uncle Frank and I went to the Lincoln Memorial, got gas at the largest gas station in the world and went to the airport and railroad station.

Sun. – Got up went to Sunday school. Then Elmer, Louise, Aunt Flossie and I went sight seeing to Custer Lee's Mansion, Mount Vernon, Arlington Cemetary and the monument.

Mon. – Messed around. Did dishes, listened to the radio and played bridge. Wayne came down after lunch and played cards. He kissed me 3 or 4 times. Thrill! Thrill! Don came home from drugstore sick. Don and I played roll game we were betting. Elmer came up and we played Battleship.

Friday – Went downtown. Got me the cutest sailor style hat. Went to the Commerce building saw some fish. Ate watermelon.

AUGUST
Tues. – Got up went down to the Congressional Library, Capital, and Botanical Garden's. After lunch went to the zoo. Swell time. Played Hearts.

Thur. – Went up to Hill's in the morning. Wayne showed me his bug collection. We played cards. I won't see him anymore for a long time. Saw Wayne for last time. Went to bed and cried.

Sat. – Aug 8 Saw my last glimpse of Hill's and Washington. We had a lot of fun on the way. It would have been more fun if Wayne had been along. Got up to Grandma's at 7oclock.

Back in New York:

Mon. – Got up early rode the bicycle down to the P.O. to mail a letter to Wayne. Went to the store. Came home made ice cream. Had it for lunch and it turned out good.

Fri Aug. 21 Listened to Hollywood Hotel program on the radio. Went out to Edith's cottage at Starlight Lake.

Sat. – Went swimming twice. Went to the store in the canoe. Went to play tennis. Played cards.

Edie and Ma would canoe across the lake, then walk the half mile distance to get to the store. They did that even when they were in their 70s.

Tues. – Rode 12 miles on the bicycles out to Star Light Lake.

(In reality, it was only seven miles, Edie said, but all uphill so it *felt like* 12 miles).

Thurs. – Wrote to Wayne. I hope he answers. Julia came home from

Washington trip. It sure seemed good to hear somebody besides me talk about the people down to Washington (the most perfect place in the world!).

Mom loved her experience of Washington and her family there. It was a perfect place to go to college after she completed high school. Her aunt and uncle Surine were kind enough to open their home to her then, too.

Sat. – Marie taught me another military tap dance. This one you do to the song "goody, goody."

Ma Turns Thirteen

October 4 – My birthday (13 years old). Charlotte stayed over the week-end. Had a party. Went to foot-ball game and movies. Had loads of fun with C.E.C. as usual

Dec 2 – Dear Diary, I am sorry I haven't been more faithful to you but I have been quite busy since I came back from Washington. School started. You know I'm in high school. I went to New York with Aunt Esther the week-end of Election. Louise got married to Elmer. Aunt Florence, Uncle Frank, Donald and Robert came up for Thanksgiving. I guess Robert hasn't forgotten old times. Nelson, Donald, Julia, Virginia Rees, (*one of Julia's friends*) Robert and I went to a square dance, it was loads of fun. I danced. I have been to quite a few movies although I have been quite busy. I listen to the Hit parade, Fred Astaire and Kraft's music hall every week.

Ma listened to Hit Parade on the radio all through school. In 1937, the "Hit Parade" showed one of the top songs was "September in the Rain", a song which Ma learned by heart on the piano and played for us often over the years. If ever I hear that melody, I immediately think of Ma playing it from memory.

December 1936 – I have to play in a trio (*Edie was in that clarinet trio, too*). I never did hear from Wayne. I hope that I can go down to Washington next summer. Memories are wonderful when you get so you can stand certain music.
I hope to get a diary an keep it every day.

Wed. ...Oh, for a couple of months ago to-day. Wore my ski pants to school. I like French.

In high school, Ma had 4 years of French, and 3 years of Latin. Years later when visiting me in Luxembourg, I was amazed to find that Ma could still remember her basic French phrases! After all those years, and never really using it either, she was amazing! She kept her tiny 1935 English/French French/English Midget Dictionary for decades, too.

Well, I just heard the Hit Parade
      so
           goodnight.

TEENS: CATS & POEMS

My Ma's love of cats began at an early age, no doubt inherited from her Grandpa Travis and all those years on the farm. From childhood and all through the various stages of her life, my mother had cats as pets.

Ma's love for these feline creatures is evident in the series of poems written in late 1938 and through 1939 back and forth between the young teenage Ma in upstate New York and her good-humored Uncle Frank Surine, in Washington, D.C. Uncle Frank teased Ma about her cats and he "panned cats in general." This developed into a lengthy poetry feud between Ma and her uncle. The poems referred to events taking place in America and some pre-World War II incidents – lend lease, etc. There is a reference to the book *Gone with the Wind* (published in 1936), how "Catty" Scarlet was.

They used the initials of their names, forwards and backwards, to create funny names to make their point (for example, D.J.R. = Dorothy Jeanne Rood, and F.A.S. = Frank A Surine). Interesting to note here, is the order of the initials. Ma was originally named Dorothy Jeanne, and this is reflected in the order of the initials used in the poems. However, in Ma's latest birth certificate, the order is shown Jeanne Dorothy (Ma never liked Dorothy so I wonder if she might have changed the order herself?).

Already at just fifteen years of age, Ma's creative capacity shines in these poems. The fact that she treasured them and her special uncle Frank is clear by the fact that she kept them for decades and passed them on to her niece Lana (some of Ma's poetic responses are probably missing).

The Cat Poems

December 1938
Dear Jeanne,

While in the stillness of the night
You hear the cats begin to fight
Get out of bed and make a light,
And find the things with which to write
And tell me why you think you are right
About those worthless parasites.

And if you don't know what to say
To help that beast of muddy grey,
Just tell me how you hope some day
To see the darned thing pass away,
And on its grave you'll gently lay
A bunch of Grandpa's weedy hay.

Fine As Silk

—————

January 1939
Dear January Rambler,

Since Elmer comes from out of town
Where Night clubs serve strong liquer,
To all the cats there on the farm
He is just a city slicker.

He likely doesn't know a mouse
From woodchucks, squirrels or chickens
So you better keep him in the house
Or he is apt to raise the dickens.

But after all he's just a cat
And being on the farm,
He'll soon be numbered with that bunch
That hang around the barn.

Fresh Apple Sauce

Dear Jeanne,

There's very little to be said
To help that green-eyed quadruped,
The only thoughts of which I know
Are stated in the lines below :

O gentle pet of highest rank,
You're always panned by Uncle Frank.
He only know the alley cats
And not the real aristocrats.

Pay no attention to his kind,
And later on perhaps he'll find
There's lots of cats that're awful nice
And only catch little mice.

And so my misled little niece,
Suppose we smoke the pipe of peace,
You try and save each little bird,
And I'll not say another word.

Fine As Silk

———————

Dear Jeanne,

I wish I were a candidate,
To get the votes I'd urge,
A W.P.A. project,
For a wide-spread feline purge.

If I lost out in election,
For reasons unforeseen,
I'd claim that I was beaten
By foolish girls like Jeanne.

———————

Thought for the day
Call her a cat and she'll give you the mitten,
But she smiles very sweetly if you call her a kitten.
Give up?
Enirus Knarf

Dear Knarf Enirus,

O! Uncle, dear uncle, you've sure been led astray.
If then you write me in a poem to do
Things the Roosevelt way.
A project, and a purge are things
That you condone
But as for me and my cats, we
Let those things alone.

A purge! A purge! Oh what an awful urge
To rid us of our cats.
The result? Relief? Oh no, a direful scourge
Of little mice and rats!

So if you turn political
Be not anti-felinical,
For when the votes are counted
You will find the number mounted
If you have the favor of the cats.

Morning Gem:
Whether a smile or whether a mitten,
You'll find it pays to be good to the kittens.

P.S. In spite of your words so vicious
The kittens always bring good wishes.

Delightful June Rose

———

Dear Jeanne:

People differ in politics
Some republicans, some democrats
But we all can work together,
To exterminate the cats.

Dear Dizzy Joke Rhymer:

Now, all the cats I speculate,
Are good for nothing except for bait,
In choosing pets I much prefer
An honest, faithful, loving cur.

Yours,
For a song.
8/17/39

————

November 15, 1939

Don't Jitterbug Regularly:

Your hearing must be poor, my dear,
Because the facts appear so clear ---
I've told you why that worthless crowd
Of lazy cats should wear a shroud ---
They catch our birds and rob their nests,
They screech and yowl and spoil our rest.
They're like some lawless robber bands.
Roberta(*) says she understands.

* * *

One day she said while on my knee,
"Why Grandpa with you I agree,
I hope you won't give up the fight
Until poor Jeanne says you're right".
So you see why I still contend,
That a purring pet is not a friend,
And since Roberta agrees with me,
I know we'er right as right can be.

I won't remain as a
Feline Aid Society

Thought for the day:
Milk to pigs will make them fat,
It's wasted when you feed a cat.
(*) Roberta is a granddaughter of F.A.S. Age 2 at the time

To Felines Are Swell (you know darned well)

Though you style yourself "For a Song"
I fear there's something sadly wrong,
Your musical ear must be made of tin,
Since you fail to recognise the melody in
The symphonic strains of a kitty's purr,
While one gently strokes its silky fur.
When you cruelly twist a pussy's tail,
Of course it's only natural for it to wail.
Even that, with some rings the gong
In fact it was the inspiration for the blues song.
When Benny Goodman's "cat" give out the "B.B. Polka"
You're right there to jump and jive and jolta.
I get the same sensation listening to the ditty,
Swung on the backyard fence by my loving kitty.
By the red roarin' I've come to the conclusion
That you've been laboring under a delusion.
For Eureka ! At last to me all is clear,
My darlings, of you now need have no fear.
(Thanks to that clever Mr. Such and Such
Who said, "The gent doth protest too much".)
In so many a "pome" and rhyme,
You've tried my dainty pets to malign,
It's evident in every verse so mean,
That this has been only a smoke screen,
To hide your great admiration
For the nicest pets in all creation.

Donating Justice Repeatedly

Dear Jeanne,

Your pretty book and clever rhymes
Have been reread now many times,
But when I saw my noble head
Upon that hunch-backed quadruped,
I grit my teeth and pull my hair,
I'm full of gloom, if not despair,
How could you put my pretty face
Upon a mongrel of the race.

An then I say "she's not to blame,
The whole idea is just a game
And since she knows her cause is lost,
She doesn't figger up the cost."
With this I quit and go to bed
Content in mind with all I've said,
They cannot say I've lost my head
Although sometimes I do see red.

Since you must love that feline pet,
You may be blind the same as Rhett,
You may recall the storm and strife
He had to face in later life,
And all because he failed to pause
To see how catty Scarlett was.

Fine As Silk

————————

(Thought for the day)

If ever you are lonesome while staying at the farm,
Gather up the bunch of cats that hang around the barn,
Tie a can on each one's tail to see how fast they run,
They're bound to chase the blues away and you'll have lots of fun.

Mr. Simply Anti Feline:

Dear Sir:
You believe that I'm convinced that felines are not good.
Are you an authority ? Is it understood ?

People who believe in stupid comic strips
(on greater things) can't be authorities,
Especially when these people believe in little Orphan Annies.

"Some people grow childish as they grow older", everyone is told.
It's plain to see that you are growing very old.

It might be excusable for cats to act young.
They have nine lives but you have only one.

That you'll never grow to be a man is plain as plain can be.
So instead of the "Lion Tamers", you'd better join "Annie's Secret Society".

And so when think you have grown to be a man,
Come up here and we'll talk as only grown-ups can.

Then, and only then, will we be able to tell
Whether we should let felines live or send them straight to .....! Oh, well !

Rare Judgment Donated.

———————

Dear June Rose:

Just picture the nights at ten below
And each day cold and bleak,
With winds that blow the drifting snow
On that turn there at the Creek. *

By then you'll need a nice fur coat
A coat that's soft and warm
To get the fur just skin those cats
That hang around the barn.

*Ma had a photo of that "turn there at the Creek" at Rood's Creek.
She had her friend Lil paint it for her, years later in the 1990s.

Frost And Snow

Thought for the day:
Out at night it will hoot and howl
Tryin' to ape a hooting owl.

December 17, 1939

Davy Jones Realm:

Christmas Eve will soon be here
And there ought to be some laws,
To banish all those howling cats
That might scare Santa Claus.

Put them on a boat to Russia
And in the course of time
You will read in all the papers
Where the boat had hit a mine.

Old Santa then would be so pleased
He'd bring such lovely junk
You'd send a note of gratitude
To your dog respecting unk.

Yours,
For Aiding Santa

———————

Thought for the day:
Merry Christmas & Happy New Year.

Those rhymes of yore
That made you sore
Were not so bad at that
They told the truth
When in your youth
You loved that faithful cat.

But now grown old
You should be told
How wrong you were to fight
Don't lose a day
Before you say
Your uncle Frank was right.

For A Solution

Three years after the last Cat Poem: Uncle Frank's son Robert (Bob) Surine, Mom and little Roberta (Louis's daughter) in Washinton DC in 1942 when Mom lived with the Surine family as she attended college. Bob Surine became an engineer and helped design the USS Enterprise, the world's first nuclear aircraft carrier.

Uncle Frank Albert Surine (1890-1964) was buried in Hale Eddy Cemetery, Deposit, NY by his wife Flossie. Roberta remembers her grandpa Frank Surine as "a tall, quiet and loving man."

COLLEGE, CAREER, NORWAY

The high school years passed in rapid succession with a good balance of fun and studies. They were happy, growing up days, except for the loss of her dear Gram in December 1938, two months after Ma turned fifteen. Grampa Travis' wife, Grandma Kate, just 70 years old, slipped away peacefully in her afternoon nap. Mom wrote:

> When I was fifteen, and living in Hancock, I spent weekends at Rood's Creek quite often. I went up one weekend and got Grandma to make her "fried cakes" (doughnuts) so I could get the recipe. (She never measured anything.) So, she took out the amount and then I measured it before she mixed them up.
>
> Uncle Nelson drove me back to Hancock. When I went out to get in the car, I could see her through the living room window sitting in the rocking chair. She waved to me and I felt I should go back in and give her another hug. But I didn't do it.
>
> The next day in Hancock after school Mom had sent me downtown to the grocery store after school. As I was on my way back up Main Street, I looked at the sky and the cloud formations. There was something sinister about the atmosphere. I felt a strange sensation and thought to myself, something drastic is going to happen. I had arrived back home for about 5 or 10 minutes when there was a knock at the door. John Lee (Birdie's Dad) was there looking very grave instead of joking as usual. He came to tell us that Grandma had died in her sleep during her afternoon nap!
>
> I think people who have grown up close to Nature, etc. (and especially Libra people) are more sensitive to intuition, etc.

It felt way too soon to lose her grandma - she would be sorely missed and never forgotten, like all cherished grandmothers.

Still, life moved forward, as it does. Ma enjoyed her carefree teenage years, the everyday-kind-of-living, where memories are made. Hancock, like most small North American towns, was hardly touched by the darkening shadows falling across Europe. However, eventually, events there began to reach across the ocean, as Hitler began to consolidate his power. Ma, like her broadminded family, was always interested in what was going on in the entire world, not just in the USA. "We used to go to the movies all the time and saw the newsreels such as "The March of Time" and "Fox Movietone" which preceded the movies," she said. "It showed the military buildup in Europe and especially in Germany…when they showed Hitler at rallies, giving speeches… it was scary to us but we didn't think about it effecting us, it seemed so far away." These newsreels were about ten-minute long clips which helped inform and perhaps inspire the public.

In 1939, Ma traveled down to Flushing Meadows in Queens, New York City to attend the World's Fair. There were buildings which represented different countries of the world. "The Czechs had a popular building," she said, and with the fall of their country to the Nazis, "the mood there was very somber," she recalled. Later that year in September, Germany took over Poland, like an unstoppable spreading tumor. Ma said, "People began to wonder about war…some Americans didn't want to get involved. They said, 'America First' and they wanted to remain isolated."

This unsettling time in world history was like a quietly hissing static in the background of Ma's final years of high school. Initially, her own family was not impacted by what was happening in Europe. However, "when they started calling up the National Guard to active duty in 1939, some of the boys from Hancock got called up, then war seemed like more of a possibility," she said. "When war started in England, it became very much of a possibility but some people were trying to prevent us from being involved but the Land Lease started so that the USA could supply supplies, etc., to England to fight Germany. Seas were being mined." Of course, there was a lot of discussion on this topic in her family over meals and other gatherings.

In April 1940, Germany invaded Norway, a breach of that

country's declared neutrality. The Nazis quickly occupied all the major cities with fairly little resistance – and so another country lost its freedom as the tumor spread through peaceful Norway.

A few months later, on June 25, 1940, "D. Jeanne Rood" graduated from Hancock Central school at the very young age of 16 1/2. She was "class testator" and her friend Edith Wheelock was "class secretary." Ma had done well in school. A newspaper clipping from May 9, 1940 stated, "The Guidance Department of Hancock Central School is pleased to announce that Miss Jeanne Rood, daughter of Mr. and Mrs. Cecil Rood of Roods Creek, has been awarded a four-year tuition scholarship at the American University, Washington, D.C. Miss Rood deserves a great deal of credit in obtaining this scholarship, as it is based solely upon excellent character, scholastic ability, and extracurricular activities."

Years later, Ma spoke about her years in Hancock Central School (HCS) with fondness and a grateful heart:

> I have always been thankful for the solid academic background we acquired at HCS. In those days, we were not only taught academics but were also taught a way of life. I have many happy memories of those years. There were…things from my High School years that influenced my career and my life. One was our Class Motto, 'Find a way or make one.' Through the years situations seemed almost hopeless or impossible, and I was about to give up when I would hear a little whisper in my ear, 'Find a way or make one' and I would try a little harder to figure out a solution.

Ma and her dear friend Edie both wanted to be librarians but, unlike Edie, Ma's family could not afford it due to financial losses in the Great Depression. Despite a tuition scholarship to American University, she was unable to finance that option. Consequently, instead of librarian's school, she attended Strayor College of Secretarial Training for 2 years, living at 1326 Kalmia Road in Washington D.C., with her Aunt Flossie (Grannie's eldest sister Florence) and Uncle Franklin Surine (her friendly cat poem rival). The house they lived in was huge, with three floors and a basement, so plenty of room. The top (third) floor was a wide-open floor with lots of beds for visitors.[1]

Heading off to college in the big city of Washington D.C.

at such a young age was exciting, especially since the city felt familiar, having spent time there with her aunt, her fun-loving uncle and cousins on summer vacations. So, "Little Lightning" continued to soar through life like a bright flash, a very social and extroverted young lady, who attended dances, participated in the "Daughters of the American Revolution, Potomac Chapter" and was in the Sigma Eta Sigma Honor Society at college, among other things. She also attended church regularly with her Aunt Flossie.

Still, leaving her loving home in the countryside of upstate New York must have been a bit difficult: at times, she was homesick. She faithfully wrote to her dear Grandpa Travis asking him about all the news, the animals and life in general, and sharing her new life with him, even confiding in him about her romance. In fact, she was one of several cousins who wrote to their grandpa after leaving home. He wrote back to them all, carefully answering every question, and filling them in on what was happening back home and on the farm. His letters to Ma also encouraged her in her studies and work, with phrases such as, "You know luck is mostly what you make it…know your work a little better than the other guy and you will have luck."

A letter from Grampa Travis:

10/17/1941   Hale Eddy N.Y.
Dear Jeanne,

I guess I do owe you a letter but you have to make allowances for old people as well as for small kids. Well, it is a nice morning here, froze ice over a tub of water I had out for the calves. I have all my garden stuff gathered but beets and onions and potatoes. I am going up to the (bluestone) quarry most days just for exercise - at least that is most I get out of it… am afraid it is most done with, as the stone does not have smooth faces. Enough for this day.

Tuesday when Nelson was going up with milk etc., he saw a car leaving the road …Then the car turned, ran on across the road and into our car. Broke bumper, fender knee axle and tire rim on our wheel and do not know what else. Could not be fixed here so had to have it taken to Binghamton. Just got their estimate last night. 200$ which does not include towing charges etc. The man was from Long Island, said did not know what happened, maybe was asleep. Was insured with Great American Insurance Co. I am going to Deposit today to have lawyer write him amount of damages etc. Is why I am not in the stone quarry.

Esther was up over week-end, went back Monday afternoon.

As to the animals, old Nig the cat took all the kittens down to John Lee to get rid of them. Fetched them back once, then took them again now, all but Sassy. Curly got running off with other dogs so have kept him tied up or in the house but guess he is improving as let him loose in the morning, he went away twice but came right back.

Have been reading news + story ends mostly some articles.

My weight does not bother me, so do not know.

I have been feeling just average...some bad spells and some good.

What do you know, I do not have any craving for candy now I do not know whether that is bad symptom or good.

Tell Julia and Johnny I'd like to have them, also Robert. Think they are planning to have all here for Thanksgiving...

Sunday, Esther had a plan for us all to come to Binghamton for dinner. It was some dinner, had nice time and home for chores.

Sonny was up one day last week, talked about going up to Maine to work with some gang he worked with at Sidney. But guess was short of money to go with.

Glad you are learning shorthand easy, as a good one can most always get a job. I know you can get typing from the way you picked it up here.

Bruce Begeal and Willie Robinson are going to Binghamton to Trade School they are working 3 days per week now, get 25$ per month and transportation, as a truck picks them up here about 6:30 am with others.

Well guess have answered your questions. I must stop and get ready for Deposit.

Yours, Gramp

P.S. Write soon

Even while life on her Gramp's farm went on as usual and Ma continued her studies, the war was changing the world. Millions of American young men left their homes to "join up," including all of Ma's male first cousins. Grampa Travis kept in touch with all of them, trying to keep track of where they were going during the war. All his grandkids were fairly close as they had enjoyed summer vacations on the farm: Julia, Sonny, and Ma but also Robert and Don Surine, and Bill and Nan Travis, to name a few.

In Washington and other cities, U.S. Officers (USO) canteens were setup for those in training camps, for those being prepared to leave for service, and for those back from war duty. Dances were setup and young women would come to dance with the soldiers and sailors, there in the USO canteens. The gals catered to the needs of the troops and dressed quite formally – they were not allowed to wear slacks and they were expected to dance with soldiers. There was no alcohol involved. Of course, Ma attended many of these dances, too, for she loved the fun, the music and dance. This she shared with her Grampa in her letters and he wrote back and teased her, "Take good care of your feet – this dancing is hard on shoes."

It was in this way that Ma met her first love, a young Marine named Shelby Z. Lassiter, from Florala, Alabama. She wrote to her Grandpa Travis about him several times, for he teased her in

Mom, 18 years old, Washington D.C.

his letters back to her with lines like, "Be good and how is the Marine?"... "You behave yourself and don't depend too much on Marines"... "Tell Julia that I said she must kind of look after you – so you don't get into mischief"... "Never heard of a Marine being cute, their slogan is 'Be tough'"... and the banter continued through the letters back and forth.

Ma had been living in Washington D.C. a little over a year when the Japanese bombed Pearl Harbor. That dark day of December 7th, 1941 Ma was attending a "Soldier/Sailor tea dance at the Marine Club. I was to meet someone there, and a sailor came in with his girlfriend and said that Pearl Harbor had been bombed and no one believed him. We thought it was a joke, but we then heard it was true. Later I went to get my bus to go home and went by the State Department and it was all lit up (that was before the days of the Pentagon), and a lot of activity was going on in Washington."

With this direct attack, the USA was now "officially" at war and "...everyday life changed rapidly: gasoline became rationed, as the Army and Air Force needed as much fuel as they could get, then meat, sugar, and butter were rationed and I think, even shoes, because of a lack of leather," Ma said. Coffee beans became scarce. Certain supplies had to be diverted to the war effort. On one of Ma's War US Ration Book from 1942 it said the following:

Jeanne Rood, Age: 19
Weight: 110 pounds
Height: 5' 4:
Occupation: Stenographer.

(Ma might have added, as she used to tell us, a 26" waist!)

The instructions in the booklet included: "This book is valuable. Do not lose it." Also, "Give your whole support to rationing and thereby conserve our vital goods. Be guided by the rule, 'If you don't need it, DON'T BUY IT.'"

Aunt Florence took the ration books and went early to take a number and stand in line for hours at the butcher's for when meat was delivered. It must have been a bit frustrating for sometimes she would get right up to the front of the line only to find that no meat remained, so she had to try again another day. Sacrifices were made by every American household and this was the kind of thing that contributed to a sense of solidarity, and even, you might say, identity. 'This is who we are, this is America, *together* we are finding a way to fight this war as one.' (This unity has all but disappeared in our day.)

Air raid wardens were appointed in the various residential districts. There were air raid drills and black out requirements (covering up windows and doors so no light escaped) to reduce the risk of being seen and bombed. "Uncle Frank blacked out the windows upstairs," Ma said, which allowed them to keep the lights on at night, so they "could read or listen to the radio. There was a fear that Washington might be bombed since it was the capital."

Back in Hancock, it hit close to home with family members now gone to join the war – Ma's uncle Walt (who had already been in World War 1) and her brother, Duane (Sonny), cousins Bill, and Robert. Black outs were imposed even in upstate New York out in the countryside, too, to reduce the risk of being bombed. Grampa Travis wrote:

Jan 14, 1942
Dear Jeanne.
I do not know what ails me. I was always slow, know enough - if could think of it quick enough…can't write much as I have family troubles up at the barn – 3 nice heifer calves…

Esther wrote that she'd heard from Robert – they are all packed to go somewhere…

…in your work I should think you'd have to think of the future advancement, etc…am very glad you have done so well (but of course I knew you would.)

I do not hear much about Donald. Last I heard from Bill he was making practice flights over US. They had to land in New Mexico due to fog.

Duane enlisted in the US Air Corp on February 2, 1942.

Dear Jeanne.
I do not know if I owe you a letter or not but I get kind of lonesome for your melodious voice and chatter, you know what I

mean. Well, it was 5 below zero this morning but kind of nice to look out the window as the sun is shining.

...Have not heard from Duane since he left. He called me on phone 10 p.m. or after, said was leaving on the 12.25 train...Esther and I have heard nothing more from Walter.

There were 5 went down to Hancock last night ... for instructions on Black Out, etc. Told they were under Army orders now. Fred Gardenier said 'they have got us now: we are in the army now.' The sheriff and Air Wardens etc.

P.S. Our country is all Blackout Feb. 17th.

Yours,

Gramp

Ma continued to write faithfully to her Grandpa Travis, despite her busy schedule, and occasionally she called him. She always asked about his health, told him all the latest in her life and she sent him cookies (as big as the ones her Grandma used to make!). He kept her informed about anything he heard from her brother or cousins, and how life was back on the farm as they began to feel more effects of the war (limits on gasoline and the rubber "famine" – Japan had taken control of almost all USA sources of natural rubber).

Monday a.m. April 20, 1942
Dear Jeanne,

Remember I wrote you that I was getting light in the head. Childish old man – guess I didn't lie any – had to go to Deposit after chores one night ..to see Dr who said my blood pressure was 210...gave me some kinda pellets – strychnine <u>maybe</u>... am some better today...

Everyone that writes me say you are getting high marks, etc. Knew you would not disappoint me.

How is the Marine?

Guess Sonny has made up his mind to go on the line mechanics- which I tried to -get him to do in the first place – would know about planes and get over to fighting just as quick.

We get B_3 (*ration*) card for gasoline that gives us 57 gallons to last (3 months) until July 1st. We had the tank filled the day before it took effect. Tires will be the worst, all but one of ours has been on 2 years or over.

I am very glad you are getting along so good, that 100 – 120 words a minute don't seem possible. I know you talk quite fast at times but don't think you could even talk that fast.

If I don't get over this Spring Fever don't think will do much farming can't seem to get any help – everybody has more than they can do themselves – guess I will have to get a Farmerette, what do you think? Well my head begins to go round and round and 'spose the calves would like their milk. Now be a good girl...

- Gramp

With gasoline being rationed, there were times when Gramp Travis' daughter, Esther (Ma's aunt), couldn't get enough gas to be able to drive up to see her dad. However, Ma once got up to NYC to see her dear Aunt Esther - they went shopping *big-time*. As Grampa Travis said, "Well, Esther says you had a fine time. Am glad you could. Says it about bushed her – shopping – says you looked grand when you started back (I suppose Upper Crust) am glad you could go... tell me what was in the store you bought out."

(By the way, US postage stamps cost 3 cents back then, and said "WIN THE WAR".)

Thursday June 11, 1942
Dear Jeanne,
    No special news that I know of.
    John Lee's horse ran away with the lime spreader and Burt was on it...he got <u>some</u> ride – everybody ran and Bertha had one of her spells they telephoned Nelson to come help– Burt fell off and the horses ran into a ditch and throwed themselves. John got them out, Burt wasn't hurt and Bertha came to and everybody was happy ever after except they broke a lever off the sulky plow...

    I don't know how you will stand it – in college until 19ᵗʰ of July. I bet it will seem good to get back in God's Country – even if there are no Marines here.

Love, Gramp

The Norwegian Embassy
Mom took her last exams at Strayor College that summer, completing the Secretarial Course "with high distinction" on July 25, 1942. Already in August she began her first job at the Bureau of Internal Revenue, Income Tax division, staying only six months in that job. College days had ended, but her relationship with

the Marine continued. Grampa Travis wrote in his Christmas card, "...thought possibly you might be home and you could kind of tell me <u>Confidentially</u> about the Marine..." Mom did get back home for a visit but not until the following January before starting a new job. The local Hancock paper of February 3, 1943 said, "Miss Jeanne Rood has returned to Washington, D.C. after spending a week with her parents, Mr. and Mrs. Cecil Rood. She has accepted a position as private secretary at the Norwegian embassy." Her whole family was surely proud of her. I wonder what her parents thought about it – not many Americans gave much thought to that small country across the ocean in Scandinavia - yet important history was being made exactly there in Norway, where a peaceful nation was oppressed by Nazi invaders.

The USA had been involved in the war almost a year by now. "If there is anyone who still wonders why this war is being fought, let him look to Norway," President Franklin Roosevelt said in a speech highlighting the brave Norwegian struggle. "If there is anyone who has any delusions that this war could have been averted, let him look to Norway: and if there is anyone who doubts the democratic will to win, again I say, let him look to Norway...Norway, at once conquered and unconquerable... At home, the Norwegian people have silently resisted the invader's will with grim endurance. Abroad, Norwegian ships and Norwegian men have rallied to the cause of the United Nations." This message opened the eyes of many Americans who became more aware of Norway's courageous resistance, fighting back in subtle and not-so-subtle ways under brutal Nazi occupation.

My mother knew very little about Norway or its people until February 1943, when she procured the full-time job at the Norwegian Embassy in Washington, where her sister Julia was working. Not everyone that worked at the Embassy learned Norwegian but Ma was intent on mastering the language. She heard Norwegian at work all day long. As she began to learn, she was grateful for the high school French teacher she had had back in Hancock. She wrote, "Mrs. Laura H. Rexford, language teacher par excellence. She was known throughout N.Y. State as a superior French teacher. When I started working at the Norwegian Embassy and was learning Norwegian, I applied many of her methods which greatly facilitated my learning. I became fluent in Norwegian --- speaking, reading, writing and taking dictation." As secretary and stenographer, she became just as proficient on the typewriter in Norwegian as in English. Of course, Mom's interest, her aptitude for languages and her impeccably good memory also played a role. This love of the Norwegian language, with its simplicity and melodious rhythms, never left my mother's heart.

In her youth my mother dreamed of becoming a librarian, as mentioned earlier - not a surprise, for she loved learning, history and books. Although she was initially very disappointed that her dream could not be realized, she told us often, "If I had become a librarian, I would have never ended up at the Norwegian Embassy, which led to a wonderful career and many fantastic experiences. You see, when God closes one door, He opens another one." (We're glad He did, else she would have never met Daddy nor had us kids!)

Being led to this job did indeed set the course of her life, leading to adventures she had *never* even *dreamed* of. Assigned to the Press and Information section, she translated classified information during the war. It was an incredibly exciting time. Information is critical in any war. The Embassy received cables from London regularly from the Norwegian government which had fled the Nazi's occupation in April 1940 and was set up in London in exile. (The government ministers and royal family narrowly escaped capture in a harrowing flight from Norway, the Nazi's nipping at their heels.) The King and the government authorities had refused to accept the German ultimatum to create a new government in Norway under the thumb of Nazi control. From free London, they were able to dispense information from the BBC. Cables out of London came from information smuggled out of Norway or from illegal radio contacts. At the Embassy, they wrote news releases published in Norwegian language newspapers in the USA and Canada.

At the Embassy, workers from various departments helped

each other out as the need arose. Ma said, "As the Press Department had all the duplicating machines on their 3rd floor, we press secretaries would assist the other gals if they needed it." Remember, this is before high-tech printers and copiers – it took a lot of time to create many copies of anything. They helped each other out, they worked hard but they also knew how to have fun.

The work meant jumping from one thing to another and long hours during those war years. Ma wrote:

> I was used to interruptions during my war years at the Norwegian Embassy…I had about 3 or 4 bosses. I might be working on a special project when we would get a cable from London (Norwegian government in exile) with important new for UP, INS, AP (Press). So would have to do that and then go back to what I was doing before.
>
> Often if we had to work overtime, the staff went out to dinner and came back. Or if it was going to take not quite so long, we would finish and then go eat. That's how I got introduced to Pink Ladies and Brandy Alexanders.

At the Norwegian Embassy, Ma met many interesting people from several different countries: one gal she and Julia worked with was from Iceland, her name was Ragna Fossberg. Ma had various bosses over the years, who were journalists, news reporters, or authors: Trygve Ager (an American who had studied

Party at the Norwegian Embassy from Ma's album Ma on far left, her sister Julia on far right

journalism in Norway) was her immediate boss. Others were Norwegians Tor Myklebost, Arne Haugland, and Hans Olav (a journalist and diplomat who eventually became ambassador to several countries).

Ma interacted with an interesting group of people, indeed many who had escaped from occupied Norway. Per Høst, a Norwegian documentary filmmaker, made films at the Embassy about Norwegians in war as well as military instructional films for the Allies. His dark room was directly under Ma's office. Arne Skoen was a Norwegian journalist who had worked in the resistance in Norway and eventually came to work at the Embassy in 1943. Arne Skaug, Norwegian economist was Commercial Counsel at the Embassy (later he became director of Statistics Norway, Norwegian Minister of Trade and Shipping and then, an ambassador). Besides all of these, lots of other well-known Norwegians would come to the Press section to learn the latest news from Nazi occupied Norway during the war years, Ma said.

Although the work was serious, they also had fun at the Embassy. There was often music involved, and they taught Ma to sing the Norwegian National anthem, "*Ja, Vi Elsker Dette Landet*" ("Yes, We Love This Country"). It was sung at the start of most receptions. There were many other Norwegian songs she learned in those years. They seemed to love singing and working together, Norwegians and Americans and others, side by side.

Ma Meets the Royal Family

Once Mom had the pleasure of meeting the Norwegian crown prince Olav and his family.

With the Nazi invasion of Norway in 1940, the royal family also escaped, travelling to the USA at President Roosevelt's invitation. Prince Olav, however, remained in London, working closely there with his father, King Haakon and with the Norwegian government in exile. A reporter for "Sons of Norway" magazine asked for stories about personal experiences with the Norwegian royal family so Ma wrote:

Crown Princess Martha and the children were living on an estate near Bethesda, MD called Pook's Hill, and they often attended receptions at the Norwegian Embassy. We saw little Prince Harald (future King Harald V) even more often, as he would accompany the chauffeur and "courier" from Pook's Hill on errands to the Embassy. He was such a cute little fellow!

One day, in the middle of a busy schedule, we were informed to drop whatever we were doing and assemble in the large reception room on the 2nd floor of the Embassy. This was unusual, as we always knew in advance when there was to be a celebration or reception. Everyone lined the walls of the room, the door opened and in came Crown Prince Olav, Crown Princess Martha and the 3 children (Ragnhild, Astrid, Harald). It was the Princess's birthday, and Crown Prince Olav's visit to America was timed as a surprise to coincide with the event.

What impressed me most about Crown Prince Olav was the way he greeted you: saying "Hello" he would shake your hand, look straight in to your eyes and gracious smile. It was a delighted smile, as though it was his great pleasure to meet you. This was repeated when it was time to say goodbye – the same handshake and gracious smile.

In May 1944 Crown Princess Martha hosted a huge party at Pook's Hill for the Embassy staff and the Norwegian Colony in Washington DC. I have pictures of the group as well as of the children, including the royal children, waving their flags in a small parade.

The Princess Martha and her children were safely protected there at Pook's Hill, under the watch of the Secret Service, assigned by President Roosevelt. It must have been terribly hard for Martha and for the children to be away from their father so long.

Every family was affected and/or pulled into the war effort in some way. Lives were interrupted. As mentioned, Mom's five male first cousins were in college or were working when the military draft began in 1940. Ma's brother, Duane, and 3 of their cousins enlisted in the service. The remaining male cousin, Don, was already in the FBI. Ma's cousin, Bill, William Clifford (Uncle Cliff) Travis' son, "was a navigator for the Air Force, and had been stationed in Africa," Ma said. Each family feared that their loved one might not return and they followed their sons' or grandsons' movements as closely as possible.

In December 1942, Grampa Travis heard from both Sonny and Bill, that they would be done with their training about the same time. Bill was to get his "Bars & Wings" soon. They worked so hard during training, having little time off, about 24 hours only on weekends.

Grandpa Travis wrote about his grandson Bill and others in the spring of 1943:

March 1943
I received a very nice book from Bill, history and pictures of all the Cadets in all branches of Pilots – Bombadiers, planes…Mather Field (California) – grounds, etc. Bill's name and picture was in it. As guess I wrote you, he is Lt now…

April 1943
…I heard your father quit the Scintilla (*later called Bendix plant in Sidney*). I presume he is going to help build the feed store for Robinson.

…We had quite a good visit with Duane & girlfriend, he certainly looked fine in his uniform.

…Bill wrote me they were flying all over the country if got anywhere near here would try to get a stopover and see us…he is on one of the B24's.

…Bob sent me a fruit cake tin with… cigars in a few days ago…

…Suppose the Marine is in Africa or some other heathen country. Don't suppose they've heard anymore from Robert?

June 1943
    Bill called me from Akron, few days ago. He was just home for a short time. He is just polishing off I think in Texas...then expects to go across.

Just two months later, on August 27, 1943, Bill's mom and dad (Cliff) received a telegram from the war department, the sort of telegram every family dreaded. It stated,

    "I REGRET TO INFORM YOU THAT THE COMMANDING GENERAL MIDDLE EASTERN AREA REPORTS YOUR SON SECOND LIEUTENANT WILLIAM C TRAVIS JR MISSING IN ACTION SINCE SIXTEEN AUGUST IF FURTHER DETAILS OR OTHER INFORMATION OF HIS STATUS ARE RECEIVED YOU WILL BE PROMPTLY NOTIFIED."[2]

September 1943
    Have had no more news about Cliff's (son) Bill. We lost 58 planes on that trip, it was over the oil fields, as Cliff thought...

The bombing of the Ploesti oil fields of Romania, was known as "Operation Tidal Wave," an attempt to deprive the Germans of fuel needed for tanks. A third of Germany's oil was produced and refined there, so a successful bombing would have hindered the war. Fifty-four Allied bombers and their heroic crews were lost in the first part of the operation.

How horrific for his parents (and his sister, Nan), not knowing what happened to their only son for so many months, hearing nothing, expecting the worst.

January 1944
    "Cliff still does not get any news of Bill..."
March 1944
    "Cliff thought he might hear something about Bill this month..."

According to the American Air Museum, Second Lieutenant William (Bill) C Travis was on the plane "Suzy Q" shot down in Italy a few weeks *after* "Operation Tidal Wave." Ironically, the plane had survived "Operation Tidal wave." Bill's parents received a letter in 1945 from the co-pilot of Bill's crew who did not go on the mission with the crew (he was later shot down elsewhere and ended up in a German prison camp, but survived). The co-pilot told them that the Foggia mission was that crew's first and only mission. Bill had gone on one mission and did not survive. He had enlisted when he was 20 and died at 22 years of age. Such a tragedy: the Travis, Rood and Surine families were all deeply touched. So many families suffered losses in World War 2.

"August, 16, 1943, 'Suzy Q' was shot down and lost, along with the bomber, Buzzin' Bear, with all of Suzy Q's crewmen killed in action on a disastrous mission to the German-held airfields at Foggia, Italy. Both planes were intercepted and shot down by ME-109 fighters. Suzy Q was last seen burning on the Italian beach believed to be Capo Stilo." [3]

A memorial for Bill is found at the Florence American cemetery in Italy and in the North Canton, Ohio Episcopal Church there is a stained-glass window dedicated to him. [4]

Meanwhile, the family had another scare, this time about Duane. In March 1944, Grandpa wrote, "Your mother said

Second Lieutenant William (Bill) C Travis, Ma's cousin

she had a letter from Duane, said they were only killing time where he is, thought they were going across very soon…have not heard anything since he may have gone…" Duane had joined the Air Force back in February 1942 and was eventually trained in "a bombing course" at Westover Field, Chicopee Falls, Massachusetts. He ended up stationed with the 8th Airforce in England. He was a tail gunner, which was a terribly stressful job. Tail gunners sat in the tight and frigid space at the very rear of an aircraft, operating a machine gun and on the lookout for enemy attacks, conveying what was happening behind the aircraft to the rest of the crew which faced forward. By at least May 1944, Duane was in England, and Grandpa Travis wrote, "…the way they are sending out Bombers and Planes, he may get action quick." Grandpa Travis wrote on June 27, 1944, "…last letter from Sonny said he had been over Enemy territory…" Mom said she thought Duane went on a lot of air raids over Hamburg and Frankfort, Germany.

Duane's son, Tony, said his Dad told him about those war years. Some nights, he'd sit on the edge of his son's bed and talk. Tony said:

> Dad ran dual machine guns, 30 caliber, 7" long. (He brought home some bullets with him after the war.) The planes had cameras on them (or some kind of registration of audio) and after a flight, there were flight reviews. When a plane went down, you'd hear them say, 'Did they get out?' Because sometimes they couldn't actually get out of the plane in time. Dad said that when they wanted to take off on a bombing run, the plane was loaded with fuel, ammunition, bombs, etc., and was so heavy the crew weren't sure it'd even get off the ground … sometimes they'd hit the end of the runway and pulled the wheels up… they thought they'd crash but then it didn't… there was the stress that came from not knowing if you could even take off, add to that the stress of German flak and fighter planes, and seeing your buddies' plane go down.

Flak was Germany's main anti-aircraft weapon which exploded up in the air, sending out jagged metal fragments (shrapnel) that tore through nearby aircraft.

It was on June 21, 1944, in the 789th unit of the 467th

Bombardment Group (H) Staff Sergeant Duane Travis Rood, Gunner, Serial Number 12055190 of the 8th Airforce was on a raid to bomb Berlin (Genshagen) in the B24 plane "Six Bits'⁵ when: "…they ran into German flak and the pilot said 'OK guys, get your parachutes, we are gunna jump,' so they rode it down and crashed in Sweden," Tony's father Duane told him.

"They were unable to get back to their base in England so they crash-landed in Sweden, which was a neutral country," Mom said, too. Tony said that after they crashed, the local Swedish authorities came to the plane, but Duane could not understand what they said, so he got poked in the back with a bayonet by Swedes who had said, "Put your hands up!" The local Swedish authorities were apparently, at first, not so clear about who they were, which side they were on.

Duane's wife, our Auntie Helen, Ma's sister-in-law, was informed that he was missing in action. Auntie Helen was pregnant and had stayed in Detroit with relatives as she was from there. Auntie Helen had been receiving the letters which Duane faithfully wrote, when suddenly, the letters stopped coming. Ma said, "Helen had gotten a telegram saying all was fine <u>before</u> she got notification from the war department" (that he was missing in action). How confusing! Mom's connections in Washington came in handy at this point. Mom said, "… through some friends in the Air Force section of the war dept I found out that he was safe. So, he was in Sweden for a time… eventually they exchanged political refugees and he was sent back to the USA."

On October 5, 1944, Grampa Travis wrote how he'd heard that Sonny was getting around by bicycle and enjoying music in Sweden:

Dear Jeanne,
    Just a line. I hear you are ailing. You know what I told you about jitterbugging would get you in bed.
    Your mother sent me up a small jar of Maple Cream private stock but is gone now.
    Willard Begeal has been home on leave, he has been gone 2 years or more and this is his first time home.
    …Guess Sonny must be having good times with his bicycle and his music…

I hope you get better soon.
Write write write write when you can.

Love Gramp

Grandpa Travis wrote to Mom on November 3, 1944, "…I think Sonny and his crew was lucky to land where they did…" Allied personnel that ended up in Sweden had a reprieve from the horrors of war. Duane was able to bicycle around, and bathe in pools, Tony said, too.

"Several Western Allied servicemen, primarily crew members of the aircraft damaged during bombing missions over Germany, found themselves on Swedish soil, and were interned by the Swedish authorities. Unlike civilian refugees from Germany, who were kept in internment camps, Allied airmen were placed in hotels and bed and breakfast establishments in the Falun area, and enjoyed relative freedom. They received their regular military pay from their home countries, which allowed them to be much better off than the local Swedish residents."[6]

While Sonny was away, his son Tony was born, in November 1944. By January 1945, Sonny was back in the USA and "lucky to be headed to Florida for reassignment," Grampa Travis wrote. Perhaps that "reassignment" included treatment from the inordinately high levels of stress from war, for Tony said that his father had to go for some kind of psychiatric treatment, shell shock treatment. Duane finally got to see his son Tony when he was 6 months old.

Another of Ma's cousins, Earl Travis, was an officer in the army, stationed in France. The Allied group had taken some German prisoners and they were interrogating one officer who they believed knew some important information. He kept behaving like he was a non-English speaking German, but when Earl went into the interrogation room and saw him, he said, "Oh my goodness, FRITZ!" Earl recognized him as "a German student who had studied with him at Union College in Schenectady, New York!" Then they knew it was a fraud, and that he understood English perfectly so they indeed "found out what they needed," Ma said.

Yet another first cousin of Ma's, Bob Surine, Uncle Frank's son, was "with Patton in the invasion of Palermo, Italy," she said, in July 1943, where the Italian civilians cheered them as liberators. It was the first city liberated by the US forces in World War 2. Bob wrote to Grampa Travis in February 1944 that he was "well and healthy, living with an Italian family." He eventually returned home safe and sound at the end of the war.

These cousins and her brother, although fortunate to have returned after the war, had nightmares and other troubles from their horrific experiences: "...some of these effects lasted for several years," Mom said. Post-war trauma affected the health of so many, for years to come, alongside the sorrow of those whose loved ones never returned at all, like Bill's family.

At the Norwegian Embassy, all eyes were fixed on the changing current of the war as countries in Europe were freed by the Allies from Nazi occupation. A wall map of Europe had been set up in the office and Trygve Ager had been gradually coloring each country red as it was liberated. Joy abounded on the day in May 1945 when "Arne Skouen, with great gusto, colored Norway red," Ma said, freed after five long and terrible years under Nazi oppression and brutality.

My sister Julie interviewed and recorded Ma in the late 1980s describing her memories of the war ending in August, 1945 (Victory over Japan Day): "When the war ended," she laughed, "I was in Washington. It ended in May in Europe but it was in August it ended in the Pacific, and the funny thing was, my girlfriend Joyce and I got on a bus and everybody was going to downtown Washington, we went to downtown Washington to join the crowds, going down 16th street and we had to laugh because here it was August and there was a fir tree all decorated with lights... somebody...you know..." (her eyes filled with tears, and her voice cracked with emotion. Julie turned off the tape recorder so she could recover). "There were just crowds milling all over the streets down on Pennsylvania Avenue, and F Street... and people were whooping it up...(not in a bad way.) It was... a lot of people." It was a huge and happy victory party.

When asked what changed for her after the war ended, she

said, "For me, not that much changed after the war, but it did for so many. Folks came back wounded, and some never came back at all. Another change was the American attitude towards the rest of the world. People were happy it was over, it was a great relief, but then, there was such a mess internationally. The USA realized we could no longer be isolationists anymore. Whatever happened in the rest of the world affected the US and vice versa, especially with the increase in communications and travel after the war. It's so much quicker now, one place can't be indifferent to another." (How quickly we forget or try to re-write history!)

Although she never spoke to us kids about it, Shelby, the Marine that Ma had fallen in love with, returned after the war a different, broken man, according to Lana and Kat, my older cousins. Shelby had been in the South Pacific, had received a citation for meritorious conduct in action in August 1942 (this I saw in my mother's dresser in 2010, where she had kept it for decades), and later was recipient of the Purple Heart (October 8, 1942 PH CO. A, 1STRDRBN, 1st Marine Division, FMF, Solomon Islands battling the Japanese) where he was wounded in action.[7] Who knows the trauma he went through? "It broke her heart. She never forgot him," Lana said. (This is why whenever we had philosophical discussions about love and marriage growing up, Ma always said, "Oh yes, you can truly love more than one person in your life.")

In 1946, after three years working in the Press and Information Section of the Norwegian Embassy, Ma was sent from Washington to the Royal Norwegian Information Service at 30 Rockefeller Plaza in New York City. This Information Service was a department of the Norwegian Embassy in Washington, with Hans Olav still overseeing their work. Their offices were on the 18th floor of the RCA Building and the back-office windows looked down on the skating pond (at the front of the RCA Building). When Ma was in the back library room addressing envelopes or sending out information about Norway, she often enjoyed watching the skaters.

At the Royal Norwegian Information Service, Ma made the acquaintance of radio broadcaster Mrs. Gladys Petch, a radio consultant whose wartime series included interviews of Norwegians

Mom with Kåre at China Doll Restaurant New York City January 1947

who had escaped during the war and described life back in the "Old Country."[8] Ma went out with a Norwegian musician, Kåre, who sent her two letters back to NYC from his tours around the world, and asked her to give his regards to Mrs. Petch.

Ma lived at the Katharine House, a residence for young women on 118 West 13th Street in New York City. She stayed in NYC for one year, and during that time, was able to see a lot of her dear Aunt Esther, who lived quite close by in Hastings-on-Hudson where she was a well-loved teacher. Aunt Esther's proximity was to be especially important for Ma, for on February 18, 1946, her dear Grampa Travis passed away. He had loved her so well, taken her to Sunday school to learn about God and taught her to do her best, to work hard and to set her sights high. His affectionate care remained a treasure in her heart to the end of her days. (Grandparents can play such an important role in our lives!)

It was about this time that Ma decided she wanted to go to Norway, this land she had been learning so much about from the many Norwegians she met and worked with. Hans Olav, the Norwegian Embassy Counselor (press advisor) wrote in a glowing reference letter dated Feb 4, 1947: "Miss Jeanne Rood has been employed as secretary – stenographer with the Norwegian Embassy's Division of Information since 1943...She is thoroughly capable even to the point of having become an excellent typist in the Norwegian language, although she is an American. Congenial, willing, and hard working (and indeed, no clock watcher) she has endeared herself to her superiors and her co-workers. We regret very much that she now wants to leave us, but she intends to go to Norway to see for herself the people and country with whom she has been associated for 4 years. I am pleased to give Miss Rood my best recommendation."

Sven N. Oftedal, experienced Norwegian journalist and Director of the Royal Norwegian Information Services, also wrote a wonderful reference letter for her: "Miss Jeanne Rood has been working with this office since March 1946. She is now leaving to take over a job in Norway. It is with regret we see Miss Rood leave us. She is an extremely versatile, conscientious, and willing worker and never shirks an extra burden. She gets things done and uses her own judgment in a very commendable way. We have been extremely well pleased with her work and her whole attitude."

Now, it was time to get ready for the next adventure – moving to Norway!

Aunt Esther "chased all over New York City shopping for me," Ma wrote, and helped her to pack for what was to be the most exciting trip of her life. Aunt Esther and a friend, Sverre Sandberg, accompanied her to the ship. Sverre kindly "carried all my bundles and suitcases," she said. Her cousin Lilian and Aunt Esther "endured me the last day in New York. Lilian said I did nothing but giggle all day." Aunt Esther, Lilian and husband George all accompanied her to the pier, to say goodbye to young Jeanne.

So, on a Wednesday, March 12, 1947, the next adventure began! She left for Norway at the young age of 23, riding a cargo freighter, the *S/S Norefjord*, from New York to Oslo, via Canada. This first stay in Norway was to last for 1½ years and was really the beginning of a lifelong love for the country – she had already fallen in love with the Norwegian people.

In her diary she wrote:

> When we finally pulled up anchor, I went out on deck and watched New York disappear! It was a beautiful sight with all the tall buildings lighted, but I could only think of the dirty, sooty smell, and all the people rushing around, and I felt a bit relieved. This made me feel guilty so I tried to feel sad – but to no avail. It just seemed right that I should be going to Norway. Even when I saw the Statue of Liberty, I didn't feel sad, I felt like everything was as it should be.

> Thursday, March 13, 1947
>   Sea sick slightly! Lost breakfast, but spent whole day up on Captain's deck in a beach chair. The Steward brought up lunch and later tea, so I'm really spoiled. We all lounge around in slacks and do as we please. Everyone is swell.
>   There were only six other passengers on the ship, a dog named "Beauty" and the working crew.

From Ma's Scrapbook of her boat trip to Norway.

Friday

It rained but I put on a million sweaters and my raincoat and went up on deck for a walk.

In the evening we came to Canada. The captain invited us up to his cabin for a party. A few cocktails and lots of fun. The Captain played the accordion and sang some long songs of the "tranoy" variety. The steward is a riot.

Saturday

The Canadian immigration officer came on board and nearly got seasick from the rocking boat.

Sunday 16th

After dinner the 1st officer took us up in the steering room and the outlook decks. Then to his cabin for music and drinks. Everyone is so nice! Talked some more with the sailors. It is some fun since they speak no English.

Tuesday

Walked around the deck after dinner and talked with the sailors. They were loading the boat and it made terrific noise. All of us watched the men loading flour, etc., and unloading sardines.

Wednesday

The Captain officers and us were invited to a dance given by the St. John Ski Club. We had a wonderful time. The radio operator and I had lots of fun jitterbuggin' but the Tango was the best. The Steward and he got in a fight over me so now the 1st officer insists on calling me "Glamour Girl." We got back to the boat at 4:30 and ate sandwiches. Bed at 5:30 a.m.!

Thursday

Steward couldn't find Randi and I for we had moved into the extra cabin which was much warmer. He insisted on singing to me before I could even comb my hair and of course the 1st officer keeps calling me Glamour Girl. I helped the tall, funny sailor from Bergen paint the boat!

Her diary of the trip is full of laughter, playing cards (poker, etc.), eating, putting puzzles together, washing clothes, reading, and walks on deck. Carrying hot water in tin pails was also a common pastime. When they stopped at port, they would visit a bit and walk by the sea. In Canada, she bought some dungarees "so now I can really paint," she wrote.

Wednesday
There was a rough sea so we had to go out and anchor in the bay in order to keep from wrecking the ship against the harbor. Some fun. It rocked quite a bit.

Friday March 28
The great day arrived! The final cargo was loaded and we pulled out of St. John a little after 4 in the afternoon. Fellows from the other ships were whistling and waving to us. You should have seen the ship's dog when she left her pal on shore. (*She always had an eye out for animals!*)

There was the most beautiful sunset I have ever seen. Everything was pink and blue and gold. It was just like a fairytale. I'll never forget it: it looked so unreal. Just beautiful.

After they finally took off for Norway from Canada, Ma was

Ma On the Ship

seasick for 3 days. "Why must the boat always rock so much? Always moving. I spend a great deal of time lying around, trying to feel better."

While on board she wrote to her dear Aunt Esther on April 1st saying, "I am all over the boat, especially in all the places where you ordinarily don't go (*Typical mischievous Ma*) ...I was a little seasick the first day, but only lost my breakfast..." She tells of lots of eating, singing and dancing with the crew and her girlfriend Randi. Randi taught her how to knit Scandinavian style. It took one month to get to Norway, but she said, "We had so much fun I wouldn't have minded if we had stayed longer." While on board, she "helped the boys paint the boat and also ironed shirts for several different ones. I had to speak Norwegian to them so I got lots of practice."

> April 6, Easter Sunday
> Randi & I got up at 5 o'clock to see the sunrise. The *Styrmann* (helmsman) invited us up to the bridge for coffee and 6 when the Steward came up. More fun! The *Styrmann* showed us how to chart course, etc.

On April 9th, they passed the Orkney Islands, Scotland, and headed for Norway. The next day, the North Sea was very calm and she had her first glimpse of Norway as they approached Kristiansand.

One full month after departure from New York, they arrived. Mom had just loved the boat trip over and afterwards made a fun-filled scrapbook to record her adventure.

> Friday, April 11th
> We are truly in Norway. We went to town and it was fun to see the stores and quaint houses. I didn't feel the least bit strange when I first stepped on Norwegian soil...

The last day on the ship was Saturday April 12. There was a lot of fog so they had to anchor in Oslo harbor. Friends she had met in either Washington or New York were on the reception committee:

I was talking to Johnny on the deck when I saw a small motorboat coming and I recognized Ellas's mother and sister! We went crazy laughing and waving. I ran around to where they came aboard and fell into their arms. They had brought me some tulips and other Norwegian flowers.

After customs had searched our baggage and after saying good bye to the crew we head for shore. When we arrived, there was Signe. "Are you really here, Jeanne?" she said.

And so, I arrived…

Mom was about to discover Norway, country of majestic mountains, fjords, forests, waterfalls, and glistening sea. She would be staying in Oslo, the capital city, where she had the joy of experiencing Constitution Day with its fun and parades on May 17, 1947. She remembered the sounds of the patriotic song, "Norge i Rødt, Hvitt og Blått" resounding "everywhere in Oslo, all day and half the night." It had just been two years since Norwegians could not celebrate the 17 of May because of the Nazi occupation. While the post-war economy had not fully recovered and many goods were still unavailable, the taste and feeling of freedom was everywhere.

While Mom was discovering this Scandinavian people and its country, Norway was about to "meet" and "adopt" this unusual American farm girl.

Edna's Child Becomes Norway's Daughter

Ma found a place to stay in Oslo with a kind Norwegian family, the Gudmundsen's. They offered her a couch in their living room until she could find a better place to stay and made her feel right at home from the start.

Her stay in Norway was undoubtably one of the most fulfilling times of her life. She was positively overwhelmed by Norwegian hospitality, fun and humor. She absolutely adored the country and its people (not to mention "the cakes and pastries" as she wrote on her "List of things to remember"). Impromptu parties were always popping up, and she met so many people who invited her for visits and trips. They often went for weekend hiking or skiing trips in the areas around Oslo. For example, Ma once hiked up a mountain with the Rund family. Recalling that hike years later she said, "The two boys wanted to take me hiking but didn't think I could keep up (they thought American girls couldn't climb mountains or hills!). Did you ever see the picture of me sitting on a strip of snow with my shorts and hiking boots on? Enough reminiscing. That was the occasion."

Ma had about six weeks to get settled before starting work at Elektrokemisk (EK), (*Det Norske Aktieselskap for electrokemisk industri*) 23 Radhusgate, in Oslo from June 1, 1947 until Sept 30, 1948. Elektrokemisk was Norway's largest private electrical engineering and entrepreneur firm in the field of electrical smelting furnaces. They developed technology and industry based on hydropower and were involved in the startup of Norsk Hydro.

Ma wrote many letters from Norway especially to her parents

Ma hikes in Norway in 1947

and her aunt Esther. She asked them to save her letters as she was "too busy to keep a diary." Aunt Esther such a generous person by nature and she spent lots of money on her favorite niece.

Ma wrote to her dear Aunt Esther on July 25, 1947:

> To one A-NUT from Another…The girls I work with are swell and we have quite a gay time at the office. Yesterday we were eating all day…melon, bananas (a rare treat)…huckleberries…Then to top everything off, Greta had slipped out to the store and bought some *Napolean's kake (a multi-layered pastry we called "mille feuille" in Luxembourg)* which was really good.
>
> Love, Jeanne, Jeanne the Village Queen."

The latter was a nickname coined by her brother-in-law, Emile Passman.

> Oslo July 5, 1947
> Dear A-Nut,
>   It sure was good to get a long chatty letter from you! …I am still having a most wonderful time and I hope it lasts. I like my work so much and my social life is something! I am invited here and there and everyone is so nice to me. Here at the office, they all absolutely spoil me since I am the only American here…I love all the crazy parties…everyone can be as crazy as they desire: not necessarily bad or anything like that but just crazy like me and you!

Even two years after the war had ended, there were many shortages of goods in Norway and "very strict rationing of almost everything in the food and clothing line. What is more, there are things that aren't even available."[9]

Many a letter to Aunt Esther refers to purchases and requests for stockings, shoes and the like. In one letter Ma wrote, "I hope everything is OK with you and that you are going strong. I am glad you bought some clothes. It is about time you got rash like your little niecyyy. Drop me a line and tell me what's cookin'." Aunt Esther was always sending packages to her in Norway: cheese spread, peanut butter, and CHOCOLATE, Ma's favorite. In every second letter she refers to how grateful she was for the chocolate Aunt Esther would send.

On Sept 6th, 1947 she wrote, "Mrs. Bache is arriving tomorrow so I am going down to meet the boat. She is bringing <u>a brief case with some chocolate</u> to me from Lilian."

(Ma once told me that her Grampa Travis used to buy chocolate and stash it so it would not get eaten up so fast. Her father Cecil did the same. So, you see that we really come from a long line of chocoholics. Once Ma sent me an article from Jan 1995 Good Housekeeping magazine entitled, "Why Women Need CHOCOLATE").

In another letter to Aunt Esther, Ma wrote about receiving shoes and other things, which her friend Randi brought back after a visit to Ma's family in NY. It wasn't that Ma had asked for all that, since she wrote, "Thanks a million for thinking about the slips, pants and garter belt. You seem to know what I need. I had been hoping for such a supply but didn't feel that I could ask for them, and would have tried to get along with the ones I have until I come home. Thanks a million for thinking about it." Ma was always a grateful lady, appreciative of gifts: she was not one to take things for granted. [Years later when Dad had retired and they were enjoying the "golden" years, she wrote, "Maggie, you are so good to us, as are all our kids. Really means a lot to us." She was a thankful person her whole life.]

Ma's sympathy for the downhearted comes out in a letter to Aunt Esther dated Sept. 6, 1947.

I was invited out for coffee at the home of Ingeborg Rosted (one of the girls from the office). Her mother was born in Finland. Ingeborg's father and 2 of her brothers were lost in the war. One killed by the Germans, one went down at sea, and the other died of hunger in a concentration camp. I feel so sorry for her mother. There are many families here like that. It makes me wonder if most Americans realize how lucky they are.

Over 10,000 Norwegians were killed in World War II.

October 22, 1947
Dear Aunt Esther,
We are still having a very nice time here at the office. I have had quite a lot to do but we in "hønsegården" (the henyard) get time to

enjoy ourselves...We have been writing poetry about each other – ½ in English and ½ Norwegian...I am still meeting people from New York when I walk down the street. The other day I was up at the American Embassy and there bumped into a Norwegian who had been in NY last winter. So it goes."

She found another living arrangement sometime in October:

Oslo, November 4, 1947
Dear Anut,
    I've found a very nice room to rent nearer town with a private family, named Vethe. He is the Director of Citroen (French automobile corporation here in Oslo)....I get the room very reasonably since I'm helping them with English. ...You usually have to pay at least 60 kroner, but I am paying only 30...Also, I am eating dinner every day with Randi at a sort of boarding place run by an old lady, Tanta Olava Øvergaard. There is a little sitting room where you can sit and read the newspapers or talk with the other people after you have eaten. Of course, I make my own breakfast where I am living. I like this arrangement I have now very much."

Despite all the eating, Ma now weighed only 121 lbs (55 kg). Each letter tells of all her invitations to dinners and parties.

Oslo, November 17, 1947
    ...My hair is getting lighter and <u>redder</u>. Must be sign of the old fiery spirit.
    Love, Your Adopted Mama.

Oslo, December 1
    I received the 2 packages from you. BOY! They were something. It is wonderful to get all the sugar for Christmas. And the vitamins. You thought of everything. I think I am lucky to have A-nut like you.
    I went skiing yesterday for the first time and I can just about move my arms today...I got along very well and had only 1 bad fall. The other falls weren't bad ones....we went on one path up to a place called Ullevåll Seteren. There we bought coffee and *wienerbrød*. Then we took another route to Froggnersetern, where we ate dinner. There we can sit in front of the big fireplaces while we are eating Then it was dark: it was beautiful skiing after dark and to look down on the lights of Oslo. We were on skis about 5 hours. It was loads of fun.

(Skiing and skating are the only sports I'm aware that Ma did as an adult. Years later, Ma gave her niece, Lana, her first pair of skis, and got her into skiing, something for which Lana was always grateful. However, I do remember her mentioning that in her schooldays, she spent hours on the tennis court, often playing until they could no longer see the ball. They played baseball, too. After her marriage, her main sport was chasing wayward offspring).

> I have loads of energy and am never tired.
> You should see me at the eating place. I am having more fun, for it usually ends up with me and Randi and about 6 – 8 fellows discussing things. I have all of them trained to hold my coat, etc. The Norwegian fellows aren't bad if you train them right. I think I have revolutionized a few things here and, of course, I am enjoying it."

There were more dinners and dancing, special times with friends (Gudmundsens, dinner and a movie (Disney's "Dumbo") with Kirsten, a visit with the Tranoy family. Ma tells how lucky they were to get a meat dinner (usually they had meat only once a week, as it just was not available in these post-war years).

> January 4, 1948
> The people where I am living are very nice and I have a wonderful room. It's quite large but very cozy. The maid spoils me because no matter what time I come home at night, if she's up she makes sandwiches and tea for me.
> The wind is blowing to beat the band and it's trying to snow. It's been mostly between 4- and 10-degrees F. They say the majority of the coldest weather comes in Feb/March so we shall see how it is.

Ma also enjoyed skiing on Sundays.

> January 21, 1948
> This time I went with the Lindstrøms – a short ski trip, only 2 ½ hours. I went to some skating races. Interesting but quite cold standing there. I was good and warm. I have never heard people complain about the cold as much as the Norwegians do.

While working one day, a middle-aged interoffice courier

named Olsen, who made the rounds with the mail, came into the office. He rushed over to Ma all excited.

"Yenny!" he said (they sometimes called her Jenny instead of Jeanne but with his accent, it came out Yenny). "Yenny, they told about Hancock on the radio travelogue last night!"

"Oh Olsen," she said, "Quit your spoofin,' they never heard of Hancock."

"Oh yes," he said, "It was Hancock all right."

Ma replied, "Olsen, do you know how many Hancocks there are in the United States – at least 10. There's Hancock, Maryland, Hancock, New Hampshire, Hancock, Maine..."

"No, Yenny, it was your home town," he responded.

Ma was acquainted with Karl Lyche, the head of the News Department of the Norwegian Broadcasting Corporation, so she called him and asked whether he'd listened to Julius Hougen's travelogue the night before. Karl said he would check with Mr. Hougen, a famous radio personality in Norway. A little while later Ma's phone rang and a very familiar Norwegian radio voice said, "Are you the gal from Hancock, N.Y.?"

She said, "Yes, Mr. Hougen, were you really there?"

"Yes," he replied. "It was such a picturesque little village surrounded by hills so we stopped there. We had been collecting material all through New England and we needed to spend a couple of days coordinating the material."

Ma got such a kick out of that! What a small world it truly is.

Ma was having such a great time, that she decided to lengthen her stay.

February 16, 1948
    Did I tell you I don't want to come before September? I can't get all the traveling done I want to if I come in July. Also, there are so many I know who are coming here this summer. And then too, besides all that I am having such a good time that I don't want to leave yet. It isn't definite yet but I am hoping that I won't come until September.

Ma's independent streak comes out in the letters from March, 1948. With World War 2 just having ended a few years earlier, her family worried about the Soviet communists possibly attempting to invade Norway, and they wanted her to consider coming home. This was the era of the Cold War, a period of tension between the Soviet Union and the USA (and its allies). She wrote:

I don't think they have anything to worry about as far as Norway is concerned – at least not at the present. The opinion here is not as aroused as it seems to be in America. That is, of course people are concerned about Czechoslovakia but there aren't many here who could begin to believe such a thing could take place in Norway. Besides, there aren't as many communists here. 2ndly, they couldn't take Norway by force unless they were ready for war with the whole world and no one here thinks they are prepared for such a thing yet, Hitler decided that the dumbest thing he ever did was to invade Norway and the Soviets would find it the same way if they came here. There would be so much sabotage, they wouldn't have much use from the airfields, etc. ...I hope everyone will stop worrying about me. You are about the only one who hasn't told me to come home. However, I intend to carry out my present plans as far as logical and possible and come home when I think it necessary or advisable.

Later in March she wrote:

I am glad to hear that at least you understand my desire to stay here as long as possible...I feel the way that you do that "what will be will be." I don't at all worry about being here and I feel worst about the fact that Mom and Dad are probably worrying their heads off. Of course everyone is probably thinking it is only because of Lars, but I am not so dumb that I would stay a place just because of a fellow. I like it here so much, my work, where I live and my social life, so why shouldn't I be here!

(There are a few references to her friend Lars in letters here and there, but it didn't seem to be very serious by the tone of her writing).

By now, Ma has been in Norway for one year. What a treat to be able to travel to other countries as well! She and friends enjoy travels to Sweden and Denmark.

April 1948

Dear Suze (*another nickname for Aunt Esther*), ...Monday night Randi and I are going to have a little party at my place to celebrate our one year in Norway. There will be 4 fellows and 4 girls all of whom eat at Tante Olava's.

Signe Lund and I are planning on going to Stockholm April 27th with the night train and be there for 5 days.

P.S. Am still enjoying the chocolate you sent some time ago. Am stretching it as far as possible.

From a Stockholm, Sweden postcard dated April 30, 1948:

Dear Suze,

Signe and I have just completed 3 days in Stockholm. We are having a wonderful time. It is one of the most charming, picturesque, and interesting places I've been. It is really "the Venice of the North" with all the bridges, etc. The cars drive on the left here so we are having a time crossing streets. Love, Jeanne.

Oslo May 10, 1948
Dear Aunt Esther,

Stockholm was wonderful...beautiful, and romantic. The bridges and waterways add to the beauty of the city and the architecture is a mixture of old with new. Each building is itself a work of art. ..There is a very old part of the city which is most interesting. I really realized how old Europe is and how young America is when I saw some of the buildings which were built in the 12th and 13th centuries.

There are lots of parks and lovers' lanes spread over the city.

I'll probably be coming home in September or early October. I am not sure yet.

May 6, 1948
Dear Grandma (*this postcard was sent to her father's mother, Julia Rood, who loved gardening*),

This is a picture of one of the main streets in Oslo. You can see the King's Palace...and the Grand Hotel, one of the best in the city. Oslo is really beautiful and I wish you could see it. I am having a wonderful time. Everyone is so kind and I have so many friends here I am never homesick. I think about you often and I hope you are feeling O.K. and will write to me sometime. Tell Uncle Roc hello. I bet your flowers are all out now. Take good care of yourself and don't pull too many weeds. Love, Jeanne.

Oslo May 31, 1948

Dear Aunt Esther,

The trip down to Copenhagen was quite nice. I went on a night train. When the train gets to the point where it crosses from Sweden over to Denmark, the whole train is loaded on a ferry and ferried across. I saw the famous Kronbork (Elsinore) Castle which is supposed to be the setting for Hamlet, and where Hamlet is played every year.

Copenhagen is big with about 1 million people. It's often called the "Paris or Paradise of the North." The influence of the architecture, art and culture from the Continent is very apparent. It has a much friendlier atmosphere (than Sweden) and there is much more to do. We visited several castles and saw the crown jewels.

The Stock Exchange was the most interesting, completed in 1640 and very unusual. We went to the circus, to the Royal Theater (for the "Marriage of Figaro") and to the Botanical Garden.

We saw the traditional stork nests on the chimneys in the country in Denmark - - and the storks were kind enough to be sitting there, so we got quite a show.

We saw the famous cigar-smoking women. I almost didn't believe it until I saw it.

Denmark is much too flat to suit me. Of the 3 Scandinavian countries, Norway is by far the most beautiful. However, it is also the most rugged and it is very apparent that Norwegians have a much heavier and harder life than either the Swedes or the Danes.

Indeed, about two-thirds of Norway is mountainous, making it the most mountainous of all the Nordic nations.

In a letter dated June 10th, 1948 Ma wrote how disgusted she was that the American government was thinking of cutting short the Marshall plan, which was so important in helping Western Europe to rebuild and recover from the effects of the war. "I wish they would throw Tabor out of congress," she wrote.

Aunt Esther had sent a package with cocoa, coffee and other goods which were scarce in post war Norway. Ma wrote:

June 22, 1948

Monday night I went home early and made a devil's food cake since our gang that plays cards was coming to visit me on Tuesday. I made the boiled icing and I must say I never have seen a cake disappear so fast in all my life. Randi was there and Lars, Jens, etc. The coffee was swell and everyone though it tasted so good. I made hot chocolate too. Of course, everyone thought it was quite a treat so you can see that everything you sent is being thoroughly enjoyed.

I wrote to Mr. Olav in Washington that I'd be home this fall but hadn't decided exactly what I was going to do. Immediately by return mail I got a letter from him saying that he was "really delighted" to hear that I was coming back to the USA and that nothing would "please them more" than to have me come back to my old job for which I am so "highly qualified."

She was interviewed in Norway, for the job at the Norwegian Embassy and all was arranged ahead of time.

I want to spend a couple of days in New York if I can stay at your penthouse with you and then go on to Hancock for a few weeks. The office here does not like to think that I am leaving.

I had a nice long letter from Lilian. I still think she and George make the best pair I've met. There ought to be more people like George, then even I might take the fatal step.

In the summer, after work (she finished work around 3 p.m.), if it was nice weather, a gang of friends and Ma would go to the beach any chance they could.

Ma was busy trying to pull things together to go back to the USA. She wrote on September 8, "Right now I have so much to do and think about that I am not only going in circles but feel as though I were standing on my head sometimes. I am someplace almost every night. I will stop working Oct 1st so that will give me some time to get half way organized. The boat leaves on the 19th."

Sept 30, 1948 Oslo
Today is my last day at the office so I am a little bit off!! We are going to have coffee and cakes in my honor a little later so I am a bit excited. If we have good weather the *Stavangerfjord* should arrive sometime Friday a.m. October 29th. I am traveling Cabin class. Gee it is going to be good to come home again and to eat some of your good cooking. You might even get your hair brushed! I hope Nelson and Uncle Walt will make me a spaghetti dinner. I haven't had any since I left the States. Also, Mom wrote me about some special cake Uncle Walt makes which sound mighty good. (I have never been so interested in food before in all my life. I shall probably start yelling at people if they don't eat up every bit).

The days were filled with goodbye parties and get-togethers. Friends from work gave her a huge, more than 800-page, Norwegian cookbook and wrote inside, "When our friend Miss Rood in future is preparing food we hope that she will be so kind to have her friends in mind."

> ...We had a lovely party here with cakes and coffee, flowers and candlelight. There were 20 of us office gals. They held speeches and so forth. The girls gave me a beautiful silver Norwegian filigran pin like they use on their national costumes. Then the *kontorsjef* (office manager) and some of the men came in and gave me flowers and a gorgeous silver salad set of a fork and spoon, which is enamel painted similar to Lilian's spoons. I was really overwhelmed. Everyone sure has been swell to me.
>
> Well , dearie, I guess I must sign off and start cleaning out my desk. It will soon be time to go.
>
> Love, Jeanne.

Having worked now with Elektrokemisk for a year and 3 months, and having loved living in Norway, it was with regret she left Holmenkollveien 48, Oslo. The glowing reference letter they wrote for her said, "Miss Rood's work has consisted of secretarial work with shorthand, typing and translations from Norwegian to English and from English to Norwegian. Miss Rood is a very efficient stenographer. She works neatly, accurately and quickly. She possesses personal initiative and has a large working capacity. It seems to be easy for her to familiarize herself with the different matters. It is astonishing how she, during the time she has been here, has acquired to excellent a knowledge of the Norwegian language.

Miss Rood has an amiable disposition and a pleasing manner. She has the ability of getting along well with her associates who have prized her greatly. We regret very much losing her as a fellow working and wish her all happiness in her future undertakings."

After this first trip to Norway, and her return to the USA, Ma worked again at the Press Section of the Norwegian Embassy in Washington from November 1948 until June 1950. She then went back to Norway for what was meant to be a 6 week visit but became a 2-year stay, working initially at Elektrokemisk (ELKEM) again.

The next letter to Aunt Esther is dated September 15, 1950:

Dear A-nut,

It was good to hear from you yesterday. As usual, I have been having a good time. In fact, I am almost getting tired of being out so much. Mrs. Smith is very nice and really spoils me. The apartment is very old but very cozy and full of interesting furniture, antiques and knick-knacks. It is just like a museum.

Mrs. Smith usually gets up and gets breakfast and I awake to the morning concert on the radio at 7:30. So I go into the bathroom and get dressed and washed and sit down to a nice breakfast with music while we eat. She even puts up my lunch so I am terribly spoiled. She sure is fun. She has had so many interesting experiences and in spite of the fact that she is 58, she is so youthful that it's lots of fun to be with her. When I met her in Washington last summer, I never dreamed that I would be living with her in Oslo.

I walk to work every morning – 20 minutes. Aren't I ambitious.

Perhaps you read my letters to Mom so you know what all I have been doing. Anyway, I had a wonderful summer swimming, sailing and hiking and going to parties. It has been lots of fun. It was nice to start working again and the office is the same as before. Everyone is so wonderful to me that I am absolutely spoiled.

On one trip hiking with friends, they stayed at a rustic cabin, high up the mountains with no indoor plumbing but with an incredible view. The beauty of her surroundings made a big impression: "I got up at 6:30 a.m. and went out and washed in the cold brook. As I looked around me all I could think was Grieg's "Morning" song." Ma loved Edvard Grieg's music. She later wrotes, "Edvard Grieg's music *is* Norway.... He composed much of his music near Hardanger Fjord. Norwegians are robust, stoic people, and Greig's music gives ample expression to this. He was far more than a folklorist. He succeeds in singing of an entire nation and its geography extraordinarily well."

Dear A-nut,

At the moment, I have not made any plans about anything but just intend to enjoy myself and take each day as it comes. You never can tell what may happen. I suppose you would like to hear about my boyfriends. (*She writes about a few, among whom is Lars, who she now finds* "rather dull"). ...Eystein (the engineer) came to town and then we went to a vaudeville show and after to dancing at the Bristol... I went to a concert with Haaken. I had a hard time keeping awake but it was a very lovely concert with a very clever conductor.

Last night I went to a party given by one of the girls...we were 10 girls from the office. We had to dress like kids and we got a big kick out of looking at one another. Everyone had big ribbons in their hair and some had actual girls' dresses, which they managed to get on but which barely managed to cover their rears. Golly, it was a riot and who should ring the doorbell at 9 o'clock but the *kontorsjef.*

Oslo November 20, 1950
Dear A-nut,

I hope you don't think I have forgotten you completely. It seems I am going around in circles so much...I went to three dinner parties from Friday to Wednesday last week so you can see how it is.

We are all getting ready for the Elektrokemisk big Christmas party at Oslo's swankiest hotel (the Bristol). It is to be held Dec 6th, banquet at 7 with dance afterwards – formal. Of course, there will be especial songs and speeches and the festivities committee have chosen me to give the speech to the men! It is in Norwegian and rhymes- praising and sarcastic at the same time.

Giving the speech for "the men's *skål*" at this formal banquet was a big deal. Ma wrote it herself with the assistance of a rhyming book. The committee had asked her 6-8 weeks ahead of time. She said, "I started right in with ideas (sometimes I would be on a bus or street car going someplace and would get a bright idea, so I'd scribble it down on a notepaper in my purse.)" Once she was done creating the speech, her friend Irene Smith helped her with her delivery – what words to emphasize. Irene was an operetta singer and had attended the Norwegian Music and Acting Academy.

The next letter was sent to her parents. [Ma sent it to me in my birthday card in 1995. She was so glad I had learned Norwegian and that I, too, made up plays, songs and poems for my workplace parties in Luxembourg just as she had done in Norway, and she wanted to share it with me.] The poem she wrote is incredibly clever, with humor and rhyme, making great fun. Her command of the Norwegian language was simply amazing.

Oslo 9th December, 1950

Dear Mom,

Wednesday was our big party. I had on my red evening gown, with my rhinestone necklace, blue and white rhinestone earrings and bracelet, opal ring and pearl ring (which is that Christmas present I bought) and my blue foxes fur stole. Ragna and I took a taxi together.

ELKEM had 3 salons plus the big dining room (later converted into ballroom) at the Hotel Bristol. Everyone looked so nice in their evening gowns and tuxedos. The table was arranged in a horseshoe form with an extra table in the middle. It was very well arranged so that all the directors were spread around and different types were well mixed up.

First, we had a cocktail and stood around and talked. It sure was quite a crowd (about 120). Finally, when all the men had found their table partners, we marched into the dining room to music and there was a string quartet which played all kinds of music during dinner.

We had soup, a special French pate filled w/ some kind of a lobster mixture, deer meat and potatoes, *tyttebaer* (a kind of red berry which we don't have in America).

Some super ice cream for dessert and little cakes. Of course, there was different wine with each course. I wish you could have seen how beautifully everything was served. All the waiters and waitresses marched in together and it was really quite a sight. When they came in with the dessert they turned out the lights because they had huge ice blocks with a light fixed under them and the huge platters of ice cream up on top of the ice blocks.

Well, I came with the dessert. Thank goodness Schanche (my table partner) had good influence on me so I wasn't the least bit nervous. When the toastmaster introduced me and I stood up and "*Mine Herrer*" (Gentlemen), everybody started clapping already. So I began and it went off fine. It took a little longer than I had expected because they laughed so much I had to pause a lot. It was really terrific. I guess I had gotten so tired of it that I didn't think it was so funny longer, but they laughed several places where I hadn't expected them to. They just roared when I got to the part about Hagerup-Larssen's stinky pipe. It sure was fun. Afterwards they clapped like mad and all the men were just nuts. The head director drank a toast with me immediately afterwards and the *kontorsjef* started calling to me to drink a toast and Hagerup-Larssen, he stood right up and yelled from his end of the table and will absolutely drink a toast with me. Everyone was so wonderful. Afterwards they all kept coming over to me and telling me how much they enjoyed it and how impressed they were. Elna Jensen (the one who sent me the perfume bottle and who thought Dad was so handsome) said she was so proud of me. So it was a big success. Afterwards all the fellows wanted to dance with me. I danced so much I got blisters on the bottom of my feet. And I was plenty lame the next day. At the office the next day all the engineers kept coming in to see me or called on the office phone to again thank me for the lovely speech. It sure was fun. The Director of our department, (Hagerup-Larssen) called me into his office and again told me how he couldn't get over that I had written it myself, etc. He also said he had decided to give me his old pipe when he was through with it! So there has been lots of fun here lately. All day at the office, everyone talked about the party.

I forgot to mention that after the dinner we withdrew to the various salons for coffee. Then we had a grand march and the dancing began. During the dinner there were other speeches and loads of special songs different ones had written. They always write special songs and put them to well-known tunes for such parties. Well, I'm glad it went off so well. The head director's wife (who was once a well-known Norwegian actress) congratulated me several times and said I had been so clever to get it off with emphasis on the right words, etc. So I felt pretty good. I felt like a Queen that evening the way everyone made a big fuss over me. Everything was just perfect and to think that I had EK's most handsome bachelor as my table partner made it nice too. So it was a big success.

Those were the glory days Ma kept in her memories forever. She was truly in a place where so many of her talents were put to use. She translated, interpreted and tutored, as she wrote, "I was invited to dinner at Trygve Bratteli's (he was one of my English pupils – assistant to the Prime Minister of all people!)." Trygve Bratteli went on to become Norway's 26th Prime Minister in the 1970s: to think that Ma tutored him in English!

Dip (*her sister Julia*) sent me a whole lot of pictures of Tina. (*Tina was Julia's first adopted daughter*). She sure is cute. Also, I have received already 3 prs of stockings from her. The package with my ski pants arrived all o.k. I must write to Dip and Flossie soon but I haven't had time. Last night I worked overtime again. This afternoon after going to the shoemaker, the dry cleaner, and to Inger Marie to give her your present and Julia's jacket. I am going out to Gudmundsens. Sunday I hope to spend a quiet day at home.

I hope you are feeling better now and taking it easy. (*Aunt Esther battled tuberculosis and had to spend some time in a sanatorium to recover).* I don't think you should work at all. Just take it easy and rest and please don't worry about me because I will be all right. I am always in touch with the American Embassy and I talked with them just the other day.

I hope Pa is o.k. and that the Christmas package arrives in time.

Love, Jeanne"

Oslo Decembre 15, 1950
(*a Christmas card which says "GOD JUL," Merry Christmas*)
Dear Aunt Esther,

I hope you have a nice Christmas. Am enclosing some handmade Hardangersom doilies which I hope you can use. The dinner party went off fine. The men sure were impressed.

We have lots of snow. I hope you are feeling better. I am taking cod liver oil every day and have so far managed to escape the colds and flu which are going around. I still walk to work every morning so I am quite a Viking now.

(Notice the cod liver oil or *tran* as it is called in Norway. It is rich in Vitamin A and D as well as Omega-fatty acids. Taking cod liver oil was nearly a religious rite in Norway and still is. This is proof that Ma *truly* had become Norwegian!)

Monday I went to hear Ralph Bunche give his Nobel Peace Prize speech. It was quite good.

Bunche, a brilliant US civil rights leader, was a diplomat for the United Nations. Through extended and intense negotiating, he and his team managed to obtain signatures on armistice agreements between Israel and the Arab States. His Nobel Peace Prize speech, which Ma enjoyed, closed as follows:

In a dark and perilous hour of human history, when the future of all mankind hangs fatefully in the balance, it is of special symbolic significance that in Norway, this traditionally peace-loving nation, and among such friendly and kindly people of great good-will, this ceremony should be held for the exclusive purpose of paying high tribute to the sacred cause of peace on earth, good-will among men. May there be freedom, equality and brotherhood among all men. May there be morality in the relations among nations. May there be, in our time, at long last, a world at peace in which we, the people, may for once begin to make full use of the great good that is in us.[10]

There were also trips to various places around Norway.

Wednesday I played Canasta. This weekend I am invited to Drammen to visit some friends of some friends of mine in Washington.

Monday the "*hønsegården*" are going to have a little Xmas party at Riborg's. Well, I hope you'll have a nice Christmas and Happy New Year,

Love Jeanne.

Oslo, February 19, 1951
Dear A-nut,

We've had more snow than ever heard of before and every once in a while the trains to southern Norway get blocked. Yesterday I was on skiis for 3 ½ hours and had a really nice time. We didn't take such a long-trip – took it easy but it was nice.

They sure are good to us here at the office...everyone received a gift of 10 lbs of reindeer meat. It is really good, too.

The other day the *kontorsjef* called me into his office. I thought he was going to dictate but when I came in, he was getting ready to go out. "What do you want," he asked me. "Janneke said you called for me," I said. "Isn't it you who usually talks about sweet things in speeches and songs?" he asked. Suddenly he took out two bags of caramels and candy. "Here is something for you girls to break your teeth on" he said. I just about fell over.

Thursday I was invited out to coffee with Lars. I enjoy meeting him once in a while but am not interested in him other than a friend. Had a long chat with Randi last night over the phone.

Ma once told me about a date she went on which surprised her somewhat. She had gone out with a guy to someone's house for an evening meal. They were at least three couples. After the meal, suddenly she noticed that the other couples had disappeared and gone to various rooms. Her date looked at her expectantly and she realized the others had gone off for some kind of physical encounter, to put it subtly. Ma turned to her date and told him to please take her home because she "wasn't that kind of girl." Cecil would have been so proud, I think.

Oslo March 31, 1951
Dear Aunt Esther,

I'm sitting here enjoying some of the quick fudge you sent and thought I would finally get a letter off to you to tell you how much I've been enjoying the things you sent. Have been using them sparingly. Wish you were here to enjoy some of the fudge with me.

It snowed last night. I've never seen the likes of it. We've had so much snow there's sure to be a flood when it melts.

Love, Jeanne"

Ma was thoroughly enjoying her life in Norway and working at ELKEM – but something new and unexpected was just around the corner.

The American Embassy Finds "The Norwegian American"

In 1951, Ma was offered a job at the American Embassy in Oslo, having been recommended for a position she never even sought out. She filled out all the forms[11] and was interviewed.

Oslo April 26, 1951

Dear A-nut: Sounds like you've been busy. There has been so much going on the past 3 weeks I haven't written very many letters myself. We've been extremely busy at the office. I may have a new job in the next few months but this is strictly confidential so don't tell anyone. I have been offered a job at the American Embassy. Without my knowing it, Haugland had recommended me to someone at the Embassy. So, I met the American press attaché who interviewed me and gave me an article to translate. Then Monday I was to go to the Embassy for another interview with a man called, Mr. Mean. He took one look at me and said, "I've seen you before." It wasn't in Washington or in Norway. So, we began talking and when I said I'd been to Strayor College he said, "Oh, I know a professor who taught there, Mr. Crouch." "Oh," I said, "He was my shorthand teacher …He happens to go to the same church as my aunt. "Oh, Calvary Baptist, THAT's where I've seen you." He knows all Aunt Flossie's friends. It sure was funny.

Then I had 2 more interviews and a typing test and a whole mess of papers to fill out. Mr Bell, one of the interviewers later told me "It looks like we are going to get you into Foreign Service." No one knows about this, just Mom and Julia.

The setup will be a good one. I get an American salary in dollars – that salary in Norway is equivalent to a VP's salary so I should

Ma - American Embassy, 1951

be able to save nearly $100 a month (salary from $2850 – 3000). Besides that, they pay house rent up to $62.50 per month. That means if I can find one, I will have a furnished apartment with a cleaning woman or maid to come in once / or twice a week. Besides that, we can order all kinds of things from home at cheap prices.

When I was interviewed at the Embassy they asked me if I knew of any reason why I might not be approved and I said the only thing I could think of was that I have a cousin who works for McArthy (*her cousin Don, Flossie and Franklin's son*). They said that wouldn't make any difference.

You're usually at one post for 2 yrs and then are sent home with 2 months vacation and then sent to another country or back to the same one if the job you are doing there is important enough. (*I remember Ma telling me once that once she got this job, she thought she would give up on the idea of marrying and instead be a career woman and see the world*).

The reason they are so crazy to get me is that I can speak, read and write Norwegian. There aren't many American girls who can do that.

Anyway, it tickled me to think that they came after me!

That's that. Otherwise, I am busy as a bee. Looked at my daily record book and found out that I have been home 3 evenings the past 3 weeks – and then one of those evenings there was a party at home. You asked about the Doctor, Anders. He called to invite me to a celebration but I was already invited elsewhere which was too bad. It would have been fun to have celebrated with all the young doctors.

Ma tells about her girlfriend Randi who had been on the boat over with her. Randi was being transferred to Moscow. Randi had requested an assignment in Russia and had been studying Russian for 2 yrs. This friend had in common with Ma an adventurous spirit. Ma said that at this point in her life, she had decided "to take the job at the American Embassy to learn all the languages I could, as one would get transferred every 3 years and so probably I wouldn't get married." Like her friend Randi, Ma had decided to be a "career gal."

Oslo May 21, 1951
    Dear Aunt Esther, I am supposed to begin at the Embassy Monday, June 4th. I may be working in Randi's section to begin with. She leaves June 28th. She craves excitement I guess. I sure will miss her. But lucky me, I get her apartment.
    I keep forgetting to tell you that I got a lot of use out of that blue tooth-checked suit this winter. Remember that one you gave me. Also, today I am wearing the pale blue gabardine you gave me, remember. It looks swell and fits well.
    Last night I was out with Haaken. We went to see *Fancy Pants* with Bob Hope. We got a big kick out of it. Afterwards we played cards and then we walked around and walked home.
    We are having one of those light nights again and it is so beautiful out that no one wants to go to bed. I wish you could be here sometime just to see how they are. It is very hard to describe. The sky is a dark-light blue if you know what I mean. The past couple of days there has been a full moon and the view from our living room has been something out over the fjord, etc.

There is something very special about evenings in Norway in the late spring and summer months. Those long hours of daylight seem magical, and give you an energy and a desire to be outside to savor it as long as possible.

Ma loved Norway, but she also remembered fondly her hometown. One time in 1951, while working for the American Embassy, an economic expert named Whitman was on loan to the embassy from the Department of Commerce (this was in the days of the Marshall Plan and the Economic Cooperation Administration). When Ma was introduced to Mr. Whitman, he asked where she was from.

"I came here from Washington, but I'm originally from N.Y. State," she said.

"Oh, where in N.Y.?" asked Mr. Whitman.

"Oh, a small village in upstate, you've never heard of, Hancock., N.Y."

"Oh, really!? I know where Hancock is because I used to visit Deposit when I was a kid."

"Oh!" she said, "Did you have relatives there?"

"No," he said, "When my father was going to college, summers he earned money for tuition working in a feed mill there. So later on, every once in a while the whole family would make a pilgrimage to Deposit."

After that, whenever he found Ma in the outer office of the Charge d'affaires or the First Secretary, he would come and look over her shoulder, shaking his head and saying: "I don't understand how a girl from Hancock can translate Norwegian!"

Ma was not your typical American – she almost seemed to be half Norwegian. Her favorite role at work was that of interpreter. People at the American Embassy recognized just how special she was and began to call her: "The American Norwegian." She had truly been assimilated into Norwegian culture to an unusual degree and in such a short time.

July 24, 1951
Dear Aunt Esther,

I guess you'll faint getting a letter from me.

I wish you were here to enjoy my apartment. I am busy fixing it up and since I don't get home until 5:30 every night and sometimes later I am very busy. I wanted to fix a divan, so first of all I had to cover over the springs and the stuffing since the old cover was coming off. I ordered a big spread from Montgomery Wards and had to cut it to fit. It is real nice and was so big that the pieces I cut off can be used to cover pillows to match. Next thing is curtains and drapes. The maid I have had is on vacation so at the moment I am doing all the cleaning too. Another girl from the Embassy has the apartment on the first floor so there's usually a gang from the Embassy around. Sometimes our place is like Grand Central when we all have guests.

I had to have so much company in the beginning that I haven't had time to breathe. I have lived there a little over 3 weeks and I have been out just 3 times. All the rest of the time I have had company. Whenever any fellows come up, I put them to work.

I am getting fat since I am eating so much steak and ice cream. In the beginning, when I had company, I always served steak but I guess I'll have to stop that.

My apartment is so cozy. I'm sure you would like it. I want you and Mom to come over. Would like to figure out how she and Dad could both come over but we'll have to wait and see what happens.

Summer's been pretty rainy and cold. I'm not very tan and I haven't even been swimming once. I think that's terrible.

I have lots to do at the office and I like it very much. The work is very interesting. I am one of the very few who can speak Norwegian so I get a big kick out of it—having to explain things to the bosses. Mr. Whitman and especially Mr. Birkeland are always kidding me about Hancock. All the men in our section are very nice.

…Have to get busy. I've got a long article to translate and it has to be done today. They sure keep me busy. I think it's most fun though when I am interpreter…it's lots of fun.

Well, I hope you are taking it easy and getting a rest. Drop me a line and tell me all the news and gossip. Tell Uncle Walt and Nelson hello.

…Guess who was in the office yesterday, Will Hays from Hollywood. He was real nice to me… a real regular guy.

[William H Hays had been a prominent American politician who became president of the Motion Pictures Production and Distribution of America.][12]

There were other important people coming to the Embassy: one day in 1951, an interesting young Norwegian man came to work there. When my mother first met him, she found him attractive but thought to herself, "Oh, he's probably married and has five kids." Ørnulf, called Ernie by the Americans, was a handsome and athletic young man, and Ma said that "all the girls in the office were crazy about Ernie."

When Ernie called to ask her out on a first date, her schedule was so filled she had to turn him down on two tries.

"I guess you didn't want to go out with him," her colleague/

friend sitting next to her said.

"Oh, but I *did*!" Ma said, "But I was already busy those times."

Her colleague said, "You call him right back and tell him he can come to the Red Cross function where you've volunteered."

And so, she picked the telephone back up and called him, "Hello…Ernie? This is Jeanne…"

DADDY'S CHILDHOOD

Who was this man, Ørnulf, called "Ernie" by the Americans, who captured my mother's interest there at the American Embassy in Oslo?

Ørnulf Hoff was born and raised in Trondheim, Norway. Ørnulf's parents were Harald R Hoff and Margrethe Oetnes Hoff (we called them "Farfar" meaning Father's Father and "Farmor," Father's Mother). The family lived at 1, Gregus *Gate* (street) near Lademoen *Kirke* (church), not far from the city center. They left this humble neighborhood just before the war, when the family moved to 37, Stadsingeniør Dahls *Gate*.

Ørnulf, my Dad, was born on August 11, 1925. He was blessed with a stable, good and loving family full of good humour and fun, balanced with respect and solid Christian values. His parents quietly loved one another and were calm, peaceful souls. "Growing up in our family was always *"en koselig, hyggelig stemning,"* (a cozy, pleasant ambiance) his sister Gerd said (we call her Tante Gerd). In their home the children felt love, belonging and security. Boundaries were very clear. Gerd said, "It was rare that our parents got angry with us, but if they did, there was always a valid reason for it – something we had done wrong." Dad described his father as "a serious man. Strict. People called him 'Chief' *(Høvding)*. He told us kids, 'Be good' and expressed his approval with a warm smile - worth more than a hug."

Ørnulf adored his elder brother Rolf, born September 9, 1922, whose gentle ways and fragile disposition endeared him to all. Farmor told me how little Ørnulf would stand up and fight against bigger boys, defending his frail brother who sometimes got picked on.

The saddest event of Dad's early years was the loss of his

brother Rolf, who died on December 28, 1929 of "croupous (now called lobar) pneumonia" at Trondheim Hospital. Rolf was only seven years old. (Sadly, the first sulphonamide antibiotic which would have saved his life was not available on the market until six years later, in 1935.)

Rolf's death was a tragic loss. Although Dad was so young, he clearly remembered his good brother fondly, and years later said that he thought Rolf might actually have been "an angel unaware."

Who knows how a mother can overcome such a tragedy? But, overcome she did. She poured out all her love on her family: her husband, her 7-month-old daughter, Gerd and four-year old Ørnulf. She cared deeply for each one and set her grief aside as best she could. Another child was given to the family three years later in 1933, when gentle Kari Margrethe was born, their last child.

Trondheim Newspaper Dagsposten Thursday the 2nd of January 1930 translation: "Our dear, kind Rolf, left us December 28, 7 years old"

"Mother took us up on her lap and in her arms the most," said Tante Gerd, "for father was at work during the day. She was always so happy," said Tante Gerd, "Always in a good mood." She was jovial, with a hearty laugh. "<u>But</u> my mother always expected us to obey what she told us to do," Gerd said, "She taught us to be conscientious and to do our duty."

Farmor kept a positive attitude through all the difficult times of her life. She remained a bright and fun-loving mother who loved singing and enjoyed many kinds of handiwork. She sewed and knitted beautifully. Her fingers were incredibly deft. She once worked in a boutique designing and sewing hats and she sewed all her family's clothing, not surprising since her father was a tailor by trade. They were so well dressed that Gerd and Kari were sometimes called "the princesses" by children on the street. Farmor was talented at working with her hands beyond sewing or knitting, for she was highly skilled at picking berries, a pastime she greatly enjoyed. She and a neighbor friend went up to the mountains when berries were ripe: *multe*r (cloud berries), *tyttebær* (lingon berries), or *blåbær* (blueberries). "She was so fast at berry picking that she would fill an entire pillowcase full of them rather than use a bucket! She was phenomenal. We <u>always</u> had *tyttebær*. The cellar was full of it," Gerd said.

Farmor also cooked for the family. Breakfast was usually slices of bread with butter, cheese or other toppings (*pålegg*). On Sundays they often had eggs and bacon. Farmor's fish dinners were simple but delightful. Ørnulf would sometimes accompany her down to Ravnkloa, the fish market downtown in Trondheim, right near the wharf area. For hundreds of years fishing boats came there into town daily to deliver and sell fresh fish. His favorite was fried fish burgers (*fiskekake*): he would pop them whole into his mouth, *if* allowed. (Ørnulf also loved *lefse*, the typical thin soft pastry made from potatoes and smothered in butter sprinkled with cinnamon and sugar. This was bought from bakeries in Trondheim which even specialized in making *lefse*.) Farmor made delicious blueberry pancakes. When I stayed with her in the summer of 1982, she would ask me what I would like for dinner and as often as I could get away with it, my answer would be *"PANN'KAK" med blåbær*! (PANCAKES with blueberries!)"

Besides all this, Farmor was an energetic person who loved to watch a good soccer game. She stayed up late into the night watching the World Cup even into her '90s. (This love of soccer was passed on to her son and several grandchildren, including me).

Farfar worked for the Norwegian government as district manager (*fullmektig*) for the Railroad system in central Norway. It was an important job as rail was the principle means of transportation between north and south. At Christmas parties and other affairs, Daddy and Gerd remembered how people would flock to Farfar, to shake his hand and speak with him, as if he were a celebrity. He commanded respect, yet was a gentle, humble man.

He liked to write and he was a great orator as well. He was also a highly skilled organizer. He once spearheaded a project whereby the railroad bought a lovely little house known as Bjørkholt on the coast, in the countryside at Vikhammer. The office railroad personnel vacationed there. Dad said it was a beautiful spot not far from Trondheim, about twenty minutes by train. The house was on the water, with a boathouse. Every summer the family spent holidays there, enjoying the long, leisurely summer days and fishing for *torsk* (cod) or *sei* (pollock) in the good old way: just holding in your hand a fish line with several hooks (called *pilker* in Norwegian), bobbing the hand up and down slowly until you felt a nibble. They learned to row a boat there, and felt the excitement of that first time going out by themselves in the row boat.

Farfar and his good friend from work, Herr Georg Stamnes, telegraph operator (who was born in Rice Lake, Wisconsin USA! His wife was Olga) would enjoy fishing together there, along with their son, Per Stamnes (who later became an engineer in Oslo, Dad said). Both Dad and Gerd said that they enjoyed getting to know and playing with all the other "railroad" children. It was a place for building family memories and they enjoyed it "...*hver eneste sommer* (every single summer)," Tante Gerd said. Besides the big house which was like a villa there was a child size house with other mini-houses nearby. All three of the Hoff children retained wonderful childhood memories of swimming, boating, fishing and simply enjoyed relaxing moments with "*Mor og Far*" (Mother and Father) and all the other railroad folks' children at Vikhammer.

Enjoyment for the whole family also included music: Farmor and Farfar *loved* music, and they both had lovely singing voices. The two had met through the "Toneveld" choir of which they were both members. In fact, they married on one of the choir tours in Hamar, in southern Norway, in Vang church on May 17, 1921 when Farmor was 22 years old! Thinking about her parents' wedding, Tante Gerd said, "Singing was very important to them."

As a married couple, they also participated in the *Gjernbahn's Sangforening* (Railroad Singing Association). People from Norway, Sweden, Denmark and Finland had such choirs, and they all came together for singing conventions, travelling all over Scandinavia. It was great fun for them, and Dad remembers them all wearing this funny hat (*en sangelue*), white on top with a black brim, which was a sign of being a member of the choir. Farfar was influential in getting one of these railroad choirs set up in Sweden, too, Gerd said, for he was clever at organizing and had many connections.

As far as other relatives, Dad remembered most his paternal grandmother, Petrine (Severine Petrine Pettersen Hoff), with great affection. She baked delicious cookies and always had them ready for her grandchildren. Her husband, Anton Rikard Hoff died on June 28, 1911 up North in Stokmarknes[13] (in Nordland county above the Lofoton Islands), when Farfar was just 18 years old. Dad was told that he had gone down in a storm, when working on a steamship as the steam ship's engineer/machinist (*dampskipsfyrbøter / maskinist*).

In her old age, Petrine's granddaughter Inger (Dad's cousin) and her kind, gentle husband Finn took her in to live with them until she passed away. They lived for a while below Dad's family, downstairs at Statsing Dahls gate 37.

Another dear relative was Tante Astrid, Farfar's sister who

married Aksel Soknes. They had four children: Inger, Ruth, Odd and Per. "We were together with Tante Astrid quite often. She was kind and calm, not an out-going person, but very careful. (*Far* was more outgoing.) She was a great cook," Gerd said.

Dad's maternal grandparents were Jakob Johanson Otnaes and Jannye Antonie Sekander Otnaes. She was a very religious woman. She sang, played guitar and gave guitar lessons. (Dad says their name used to be Gevig, and they changed their name for some reason ("There's got to be some skeleton in the closet," Dad said but Tante Gerd has no idea what he was talking about).) These grandparents lived near enough to visit quite often before the war. "They often ate porridge (*de spiste ofte grøt*) which I loved," said Gerd, "so I went over to their place on foot and by *trikk* (tram) to eat with them, crossing over the bridge in Trondheim city." Jakob was a tailor, and later sold insurance. Jakob and his son-in-law (our Farfar) used to spend many a Sunday afternoon sitting for hours (at Statsing Dahls street) playing chess together in total silence. "Not a word passed between them: it was real social-like," Dad said, with a grin. Tante Gerd remembers the

Farmor and Farfar's wedding with the choir in their hats
Photographer: Christian Grundseth, who trained as photographer in the USA

same. "Jakob played with such an intensity he even got a bloody nose from the stress," said Gerd.

Family Holidays

The family enjoyed celebrating holidays often with friends and relatives. One of the most festive was Norway's Constitution Day on May 17th. There were parades full of people, many wearing colorful, traditional national costumes (*bunad*) from the different regions of Norway. Children were everywhere waving small, Norwegian flags. (It is the same today.) On May 17th they had a big family party with lots of extended family getting together to celebrate. There were all kinds of cookies and cakes, Gerd's favorite was *krumkake.*

A long weekend away for Pentecost was also anticipated in early spring. We often "spent the days of Pentecost at Bjørkholt together with all our friends," Farfar wrote, "...the Pentecost bonfire burned down late into the night until flames were carefully put out..." These holidays passed far too quickly with "pleasant chats and much food and drink."

There were also wonderful celebrations of Midsummer on June 23rd (known as "*Sankt Hans Aften*," commemorating St. John the Baptist), with more large bonfires on the beach, food and playing games late into the night. This was the time of year with the longest days, and the sky remained bright until midnight in Trondheim and even further south.

Christmas was an exceptionally wonderful holiday, anticipated by the three Hoff children with great joy. Even at 94 years of age, Tante Gerd, with youthful excitement, spoke these words, describing their childhood Christmases:

> Mother would be cooking and baking all kinds of treats on the days before Christmas: *gorokakker, serinakaker* (topped with sugar), poor man's cookies (*fattigman*), pretzel-shaped Berlin wreath cookies (*berlinerkranse),* fried cakes and more! She was also busy cleaning house from top to bottom in preparation for Christmas eve. Father was in charge of bringing home the Christmas tree. It was kept in a bucket of water until December 23rd when it was then set up in the living room and we decorated it altogether. There were many fine

glass ornaments, alongside things we kids had made. The Norwegian flags ran from top to bottom and a star crowned the top. The candles on the tree weren't lit until the next day, Christmas Eve, at mid-day.

We always went to church on Christmas Eve before we began celebrations at home. The gifts were placed beneath the tree on the 23rd so we had a chance to snoop around and see them, and I always hoped I had some that weren't soft (like clothes of some kind). I wanted to have packages that were firm rather than soft. When we were old enough to read, we kids would read out the names on the Christmas gifts and hand them out. In the excitement, we opened them all at once. Then, sitting with our treasures, when all was opened, we would show one another, saying with glee, "Oh! Oh, look at this!!"

After the gifts, melodies of Christmas filled the air, like the sweet aroma of cookies being baked. "We sang all the classic Christmas carols we could think of, like *"Glade Jul," "Du Grøne, Glitrande Tre, God Dag"* and then we sang my favorite, fun song, *"På låven sitter nissen med sin julegrøt, så god og søt."* (The Christmas elf sits with his Christmas porridge, so good and sweet). Every year the traditional circling of the Christmas tree was an integral part of the celebration along with the singing. That is, as they sang, they held hands, moving slowly around the tree. On Christmas day the family often visited Tante Astrid (Farfar's sister) or other family members but Christmas eve was celebrated with just the immediate family.

All these joyful holiday memories lasted a lifetime.

School, Sports & Music

At school in Lademoen, Dad joined his comrades each day hoping for some fun. There were only boys in the classroom, for the girls had their own classes and teachers. Dad had a strict teacher, *Herr* (Mr.) Moeske, who was a challenge, especially for a lively youngster with a thriving sense of humour such as my father.

Herr Moeske remained his teacher all the years of primary school. Herr Moeske smoked cigars that spotted their homework papers brown. He sometimes smacked the students across their fingers with the pointer. "Therefore, we paid close attention,"

Dad said, but he sometimes got in trouble none the less for "he was not the most obedient of the students," Gerd said. They learned all the usual subjects, like math, reading, writing, science, geography, etc. Dad remembers an old lady that taught them *skjønnskrift,* a beautiful style of artistic handwriting, something close to calligraphy. Dad said it was "fluid letters," a cursive writing in penmanship class (he said he had "never seen such beautiful handwriting ever since"). They also had gym class and music class, learning many songs in primary school, so the schools were "full of singing," Gerd remembered. Dad had a good friend, Gunnar Andersen, who used to sing all the time as they walked the streets of Trondheim.

There was no organized sport in the school, but many of the boys played soccer together after school in various open fields (like Ravn or by the old fortress (Kristiansten Festning)) whenever weather permitted and they could get away to play. He *loved* to play soccer. His love for the sport lasted a lifetime. Girls often played handball and went ice skating outdoors in winter, which Gerd enjoyed.

Young Ørnulf ready for soccer

Norwegians are generally an 'outdoorsy' people and the Hoffs were no exception: they loved to hike or take walks. On Sundays, they sometimes took a walk up to Bymarka, a large nature reserve west of Trondheim. Another Sunday walk was down to the pier. If Farfar took Gerd on a *tur til brygga* (trip down to the pier) she had to be dressed in Sunday-best clothes *including* nice shoes if she wanted to join him. "Wherever we went, people knew my father," Gerd said. She had to be on her best behaviour in his company. "*Han var streng, ingen tulle*," (He was strict, there was to be no fooling around), she said.

Skiing was another family activity. It was great fun but also a good workout. Ørnulf enjoyed cross country skiing like all good Norwegians. The children learned to ski so young that they did not even remember when or how it happened, it felt like they had always known how to slide through the crisp, white snow with the pleasure of smooth, continuous gliding. Their skis were wooden with leather boots and bindings. If they were out for a long ski trip for several hours, they took food and drink with them in backpacks. If the snow was deep and no tracks had yet been made, it was their father who led the way, creating the first set of tracks and the family followed behind, one by one. Up in the mountains they found it interesting to look for the footprints of animals who had passed by in the area: reindeer, fox and occasionally musk oxen, with their long, curved horns, when in the Dovrefjell area.

On wintery Sundays the family might ski west of Trondheim in Bymarka. Longer ski vacations took place during the week of Easter break and Autumn break (if there was snow). Then by train they headed south of Trondheim towards the Dovrefjell mountain range, staying at Grunbakken *hytte* with the great Snøhetta mountain (2286 meters / 7500 feet) in sight. Kongsvoll, an old mountain lodge, was typically part of the journey. "If we were lucky, we could take a draisine on the train rails up from Kongsvoll up to the cabin where we stayed, (we thought taking the draisine was very cool.) We carried with us all the food and drink we would need during the vacation," Gerd said.

It was also at Bymarka, Tante Gerd thought, where Ørnulf

had learned to ski jump. Ski jumping originated in Norway. There was ski jumping in the Gråkallen mountains in Bymarka as far back as the early 1900s.

Another family enjoyment was going to the theatre, both for adults and children. The Hoff family was often in attendance at the Trondheim theatre. (Trøndelag Teater was built in 1816, the theatre is the oldest stage in Scandinavia in continuous use.)[14] Norwegian actor and theater director Henry Gleditsch took charge of Trøndelag Teater in 1937.[15]

On special Sundays the family attended church. Gerd remembers sitting in a row at home with her siblings, all dressed and ready to go, "waiting for Far" who was the last to be ready. He took his time, but off they would go together as a family to Lademoen Kirke: the church where Ørnulf, Gerd and Kari were baptized and confirmed. When young Ørnulf was confirmed, he used his mother's Bible, which said inside the front "*Kjaere Margrethe min, laes din Bibel hver aften er du snil. Din Mor.*" (My dear Margrethe, please read your Bible every evening. Your Mother.") Young Ørnulf wrote on the front page, too, all underlined, "*Den Hellige Ånd er vår styrke til å tro på Jesus.*" *Ørnulf Hoff* ("The Holy Spirit is our strength to believe in Jesus.")

When he was just eight years old, Ørnulf tried out for the all-boys' choir (*Guttekor*) of the great Nidaros Cathedral (Domkirke), a place which was to hold further significance for him as an adult. The Nidaros Cathedral Boys' Choir is Norway's oldest boys' choir and "continues to this day a 900-year-old tradition" in Trondheim. It was a great privilege for the young Ørnulf to be chosen to join this choir which began centuries ago. Only the best voices were chosen by means of a rigorous selection process. The Trondheim Guttekor archives show that Ørnulf Hoff started in the choir on April 29, 1934.[16] In the year 1934/1935, there were 52 sopranos and 40 altos: 92 boys![17] Boys were usually between 9 and 15 years old. They went on tour, travelling outside of Trondheim, giving concerts but most often in the home cathedral. Dad said that they usually sang there from just beneath the gorgeous Rose Vindu (Rose Window) but on special occasions they were positioned way up in the church loft, so that their voices descended from on high like that of angels.

After Daddy started singing in this elite boys' choir, the family regularly attended the grand Nidaros Cathedral in Trondheim.

The cathedral itself is an architectural masterpiece and the largest medieval building in Scandinavia as well as the northernmost gothic cathedral in the world.[18] It is Trondheim's most famous and revered symbol, built early in the Middle Ages. The cathedral is built over the tomb of St. Olav, the Viking king who converted Norway to Christianity. Over the centuries, pilgrims journeyed to Nidaros from all over Northern Europe.

Though the cathedral itself is made of stone, much of its interior and roof trusses are still wooden. In 1869, the church was completely renovated -- a process that took, in the true spirit of cathedral building, 100 years. When the restoration began, only five medieval statues on the building's front had survived. So, in 1933, Norwegian sculptors, including one of Norway's most beloved artists, Gustav Vigeland, (whose park you can

Gerd & Kari with Ørnulf in his Boys' Choir suit

visit in Oslo), replaced the missing sculptures. It took decades to replace all 54. In the basement crypt, there are 700-year-old tombstones. The magnificent Rose window is a multi-coloured stained-glass masterpiece.

To sing within the wonder of such a place was awe-inspiring. Ørnulf was the first of the family to sing there. Afterwards, their mom joined a mixed choir. Then, when Gerd was 16 or 17, her mom invited her to join her in the mixed choir. Gerd greatly appreciated that her mom introduced her to singing in church and that they could enjoy being in the choir together. The choir lead hymns singing in the service standing right in the middle of the church, with the rose window up on the right side. (*"Vi ledet salme sangene mitt i kirken, rose vinduet opp på høyre siden, da vi sang," sa Gerd.*)

Music truly filled Ørnulf's family life: his parents loved to sing, as did his maternal grandmother, as mentioned earlier. In the early years, Dad remembers his father playing the accordion, too. "We sang at home all the time," Gerd said. "There would be one who began to sing and the others joined in. One time, Ørnulf and I, we danced in the kitchen! *Vi var sa opptatt av sang, musik og glede, rett og slett,*" (We were simply obsessed with singing, music and joy).

Tante Gerd remembers that "when Ørnulf wasn't singing like an angel in the Nidaros boys' choir, he was a real rascal *(en ordentlig røvver).*" He once got in trouble for "climbing up over the wall to see Tante Kristina in *barnehagen* (kindergarten)." Tante Kristina was a second cousin who directed the kindergarten and lived up above it in an apartment, near Lademoen's station. Ørnulf climbed up over the wall just "to prove he was capable to do it and show that he didn't have to go through the door like the rest of us," Gerd said.

"Ørnulf would sneak down to the cellar at home with a spoon in hand to sneak some *tyttebær* (lingonberry) from the crock. He did a lot of mischievous, crazy things; it was fun to be with him. He always found many odd things to do that made us laugh," Gerd said. "Ørnulf and I were quite like one another: the same things made us both laugh and we went about life 'full-speed ahead' while little Kari was gentle, quiet and kind," Gerd recalls.

For example, once when Ørnulf was older, he went out to a dance party with friends; Farfar told him to be home by midnight but he was *not* home on time. "*DA var Far sint* (*THEN* Father was angry)," Gerd said. So, Farfar went and picked him up at the dance, which, of course, was embarrassing. "Yes," she

Young Dad with friends on ship

says, "Ørnulf was a rascal, but a very good-hearted one." He sometimes joked and called himself *gullgutten*, (the golden boy) Gerd told us, between hearty laughter. "It meant he was the best that one could have. That was typical Ørnulf. He was a real *tulleboka* (jokester)."

Young Ørnulf once joined his parents on a short trip on the Hurtigruten postal ferry and remembered singing from the front of the boat when they stopped in Trollfjord, a small but famous fjord in Lofoten above the Artic Circle. The melody echoed all around and back to the ship.

The boys' choir member lists and photos from 1936-1940 were destroyed in the war,[19] so we don't know how long he was in the choir but when he hit puberty, his changing voice meant he had to leave the boys' choir, and "that was a sad day," he recalled.

Unfortunately, much bigger sorrows were up ahead.

The Invasion of Norway

In the late 1930s troubles began to brew in Europe, with the Czech annexation by Germany in 1938 and the 1939 Polish invasion. Dad heard of this and said, "I thought those events were outrageous, but still, at the time, I certainly did not think it would become a full-scale war." Neither did the rest of Norway.

Both the Allies and Germany were very interested in Norway because of the need for iron ore and the strategic advantage of having ice-free harbours available for their fleets in the north Atlantic. Norway (as well as Sweden) had been neutral during World War I and expected to do the same in the "unlikely" event of another world war.

However, Norway was invaded by the Nazis early on April 9, 1940.

In the Trondheim Police Chamber Guard Journal, it was reported at 4:30 a.m. that two German warships had entered the harbor. By 5 a.m. the quays were full of German soldiers while most of the people of Trondheim slept.[20]

At seven o'clock in the morning the German colonel in command came with his adjutant to the Trondheim central police station. "He was completely appropriate in his behaviour and said he sincerely hoped that they did not have to shed any blood on the occasion of the Germans' arrival, for they came as our friends – so he said."[21]

(An interesting approach to friendship: so long as you comply, we won't have to kill anyone! It was a great starting point to convince the Norwegians that the Germans came to defend them from the Brits – who, the Nazis said, were the *real* bad guys.)

Dad described the day this way: "I was at home the morning they came. We didn't know what was going on, so we went downtown and there they were! We heard the airplanes...they were bombing several places (not near where I lived) so we knew what was going on."

His reaction to all this was one of confusion. "Frankly, I didn't know what was going on, or what my feelings were, to begin with. We listened to the radio but, of course, the radio had been taken over by the Germans and they were telling us they 'came in peace' but down in the harbor we saw the war ships so we knew it was war. We just waited to see what was going to happen next."

"Confusion was rampant in all quarters those first hours and days after the German attack...One of the chief causes of the confusion was, of course, the surprise attack. Event followed unexpected event at a terrific pace. In a flash, the old familiar concepts crumbled in dust...the world was out of kilter."[22]

Dad was 14 years old. The carefree days of childhood had just come to an abrupt halt.

Life Under the Darkness of Nazi Occupation

It is nearly impossible to fathom the psychological stress that came from being occupied by a foreign, dominating, and brutal power, especially in such a peace-loving, stable, and quiet society as Norway. The Hoff family tried to go about their life as normally as possible, what else could they do? "Our parents shielded us from the war as best they could," Gerd said, trying to maintain some kind of continuity. "We carried out life as usual: my dad went to work, we went to school," Dad said. At school, children received their usual dose of cod liver oil (*"tran"*).

German soldier puts up the Infantry General Falken-horst's proclamation April 9, 1940 in Trondheim

Photo credit: FotoWeb Digital archive foto.digitalarkivet.no

Nazi-imposed changes came in spurts, disrupting their world sporadically, as least from the perspective of children.

One month after the Nazis arrived, the soldiers took over Lademoen school using it as a barracks, so Gerd and her neighbourhood friends had to walk further to Singsaker *skole* (school) for their classes. This Nazi confiscation of school buildings happened in many places all over Norway. "In Oslo, for instance, only seven of the city's thirty-three public schools were available for their intended purposes, education."[23]

This gave a clear message: we are in charge here and we have the priority.

Life took on an element of uncertainty perceived even by the children. It all seemed so absurd. "The Norwegian government had fled to England in exile. We didn't really know about what was going on. We were blasted with propaganda of the Nazis," Dad said. The "new order" government tried to shape the thinking of the Norwegians by controlling and censuring newspapers, radio and even theatre. The "new order" put in place was full of Norwegian Nazi sympathizers who collaborated with the Germans, including the infamous Norwegian traitor Quisling, who had met with Hitler before the war. The German soldiers were there to enforce the new order and compliance with all the new regulations. The far-right Nasjonal Samling (or NS, about 1% of the population) became the only allowed political party – essentially a Norwegian version of the German Nazis. To destabilize ideals and culture, public use of the Norwegian flag and anything patriotic was banned, including songs like the national anthem, "*Ja, Vi Elsker Dette Landet.*"

The presence of numerous foreign soldiers was unsettling to say the least. There was an incredible number of soldiers in Norway – at the peak, 380,000 in a country of 2.9 million people (or one German soldier for every eight Norwegian citizens).[24] As Gerd said, "German soldiers were everywhere: all over the city, taking everything in the stores...as children, we thought they would take us away! It was so frightening. We were afraid of them, so afraid, and we kept thinking, and thinking, *what if they take us*? It was an unreal experience."

Even bigger changes came when the Nazis "started issuing certain decrees and laws which impacted us: they confiscated the radios and they also closed the churches to begin with, later they opened them, but the priests could only preach certain messages within certain criteria," Dad said. In September 1941, the Nazi-run Department of Church & Education sent a letter to all the clergy (more than 850 men) asking them to sign a statement that they supported the Nazi occupation. If they did not agree, they were to give the reason why and sign it. Church leaders responded that the request was illegal and would be ignored.[25]

At Trondheim Nidaros Cathedral in early 1942, a Nazi-sympathizer priest, Blessing-Dahle, was setup to hold a "service" at the same time Quisling was to be appointed Minster-President in Oslo. The Nazi priest "...faced a swastika-decked church that was all but empty." Shortly afterward, a now illegal church service was held by courageous Dean Arne Fjellbu. The congregation sang "*A Mighty Fortress is Our God*" written by German Martin Luther, surely known by the German soldiers surrounding the people. They then sang "*Ja, Vi Elsker.*" An account of the event is as follows: "The police...forced the crowd back towards the street. Here and there a policeman uses his club, but no one strikes back. Not for a moment does the singing falter; it only becomes more defiant in spirit...Bishop Størens appears on the church steps and a lull settles over the square. Calmly the Bishop invokes a blessing on the congregation. Then he asks all to leave quietly. Slowly, reluctantly the crowd disperses."[26]

This event was a turning point for the church in Norway. Most bishops and priests across Norway, refusing to be puppets to the Nazis, quit their job - the church went underground.

Nazi influence also included an attempt to "brainwash" children through the educational system for Hitler believed that if he could "own" the youth he would gain the future. For the first couple of years, all seemed normal at school but Nazi ideology "...was creeping in, textbooks began to be formalized to conform to Hitler's decrees," Dad said. Nazis wanted at least one copy of *Fritt Folk* (the official Nazi newspaper) in every school. Higher grades were supposed to use books like "*Is Norway a Free Country?*" written by a Norwegian Nazi sympathizer.[27]

Despite this pressure, as much as possible, an uninterrupted classroom life was provided by the teachers, who taught according to their conscience, ignoring the new Nazi School Inspectors even though they were being harassed and threatened. Already in November 1940 teachers were asked to sign a document pledging their loyalty to the Nazi regime. The vast majority refused and over a thousand teachers were arrested for not cooperating with the fascist agenda. About 650 were sent to a forced labor prison camp in the far north (Kirkenes) in 1942 but later that year all were freed after months of suffering.[28]

Nazi control also meant that "any kind of gathering was forbidden," Gerd said. Families could not have any of the usual celebrations/holidays with friends and extended family: no May 17, no Pentecost, no St. John's Eve, no Christmas. This was keenly felt by the children. Everything had to be small scale, just among

Demonstration outside Trondheim Nidaros Cathedral – Early 1942

"Here we bring the first pictures from the dramatic episode outside Trondheim Cathedral when the Nazi authorities forced the Lutheran priest Fjellbu away from his High Mass and replaced him with the infamous Nazi priest, Blessing Dahle, who allowed N. S. to place Hirden's symbol (the Norwegian swastika) and N. S. red-yellow flag in the choir of the church. Fjellbu quietly announced that his congregational service would still be held at 2 p.m. A large crowd showed up and was chased out by the police, who also closed the church door. The church-seekers responded to the Nazis' challenge by singing hymns outside the church gate. This episode was one of the reasons why the Norwegian bishops resigned from their positions in the service of the Norwegian state. The crowd sings Luther's old battle hymn: "*A Mighty Fortress is Our God*" outside the church gate. Everyone, as you can see, has bared their heads in the winter cold. The picture shows Nidaros Cathedral in Trondheim, the Norwegian national shrine (from the original captions on the photos)."

149

the immediate family. Christmas during the war meant no more store-bought packages, only homemade gifts, and no cookies. "Mor would undo sweaters or clothes and remake something else, knitting something else out of old things. Far still brought us a tree, and we sang," Gerd said, "But there were no church services and simply no normal celebration of *Jul* during the war."

The oppression, looting and violence of the brutal military forces which occupied Trondheim (and all of Norway), made for an increasingly uncertain and unsettling existence for a young teenage boy, who was at the same time experiencing the challenging ups and downs of puberty. What a strain it was on the whole Hoff family, never knowing if the Nazis would be banging on their door day or night to take a loved one away!

In those terrible days of the occupation, it was confusing to know who you could or could not trust because the German Nazis (and those few Norwegians that embraced them) ran the country through fear and violence. "The occupying power… resorted to the only means it know when it comes to holding a people in check: terror and more terror."[29] Cities, like Trondheim, felt it the most. "You were never sure who was a 'good Norwegian' and who was a Nazi sympathiser. We called them *stripet* ("striped")," Tante Gerd said, "You could not be open with people unless you really knew them. This was terrible for us, who had always been able to talk openly about everything in the past." Some who became sympathizers possibly found themselves with "their backs against the wall" and perhaps did things to accommodate the Nazis to avoid being imprisoned or having their loved ones hurt, actions they may have regretted later. Others simply joined the "new Nazi way" hoping to find power – but these were the minority in Norway, thankfully, although this group was often more brutal than the Germans. Trondheim's Henry Rinnan became a notorious Gestapo agent who led a group that would infiltrate the resistance movement pretending to be anti-Nazi. They arrested, killed, and tortured many resistance people. There was another category of what *appeared to be* Nazi sympathizers but were, in fact, double agents, reporting information back to the resistance groups, taking enormous risks. Again, in this context, how very hard it was to know who you could trust.

The frustration of being unable to respond or react to the outrageous German demands was keen, but very early on, the Norwegian resistance movement (or, the underground) was developed and organized to fight back against the German regime but under extreme secrecy. This struggle, which was both civilian and military, was also called "the home front." They sought unique ways to undermine the Nazis. "The two largest resistance groups were a civilian and a military organization, Sivorg and Milorg respectively. Its civilians formed a link to the government-in-exile in London, while the military came under the Norwegian Armed Forces High Command in London. Intelligence Service XU was directly subordinate to the Norwegian High Command in London and managed, inter alia, a large part of the courier (information) traffic between Resistance Movements and London. The correspondence between London and the resistance movement went mostly through couriers who crossed the Swedish-Norwegian border with the Norwegian legation in Stockholm as a hub...."[30]

In the autumn of 1941, "...the German technique of mass arrests...produced results. The home front lost many of its most valuable leaders, people who during a year and a half of occupation had mastered the art of conspiracy...Everybody arrested was locked up and rendered harmless. If the concentration camps became crowded it was an easy matter to set up additional ones."[31] Yet, slowly new leaders rose to take the place of those arrested and the struggle against the occupying power continued.

These were times of despair. "Winter was at hand, with long months of hunger and loss and black-outs...Hope was far, far off – the hope of liberation, peace, and happiness...Then America entered the war (*on December 8, 1941*). The effect was tremendous. Nearly everyone had almost given up hope that the United States would actively join forces with the fighting democracies...Far, far ahead in the tunnel a faint light had appeared."[32]

The Hoff family tried to meet the challenge of living a quiet life and carrying on with hope and with calm. But stress came from every side. "There was less and less food available," Gerd said. "We had no butter, no cheese. It was hard for my mother to bake bread anymore because she couldn't get yeast, for example," (and as time went by, the quality of the flour was worse and worse) "...but at least we had herring." Very early on sugar, coffee and flour were rationed, followed by all imported foods and then bread, fat, meat, eggs, dairy and dairy products. "In the summer of 1942, vegetables and potatoes were also rationed. (Notice potatoes are in their own sanctified class, not merely a lowly vegetable, so important were they to the Norwegian dinner table.) Each household was given one ration card per family member – this was a kind of ticket that gave the right to buy a certain amount of a particular food item."[33] Procuring food was an enormous hassle. On the black market, if you had something to exchange for food, of course there you did not use any ration card and you hoped you did not get caught.

"During the war there was a lack of almost everything. All import of goods from the countries Germany was at war with was stopped, and in addition the German occupation force requisitioned food and equipment for their own forces."[34] Farmor had to stand in lines at the stores, waiting for a chance to get food but sometimes to no avail. By the time it was her turn, all the food might be gone. She used all her creativity to make meals from whatever was available. "We were scramblin' for food," Dad said, so he was sent for a time during spring and summer to live and work on a farm outside Trondheim, "where he could get enough to eat," Farmor told me when I was visiting her in Norway in 1982. Tante Gerd remembers her brother being with them off and on at that time, so he went back-and-forth from the farm to home in Trondheim, "I don't know how often, but I remember him being there from time to time in that period," she said.

Dad loved life on a farm: the proximity to nature and animals and the pleasure of making things grow. Being outside the city, coupled with honest, hard physical work was a blessed distraction from life in occupied Trondheim. At the farm, he enjoyed joking around with one of the men he worked with, a kind, Hungarian man. Dad always liked to try to get folks to laugh. For instance, one time the two of them sat together companionably, a young teen and an older man, driving the horses pulling the wagon with a load of milk cans. There was a certain horse that often had terrible gas, worse when it had cholic. The Hungarian would comment after an especially powerful fart, "Step aside!" Dad would turn to the Hungarian man, a grimace on his face, and say, "Mmmm, breath that in. *FISE MEISTER!*" (Fart Master). "How he would LAUGH!" Dad said chuckling at himself, laughing at his own humor, as he so often did.

With her son working on the farm, Farmor at least knew he had enough to eat. Other challenges weighed on her, like clothing her family. Children grow quickly and it became impossible to find material for sewing clothes: "Mother had to re-create clothes from older clothes they could get, some from our grown aunts." Shoes and boots were not to be found. "We had to wear these very thick, wooden-soled shoes (*tresko*)," Gerd said, "they were painful to walk in. Very hard to walk in. When you are so young, it was troubling to walk in such shoes, you couldn't possibly hop around freely, terrible for children." Kari got the hand-me-downs from Gerd and everything they had was used and reused ("*Alt blir brukt.*") When it was time for Gerd's confirmation, her mother managed to procure some white parachute material on the black market and she made Gerd's dress out of it!

During the whole war, heavy blackout curtains had to be placed on every window and door at sunset. No light should be seen from the outside - everything had to be completely dark, to lower the risk of being bombed. The streets, too, were kept pitch black. "We were afraid to go out since it was so dark, there was no light on the street," Gerd recalls. The darkness itself was depressing, but especially in the long, already dark months of winter.

War equals darkness in so many ways. There were such terrible things that happened in those days, that afterwards, many folks blocked them out of their minds – they simply drew a dark curtain across – which is partly why my father and many others rarely spoke about the war for decades – or never.

Beyond the lack of food, the lack of clothing and the

imposed ever-increasing regulations, the most devastating effect of the occupation was by far the blatant Nazi brutality, used to instill fear and to attempt to enforce obedience. This impacted every soul in ways which cannot be measured. Etched into Tante Gerd's memory was the most dramatic day she would never forget. She was thirteen years old the day her father came home from the railroad station thoroughly distraught. He came into the kitchen and leaned against the wall, his head on his arm, sobbing inconsolably. "It was the only time I ever saw my father cry," she said. "It was because he had heard that two of his friends had been shot by the Nazis due to their work in the resistance movement. One, Henry Gleditsch, was either an actor or chief of the theatre," Gerd said explaining who he was. "Henry had worked with your grandfather in the same group doing resistance work." The other friend was Harald Langhelle, who Gerd said her father had worked with earlier and they were active in the same resistance group with Henry. "Harald was a journalist and had a newspaper in Trondheim," she said. Both men had been outspoken and defiant in various ways about their anti-Nazi position.[35] After Henry's assassination, the Nazis took over the theater and no one went there anymore, Gerd said, it was totally boycotted.

The execution of Henry, Harald and eight other well-known men from Trondheim took place on October 6, 1942 without trial. On that day, the voice of Nazi madman Terboven, the "Reich Commissioner," blasted from loudspeakers set up "in the streets of Trondheim, at all railroad stations, and in all thickly populated sections of Trøndelag. As the executions took place the names of the victims were shouted through the loudspeakers."[36] The ten prominent residents of the area were executed as "atonement sacrifices" (*soneofre*) at what became killing grounds in the forest near Falstad concentration camp north of Trondheim. All the victims' financial assets were confiscated.[37] Terboven said that he was pleased "...to grab the big ones, the ones who pull the strings."[38] He then declared a state of civil emergency. "In the days that followed, a further 24 people were executed by trial in Falstad and... marked the start of the persecution of Jews in the district."[39]

The Gestapo had taken over. "In the course of three hectic days thirty-four Norwegian patriots were executed and hundreds of persons were arrested. The Germans exploited the situation to the utmost for the purpose of spreading terror...Thus the Germans hoped to warn and intimidate the Norwegians. At the same time the occupying power let it be known that complete hostage lists had been prepared for all towns and localities throughout the country, lists of persons who would be instantly liquidated if an invasion of Norway *(by the Allies)* would be attempted."[40]

This was the Nazis' response to several acts of sabotage which had been carried out earlier by the resistance: "mysterious fires blazed up; inexplicable train wrecks occurred."[41] An explosion in German-owned iron mine Fosdalens Bergverk in north Trøndelag had taken place October 5, 1942.[42] Also, an underground smuggling of weapons and plan to build a military group that would disrupt German communication lines had also been recently discovered by the Nazis. During a skirmish, three Germans were killed by resistance men. The result was the twenty-four men executed, ten innocent Trønders shot as "atoning victims" – reprisal for the loss of German lives. This tragedy was known as the Majavatn affair. The Rinnan gang was involved in uncovering this activity.[43]

The Nazis' response to overt actions of the resistance was to kill civilians as "punishment": this made any important act of sabotage extremely costly. Besides the threat of death, the Nazis had set up several hundreds of concentration camps in Norway, one of the worst and largest being Grini, where some 20,000 prisoners were registered during the war.

This kind of threat of violence loomed even more heavily over those who found themselves forced to work with the Nazis as they carried out their normal jobs, like my grandfather. Those active in the resistance rarely told anyone else about what they were doing. Farfar probably never spoke to his wife about anything in relation to the resistance activities in which he participated. For one reason, Gerd said, because of the great burden of carrying certain information. Secrecy became the norm during the war, to protect people from knowing things that could be incriminating

155

or be dragged out by means of torture. (It was also the norm after the war, as a kind of bandage over deep wounds of sorrow).

The choices that leaders were forced to make meant, in many cases, weighing out consequences and choosing the lesser of two evils. Life in such a context is not always "black and white:" one cannot easily judge decisions made under such extreme pressure. The Nazis took slave labor and extended the railroad tracks further north, with no regard for human life. What could the railroad personnel do in such a situation and under such extreme pressure to comply (otherwise, be shot)? Railroad personnel, at the same time, were deeply involved with helping people in trouble escape by rail to Sweden right under the nose of the Germans. Being part of the railroad organization must have meant difficult choices for my grandfather and his colleagues, who walked a fine line to comply with Nazi instructions and still live with a clear conscience.

Sometime either just before or after the shooting of the ten citizens, "Nazi soldiers burst into our home," Gerd vividly remembered. As if in a frenzy, the barbaric soldiers pulled out drawers, dumped the contents on the floor of the living room and made a total mess of their home. As Gerd described it, "… it was so frightening. They were apparently looking for hidden documents or anything incriminating they might find." It was shocking to have these brutes burst violently into their home. One's home is one's refuge, a peaceful place away from the world. This was a terrifying invasion of privacy. It was the kind of event that one cannot forget, she said, and looking back on it, she thought it was probably because of her father's work in the resistance related to illegal newspapers or helping Jews via rail to escape into Sweden during the war.

The Meråker Line (*Meråkerbanen*) was the train line from Trondheim Central Station to the Swedish border, 102 kilometers (63 miles) away. When it became clear that Jews and others were in great danger from the Nazis, Farfar and his colleagues at the train station would assist in smuggling people via rail across to Sweden, which was neutral.

People could be hidden in a compartment or crate (Gerd

called it a *kasse*) inside the locomotive which housed the coal bunker (where coal was kept). Trondheim railroad personnel helped Jews escape from the Nazis in this and other ways. "The hidden coal compartment was one of several ways to hide the refugees. Railway staff on the trains and at the stations along all four lines to Sweden were involved in these transports which were called "export"."[44] One means of hiding was by completely sealing the door of a train compartment, that it could not be opened.[45] Farfar would have been in big trouble if this was ever discovered. It took courage to take such a risk, Daddy said, especially since his father was "head hancho" of scheduling so he would have been held responsible.

"...the Trondheim railway personnel were acting as part of the Norwegian resistance movement. Swedish newspapers and literature were smuggled into the country, primarily by stokers, who hid the material in the coal. Also, people who were not able to flee to Sweden via the mountains, or needed to get out in a hurry, were sometimes smuggled on board the trains... Illegal documents and microfilms were also smuggled out. For German transport trains, track-side employees tried to create "delays". [46] There were many railway employees who were quiet heroes, and never acknowledged.[47]

The greater the Nazi suppression, the greater the Norwegian spirit of defiance. There were many "regular" people that took part in various types of acts of resistance in ways too numerous to describe, but a few examples follow. Some carried rolls of film and coded letters bearing important information. A Lutheran priest, who ministered to deaf people in the area of Bergen, carried secret messages for the resistance along with him, up and down the coast until he was discovered and had to escape to Sweden.[48] In all parts of Norway, families hid those in trouble in their homes until they could escape over the border. Women sewed clothing and prepared meals for those they hid. Families that lived close to the border of Sweden "fought" as well, by helping guide people in need over the border to Sweden, leading them by foot or on skis, in horse-drawn wagons and on sleds. Especially in rural areas, local people found ways to give each other messages, for example, by using code words, or by "signs": placing an upside-down bucket on the bridge to mean there were no Germans around, or a shovel placed just outside a certain gate,[49] or a worn piece of clothing hanging out in an obvious place on a barn meant that Germans were in the area.[50]

People wrote new anti-Nazi lyrics to the national anthem as a means of defiance. People included illegal songs in their weddings. These actions could have serious consequences if discovered. For example, "Newlyweds Jenny and Johan Strand…were arrested because an illegal song was sung at their wedding. They spent the rest of the war at Grini. Several of the guests were also arrested, and one of them sent to a concentration camp in Germany."[51] Attempts to escape occupied Norway to join the Allies could end in tragedy, for example, in 1942, two men were shot… "18-year-old Kåre Iversen Hafstad from Kristiansund and Dutchman Paul Winnemüller. These two…had attempted to escape to England on a stolen motorboat."[52]

A newspaper editor and chairman of the Norwegian Press association, Torolv Kandahl said in May 1942 when interviewed on the radio after his escape from Norway, "For me, I either had to leave or be put in a concentration camp. It was hard to live under the tyranny of the Nazis but it was the greatest experience a man could have had, to see how his own people were united in an unbreakable solidarity to defend their right to live, only with spiritual weapons against the weapons of brutality which are used in the Germans armament factories. In my country they are carrying on the fight in every family and every home…"[53]

Tante Gerd said that the family also participated in acts of civil disobedience like many other courageous folks in Trondheim and around the country, during the Nazi occupation. They read illegal newspapers from the underground which popped up secretly all over Norway. This was especially important after radios were taken away. Some 350 different illegal newspapers appeared over the length of the war.[54] These newspapers gave information about what was really happening in the outside world as well as within Norway, and they inspired Norwegian citizens to carry on in their struggle to resist the Nazis. Despite the danger, "new illegal newspapers appeared constantly, produced and distributed by men and women who risked their lives by spreading information to Trondheim's citizens."[55] Gerd said, "News came from London and America on the radio and this was put in the newspapers."

The primary source of news for the newspapers came from London Radio, with messages from King Haakon and the government received by resistance people with secret radio receivers. Secondly, home front news came from double-agents *inside* Nazi offices. The latest arrests, confiscations of properties, or plans to mobilize Norwegian youth would leak out and promptly be written in the illegal press. Thirdly, local agents all over the country kept their eyes open, too, and got information to Homefront people, who then sent it back to London.[56]

Illegal newspapers were type written or on mimeographed sheets – not made on big presses. Editions were small, standard letter size, due to paper shortages. News was the bulk of the content, for it was the key to understanding the whole situation. However, reviews of books or movies might be included at times, for these topics interested the Norwegians, too. Various groups such as the church, labor unions, teachers, and the medical world had their own newspapers, while remaining non-partisan and with one voice expressing the national attitude against Germans and quislings.[57]

Newspapers were distributed in carefully organized ways. When printed or typed, they were sometimes sent to readers by mail, fooling censorship by using envelopes with German letterhead. Voluntary "postmen" helped distribute although it was severe punishment if you were caught with an illegal newspaper. Some would place it inside of German papers so if caught they could say they were on their way to the police to report that it was received in the mail.[58]

"My father was very busy with distributing the newspapers," Gerd said. "Sometimes we children were carrying them along without knowing it." Like his father, Dad was also involved in helping to carry "both messages and underground newspapers, which were printed and circulated through a system of messengers," who often did not even know each other's names. Although he classified his role as only being "…partially involved in the underground, since I was quite young at the time," this meant he was effectively engaged in illegal work, and the danger of arrest or even death hung over all those that did such things. ("Between 3,000 and 4,000 people were arrested for writing or distributing illegal newspapers in Norway during the war…Of these, 62 were executed and 150 died in captivity.")[59]

"Trondheim was one of the most dangerous places in Norway to engage in illegal press activity. The notorious network of Henry Rinnan had infiltrated large parts of Trondheim city, and this in many cases made it very difficult to publish illegal newspapers without being reported to the German occupation authorities."[60]

Some of the names of Norwegian illegal newspapers were "*The Home Front,*" "*Forward,*" "*We Want Our Country,*" "*Freedom,*" and "*London News.*"

The secret resistance movement was called the Home Front (*Hjemmefronten*), and consisted of many different groups that carried out both civil and military resistance.[61]

As one Norwegian wrote, "Living in an enemy-occupied country can never be fully understood if not experienced. The Nazi's initial step was to seize the newspapers and the radio stations, and from then on, we were fed their lies and distorted truth."[62] Only one way of thinking was allowed: Nazi ideology.

So, most people cancelled their newspaper subscriptions, read

Examples of Illegal newspapers

only illegal newspapers and listened to the "free" radio in secret. If you were caught listening to the radio or even reading illegal newspapers, the official penalty was death. The Nazis hoped to control every piece of information going into the minds of the people. As mentioned above, the Nazis tried to tighten their control over information by outlawing radios in 1941. The Hoff family kept their now illegal radio but they hid it in a hole in the wall which was carefully covered with a picture. They listened to it secretly up in the attic (*opp i lofte*) so no one knew they were listening. Thus, they could hear news from the "free" world, including communication from the Norwegian government in exile in London. The radio messages began each time with the words, "*Dette er London!*" ("This is London!"), words that signalled hope. Gerd remembers hearing King Haakon speak from London on the radio. "People connected with the resistance would be given a message to know that at such and such a time there would be an important radio message so we set up to hear it. *Det var nok en glede* (it was quite a joy)," she said, "for the king and the whole royal family were truly very much loved by Norwegians. They had to escape from Norway early on, for the Nazis were after them," she said. "The king inspired us."

The King was a figure of hope and of standing up against the Nazis. His motto was "*Alt for Norge*" ("Everything for Norway)." He embodied the fight for a free and independent Norway. When the Germans had invaded Norway, they pressured the King to appoint Quisling, puppet of the Nazis, as Prime Minister. The King responded that he would have to confer with the legal Norwegian government. In a trembling voice, the King, 68 years old, said to the government ministers, "I am profoundly moved at the idea of having to assume personal responsibility for the woes that will befall our country and our people if German demands are rejected. It is such a heavy responsibility that I shudder to hear it. The government is free to decide, but I shall make my own position clear: I cannot accept the German demands. This would conflict with everything I have considered to be my duty as a king ever since I came to Norway almost 35 years ago… I have endeavoured to embody a constitutional monarch that was entirely loyal to the people who elected me in 1905... I cannot name Quisling Prime Minister, because he had neither the confidence of the people nor that of their deputies. As a result, should the government choose to bow before the German demands, I would understand their motivation perfectly, in view of the imminent peril now threatening, and the prospect of seeing so many young Norwegians sacrifice their lives in this war: yet I would then have no other alternative than to abdicate."[63] The government agreed with the King and Norway refused the cave in to Nazi demands.

The King's speeches on BBC World Service radio from London truly inspired his people struggling back home. To honor King Haakon on his birthday in August, people in Norway put a flower in their jacket buttonhole (which also quickly became an illegal action.) There were folks put in prison in Trondheim because of the flowers worn to honor the King and to spite the Nazis.

Another act of rebellion was "wearing paperclips on our jackets," Gerd said. "Paper clips keep papers stuck together - these paper clips symbolized that the Norwegian people would stick together against the Nazis. *Vi holder sammen!* (We stick together)," she explained. It was illegal to wear paper clips on your jacket ("*fikk ikke lov å bruke binders på jakken*") yet they wore them anyway. This obscure symbol could hardly be noticed but, for the Norwegians, it gave a clear message of solidarity.

In many and diverse ways, Norwegians stuck together and stood up against the Nazis. A journalist was once carrying a briefcase of 500 illegal newspapers on a busy street in Oslo. As he crossed the street, the briefcase slipped out of his hand, fell to the ground and to his horror, opened, spilling bundles all over the street. Others on the street spontaneously surrounded him and helped him gather them up quickly and return them safely back in the briefcase. A German soldier, seeing a gathering, approached them asking, "What's going on here!?"

A man quickly piped up with an answer: "We were discussing the price of potatoes."[64] (This, apparently was a common occurrence or in any event did not surprise the Nazi.)

He commanded them to break it up. The Norwegians went on their way, probably smiling to themselves. Yes, we stick together.

At the end of January 1943, German forces were forced to surrender to the Soviets at Stalingrad at great cost. With every year that followed, the weight of German oppression increased as their losses became more frequent in Europe. With great numbers of people dying, the Nazis needed more cheap labor: they would steal any able-bodied person available from the countries they occupied. An incredible number of people were coerced by Germany to join their war effort all over Europe. Millions were forced to work in horrific conditions and many did not survive.

In Norway, "in the spring of 1943…measures were taken to mobilize all available labor." The Nazi-run government inside the country headed by Quisling issued the General National Labour Act of February 22, 1943. It stated that the Norwegian people "must 'put all their strength into the life-and-death struggle that Europe is waging against Bolshevism.' Men aged 18 -55 and women between the ages of 21 and 40 were obliged to register with the employment service. Most of those who were summoned were sent to the Organisation Todt's facilities…"[65]

Forced laborers sent to Germany from occupied countries were "effectively treated as slaves and existed in the complete and arbitrary service of the totalitarian state. Many did not survive the work or the war." [66]

Ørnulf would be turning eighteen that year, on August 11, 1943. He would then be legally required to register and join the Nazi work force. Although the law was issued as a required action, the government in exile announced by BBC radio and through the resistance network of communication that young men should not at any cost register their names to join in the *arbeidsmobilisering* (labor mobilization*). These messages coming over the radio from the Norwegian government in exile made it clear: Do *not* comply with the Nazi worker mobilization program! The resistance movement took this instruction so seriously that they destroyed many paper records, eliminating the registers of the German-controlled Norwegian employment offices to make it more difficult for the Nazis to locate eligible young men in Trondheim.[67]

It was time to make a move to escape to neutral Sweden – even if anyone caught crossing the border would be shot. Two comrades close to his age agreed to steal away with him to avoid joining the Nazi workforce. Dad had connections with the resistance (underground) as he was carrying around illegal newspapers and messages. Through them he obtained information for the safest route to leave Norway.

Dad said, "Well, the minute I found out they were 'recruiting,' as they called it, youth labor for their industry in Germany, I didn't want any part of it whatsoever, so we made plans to escape to Sweden. At the time, the underground in Norway had various routes to Sweden whereby people who were in danger could escape. I contacted the local underground people and asked them for some advice as to how to get over to Sweden and they set up a route for us whereby we took a train from the city of Trondheim… up to the peaks, from there on we went on skis to Sweden."

"The organised Norwegian refugee traffic took place mainly through… resistance organisations."[68] For example, twenty-eight Jewish refugees who fled from various parts of Norway to Sweden in 1942 and 1943 and were interviewed later stated that they had assistance along the way of their escape. The majority of these said that the resistance organized the escape and that people associated with the resistance movement helped them and guided them on different parts of the escape route. Of these, five fled from Trondheim in autumn of 1942 over the Sylane mountains and had detailed knowledge of who was involved at different stages of planning and completion of the escape. The resistance movement was to a greater or lesser extent engaged in their extensive escape route, even to the extent of knowing the names of the border guides.[69]

The advice and assistance of the underground (or resistance) was essential for more than one reason. Firstly, the border area is treacherous, especially in the Sør-Trøndelag region– crossing over would be dangerous without the intimate knowledge and help of local people who knew the mountains, forests, and the risky, open areas of high visibility.

Secondly, the German patrols moved along the Norway/Sweden border areas to catch people trying to escape and especially resistance people. One could not simply use the main roads over to Sweden because soldiers were stationed exactly at the border. Local people knew the pattern of the patrols' movements and were critical in helping refugees escape, reducing the risk of getting caught while crossing over. "The Norwegian resistance movement gradually established systems with transport routes for refugees, in which locally known border guides (or border pilots, *grenseloser*) were the last link in the chain that took them to safety."[70] These folks lived close to the border, knew the geography well and were willing to take the risk to help others to get across. "Many refugees were unaccustomed to the forests, and for them it was critical to be piloted to the border by persons with knowledge about local forest trails as well as the Germans' guarding/patrol routines."[71]

In the region where Dad and his friends would get off the

"Barbed wire between Norway and Sweden. Photo taken on the Norwegian-Swedish border last winter when the Germans had set up barbed wire barriers and reinforced guard duty. London files, May 24, 1943" Riksarkivet (National Archives of Norway)
Piggtråd mellom Norge og Sverige. Et bilde tatt på den norsk-svenske grensen i vinter da tyskerne hadde satt opp piggtrådsperring og forsterket vakttjenesten. London, 24.5.43"

train, they could not simply head east straight to Sweden following roads because the German soldiers were "...patrolling from Fjällnäs, Bruksvallarna and the border post near Vauldalen."[72] Vauldalen was the Norwegian customs station directly east and just before the Swedish border, while Fjällnäs was the station just over the border, in Sweden.

Once they knew the outline of their journey, as advised by the resistance, the three young men discretely prepared for departure. No one should know that they were going, because leaving the country was strictly forbidden.

Everything had to be done in secret.

ESCAPE: THE JOURNEY TO SWEDEN

On April 6, 1943, the three youth left their homes without telling a soul. Dad's family knew absolutely nothing about his decision to leave – it was safer for them *not* to know. When their parents realized that Ørnulf was gone, they were totally taken by surprise. Gerd said, "It was a big shock to both Mor and Far."

What turmoil must have filled his mother's heart when her one remaining son departed into the unknown and he just seventeen years old! Would he make it over the border safely and what would happen to him away from home? It was already hard when he was away, working on the farm. Of course, every mother who has carried a child nine months and given her life raising a little one finds it hard to let go of a child when they reach maturity, but releasing a son in such an uncertain situation was cause for great distress. In the months and years that followed, the two sisters observed their mother's heartache as she missed and worried about Ørnulf – it brought sorrow to the whole family.

The family did not talk about it but the girls felt the weight of the burden their parents carried. Gerd said, "I only knew that he had left for Sweden, nothing more. Everything was done in secret." ("*Alt ble gjort i hemmelighet*").

Dad and his friends left family and homeland behind, not knowing what lay ahead. However, there must have been a feeling of safety in numbers: the band of three journeyed together. Besides apprehension, they probably felt that an adventure had begun. One of the two boys was nineteen-year-old Ragnar Sundseth, "but we called him 'Barabbas' as he was such a rascal,"

Dad said with a smile. The other was Sverra Johan Aune, who was eighteen. They were all from Trondheim and they were all good skiers.[73]

They boarded the train with their skis at Trondheim and headed southeast to obscure Reitan Station (before Røros). They looked like three mates heading out for a recreational ski trip. Dad said that travel was not restricted inside of Norway most of the time but no travel was allowed outside the borders of the country. I can imagine them joking with one another as if everything was normal, to cover up their anxious feelings during the approximately two-hour train trip. They got off at the remote and tiny Reitan Station according to the advice the resistance contacts had given them. Somewhere near Reitan, they slept under the snow. (Norwegians are trained to create snow caves in case they ever get stuck in a storm.) From Reitan, they were supposed to head North towards the abandoned Kjøli copper mines (more than a thousand meters above sea level and quite rugged terrain) and they were surely anxious to get going.

The trip from Reitan over to Sweden would not be an easy one. Travelling up and over the mountains and through the fields was a challenging trek. The journey was not along nicely groomed ski trails: they had to make their way through. This was not a trip for the faint-hearted. It was cold, mostly below freezing, and it snowed off and on. In April, snow can be quite icy, making it tricky to ski without slipping and hard when you fell.

We are not sure how the three young men found the way from Reitan to Kjøli but the following story, shared by Jørgen Storrønning when he was 91 years old, may fill in some blanks. Jørgen lived at Storrønning farm close to Reitan. Shortly before his death in 2023, he shared this memory with his step-son Putte (Idar Oliver Putte Aspèn) when asked about helping refugees over to Sweden:

One morning during the occupation, three young men came to the Storrønning farm in Holtålen. They had first traveled by train to Reitan station, then used a draisine and traveled back to Graftås (2.5 km back towards Trondheim) before reaching Storrønning farm nearby. Jørgen, who at the time was ten years old, met them in the farmyard. They asked whether any adults were home, so he fetched his uncle, Ingvald Storrønningen (32 years old). They told him they needed help getting to Kjøli because they were escaping to Sweden. Ingvald asked them whether they were refugees or saboteurs, and they answered that they were refugees. He then responded – "I will come with you." They ate at the farm before they left. Jørgen could not remember their dialect but recalled one of the three saying during their meal that he "hadn't had milk since Ålesund burned," meaning, it had been quite a while since he had tasted milk.

Ingvald took the three young men to Kjøli Cabin. From there, the terrain is quite open, and you can see all the way to Sweden. He pointed out the direction and told them to pass by Langen Lake and Langen Farm. Ingvald was exhausted when he returned to Storrønning farm after guiding the three young men to Kjøli. He had never traveled with such a fit group of people – he struggled to keep pace with them.

(Jørgen could not remember if it was 1942 or 1943, Putte said.)

Whether they travelled with Ingvald or by some other means, the three friends indeed skied the approximately 14 kilometers (9 miles) up to the Kjøli abandoned copper mining area, and from there skied in the direction of Stugudalen (another 14 kilometers). From Stugudalen, they would ski over the Swedish border.

Stugudalen is a village in the region of Sør-Trøndelag situated along the lake "Stugusjøen."

> 5.   Han reiste hjemme fra sammen med Sverre Aune og Ragnar Sundseth begge kammerater av vitnet fra Trondheim.
>   De tok toget til Reitan st. Overnattet der. BDen neste dag gikk de videre over fejllet til Kjøli gruber. Derfra fortsatte de til en hytte som de hadde fått anvist. Fra hytten fikk de følge vid dere til grensen ved Stugudalen.

Description of Dad's escape to Sweden. Excerpt from police interrogation - Isle of Man, June 1944. See Appendix G.

TRANSLATION: He left home together with Sverre Aune and Ragnar Sundseth both friends of the witness from Trondheim. They took the train to Reitan station. Spent the night there. The next day they continued across the mountain to Kjøli mines. From there they continued to a cabin they had been shown. From the cabin, they were accompanied over the border by Stugudalen.

Stugudalen had two farms with humble, "good Norwegians" who were known to help escapees over the border: Nedal Farm, towards the north, and Langen Farm, by Langen Lake, south of Nedal. Langen is on the more direct route for a safe entry into Sweden from Kjøli and very likely the farm where the youth stopped for help.

Langen farm had been around since the 1800s and was accessible only by foot or by ski or by horse (even today there is no road to the now abandoned farm). Ole. O. Berggård and his wife Berit leased Langen farm from city people in Oslo, farming it since 1926. They were hard-working, ordinary folk who loved animals and farming. Ole and Berit assisted many people to escape to Sweden: fed them and helped get them properly equipped for the journey before leading them over the border (often on skis).

To the north, at Nedal farm, young Jon Magnus Rotvold (Magnus) helped his parents, Oliver and Ingeborg, with refugees

Langen Farm

that came for assistance. In October 2023, this humble man reluctantly described to us what it was like, helping refugees in the Stugudalen area over to Sweden. Even with "German soldiers right nearby, the entire village of Stugudalen was united in helping the refugees" by discretely bringing clothing, shoes, and food out to the two farms. Their generosity was great, for these were times when everything was so terribly scarce. Their hearts were moved to help the refugees – complete strangers - who "were in *such* dire need and were *all* afraid," Magnus said.

Border zones were established as the Nazis especially needed to control areas of escape. It was required that "everyone over the age of 15 had to have identification papers on them once the border zones were established."[74] Dad and his friends most likely did not have any such papers.

Everyone knew this illegal activity which was going on at these farms, but no one ever mentioned it, for that was safer for all ("...*all visste mye, men ingen måtte vite noe*").[75] "Many had illegal radio sets tucked away and listened to London, and the message passed by word of mouth from one person to another in 'the silent ring.'"[76]

Refugees were mainly Norwegians but there were also Poles, Frenchmen, Russians and even Germans wanting to escape the Nazis.[77] Those coming to Langen farm were shown to the cabin adjacent to the house where they might stay until it was the safest time to leave. That is, unless the cabin was occupied that day by German soldiers because this very cabin was taken over by German soldiers as their base whenever they came to patrol nearby! A well-known resistance man, Tormod Morset, who quite often passed through Langen farm on his trips back and forth to Sweden carrying information and other illegal goods, would sneak up to the farmhouse and knock on the door, and quickly go and hide again. Ole's wife Berit would come out, look around, and if there were Germans there at the time, she locked the door behind her as she went back inside. If no Germans were there at the time, she would leave the door unlocked so Tormod would know it was safe for him to stay there that night.[78]

Both farms had the added stress of German patrolling soldiers in the vicinity. "There was a German station 150 meters away from Nedal farm and the patrols went all around the area."[79] Yet both farms and the citizens of Stugudalen cared for the refugees coming for help even if such actions were "punishable and dangerous to the highest degree."[80] Across all of Norway, hundreds of refugees and several hundred border pilots were caught and were arrested and imprisoned. Approximately 180 people (including refugees and border pilots) were either shot while fleeing, died or were executed after they were caught trying to escape over the border to Sweden.[81]

Ole and Oliver led many a refugee over the Swedish border, (it is not known just how many). These clandestine trips typically took place at night, as it was quite a long stretch and to avoid encountering anyone. The area is high in elevation, and it is open landscape, with little vegetation, so one could be seen from a long distance in daylight. Nighttime travel was therefore necessary to

Ole O. Berggård on Langen Lake

172

avoid being seen. As Magnus said, "Day and night, night and day, we took them over. We knew the land so well, every branch and twig, every turn of the path, so it was no problem for us to take them over at night, too."

Years later, Ole and Berit's daughter, Reidun, spoke of one of the times she remembered distinctly her father's border guide work: "One evening, Father brought home with him two young boys who he was going to accompany over the border the next day. They were not equipped properly, so there was no other choice than to give one of them my own new skis."[82]

Ole was arrested by the Nazis in September 1943 for "illegal business." He was a courier as well, taking information back and forth between resistance contacts in Norway and Sweden. He created a hidden compartment under the ski bindings where these letters were hidden.[83] Eventually, he was released from prison in Bredveit.

Fortunately, Dad and his friends had their own skis so, on their last day in Norway during the war, early April 1943, they set out from the farm, very likely skiing after Ole, on the segment of the trip fraught with the most danger. It is hard to imagine what it must have been like, but surely their hearts were racing as they travelled under the cover of darkness, coming closer to the border and further into the unknown. There was only a sliver of a waxing crescent moon that night, but perhaps the stars that shone helped light the way.

The area from Langen Farm to the Swedish border included more rough terrain: rocky, areas of great snow drifts, steep in places and very difficult to traverse. The cold air would sting their eyes and chill their bones – but the brisk pace kept them warm. A Danish refugee once came through this very same area trying to make his way over to Sweden *without* a border guide: sadly, he was found frozen to death near Vigl Lake.[84] "Numerous attempts to escape over the border mountains ended tragically. The graves of Anna Ingeborg Feragen and Leif Båtne at Hållans cemetery near Funäsdalen testify to this."[85] They were caught in a snow storm in November 1942, five months earlier and not far from where Dad and his friends traversed the border.

Skiing on, passing by way of Vigl Lake, still in Norway, the small group would most likely have avoided the open area of the frozen lake which, although easier to ski over was too risky because of visibility. Instead, they probably skied beside it, ready to quickly cross up over the mountain in case they met patrol soldiers on skis.[86] Patrol soldiers were mostly Eastern German soldiers sent to the border area, and they had to be "good skiers, which was absolutely necessary… to be capable to patrol such an area in winter."[87]

Even if one made it just over the border in to Sweden, it did not necessarily mean immediate safety: the area closest to the Norwegian border on the Swedish side was considered "no man's land" and Swedish police sometimes arrested refugees caught in those areas and sent them back. This meant refugees had to get beyond these areas and further into Sweden before

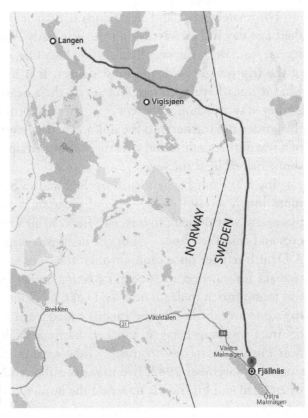

Dad's route
to Sweden
from Langen

being admitted by the Swedish police at a border station. There was great "risk for the border pilot (helping refugees), for the Swedes looked after the border at least as well as the Germans. Many Norwegians experienced being caught by Swedish border police and detained for shorter or longer periods of time in Sweden."[88]

At the start of the war, Swedish refugee policy was very restrictive. From 1940 to early 1942, many Norwegian refugees were stopped after crossing the Swedish border and were forced to go back.[89] For example, "In 1940, about 800 Norwegian refugees were rejected by Swedish authorities. This amounted to about a third of all those who tried to flee from Norway to Sweden."[90] Part of the reason may have been because early in the war, Swedish authorities did not believe that the refugees needed to leave Norway for their safety[91]: this changed as they became aware of Nazi brutality. In addition, Sweden wanted very much to protect their neutral status. There were also those Swedes who just wanted to avoid being overrun by refugees. Thankfully, by the time Dad left Norway in April 1943, Sweden was far more open to accepting refugees and gradually, unconditionally admitted all who fled there from Norway in the final years of the war.

Passing on to Hyddal, on the border between Norway and Sweden, above Hyddsjøen by the mountain Haftorstøten, they probably followed down the valley, south to Gröndalen on the Swedish side of the border just south of Haftorstøten. But how to find the Swedish police station where they could sign in as refugees and finally be safe? The Norway-Sweden border is more than 1600 kilometers long with rugged terrain, so the military and police resources were spread along the border at various locations. The closest Swedish local police stations where refugees could be safely signed in were often many miles from the border. So, it was still quite a trek south to the small cabin at Fjällnäs which housed the Malmagen Customs (border) police station.

It is very likely that Ole led them over the border to Gröndalen, about 16 kilometers from Langen based on information from

Sámi Border Guide (grenselos)

others, like the Morset brothers, who also passed via Langen Farm into Sweden.[92] Gröndalen was a very rural area with no real roads in or out, and just two Sámi settlements (the families Middagsfjäll and Nordfjäll.)[93] From Gröndalen, the Sámi (formerly known as Laplanders) led refugees on the final step south to the Malmagen border police station. This semi-nomadic, indigenous people, most of whom live in northern Norway, Sweden and Finland, had the legal right since "the codicil to the 1751 border treaty"[94] to cross between the countries' borders fishing, trapping and following their reindeer herds. So, the Sámi helped refugees on both sides of the border, sometimes even crossing back into Norway to help people who got stuck for one reason or another.[95] Their freedom of movement and generous and courageous spirit made them perfectly suited to aid refugees in their flight. For example, two Sámi brothers from Gröndalen, Nils Ott Nordfjäll and Arne Nordfjäll helped refugees in this way besides other resistance activities.[96] It was probably one of these two brothers, who were close to Dad's age, that led Dad and his friends the last 15 kilometers of their journey on skis from Gröndalen to the Swedish Customs station at Malmagen.

Some forty years after his escape, in the late 1980s, my father briefly described what he remembered of his journey to my sister, Julie, which she recorded on cassette tape. Dad said, "We took a train from the city of Trondheim… then up to the peaks…North. We went on skis, from there to Sweden. It took us 3 days. We could only travel during the night because in the daytime it was too dangerous to travel as it was constantly being watched by planes overhead and various ski patrols in some areas by Germans. So, we dug in, during the day, we built ourselves some snow huts and if we found some barns we used them. We travelled only by night, and on the third day came to Sweden."

Dad, Ragnar, and Sverre's names were indeed registered in Fjällnäs, Sweden at the Malmagen Customs (Border) Station log on April 8, 1943, the third day of their journey.[97] They had skied 31 kilometers (about 19 miles) from Langen farm, over the border and down to where they were signed in at the border station. I can imagine that they were exhausted.

They were the only refugees to arrive that day. Each was assigned a refugee number in the Swedish registry: Dad's number was 15307.[98] Each one was interrogated by the Swedish local police (but no record of this could be found). I wonder what that felt like. Perhaps the relief of being away from Nazi-run Norway overshadowed the uneasy feeling of being interrogated by Swedish authorities and the stark reality of an unknown life which loomed ahead.

36495 Hoff	Per Odd	091124 011144
35641 Hoff	Reidar	300610 211044
23513 Hoff	Svein Marius	220413 281243
02906 Hoff	Sven Helge	281115 041141
34458 Hoff	Sverre Asbjörn	160619 260944
01814 Hoff	Thorbjörn Kåre	300617 240841
30270 Hoff	Willy	150222 180844
06177 Hoff	Willy Hartvig	100623 050842
15307 Hoff	Ørnulf	110825 080443

Flyktningar i Sverige - Arkivverket (Refuges in Sweden – Archives)
Political Refugees can be searched by last name.
Assigned Refugee# | Last name | First name | Date of birth (day/mo/yr) | Arrival Date

The youth were eventually taken nearby to the very small village of Funäsdalen. The customs chief there, "Rickard Larsson, was a key person for the resistance movement on the Swedish side. He worked together with the sheriff in Funäsdalen who sympathized with the Germans. This was everyday life at the time."[99] Pro-Norwegian and Pro-Nazi worked side by side. Again, you always had to be very careful who you trusted, even inside of Sweden.

On April 10th, the three young men were paid a "travel allowance for the transport of refugees from Funäsdalen to the refugee camp." Each one was given 17 Swedish crowns and 14 cents (the equivalent of pay for a nine-hour work day back then, or about $30 today) to facilitate their trip.[100]

Dad, Ragnar and Sverre took the train to Vingåker station and from there continued on three kilometers (1.9 miles) to the political refugee camp in Kjesäter. They were registered there on April 11, 1943, three days after crossing the border into Sweden. Every single person who arrived had to be interrogated as part of a screening process. "They were seeking out traitors, 'Quislings'... who could give the Germans in Sweden information about the escape routes from Norway."[101] They did not want any Nazi-collaborating spies infiltrating and spies could be anywhere. They also warned newcomers not to contact anyone back in Norway to avoid causing problems for them and never to speak of how they escaped. "It was a very strict regime, almost military. It had to be. Not only because people were constantly coming there and they needed routines to process all the people. They were constantly afraid of infiltrators and were on the lookout for such. Spies were also exposed and caught at Kjesäter. Fake refugees who were looking for information to destroy the resistance work back home (in Norway)."[102]

The day after their arrival at the camp, Dad and his companions were individually interrogated by Police Constable Leif Berg.[103] Each one gave information about his identity. As Sverre and Ragnar were adults, their pictures were taken and they gave details about their short work history in Norway. All three mentioned that they had come over the border together because of the Nazi worker mobilization. Sverre and Ragnar also stated that the companions with whom they had escaped were "trustworthy."

Was Police Constable Berg a kind man, treating the youth before him with patience, or was he short and impatient? There were many refugees to deal with. The refugee's signature at the bottom of the report looks a bit shaky, or am I imagining?

In Dad's Interrogation Report, refugee #15307, described himself as follows:

- Ørnulf Hoff, born August 11, 1925 in Trondheim of Norwegian married parents, Harald Hoff, Train Station Commissioner, and housewife Margrethe Hoff (maiden name Otnes).
- Baptized and confirmed in Lademoen church [an important identity]
- Student [equivalent to 11th grade of high school in USA]
- Living at 37, Statsing. Dahls Street, Trondheim
- No involvement with NS [Nasjonal Samling – Quisling fascist party] or any political party.

Constable Berg asked him if he knew anyone in Sweden or did anyone there know him. He named two Norwegians: an older cousin, Per Soknes (son of Aksel and Astrid Soknes. Astrid was Farfar's sister. Per came over to Sweden on July 28, 1942, a year earlier). The other he named, Egil Alstad, had lived nearby the Hoff family in Trondheim, Gerd said.[104]

Ørnulf explained that "he left school and just now escaped over the border because of the (Nazi) worker mobilization. He came over the border on April 8, 1943 together with refugee numbers 15205 and 6. He had never participated in any illegal work or other doings which made it necessary to escape."[105]

Here was a kid, 17 years old, far from home, no longer surrounded by his loving family, no longer under the stable security of his respected father. He had left everything behind.

His refugee index card sums him up well, and poignantly attests to how little he had:

A Student. 175 cm tall (5'9"). Blue eyes. Blond hair.

No Military experience. No driver's license. No money.
A pair of skis.

```
RK.                        15307
                                                                        V
Hoff Örnulf                      F. Tr.heim 11.8.25
Skoleelev                        Statsing. Dahlsgt 37 Tr.heim


175              Oval            BIÅ              Blond

Leg.k. 50961/42 Tr.heim          Passnr. 3094a/43 til 11.4.45

Ank. Sv. 8.4.43                  Kj. 11.4.43 fra Funäsdalen

Avbrutt middelskole ca. 1½ md. för eks. grunnet avreisen til Sverige.
                                    Reiste E. 18/6-44 F.
Mil: Ingen                       ============================

Far: Harald Hoff, Fullm. ve N. S. B. Statsing. Dahlsgt 37 Tr.heim.

Ski: Kl. 2               Ingen penger              Ikke förerkort
```

Dad's Refugee Card

LIFE AS A REFUGEE AND THEN...

The refugee camp where Dad had arrived in the spring of 1943 was a reception center at Kjesäter, a manor house in Södermanland county (not far from Stockholm). Norwegian refugees were sent there, in most cases, after crossing the border. Between 1942 and 1943, an average of about thirty Norwegian refugees arrived per day to Kjesäter from the police districts at the border, but this increased to about 100 per day in 1944.[106]

Dad had told me, "After we arrived in Sweden, which remained a neutral country throughout the war, we were put in a political camp." That camp was Kjesäter.

About a year before, Swedish authorities had agreed to allow the Norwegian government to set up and run the refugee camp. Norwegians, often refugees themselves, ran the camp. It was a secret, mini-Norwegian village in the town of Vingåker, Sweden with small roads named patriotically like, *Kongens Gate* (The King's Street).

Nr.15307.

Hoff, Örnulf
Skolelev
Född d.11.8.1925.
Hemort: Trondheim
Ankom d.11.4.1943. Vingåker.
Avrest d. 14.4.1943. Öreryd.

Dad's Kjesäter Index Card from Swedish Archives "Skolelev" means Student (USA equivalent to high school)

Kjesäter Barracks

"First, we were put up in barracks," Dad said, describing this part of his journey. Refugees were housed in many long rows of barracks.[107] The dining hall where they ate was called *Haakonshallen* (named after Norway's beloved King Haakon).[108] Despite the strict, military-like ambiance, I bet it felt good to hear Norwegian again, in its many different dialects, and to be among his countrymen in free territory. Dad probably soon noticed the availability of foods like butter and coffee in Sweden which had been so scarce in Norway.

Dad did not remain in the first political refugee camp for long. On April 14, 1943, on the fourth day after arriving at Kjesäter, he was sent to Öreryd, another refugee camp in Småland several hours south of Kjesäter. He remained there about a week. Besides registration and interrogation, he had medical checks and was issued new I.D. papers.

It seems appropriate to have received new identification papers. Think of how this boy's life had changed: from peaceful childhood to fulltime working refugee. Consider the challenges: from being rooted in a supportive and nurturing home environment, citizen of his own country to being on his own, a stranger and foreigner, cut off from mother, father, sisters and most of his friends, and his future completely unknown.

Refugee screening at the camps also had an impact on their future: some of the young refugees were sent on to schools but that was not Dad's preference. Given the choice, he would rather work than study (as Gerd said, "He was not fond of going to school.") At least he had the possibility to make this choice as he was 17.

Öreryd had a kind of job placement service for Norwegian men. They were first assigned three months of work duty before they themselves had to locate their own jobs in the Swedish labor market. "Until 1944, most of the men were sent to do forestry work under the auspices of the Swedish state."[109]

The refugees contributed greatly to the labor market in Sweden especially in forestry and agriculture. "Especially the Norwegians' contribution to forestry can almost be characterized as outstanding. Twenty percent of Sweden's needed firewood during the harsh war winters of 1942 and 1943 was met by Norwegian men who in many cases were not accustomed to doing forestry work."[110]

So, in Öreryd, the first job assigned to Dad and his buddies, was *skogsarbetare*, working in the forest at a logging camp in Reimyre, some 3 hours north-east.[111] They would be cutting timber although they had never done this type of work before. Work horses were still in use in those days, for dragging the timber. The work was physically exhausting, and he stayed in that job only one month – not three. He said with a laugh, "I wasn't going to break my back for the damn Swedes cutting wood!"

He quickly found another job and started in May continuing through the summer of 1943. He remembered it as beer production. It was here he parted company from his two escapee comrades but made new friends. "At least we could drink there, and we didn't care what they said," he laughed heartily as he said it. "We figured, we might's well help ourselves." His job was described as "agricultural worker" (*jordbruksarbetare*) at Herrborums Farm, Bottna, Söderköping. They must have been growing hops or something of the like and brewing beer. Of the various jobs in Sweden, this was his favorite (no surprise there!). Farm life must have felt familiar, and was as good a place as any to spend your eighteenth birthday in a foreign country.

After the summer, on September 20, he was sent to Lunnevads, Sjögestad, where he stayed briefly in the barracks there with other Norwegians and was vaccinated, probably for tuberculosis, diphtheria and tetanus.

In October, he moved to Norrköping, Östergötland where he had found work in a huge wool textile factory, A/B Förenade Yllefabrikerna. Textile manufacturing was a big deal there in the 1940s: there were thousands of workers employed in the city. Dad worked on the dye and weaving machines. "The weaving machines moved back and forth, back and forth," he described, moving his hands accordingly as if to illustrate, a dull look on his face for emphasis. Life as a factory worker was mindless, "Boring to death. I'd have been better off in the beer factory," he then said with a smile. He longed to be elsewhere, but he held this job in Sweden the longest, and moved a few times, having four different addresses in the city of Norrköping.

Being a political refugee in a foreign country is not an easy thing. There were cultural differences, language, customs, etc. Refugees must "try to fit in," and try to understand what is expected of them, although so many things are different from "back home." Dad had to have a residence visa, which was valid for six months. Anytime he moved to another area, another visa had to be obtained, which meant more forms to fill in, more interviews. Besides adapting to a different way of life, refugees had other worries. Many Norwegians in exile wondered if they would remain safe there or if the Germans would eventually take over Sweden as they had Norway.[112] Others did not worry, reasoning that as long as Germany could *use* Sweden for its' purposes in war, they wouldn't need to occupy it. By "use" I mean a lot of top-quality Swedish iron ore needed for the war was being sold to Germany right up until the end of 1944 and Sweden allowed the Nazis to pass unhindered through the country into Norway with their soldiers and military equipment, etc., actions contrary to a position of neutrality.

There were many Norwegian refugees in Norrkköping. "The refugee residence in Norrköping was a central meeting place and had an important social function for the Norwegian refugee community."[113] The Norwegians stuck together.[114] Probably Dad found his way to this community which likely made his life tolerable for he lived there a whole year, continuing to work at a miserable job.

Some refugees looked back fondly on their experience in Sweden and felt they were well taken care of. "The Swedes were kind to us."[115] However, Dad described his own experiences saying that "the Swedes were not too happy about having all these Norwegian refugees around," (there were approximately 40,000 - 50,000 in a five-year period). [116] Anne Jackson (née Villars-Dahl) described her experience as a refugee from Norway: "It was October 1943 when we left the (refugee) camp and went with Father to Stockholm. The war was still going in Germany's favour and many Swedes were pro-German. They laughed at Norwegian refugees and called them *Nordbagger*, a word with no English translation, but it was a very derogatory expression to us."[117] Dad, who also arrived in 1943, never spoke of such comments but he did say he felt they were "looked down upon," and he did not feel so very welcome. Could this also have been because he moved around so often during the year he lived there, which meant he never had the chance to really get to know many

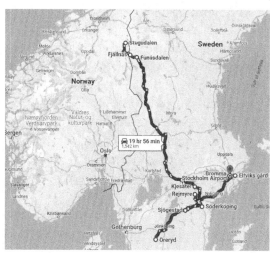

Map From Stugudalen to Many Places in Sweden

185

Swedes? He stayed in at least eight different villages or cities for various amounts of time, if we include the refugee camps, and the last city, Norrköping, he had four different physical addresses:

Fjällnäs

Funäsdalen

Kjesäter Refugee Camp, Vingåker

Öreryd

Rejmyra

Herrborums Farm, Bottna, Söderköping

Lunnevads, Sjögestad

Norrköping – 4 different addresses

So much moving around must have made him wish he was back in the stability of his home, and when Christmas came in December 1943, it must have led his thoughts back to Trondheim, to family and friends. It must have been a very different Christmas that year. He could not even contact anyone in Norway and he knew nothing about how they were doing, while they, too, were wondering about him.

Occasionally, Dad would meet someone from back home. He encountered a business man from Trondheim that he recognized and enjoyed speaking with. (He thought his name was Mr. Abrahamsen but he wasn't sure.) "He was a kind Jewish man who had run a small clothing store in downtown Trondheim," Dad said. There were about 2100 Jewish people living in Norway at the time of the German occupation. When Jews from Norway began to be deported, the Norwegian Church stood up and protested vehemently. Many Jews received a warning from Norwegian policemen or the resistance movement before the roundups began. Almost all of those that could not hide or escape were sent to their death. About 1100 fled to Sweden, which saved their lives but about 770 people were deported from Norway and only 34 of these survived..[118] These horrors took place in a world which existed *less than ninety years ago*: it is hard even to conceive of such things.

How critical the neutrality of Sweden was, for my father and for many other souls who found refuge there! So many Swedish citizens assisted the numerous Norwegians that crossed the border, helping them find their way to life in a free country, and, in some cases, saving their lives.

Dad met other interesting people during his stay, including a lovely Swedish girl, Anna Larsson who was to become his first real girlfriend. "She had dark hair and a good face, and she was so kind. She wanted to become a nurse," he said. They fell in love. "Her parents didn't want anything to do with me, but Anna didn't mind. I guess they weren't too keen on their daughter dating a political refugee," he said. They did all they could to hinder the relationship, eventually sending Anna away. When he left Sweden, he lost contact with her. Years later, he went back to Sweden twice after the war to try to find her but without success. The first time, he had become a sailor (*matros*) on the big freighter he worked on, and as they were going towards Göteborg, "I remember there was such a strong current, I had to give it my damnest to keep the ship on course. The pilot said to me, Steady, young sailor, steady." But Anna was not to be found there. The second time, he went to Stockholm. "I looked for her but couldn't find her. It's funny how life turns out," he said. He never forgot her.

There were thousands of young Norwegians refugees like Dad who wanted to get out of Sweden and join the war effort but were "stuck" in Sweden. Then, in April 1944, a special operation was set up so that young Norwegians like Dad could be secretly flown out of no-longer-so-very neutral Sweden.

Information was passed around inside the Norwegian community. Dad made it known that he, too, was interested in joining the Norwegian Armed forces, and by now he was old enough to do so (eighteen years old). He had begun to dream of being trained as a pilot. A way was set up that he could leave Sweden to join the free Norwegian Airforce.

On May 5, 1944, Dad was "*called in to Toresta, and was there four weeks. Later, by way of Elfvik until departure.*"[119]

Sweden had allowed Norway to set up Norwegian "Police" troops training camps within Sweden during the last part of the war. These "Police" – in actuality, soldiers - would be necessary to make a peaceful transition from Nazi rule in Norway when the war was over. "There were four camps for weapons training and other camps established at various locations for the training of reserve troops. The original list included the Toresta farm."[120]

Dad spent one month in Toresta, possibly for training, then on to Elfvik which was the last step before the flight from Stockholm (45 minute drive away). Conditions had to be right for any flight out to avoid being detected by the enemy. "During World War II, the main building at Elfvik's farm was used by the Swedish Defense Staff/FRA (*Försvarsstaben*) for signals intelligence activities."[121]

At various points along Dad's journey after leaving Norway, he was tested several times to evaluate his English skills. In Norway, the children learn English from a young age and Dad had a real aptitude for it. "I had English almost every day in school, I mean, how many people are there in the world speaking Norwegian?" he said with a laugh, "And Norway being a seafaring country, they needed English for trade. I always liked English and did well. I also had some German classes in school but not every day." It is possible that these tests and his language skills had an impact on where he was sent next (England vs. Canada). He was not assigned to one of the Norwegian "Police" training-camps set up in Sweden to train Norwegians to be soldiers. When he had first arrived in Sweden, he was underage anyhow.

With more testing/screening, Dad left Sweden to eventually join the Norwegian Armed Forces in the UK. However, before being sent to London, he was screened on the Isle of Man, as was the normal procedure. I had never thought about the fact that Dad left Sweden and flew to England with the war still in full swing. How exactly did he get *out* from neutral Sweden to Great Britain over Nazi-occupied Norway?

The answer comes from an extraordinary Norwegian named Bernt Balchen, who played the leading role in a top-secret operation which successfully flew out more than three thousand people who wanted to leave Sweden right out from under the nose of the Germans. Young Norwegians, Allied airmen from internment (e.g. force landed in Sweden) and others who needed to leave discretely made it out because of Bernt and teams of men that supported his plans.

Bernt Balchen Helps Fly Norwegians Out of Sweden

Who was Bernt Balchen? He was born in southern Norway in 1899, became a pilot at twenty as well as a top-notch airplane mechanic. He was a pilot on several polar expeditions, working with Roald Amundsen, Richard E. Byrd and Floyd Bennett. Bernt knew how to navigate in bad weather and knew Norway well, from a birds' eye view, so to speak. He also had many contacts in Norway and Sweden, as well as the USA and Britain. All of this, plus his spirit of adventure, made him the perfect candidate for setting up two important operations having to do with Norway in 1944. Operation Sonnie (called Operation Balder by the Norwegians) and Operation Ball, which dropped...

> ...weapons, ammunition, food, radios, and equipment with which to carry on sabotage into the hands of the Norwegian underground and for dropping secret agents and radio equipment behind enemy lines in northern Norway. The project, undertaken for Special Force Headquarters, Office of Strategic Services, London lasted from July until September, 1944. Six war-weary B-24's, specially equipped for the job, and painted with black, light-absorbent paint, dropped approximately 120 tons of cargo and personnel at designated points, mostly in southern and central Norway. Enemy opposition was encountered on fifteen of the sixty-four dropping missions undertaken.[122]

Well before the war, Bernt worked in aviation for years in the USA, and became an American citizen in 1931. He was about to be deported (by accident, so to speak), when the right people heard about it and a special bill was passed by Congress and signed by President Hoover granting him full rights as an American citizen. Bernt wrote, "This is bigger to me than any medal."[123] In July 1941, General Hap Arnold invited Bernt to join the American Air Corps and he was eventually assigned to be the commander of special Operation Sonnie. When asked by

General Spaatz at the US Strategic HQ in London if he could handle the project, Bernt replied, "Vi do it," a phrase which Bernt became famous for.[124]

Transporting people from Sweden into the UK meant both Britain and Sweden had to agree to the operation. Things got stuck in red tape. When Bernt was in Kingston House, headquarters of the Norwegian government in exile, he talked with his friend, Trygve Lie, Norway's Foreign Minister (my mother met him at least once). Trygve suggested engaging the help of King Haakon. King Haakon, in a luncheon with Winston Churchill and British Anthony Eden (Secretary of State for War), asked Churchill "Why are the Americans refused the right to fly into Sweden to take out the men we need for our Airforce and merchant marine?" After that, clearance was quickly given.[125]

Bernt and his crews flew out of Leuchars Field near Aberdeen in Scotland, using more unarmed B-24 Liberators. These planes were equipped with a kind of radar to help navigate through blind weather. They were painted dark green, and were "identified" with fake numbers, posing as a civilian aviation company. Each B24 airplane had been transformed to carry 35 passengers out.[126] The clandestine missions were manned with Office of Strategic Services (OSS) crews, American military posing as civilians, with passports issued by the American Embassy in London. These crews had been trained within the framework of "Operation Carpetbagger" – a secret allied activity of supporting agents and resistance movements in Nazi-occupied Europe.[127]

Bernd flew the first flight on March 31, 1944 into Bromma municipal airport Sweden, leaving Leuchars at midnight. It was perfectly overcast, reducing the risk of being seen by the enemy, so he told his three American crewmembers, "Our line of flight will be up the North coast to our coast-in point, then a dash over occupied Norway to Swedish territory and a final dog-leg down…to confuse the enemy our entry point will vary all the way from Trondheim down to the extreme southern tip of Norway."[128] It is likely this was the same tactic for return flights.

"A. L. Sharps, a gunner on Lt. Howard Davis' Carpetbagger trained crew, was sent north to Leuchars. He flew seven missions on the "Ball Project" from July 31 to September 21,1944." He described Bernt Balchen as follows: "I still recall him as the best flier, the best navigator, and the most deadly soldier I ever knew. Balchen had a built-in compass in his brain which worked when the regular compass went crazy."[129]

The pilots would file fake flight plans[130] so Nazi spies in Sweden would not know of their real path across Norway which varied according to relevant Nazi information they were able to glean from the underground forces in Norway.

As the first of these flights began in April 1944, Dad was fortunate to get a seat already by June considering there were some 2000 young Norwegians that wanted to leave Sweden to join the Allies.

In an earlier talk I had with Dad, well before 2015 he had said: "I flew on an army plane which had an American crew. The other Norwegians being sent over were all new faces to me. We actually flew right over Trondheim and [*eventually*] came to the Isle of Man, where we were in another camp."

I remember thinking at the time, he must be confused, an American crew? Little did I know about Bernt Balchen, the Carpetbaggers and Operation Sonnie / Balder!

Flights over Nazi-occupied Norway to Great Britain were dangerous, fraught with the possibility of being detected and shot down by the enemy. One such flight was described by Norwegian refugee, Reidar Drengsrud, another young man who fled to Sweden to avoid being forced to join the German's labor scheme. He flew from Sweden to Great Britain just fifty-one days after Dad's flight. He, too, had been sent to "a restricted camp outside Stockholm in Sweden for training"[131] before the flight out. "The flight was dramatic. There was much German activity in the North Sea. We waited 5 days to take off from Stockholm because the flights were cancelled due to German activity over Norway and the North Sea. On the night of the 8th of August, 1944 we got clearance and took off. We then went to a very high altitude over Sweden and Norway and dived down almost to the ocean surface because of the German radar coverage over the North Sea."[132]

Daddy's particular flight out of Stockholm was identified as "Balder 0807." They departed in the B24 Liberator on June 18, 1944 and landed in RAF Leuchars Scotland. From there, they left for the Isle of Man in a Lockheed Lodestar arriving on June 19, 1944 on a "bright and warm" day. That day there were four flights in, carry 68 Norwegians, as the Jurby Airport Flight log shows on the Isle of Man.

Dad was a mere eighteen years old. As he described himself years later, "I was just a kid!"

He said he "…had been sent for a short time to the Isle of Man, England after being in Sweden. That was an island where all the refugees came before they were admitted to the United Kingdom. It was a political camp where background checks were done. The royalty of UK and Norway were somehow related and

Dad's Archived Document - Operation Balder June 19th Arrival (Ankom)

Navn...... HOF , Örnulf

Født 11.8.25

Kommune ...... Trondheim

Hjemsted ....Stats.ing..Dahls gt.37

Ankom......19.6.44........ med.........Balder 0807

Militærutdannelse......00

Andre opplysninger 23.6.44

Nr. ....

L&S 2m/12/43

Jurby Airport, Isle of Man Flight Log Lists

192

*Typical Camp
Entrance Isle of Man
(Onchan)*

that may be the reason this was set up there," he conjectured, regarding the location being on the Isle of Man. King Haakon's wife, Maude was British.

The Isle of Man is a self-governed "Crown Dependency" in the Irish Sea between Great Britain and Ireland. It served as an internment (Prisoner of War) camp in both World Wars mostly due to its' location, for it provided security by isolation and distance from Great Britain. German, Austrian and Italian POW's were held there as were Norwegians who were arrested as Nazi collaborators. However, in 1944 when "Operation Sonnie" started bringing Norwegian "good guys" out of Sweden, they also all had to be screened to verify identity and to ask them about any contacts or information they might have had about people they had known or worked with who were Nazi collaborators. This screening and registration were done by Norwegian authorities in exile on the island, under the auspices of the Norwegian government in exile in London. It was set up as a separate office in the Ministry of Defense and called "The Recipient Center" (*Mottakersentralen*).[133]

Dad and the other young Norwegians were interned mainly under the guard of Norwegian soldiers in Camp Onchan, above Port Jack. Their living quarters were in long rows of pleasant Victorian boarding houses quite near the sea front which had been commandeered for the war. Each house had between 20 and 40 people.[134] They were not living among interned prisoners of war yet they, too, were fenced in with barbed wire, as you see in the photo above, "Typical Camp Entrance."

Occasionly, Dad interacted with internees of different nationality, although they could not communicate due to language barriers. While there were placements for the relatively few Norwegian refugees, most internees on the Isle of Man were political enemies. The Norwegian "good guys" were kept in buildings which were, in fact, originally boarding houses with beautiful views of the sea. Dad remembered singing there and making connections with others through music, their only common "language."

Reidar Drengsrud was another Norwegian refugee on the Isle of Man. His experience was described as follows:

> They were marched all over the island, always under guard, to see places associated with the Viking past. One lovely story he told of them being taken down to a beach for swimming and on the way back stopped in a square, it was a beautiful Sunday afternoon, and these young men asked the guards for permission to sing Norwegian songs. [*As mentioned, singing was important for Norwegians during the war: they sang even in prison camps, when they could get away with it.*][135] Locals started to gather and listen, asked the guards who these men were, and being told they were Norwegians wanting to join the Allied Forces, in Reidar's own words, 'they almost lynched the guards and we marched in triumph back to barbed wire.' Reidar was there about a week before being sent on for training with the RAF.[136]

Dad was given a "medical examination" on June 27. He was only at Camp Onchan about ten days until all his screening was completed. He found it completely reasonable that such checks were done, and he deemed it to be a necessary process. Although refugees had already been interrogated by the Swedish police when they arrived at the border of Sweden, each refugee still had to be cleared as being genuine and not a spy or Nazi sympathizer in order to join either the Royal Norwegian Air Force (RNAF) in London or "Little Norway." "Little Norway" was an Airforce pilot training camp outside of Ottawa in Canada also set up by Bernt Balchen at the direction of the Norwegian government in exile.[137] This was where Dad hoped to be sent next.

There on the Isle of Man during the screening process, Dad

and the others were given an important paper, *Til Nyankomne* ("To the Newcomers")[138] which he read and agreed to, dated and signed on June 23, 1944, the fifth day at Camp Onchan. It formally explained the absolute secrecy required regarding all operations. Here is the English translation with original underlining and bold letters:

> Messages from Norway constantly provide information that our compatriots at home are exposed to danger by careless talk outside the country's borders.
>
> The Ministry of Defense finds it necessary to exercise the greatest caution when discussing conditions and persons in Norway.
>
> In particular, it is emphasized that you are strictly prohibited from giving information about where, by what means and in what way you have left Norway.
>
> This restriction includes not only publishing that you are alive in the press and broadcasting, but also information that appears in private conversations and in private letters: essentially all communications that may give outsiders knowledge of their escape or of the experience associated with it.
>
> <u>Violation of this restriction could result in severe punishment.</u>
>
> <u>Violation of this restriction could expose relatives and friends to torture and torment.</u>
>
> **OBS: When you come over to England, it is strictly forbidden to mention the trip from Sweden to the Isle of Man and your stay here.**

So, Dad signed his name after the words of the Newcomer's paper, "I have read the present document and confirm that I have familiarized myself with the prohibition against careless mention of circumstances and persons in Norway as well as the departure from Sweden."

This restriction was true of the stay in Sweden as well. In one of his interrogations on June 28th he declared that he had "never had any correspondence with anyone back home in Norway while he was in Sweden." How hard it must have been, knowing that his family back home in Norway had no idea what happened to him: his mother and father wondering whether he was alive or not! This was one of the things my Farmor mentioned to me with great feeling, how difficult it was, waiting, not knowing of her son's situation. Dad's sister Kari keenly perceived her mother's distress during those years. From her perspective as a young child, she felt a kind of frustration with her older brother, knowing he was the cause of her mother's anguish and not understanding, first of all, why did he leave them and secondly, why on earth he did not contact them to let me know he was alright? (These thoughts and feeling were never discussed even for decades afterwards.)

Dad also said in his interrogation on June 28th that another reason he left home and traveled to Sweden was because he had been tired of being at home doing nothing and had heard that there was an opportunity to join the Norwegian armed forces. He wanted to join the action, like so many other young Norwegians who felt helpless in Nazi occupied Norway but eventually found a way out of Sweden through the Isle of Man.

London

Dad flew into London sometime before July 1, 1944. There were a lot of Norwegians in London during the war. Already on June 11, 1940, the Norwegian King Haakon, crown prince Olav and government had escaped from Norway and set up office in London in exile. A large civilian and military organization was built up in the UK, and many businesses and industries were established, including a large Norwegian State shipping company "Nortraship" which helped the Allies immensely all through the war, at the cost of losing half their own ships.

His official day of signing up with the Royal Norwegian Air Force (R.N.A.F.) in London was July 1. He was also screened once more to verify that he was not a spy. He said, "The Brits wanted to know all about us, and they didn't trust the Swedes' screening, so they did their own tests and interviews. How they picked me for the Airforce I don't know really. But

I was supposed to go to Canada, my English was good, then somehow, through the system, I got sent to the Norwegian Airforce in London and I couldn't get out of there. I had an asshole Norsk Captain Smitz, an Engineer I translated for. He thought he needed me there."

Clearly, Dad was disappointed that he was not assigned to be a pilot. As soon as Dad heard of the possibility of joining the Norwegian armed forces back in Sweden, he had wanted to train as a pilot. He wondered if the denial may have been "the long arm of my father," as he said, reaching from the resistance in Trondheim to the Norwegian government in exile to protect him from danger. It all worked out for good, he later recognized, as he said, "Still, the experience I had there in London prepared me for a future life in 'the good ole USA,'" as he called it.

Dad officially began in accounting as an office worker (Airman Class 2) on July 1, 1944. The Defense General War Commissariat document states that he had "some English and German language skills."[139] By November, he moved up one rank to Airman Class 1. Dad did a little bit of everything in the office there at Knight's Bridge: he wrote memos, translated a bit, and learned accounting.

Although his permanent address was documented simply as "R.N.A.F." (the Royal Norwegian Air Force), Dad said he lived up in Northgate, and took the underground (subway) up to Knight's Bridge, where a lovely house with a garden served as headquarters to the Royal Norwegian Air Force, the Loyalist group in London.[140] The house was known as Kingston House (Dad said, "I think that very house featured in an English television detective series some years ago, *Poirot*, stories based on an Agatha Christy novel.")

There in London, he perfected his English skills. By the time he was 20, he had already lived in three different countries and spoke and wrote in two languages fluently (he didn't have a Swedish girlfriend long enough to learn Svensk well although he understood it without difficulty, as most Norwegians do).

Dad at Hyde Park, London

Dad (on the left) in the Norwegian Air Force

He also played soccer with friends in Hyde Park, a historic Royal park in Westminster, London (see photo). He also found time to go to the pub and to the movies "and to chase the girls." Some friends who worked with him in the Norwegian Air Force were Per Tajet, Kaare Kjellsett, and Per Høst.

"I loved getting fish and chips which were sold wrapped in

newspapers," he said, reminiscing of those London days when I asked him. He also remembered seeing adult "chimney sweeps, men all dressed in black, up on the roofs, with long brushes on their shoulders, a metal pole with a brush at the end. It was quite a trade at the time."

Life in London in 1944 was certainly not all fun and games: it had its own safety risks. There were thousands of German air offensive attacks against London during the war with V1 flying bombs (no pilot) and V2 rockets (ballistic missiles). Once a public place where Dad had just been was destroyed by one of these bombs: a close call. V1 bombs killed more than 6000 people and seriously injured many, many more.

A young Norwegian named Fritz from Trondheim, just like Dad, who had been flown out of Sweden with Operation Balder (Sonnie) also made it to London in 1944.[141] He served as a mechanic in the Air Force: but he, sadly, was killed by one of these bombs just a few months after arrival.

That *could* have been my father.

A special kind of warning system was introduced at the Norwegian offices there in London, so that office workers could seek cover during office hours when the bombs got too close. At night, the Norwegians participate in the guard both as Air Raid Precautions (A.R.P.) Wardens and as ordinary fire watch guards. Some clerks lived further away or who lived in poorly built houses would sometimes sleep in the offices.

In London, he was surprised to meet up with another kind

Navn ÅBAKKEN, Fritz

Født 16.1.21 1 Trondheim

    Kommune Trondheim

    Hjemsted Nedre Mullenberg 59, T.

Ankom 20.4.44 med Balder 0036

Militærutdannelse 00

Andre oplysninger Eks. 22.4.44

    Nr.

L&S 2m/12/43

Fritz from Trondheim

Jewish man, also from Trondheim. "He was a good man. He was tall and thin with a hook nose. He became a pilot during the war, and eventually went to Israel to make a new home, which didn't surprise me at all," Dad said. He could not recall his name but remembered his face. How good it felt to see a familiar face from home. He wondered so many times how his family fared back in Trondheim, but he had no idea and no way to find out.

The Hoff Family Back in Trondheim

Back in Trondheim life was not easy. Gerd remembers hearing the air raid sirens, warning them of the approaching danger of bombing. Everyone would seek shelter, heading quickly down to the cellar. "Kari was terrified every time we had to go down to the cellar, so each time I would tell her stories and somehow make her laugh in order to distract her, for I was never afraid. I tried to take care of her." Their parents feared for their daughters' safety; just a few months after Dad left Norway, on July 23, 1943, there was an intense bombing raid on German military areas in Trondheim by the United States Eighth Air Force.[142] The nearby Lade church cemetery was torn up leaving big bomb craters. Lade is just 2 kilometers (1.2 miles) from where the Hoff's lived (a 15-minute walk). This was too close for comfort so they evacuated Trondheim for a while.

"There had been bombing in Lade. My parents were afraid that there might be more bombing so my mother, my sister Kari and I were quickly evacuated to safety out to Statsbygd to farms outside of Trondheim. My father stayed in Trondheim as he had to work." Tanta Gerd remembers being evacuated, which lasted for weeks, possibly months, Gerd wasn't sure how long. While it was a relief to be away from the Nazi presence in the city which created such palpable fear, Gerd said "...but, actually, we lived only with the hope that we could soon go home again, it was not 'koselig' to be so long away from our home," Gerd said.

The first families that took them in remained in Gerd's memories: the father of the first farm was a devoted Christian, and that was where they often had home church services, and where she first learned to "sing the Psalms," such as "*Naemere deg, min Gud*" ("Nearer, My God, to Thee.") The Leinsli's of Statsbygd were a kind farming family where they stayed next. This may have been one of the farms where Daddy worked, because he mentioned them, too, with affection. They helped the Hoffs and stayed in touch for many years afterwards.

"Father did not come at all while we were out at Statsbygd," Gerd said, "They needed him at the train station." How they missed their father, and what a joy it was when they returned and saw him again! "You can just imagine!" she said.

Little did Dad know, but shortly after his London arrival, his father was arrested and put in prison ("*Trondheim Kretsfengsel avd. C*" on Kongens gate 85 (The King's Street)). "In January 1943, Norwegian police were ordered to take hostage relatives of those who had fled the country. In some cases, these hostages were executed."[143] Farfar had been taken as a hostage because somehow the police had found out that Ørnulf had left the country, although his departure was a year earlier. A copy of the registration card from the prison states the reason for arrest was *Tatt som gissel* (taken or held hostage).[144] They arrested him at his job at the train station and imprisoned him on Friday, June 30, 1944 sometime before 3:45 p.m. by order of the *Statspolitiet,* the Nazi-run Norwegian police. At least his daughters and wife were spared the trauma of seeing him dragged away from home. There was no way of knowing how long he would be held or if he would ever come out of prison. "More than 44,000 Norwegians were imprisoned during World War II, in camps and prisons in Norway, and various types of camps and prisons spread over large parts of the world."[145]

It was now even harder to find enough food for herself and two daughters. The uncertainty of their situation must have weighed heavily upon Farmor, yet she continued to care for her two daughters as if everything was fine. She bartered for food on the black market. Once, she took the boat across the fjord taking with her the best curtains to trade them for food. She took the boat to Stadsbygd, located at the southern end of the Fosen peninsula along the north side of the Trondheimsfjord. There she exchanged the fancy curtains for food at a farm. What a prize! However, upon return to Ravnkloa, as she got off the boat, there stood German soldiers, waiting. The heartless men simply took everything that she and everyone else on the boat had just procured. "So, there she was, without curtains, and without food," said Gerd. It was devastating.

Oh, the things my grandmother went through! Her young son had left for Sweden over a year ago, and she still had no idea whether he was alive or dead. Now, her husband was in prison and she alone bore the responsibility of two young girls – and she no longer had any contact with her own father because Jakob had become a Nazi sympathizer, joining the NS, following along with one of his friends, Gerd said.

There were not only Norwegians in the prisons, for the Nazis had brought about 100,000 Soviets in to Norway as POWs. While in prison, Farfar was somehow able to procure tiny cigarettes which came in a box the length of a man's thumb with ten cigarettes in a box. Farfar gave the cigarettes to a Russian prisoner he was friendly with. The man appreciated it so much that he gave Farfar (possibly) the only thing he had, a very primitive looking small fork. Farfar cherished that tiny token and kept it for the rest of his life.[146] (Some 13,700 Soviet prisoners of war died in Norway during this war: more than the total number of Norwegian war casualties (estimated at 10,262 lives)).[147]

During the war, inmates wrote songs during their imprisonment and secretly sang as a means of boosting morale. But they had to hide their singing for it was strictly forbidden. They even used precious toilet paper to write their songs down.[148] They often wrote their own lyrics to known melodies, words about the sorrow of being occupied, or mocking the Nazis or to express personal losses. The national anthem was given new lyrics, for example the normal text which follows is on the top and the wartime lyrics are below:[149]

> *Yes, we love with fond devotion this our land that looms*
> *Rugged, storm-scarred o'er the ocean*
> *With her thousand homes.*

———

Yes, they are selling this land, that looms,
Ravaged, plundered, overpowered, sorrow
in a thousand homes.

There were literally hundreds and hundreds of songs created during the war all across Norway, in prison and out, for "...song and culture were of great importance for a people in crisis."[150] Tante Gerd said that even when they were incomplete as a family, after her brother had left, and when Far was in prison, they kept singing at home. "Song was important all throughout the war. Even when it was just Mor and Kari and me, still, we sang. Clearly, we used every means to forget that there was war going on," Gerd said. "Yes, singing and music have been an important part of our lives."

I wonder if Farfar and his prison mates found a way to sing while in Trondheim Kretsfengsel prison, too? Given his love of song, it may very well have happened as it did in many other prisons across Norway. However, the prison was very small, and therefore perhaps more difficult to hide such activities.

Occasionally, my grandmother visited her husband, as these prisoners were allowed visitors. We know this because Gerd also went with her mother to visit her father when he was imprisoned. When Gerd saw her father, she "noticed he was wearing a strange sort of jacket and his hands were wounded and bloodied." As railway district commissioner, Farfar had an office job but in prison he was forced to do hard physical labor: his injured hands revealed how unfamiliar he was with the type of work he was compelled to do in prison.

Despite his situation, being unjustly imprisoned and treated as a convicted prisoner, Farfar acted as if nothing was wrong, as if all was normal. He was calm, unruffled. Gerd said, "He came across as his usual, calm self so that we would not worry about him." He was a gentle, good man, who tried to put others before himself. The way her parents remained calm and with childlike faith, Gerd said, "I never once thought that my father would not return. It was just too difficult to imagine that he might be killed." She could not even allow such thoughts to enter her mind.

In the middle of such darkness, there were good people

ready to help, shining a ray of hope in tragic times: Tante Gerd said that after Farfar was taken, someone from the resistance movement approached her mother in secret, saying they had food for the family. So, Farmor went to a specific house which was (ironically) on Jonsvannsveien, the same street as the house (or headquarters) of a notorious Nazi collaborator group called the Rinnan gang. This provision of food for families connected with the underground was organized by a Lutheran priest and member of the resistance. He told Farmor where to go to pick it up. My grandmother and Tante Gerd went to this home and there, up in the attic, the floor was covered with food! It was a feast before their eyes. They filled their backpacks and rejoiced. The food and such acts of kindness helped them make it through a difficult time. Gerd said that none of the "real" priests worked in the church buildings anymore, they had all quit their jobs and still "they did a lot of good among the people during the war (from 'underground')."

There were also good people who were clever. The rest of Farfar's colleagues back at the railroad figured out a way to get him out of prison fairly quickly - they maximized delays and problems with the train schedules saying to the Nazis that they could not manage the scheduling well without Mr. Hoff, who normally handled that. "We were so fortunate to have a father who was sorely missed at the Railroad. For this reason, he was able to be released so quickly. He had oversight of all the rail traffic between Trondheim and Sweden and around central Norway. What father did in his job was ensure that trains came and went according to schedule and plan ... they needed him at the station," Gerd said.

What a relief for the family when Farfar was released on September 4, within less than ten weeks of his imprisonment! This was not the case for many others who were imprisoned, many stayed in prison for the rest of the war, and others never came home at all.

It wasn't until decades later when Dad returned to Norway in 1994 after his mother's death in December 1993, that he came across the papers in his father's desk showing the grounds for his imprisonment. The reason for the arrest was marked *Tatt som gissel* on Farfar's prison paper. My sister Heidi was there beside him in Trondheim, sorting through our family photos sent to the grandparents over the years. She heard Daddy cry out in anguish and quickly looked over. His face was ashen, and he kept repeating, "I never knew, I didn't know…" He had found the piece of paper that showed that his father was taken into prison as "hostage" when Dad's escape into Sweden was discovered. Again, it was not uncommon that family members were held hostage by the Nazi authorities when such an escape was discovered. Dad's parents never ever told him or his sisters the reason for Farfar's imprisonment. Gerd did not know why her father had been taken, but she always presumed it was because of his resistance work, like illegal newspaper work and helping people escape to Sweden by train.

Back in London, Dad did not know anything about his father's imprisonment and he wondered how his family fared. Back at his home in Trondheim, his family wondered about him. All this time, there was no way to get a letter to his mother to tell her he was alright. The Nazis were controlling everything inside of Norway, including mail. Many were arrested because of a letter naively sent home from a family member who had escaped over the border.

When the war ended, and there were several trains which came back to Trondheim full of refugees that had escaped to Sweden, the Hoff family was there at the station with great expectations, waiting to see if Dad was on any of these trains, but he was not to be found. Dad did manage to get a message through however, the British read over the radio a whole list of names of people that were safe in England, and Farmor heard his name. It was an immense relief. "*Hele den tiden visste jeg ikke om han var død eller levende* (All that time I didn't know if he was dead or alive)," she told me, with tears in her eyes, years later when she was in her 80s.

In London, the day the European war ended, May 8, 1945, everyone went down to Trafalgar Square. Many wanted to hear the formal announcement by Winston Churchill that the war was over - it was packed to bursting point. Trafalgar Square became a place of celebration and people from all over the country came to be there. It was a massive crowd, "We were wall-to-wall people," Dad said. "There were so many people," he said, "You couldn't get in sideways. It was a day of great joy. We celebrated a full 24 hours straight."

Gerd described how it was in Trondheim, Norway when the war ended:

> *DET var folkefest, det*! ("Now *that* was a nationwide celebration of all the people!") I told you that I was in the process of preparing for confirmation. So that day, I came down to the church and the Priest came out and told us there was 'No class today but today is a day to celebrate, for Peace has come, the war is over.' So, I headed back home and along the way to StatsIng Dahls street there were Norwegian flags hanging out from *every* single house. *All* the flags were out, and there was this atmosphere which was indescribable. People were everywhere out on the streets, there was lots of shouting and '*Hurrah*s!' and waving flags. *Det var helt utrolig... Ubeskrivelig!*" (It was completely unbelievable... Indescribable!)

It was a day to celebrate what it meant to be Norwegian, after five years of an oppressive power attempting to force them into something that they were not. As Gerd said, in spite of years of attempting to change us, "There was no one who managed to tell us to be anything other than what we were: Norwegian."

That first 17 of May was finally celebrated in the usual, pre-war fashion, Tante Gerd said, but with much more "flagging." There was a flag hanging from every house and all children were waving flags with great gusto. There was not too much good food available, she said, and some kinds of fruit weren't available for years after the war, but as Gerd said, "One can celebrate *very well* even without food."

When King Haakon and his family arrived back in Oslo the next month by ship, innumerable boats lined the way and people flooded the streets in exultation and joy. His return was another great festivity.

Yet another celebration took place after the war when Dad returned to visit his family. They had not seen him for what had seemed like an eternity.

Kari, Dad (in uniform) and Gerd standing, Farmor and Farfar seated

The family was deeply grateful to be together again. There was also thankfulness that the stress was over and the war could be filed away as "the past," at least on some level. There was enormous relief, joy and hope that life might start to be "normal" again. "We spoke of the war years as little as possible," Gerd said. They took a family photo and contented, sincere smiles are on every face. Dad wore his uniform, his hair somewhat unruly and his tie slightly askew. He had left as a boy, but returned as a young man, changed by war, his life as a refugee and his short time in the military.

Dad did not return to live in Norway immediately at the war's end because he was signed up with the military, still stationed in the UK for almost another year. "I couldn't go back until they sent me back," he said. "I had to help the Norwegian Airforce negotiate for military equipment, planes, and such. I don't know why they were working with the Brits; they didn't have squat. They should've been negotiating with the Americans."

Economically, the war had devastated Norway, for they had been plundered by the Nazis for five long years. In the north, entire towns were in ashes having been totally burnt up by the retreating Nazis. More than half of all the Norwegian ships had been destroyed. So much needed to be built back up.

Norway also had the challenge of administering justice to those that had sided with the Nazis. After the war, the government temporarily instated the death penalty after trial for notorious Nazis like Henry Rinnan and many others,. Many that sided with the NS were fined and some 19,000 imprisoned.[151]

Indeed, the war had taken its toll on many levels: entire households were wiped out (for example, 230 Jewish Norwegian families had been killed), families lost a member or more, others were scarred more than physically by torture or imprisonment. Those that had lived under constant oppression were also, in many cases, mentally and emotionally exhausted.

German became "like a swear word," Gerd said, "It was taboo to speak German." Even decades after the war's end, Farmor simply could not stand to hear the German language being spoken – a visceral reaction to the occupied years – without any animosity towards Germans themselves.[152] Farmor never again had contact with her own father after the war, and had not a single photo of him in her home. "He was ostracized by the family," Gerd said.

Nazi sympathizers were also often shamed by people who had suffered during the war and acted out of their own wounds instead of out of grace and compassion. For example, women who had children with German soldiers were often treated very badly, a misguided kind of vengeance. The post-war years were difficult in many ways and rebuilding was needed which went far beyond economics.

It was, in some ways, a broken yet determined country Dad finally returned to, but his family was overjoyed to have him back. At the start, he got a job at the Ranheim Paper Company just outside of Trondheim, in the exports section. But before long his spirit of adventure made it impossible for him to stay. He said "The work there was just too boring." So, he decided to sign up to work on a merchant marine ship since he "wanted to see the world." Wanderlust, pure and simple.

We do not know the very first ship he signed up with out of

M/S Grenanger
Ship

Norway but in June 1947, Dad signed on the *M/S Grenanger*, (a ship made in Texas!) owned by Westfal-Larsen & Co. A/S,[153] (a shipping company based in Bergen and still in existence in 2023.)

		Built by Pennsylvania Shipyards Inc., Beaumont, Texas | ex- Cape Falcon standard ship type C1-A built for United States War Shipping Administration, 1946 purchased renamed Grenanger	
Grenanger (2)	Built 1944		5,221 tons

At twenty-one years old, he began a great adventure which would last about three years. I wonder if Farmor thought, "There goes my son, again!"

The crew list for the *M/S Grenanger* reveals that most of his ship mates were from Norway, many from Bergen, but only Dad was from Trondheim. Occasionally a Finn, Swede, Latvian, Cape Verdian or even a North American would join the ship, signing on at various ports along the way.

His captain was Ole Severin Belt, born in 1892, from Tysnes, Norway.[154] He had sailed often to New York during the war (September 1941 – September 1945) serving in Nortraship, the Norwegian Merchant fleet critical to the government for the mobilization and use of resources and forces.

During his seafaring years, Dad sailed on at least four different ships, stopping at numerous ports of call, seeing and visiting places yet unknown to him. His pay at the time was decent: about 421 – 442 kroner/month (around 950$ - $1000/ month in today's currency), but what he gained in experience was far more valuable: his world expanded.

Other vessels he sailed on included the following:
- *M/S STOCKHOLT* (built 1944 as *CAPE POGE* by Pennsylvania Shipyards, Inc., Beaumont, Texas USA for U. S. War Shipping Administration)
- *M/T ALAR* (built 1939 by Sir James Laing & Sons Ltd., Sunderland, UK)

Archived documents reveal the ports where he signed on to the various ships including San Pedro, Belize (Central America), Montreal, Canada, (via the St. Lawrence River) New York City, New York, and Baltimore, Maryland.

While in the New York City port in 1948, Dad and two sailor friends visited Brooklyn to celebrate May 17. Did they did stop at the Norwegian Seaman's Church there in Brooklyn? That we do not know. But, we do know that he and a tall sailor friend from Bergen and one from Sweden stopped at Jack Dempsey's Broadway Bar and Cocktail Lounge near 49th Street, advertised as "The Meeting Place of the World."

As any sailor did, he started out as *Jungmann*, a term for a young sailor ranked between deck boy and light sailor, something of an apprentice. Then he became a *lettmatros* or "light sailor"– a designation for deck crew on a Norwegian vessel. Typical tasks consisted of maintenance, loading and unloading, lashing cargo, mooring and so on. The next role he held was designated as *matros* or simply "sailor" - a professional with a bit more responsibility associated with deck service and able to use and maintain equipment on board. This work included guard duty, maintenance, sea clearance as well as loading and unloading preparation.[155]

On these Merchant Navy (commercial) freighters, he of course learned to work with the varied crew, how to get along with all sorts of people. He also learned to tie all kinds of sailor's knots and had various odd jobs typical to ships. But he also

Dad (on the left), 22, with sailor friends in Brooklyn, NY May 17, 1948

picked up the slang and rough manner of speaking on the ships. ("He never talked like that at home, he would not have been allowed," Gerd said. "He seemed to have picked up the ugliest expressions possible after he left home and he used them to be funny.")

"There were about fifty people on the boat," Dad recalled. He enjoyed the comradery of being part of the ship's crew. They visited the Canary Islands, and parts of South America. In Brazil, they stopped at Rio de Janeiro. In Buenos Aires, he was able to attend an Argentinean soccer game. "It was incredible," he said, "the way the people went nuts--there were partitions in between the sections of the stadium with barbed wire, to keep the people apart to avoid riots. It was as bad as the hooligans."

What impressed him at another stop, was the way the natives would use just their 2 thumbs to peel mandarin oranges in a split second before popping them into their mouths. (Isn't it funny, the things that stick in our memories?) I think this was somewhere in the West Indies islands.

So many adventures at sea! Dad's last trip in early 1950 was more regional in Narvik, Norway (above the Arctic Circle). Later that year, Dad eventually returned home and worked briefly at an office job in Trondheim. Then he found out about an interesting job down in Oslo at the American Embassy.

This was to change the course of his life.

THE AMERICAN NORWEGIAN MEETS A SPECIAL NORWEGIAN

The beautiful and intelligent "American Norwegian," Jeanne Rood was working at the American Embassy, translating in the political section, the day a handsome Norwegian ex-sailor named Ørnulf Hoff was hired. The Americans called him, "Ernie." *Gullgutten* had arrived!

Their first date was at a Red Cross event where Ma volunteered. When Dad came to the tombola Ma was manning, she cleverly asked him to buy a chance, and asked how to spell his name to write on the ticket, since she could not remember his last name!

There is a big gap between Ma's letters to Aunt Esther from July to October 1951: what was taking up all her time? That was the summer Jeanne and Ernie started dating.

When she finally wrote to her aunt in October 1951 it is apparent who has been taking up her time. We can see that Ernie has a special role: she mentions seeing him *three* times in one week the first time she writes about him. (This is unlike any of the others Norwegians she has dated up until now.)

Ma told us that when she first met Daddy she thought to herself, *Oh, he's probably married with 5 kids.*

But, ...*he wasn't.*

Oct 15, 1951
Dear Aunt Esther,
    ...I have been so busy that I haven't had time to write...Have been going in too many circles.
    This is a sample of my schedule for the past 2 weeks.
    On Sunday Signe and I went for a 3-hour hike, then I baked a cake since Jorgen and Berit were coming.

Monday after that Ruth Hellan came to drink coffee with me. I got some curtain material on Monday so Tuesday I started making curtains. Ragna came up and brought her sewing too.

Wednesday, I went to dinner and the movies with Ernie (a Norwegian who works at the Embassy).

Thursday Helen Simonsens came for dinner.

Friday Ernie came for dinner. Saturday, I had to do grocery shopping and sewed and put up some curtains. I went to movies with a couple of fellows from the Embassy. I washed the storm windows.

Sunday, Margaret Guys and Dorothy Danielsen (both from the Embassy) came for dinner and Ernie joined us for coffee.

Mom was planning to go home for Christmas and seemed excited about it but then something changed her plans or maybe someone influenced her plans:

As Mom has probably told you, I expect to come home for Christmas unless something happens to prevent it. I will probably be in the States 4 weeks. I have to report to the State Dept. and see about the things I left at Flossie's so I guess I will be busy. Must do some clothes shopping too.

What have you been doing lately? What would you like (as a gift) in the Norwegian line for Christmas? How's Uncle Walt? Have you been up to the farm lately?

I don't know much at the moment. Am going in too many circles. Am looking forward to coming home for Christmas. It's only about 2 months from now and I think time goes so fast it will be here before I turn around.

I hope you are feeling OK.

November 9, 1951 Oslo
Dear Aunt Esther,

Was glad to hear from you. I got bronchitis a while back and spent the greater part of a week in bed. I slept for 3 solid days so I guess I was more exhausted than anything else.

Well, from one thing to the next. I'm not so sure that I will be able to get home for Christmas. They have cut our leave and then the plane ticket keeps going up and up. So I'll wait and see what happens. I may come later if I don't come then.

Everyone has a cold. Thank goodness I just got a shipment of oranges and grapefruit a week or so ago so I have been eating oranges like mad.

Otherwise, I'm busy as usual although I have been spending most of my time with company at home. I've fixed up my apartment real cozy so I wish you could come to visit me. I guess I was going out so much before that now all I want to do is stay home. Am cooking dinner all the time and making desserts. My maid does all my washing and ironing so I don't have that to do.

I had a long newsy letter from Randi. She is having quite some time (in Moscow) and making the most of it. She has gone to several of the churches and said that they were just packed but that she had never seen such poverty. Wish you could read her letters. They're a riot when she tells about marketing, etc.

The next letter sounds like Ma was very down and out. She and Ernie had broken up after Ernie had been home to Trondheim for Christmas. It was a huge disappointment, she was hoping to finally settle down. It is written in pencil and sounds like she's trying to cheer herself up by writing to her dear aunt and "looking on the bright side of life," so typical of her positive character.

Oslo, Jan.15, 1952 At the office
Dear Aunt Esther,

Not having any pen and not being in the mood for much of anything I am probably breaking all rules of etiquette, etc., etc., besides goldbricking in writing to you. Here I sit surrounded by clippings about Churchill-Truman meeting, women's organizations, Norwegian foreign policy and what have you. It's all bad enough in itself but try to write summaries of such dry stuff when it doesn't say anything anyway. Guess I'm in sort of a dilemma at the moment but it will probably all blow over after a while.

I should have written a long time ago but we were so busy at the office and evenings I was busy too so I neglected everyone. I had been going steady with a Norw. employed at the office and we had plans of coming to America this year to-gether (that's one reason why I didn't come home) but Christmas time his family evidently used as much influence as they could to change things and to try to keep him here (which is silly because he'll go to America with or without me) and he sort of turned color and I'm beginning to think he was more interested in the meals and refreshments he got at my place than he is in me. And I thought he was so reliable!

Well, I have plenty of friends and enough to do so I suppose it doesn't matter so much, but I had gotten kinda used to the idea of coming home for good and settling down for a change. Oh, well, there's nothing like the foreign Service: at least you can save money if you try. I guess things always take care of themselves so why worry?

I wish you could come over and see my cozy apartment. I certainly do enjoy it and would like to entertain you for a change.

What do you think of the international situation? Seems to me everything is a mess. I think the world and mentality is going backwards instead of forward and I wonder where it all will lead to. The conferences don't seem to get anyplace. What do you think of Eisenhower for president? The Norwegian newspapers seem to think he might make a good one, at least they prefer him to Taft.

(I think Ma's favorite president had been Roosevelt, "…good old F.D.R.")

How are you feeling now? Would like to see your new car, am so glad you could get it.

Am glad the earrings arrived OK. I wanted to send something else but it isn't easy to send through the mail so you'll just have to wait until I come home. Don't send anything for Christmas. You've done enough already and I got the biggest kick out of those cards.

We finally got some snow so the Olympics will be OK. I've seen quite a few movies. It goes by spells. Sometimes we see a lot and other times not. Ernie and I spent a great deal of time with a young couple Kay and Mickael. He's Norwegian and she's English. They're really swell and Kay is a wonderful friend. She and I have really become pals.

Well, I guess I've about run out of chatter. I hope you can read my writing. I don't think it has improved any lately. Guess I'm not trying. Have you heard anything about Kenny lately? Something suddenly reminded me of him the other day.

Take care of yourself and write soon,
Love Jeanne

One month later, Jeanne and Ernie were back together and officially engaged to marry! That was a quick turnaround. Mom was 28 years old when she and Dad started dating, so she was used to her independent way of life. She had already "made up her mind to forget marriage and to be a career woman instead since she was already 'an old maid' (28 years old)", she once wrote - but God had other plans.

215

They had dated about six or seven months before they got engaged officially.

Oslo Feb 15, 1952 (*a handwritten letter*)
Dear Suze,

Thanks for the Valentines. I sure got a big kick out of them. I've been wanting to write for some time but I've been so darn busy and you know how it is. As things stand now, Ernie and I have asked the State dept. for permission to get married. In order to continue working at an Embassy after marriage to a foreigner, you have to have permission, all because of security reasons.

It usually takes 2-3 months to get a reply so we can't make plans until April or May.

After we're married, we'll apply for a visa for him, and that will take a couple of months so we probably won't arrive in the States until late summer or early fall.

It's funny in a way because we've both been so independent that he started getting cold feet and got mad and then when he finally realized what he wanted to do, I started getting cold feet.

Oh, well, I guess they say the path of true love never runs smoothly or something like that.

His family sort of messed things up at Christmas but I guess they're reconciled to the fact now. Guess they didn't want him to go to America, but he would go whether we got married or not. So much for that.

I may want you to send me a wedding dress but will let you know in plenty of time.

How's everything? Randi called me from Moscow a while ago concerning 2 others from the Embassy there who were coming over for the Olympics. She sounded swell and seemed to be very happy, having a good time.

I don't have a maid any more and what with trying to do everything myself I'm all too busy. Ernie comes and helps wash the floors, etc. so that's something. Am going to get along without one in order to save money. We usually have dinner to-gether at my house and he gives me kroner since I am trying to save most of my dollars for when we come home.

My house is like a boarding house. With 2 American fellows living downstairs I never know who'll be eating with me. They contribute some food to the dinners, etc. when they come up. But sometimes it gets to be too much of a good thing. So evenings when Ernie's there we hardly get any time to ourselves.

To-night I've invited one of the girls from the Embassy & Ernie's best friend for dinner. We're going to have spaghetti but I don't know how it will be since I didn't have a recipe. I cooked the sauce last night.

Oslo has gone Olympics crazy. Most of the Embassy is at the opening this morning. I'm going to the closing ceremony. I thought that would be just as interesting. We've got tickets for some speed skating, figure skating, and ski jumping. There still isn't an awful lot of snow but there's enough. Certainly strange how all the big snowstorms are all over Europe, even in Denmark but they avoid Norway.

Saturday the English-Norw. couple we play canasta with are coming for dinner and the evening. During the next few days are various Olympic events, so I'll be quite busy. Hope you are feeling OK,

Love, Jeanne

Ma kept the *Oslo De VI Olympiske Vinterleker 1952* ticket from the Special ski jumping event she attended on Sunday, February 24 in the Holmenkollen Ski Stadium.

March 19, 1952
Dear Suze,

I was glad to get your letter. Now I shall get down to business first. Since I still don't know where the wedding will be, I cannot make too much of a plan but in the February "Mademoiselle" on page 94 is a wedding dress somewhat of the type I would like. The white dress with long sleeves. I also like the headdress and short veil style. Now that one costs $69.95 without the veil but I would prefer to pay less if possible. I would like to get a dress and veil included for not more than $60 if possible. *[$60 in 1952 = about $695 in 2024]*

According to Madmoiselle, Altman's should carry that particular dress. But that is just to give you an idea. Now my dress doesn't necessarily have to tie in the back or anything like that. Also it can have a sweetheart neckline or a round neckline. I don't like V-necklines. I like high neck but I do like sweetheart neckline too. I prefer long sleeves. I think the button effect on the sleeves and back is nice too. Anyway, that should give you some idea. Now don't go running your head off for this. Anything you pick out I am sure will be fine. The dress can be any kind of material you think is O.K. I am enclosing a check for $60 but will send more later for a few other things. If you find something for $50 that's OK too but I doubt you'll find . Don't worry about it. I might as well splurge if I have to.

I will also need some white satin or some kind of white flat or very low-heeled shoes. Louise Hirtle wore her bedroom slippers, maybe I could do that. So whenever you get the chance, I would appreciate you looking into the matter. There is no rush, just that I wanted to let you know ahead of time. It can always be sent airmail if necessary. I will know more details about the wedding after I have talked with Ernie's family. He thinks they will want it up in Trondheim, which would suit me just fine (that's his home town). Then they would have the headache of making all the arrangements.

Ernie's family are going to spend Easter in the mountains with us on a private farm. Ernie and I are leaving Oslo on April 4 in the evening and will be gone ten days. Am sure looking forward to a vacation.

Not much news. The snow's practically melted in Oslo but the air is still plenty sharp. I do hope Ernie and I can be home in August.

P.S. Thanks a million for all the trouble. I hope you don't mind but I thought you're the one who knows how to pick things out. Be sure to let me know how much more money you may need.

March 28, 1952
Dear Aunt Esther,

Will just scribble off a few lines. I was glad to hear from you and hear about Lilian. I think Phyllis Ann is a pretty name.

Now. I take size 11. Shoes I take size 7AA. The package sent regular mail should be sent to:

Miss Jeanne Rood
OSLO, FSS
Department of State
Washington 25, D.C. (If sent before April 15)

If sent after April 15 perhaps it is best to send it airmail. In such case you address it merely Miss Jeanne Rood, %American Embassy, Stortingsgate 28, Oslo, Norway. Then it comes open mail. It is best to send it through the pouch so I avoid duty and redtape.

I am sorry I have to cut this short but I am really supposed to be translating.

Ernie's last name is Hoff.

We are going to the mountains for Easter for 10 days.

I'll let you know as soon as I know anything more about our plans. I hope you are O.K.

April 1952 Gerd, Kari & Ma with Dad thrown across their laps
- From Gerd's photo album

That April, they had a marvelous time in the mountains of Dovrefjell at a *hytte* in Grunbakken together with the Hoff family, skiing together with Dad's sisters, Gerd and Kari and a few other friends. They skied between Oppdal and Dovrefjell, Gerd said, "We skied and skied, taking sandwiches and hot chocolate in our backpacks." Up and down, over hills and slopes they skied. "I got so tired," Ma said, "and Ernie started telling me, 'Oh, it's just over the next hill,' and we'd get there and he'd say, 'Just over the next one,' until we finally did get there. I wondered if I'd make it, but I did."

Gerd took a few photos which captured the fun. Dad "threw himself over the top of our laps, in the typical fashion of my brother", Gerd said.

At the end of each ski day, "Mor was there at the *hytte*, waiting for us and she cooked for us all," Gerd recalled. Farfar was still working as he did not retire until 1965.

Ma wrote to her aunt:

We had a wonderful vacation. Will write details later.

Thanks a hundred million for getting the dress and for all your struggles. It sounds just gorgeous and I'm sorry you won't be here for the big event. Am anxious to see the dress. And how wonderful you got such a good bargain. Am enclosing a check to cover slipper and other expenses. Let me know if you need more.

Thanks a million for the package: that sweater is lovely and so are the hankies. Must be telepathy but I needed just those things.

Hope you can read my scribbling. Am in a dither. Up to my ears in work and then I get the wedding information. Have to see about rings tomorrow. I asked Mom to call you since I didn't think I'd get a note off. Hope you are O.K. Will write soon.

Love, Jeanne

Dear Aunt Esther comes through: the wedding dress and slippers arrive!!

Oslo, April 29, 1952
Dear Suze,

I wanted to drop you a line right away to tell you that the wedding dress arrived all o.k. yesterday on the Stavangerfjord. It is simply beautiful and is a perfect fit. It is so nice and just exactly what I wanted. Thanks a hundred million for all the trouble you went to, the slippers are just perfect too. I don't know whether it was you or mom who put in the round garters but they sure are cute. When I go down the aisle, I am going to have the veil over my face but afterwards, I will have it back.

We are going to be married on May 24th, at 5 p.m. in the Trondheim cathedral.

Kay is going to be my maid of honor in a very pale green dress. Ernie's two sisters, Gerd and Kari are going to be bridesmaids in identical dresses of tulle, except that Gerd will have pale blue and Kari pale yellow. Ernie and his best man will have white tie and tails. After the ceremony, we are going to have the dinner at some club in Trondheim. There will be about 35 guests for dinner, during which there will be various speeches, etc.

After that we will go to Ernie's home where we will have coffee, liqueur, fruit table with all kinds of fruits and fruit desserts and champagne. Later there will be supper (smorgasbord, etc). We can dance in one of the living rooms. We are going to use both the upstairs and down.

Farmor took the train down to Oslo to meet Ma and help with their wedding plans, as moms do. I can imagine how Farmor might have been feeling: happiness for her son to find a good wife, but sad, realizing he was moving far away, more than 3500 miles, to a foreign country. She only expressed kindness to Ma and helped make their wedding back in Trondheim a wonderful experience.

> Ernie's mother has been here since last Thursday to help plan the wedding and I guess everything is all fixed now. She just has to make arrangements when she gets home. She is so nice and I wish she could stay longer.
>
> Ernie and I and the Matron of honor and her husband are going to leave Oslo on Wed. night the 21st on the sleeper, arriving in Trondheim the next morning so that will give us two days. Arvid is going to be best man. Am not sure who is going to give me away but perhaps Mr. Lindstrom. Randi is supposed to arrive in Oslo this Sunday from Moscow for a 4 weeks' vacation so I hope she can come.
>
> I wish you could be here. It would have been so much fun and I am sure you would have enjoyed it. We are going to take a lot of pictures so I hope they will turn out well.
>
> It is raining today and has rained for 3 days. Tomorrow is a Norwegian holiday and I am glad for that. Just 3 weeks from today we are supposed to leave for Trondheim. I guess that the time will go fast.
>
> Don't know any more news right now. Hope you got my other letter with the check.
>
> Love Jeanne

On May 21, 1952, Ma and Dad went up to be wed in Dad's home town, Trondheim, a city founded in 997, and Norway's 3rd largest city. Ma adored Oslo, but Trondheim also won a special place in her heart at this time.

(It also won my heart when I went there at age 19. When I think of Trondheim, I feel this way: O, dear Trondheim, birthplace of my father, with the quaint *Gamle Bybro* (Old City Bridge) I adored, and centuries-old timber warehouses standing on the canal, city full of such old wooden buildings, that gives the feel of the old wild West. How glad I am, that this town escaped extensive property destruction of World War II, unlike other cities.)

In the city's market place, she surely saw the famous Viking and King, Olav Tryggvason peering down from a tall column, a cross in one hand, a sword in the other. Olav brought Christianity to Norway.

Ma probably didn't have much time for site-seeing, preparing for the wedding and all. So, she didn't take the tram up to visit the magnificent Ringve Museum, with its thousand plus instruments, some dating back to the Viking days. I wonder if she took a boat out to the mysterious Monk Island in the fjord (the story of the table with the ridge made by a prisoner walking all his life around it, dragging his finger along the edge - turned out to be a myth to attract tourists. They're no dummies, these Trønder folk).

Nearby the Nidelva river, the Nidaros Cathedral looms above the city, calling attention to itself with its proud majesty. When my mother walked into that ancient cathedral the first time, it took her breath away. The place is awesome: you try to get a grasp on its age, its history, but it simply eludes you.

When I visited Nidaros the first time, I could almost hear

Mom & Dad's Wedding. Gerd, Mr. Lindstrom,
Mom, Dad, Kari, Kay, Arvid

sweet echoes of the young boys' choir in which my father had participated.

Over the centuries, the Nidaros Cathedral was witness to fire, the Black Death, and the annexation of Norway by Sweden, then by Denmark and the occupation of Norway by Nazi Germany. It was the venue for phenomenal boys' choir concerts, kings' coronations, a royal wedding and on May 24th 1952, the two most important people in my life walked down its aisle on the King's red carpet, adding their own story to the history of the impressive gothic Nidaros Cathedral.

After the fairy-tale wedding they continued celebrating with a fancy dinner at a restaurant in Trondheim. There were impressive ice sculptures, and flowers everywhere. Three musicians played, and all kinds of speeches were made, in the Norwegian tradition. One very lovely and moving speech was made by Farfar, who was an outstanding orator. He truly was a very kind and beloved man, and my mother always spoke positively about him.

The reception at Dad's family home held more fun and food, as well as dancing.

After the wedding they headed back to Oslo. Within a few months, the married couple left for the USA. Dad was excited to be fulfilling his dream of moving to America.

Mom's heart was torn as she was leaving her beloved Norway. It had been so fulfilling, working for and with Norwegians from 1943 – 1952. Ma wrote, "I loved Norway and never wanted to leave it. I had all kinds of friends there of all ages - - then there were all the diplomats and well-known Norwegians I knew who entertained me and 'watched out' for me. But God had other plans for me."

They left from Oslo on the Norwegian ocean liner, *Stavangerfjord*, the same ship which had brought over Mom's wedding dress! Part of The Norwegian America Line, the *Stavangerfjord* was a huge ship, over twelve thousand tons, 552 feet long with room for some 900 people. Chimes or a gong were sounded half an hour before and immediately preceding meals. There was music accompanying the meals, with a program showing the music to be played. The evening meal began at 6:30 pm. Gambling was prohibited. There was a library, a Barber Shop and a "Wireless Telegram Station" on board, too.

The boat took about a week to arrive in New York. Along with their suitcases, they brought with them some pieces of Norwegian furniture, an oak bookshelf and chair.

In marrying Dad, Ma also brought back home with her a living piece of the Norway she loved. (She may have been disappointed, since, in many ways, Daddy became more American than she! When my parents came over to visit me in Luxembourg and met my friends, more than once they thought it was my father, with his baseball cap and American slang expressions, who was the American parent and my mother, the Norwegian!)

While Ma was glad to get back home closer to her family, she always longed for her beloved Norway. Through-out the years my mother often prepared and gave talks about Norway in school and various clubs. When she finally got her own *bunad*, a Norwegian national costume, she would wear it while giving her speeches. She loved that *bunad* and the lovely silver jewelry *sølje*.

Ma kept in touch with her Norwegian friends for the rest of her life. When I went to Norway in 1982, Mom gave me phone numbers and wrote to her friends so that I could meet up with them. Johan R. Lindstrom (who gave her away at the wedding), Ragnhild Kirkhorn, "Mor" Gudmundsen's daughter, Marit, and good friends from her days working at EK, Berit Tranoy and Ragna Hansen and of course, Astrid, a friend who she had met later in life in the USA who moved back to Norway after her husband died. Mom truly cherished her Norwegian friends.

Indeed, Norway had profoundly impacted my mother's heart and soul. It was her home away from home.

Whenever she spoke of Norway, her eyes inevitably lit up and her voice became animated.

Although she was born as Cecil and Edna's child in the USA, she would always remain Norway's daughter, the American Norwegian.

Jeanne, the American Norwegian

DAD: EARLY MEMORIES

When the folks arrived in the USA, married life began in Washington D.C., Mom's old stomping grounds, but a whole new world for Dad. Ma's Aunt Flossy and Uncle Frank still lived there, and Ma's sister Julia and her husband Emile Passman were also nearby. Ma's eldest niece, Lana, came down from Hancock and visited them there, and they took her around siteseeing. The USA in the early 1950s was a booming place, with lots of job opportunities. Dad worked a while for brother-in-law Emile, who then had a business installing windows. Shortly afterwards, Dad got a job with the John C Grimberg Co., a civil engineering firm, primarily concerned with government and municipal projects, somewhat similar to the military job he had held in London briefly after the war ended.

This was also the era of the Cold War and Dad volunteered, at some point, for the civil defence organization, the "US Air Force Air Defense Command" to keep an eye out for low-flying enemy Russian planes: "Ernie Hoff is a fully accredited member of the Ground Observer Corp (for I.D. only)."

Ma took a job in an office as a secretary where she met Lil Roy, who became a close, lifelong friend. They worked for a demanding woman named Marie who ran a steno office. The girls did dictation and typing for a group of lawyers in Colesville, near Silver Spring, Lil told me. Marie was a very particular woman who used to look through the garbage pails to see how many mistakes the girls had made in typing. Lil and Ma used to put the imperfect pages inside their braziers, and then go into the restroom, rip them up in tiny pieces, and flush it down the toilets! How they laughed, envisioning Marie sitting on the pot one day when the septic system would back up from all that paper!

Ma and Daddy would spend many an evening playing Pitch and Rummy with their friends, Lil and Mel. Lil said that from the time they first met, and as long as Lil knew her, Ma was always talking about the Norway which she loved, telling stories and describing her wonderful experiences there.

At some point in Washington, Ma, ever the cat-lover, got herself a little kitten which managed to get stuck up in a pine tree, and no one could entice it to descend. Daddy was not around at the time so "Uncle" Mel, who was deadly afraid of cats, somehow turned out to be the one who braved the danger, went up the ladder and got it down for her (of course, we aren't surprised that Ma did not ask her Uncle Frank!)

The last year they were in Washington, in October 1954, Ma's father Cecil passed away– he was only 66 years old. Ma decided that her first child would be named after him, when the day came.

After three child-free years in Washington, they moved up to Hancock, Ma's hometown in upstate New York in May 1955, where Dad got a job with the First National Bank of Hancock. It was a great place to raise children and to be near family. Their first child, Cecilia, arrived in December that year. While working there in Hancock, Dad took classes and attended seminars to prepare for an examination that qualified him to be appointed as assistant bank examiner for the U.S. Treasury department. Tony, Ma's eldest nephew told me, "It was not an easy thing, those classes and exams, and another colleague at the bank, Percy, that worked with him, tried too, but failed, but your Dad soared right through it. Your mom and your dad were both *really* sharp."

"I had a very special relationship with your dad," Tony continued. "When I was little, about 10, I remember going fishing with Uncle Ernie, Great Uncle Walt and my dad, Duane, down the Delaware river, catching bass, back then, and *lots* of fun times. Also, sometimes Uncle Ernie would call me up and say 'Wanna go see a western at the movie theatre?' He was into westerns, Uncle Ernie was, and off we'd go. In one movie there was a scene where a guy had his hands tied up a certain way and afterwards, I said to Uncle Ernie, 'Let me tie you up like that,' so I did and Uncle Ernie broke that rope off like it was nothing! Your dad was tall, strong and very athletic." As Tony grew up, they became friends and had a lot of fun together. "He had a sense of humor *unparalleled*," Tony said with his own infectious chuckle, "How he could laugh! Sometimes he would say some word that was wrong with a straight face so Aunt Jeanne had to correct him and we both knew he did it on purpose and we'd laugh so hard together, your folks and me."

It must have been fun for Mom and Dad to be able to spend time with her brother, Duane and his wife, Helen who lived in Hancock with their son, Tony, and daughters Lana and Kat at the old Rood home on 17 East Main Street. Tony remembered another example of Uncle Ernie's great sense of humor and told the story about once when Lana was quite young and had received a guitar for her birthday. She wrote her own original song and sang it for her folks and Uncle Ernie and Aunt Jeanne as they sat around the table, when they were visiting Auntie Helen and Uncle Duane.

Tony said it went something like this:

"If you don't eat, (random twang, twang on the guitar, pause) *yer gunna die o' hunger,*

"If you don't eat, (twang, twang on the guitar, pause) *yer gunna die o' hunger* (twang, twang).

Uncle Ernie began to laugh as quietly as he could. Then came the second verse:

"If you don't drink (twang, twang, pause) *yer gunna die of thirst..."* etc.

Uncle Ernie laughed harder and could no longer contain himself. Then came the final verse:

"If you don't sleep (twang, twang) *yer gunna die of tiredness...."*

"Uncle Ernie's head was on the table, tears rolling down his face, as he laughed," Tony said, totally out of control at Lana's silly song.

Tony remembers one autumn when his buddy Eddy Ray, also of Hancock, said to him, "Hey, Ernie's going to come hunting with us! "Ernie who?" Tony asked. "Ernie Hoff," Eddy replied. "OH, that's my uncle!" Tony laughed. Once again, it was clear that Uncle Ernie was known and loved by everyone in Hancock. (As Tony said, he could have run for mayor and won, with his calm manner - he was friends with the higher echelon and with the lowest, treating them all with equal respect.) So, Tony said, they went hunting several times, and gave Ernie the best blinds where they usually always saw deer, but somehow, he never got a deer. I think he loved being out in nature with good people, but he didn't have the heart to shoot the deer. Gerd agreed with me, she thought he was too fond of animals to manage to shoot one.

Five years after his arrival in the USA, Dad became an official US citizen in 1957.

Meanwhile Ma was busy as a "stay-at-home" mom raising the Future of America, and Dad kept improving his work situation. A newspaper clipping Ma cut from the *Sun Bulletin* in August 1960, describes Dad's next position: "Endicott National Names Head Auditor. Endicott National Bank President K McQueen today announced the appointment of Ernie Hoff of Hancock as bank auditor...the manager of the bank had been doubling as auditor and an increase in business made it necessary to hire a full-time auditor." The new job meant they had to move to Endwell, NY with their now 3-soon-to-be 4 children.

In May 1962, Dad was "one of three Triple Cities bankers to have been elected Director of the Southern New York Conference of NABAC, the Association for Bank Audit, Control and Operation." He sometimes had work assignments down in New York City, and occasionally took his young nephew Tony with him. Dad said he hated auditing a bank in the World Trade Center, which he said he felt swaying when there was a lot of wind, up so high. Those buildings had 110 floors and indeed could sway 12 inches from side to side. Dad had a fear of heights which is crazy because he used to ski jump as a young man in Norway.

In September 1965, Ma's brother Duane passed away unexpectedly, at only 44 years old. It was thought that the enormous stress of the war had impacted his heart and contributed to his passing. What a loss for so many! He was given full military honors at his burial in Hancock. Ma had already lost her dad quite early in 1954, when she was only 31, and now, her only brother.

In 1966, Dad got a job in Deposit, NY in the Farmer's National Bank and we moved from Endwell to Deposit into the house where we grew up on River Road, the old house my mother had admired from her youth. I was three years old when we moved in. Three years later, the last child was born and the family was complete – we were now six kids and we knew how to fill a huge house with life and "rambunction" (that *is* a word, it describes beautifully the Hoff house which overflowed with energy in those early years. OK, maybe I invented it.)

I loved it when Dad worked at Farmers National Bank. He brought home accounting sheets which looked so official, and we used them to play bank and veterinarian. They had Santa there at the bank at Christmas, and one year I sat on his lap and screwed up the courage to ask for the great big brown teddy bear which sat in the window, and sure enough, Santa brought it-that very year! Sometimes on a Friday, Dad came home from work with a bag of creampuffs, a delightful type of doughnut filled with the lightest, most heavenly white cream, made in the bakery down the street across from the bank.

"Buzz" Axtell was a friend that worked at the bank with Dad and he used to come down to the house for a visit, sometimes staying for dinner. (He was lean, dark and handsome, and we girls always wondered how such an attractive man somewhere around 40 would still be a bachelor. It didn't quite fit the fairy tales of handsome people marrying and living happily ever after.) Mom always seemed to find a way to feed one more at our huge dining room table, stretching it apart and adding a table leaf to make it longer.

In cold winter months, when the roads were blocked with snow, Dad simply skied the few miles into work at the bank in town, which was just *too cool* to us kids. Imagining him gliding into town, in such a unique manner, amused us greatly. There's a saying in Norway, "there's no such thing as bad weather – just inappropriate clothing." There's no such thing as bad weather to stop you from getting to your job, either, if you are Norwegian, we kids thought. We were proud to be Norwegian and we loved that our Dad was Norwegian. His name, Ørnulf means "Eagle Wolf," which was as impressive as any Native American name we'd ever heard.

Sometime in the 1970s, he left the bank and moved on to bigger things, finding a more interesting job with BardParker, a medical supplies company based just outside of Hancock, not far from Grannie's. There he started off in the accounting department and making more friends with co-workers. Dad occasionally fished in a creek by the Baudendistel farm out in French Woods, outside of Hancock, a lovely wild part of upstate New York, down a dirt road. One time, it began to pour down rain and he took cover in the barn until it let up a bit. The rain was like a steady stream and just as it began to slow, Mrs. Baudendistel, a BardParker co-worker, appeared with what Dad said was "the most delicious homemade apple pie" he had ever tasted. Dad had friends all over the area.

He once worked with a likable young Pakistani man. Dad told him he had 5 unmarried daughters. The Pakistani bachelor was delighted when Dad invited him to dinner: he brought with him 4 of his bachelor Pakistani friends. What Dad failed to mention was that most of the daughters were under 12 years of age! How Ma laughed about Dad's sense of humor that time! Dad worked at BardParker the rest of his career, learning more and more about IBM computers as they sent him to training, etc. He sometimes was sent down to another branch of the company in El Paso, Texas for short business trips. Sometime during those years, he became computer systems analyst, a position he held until his retirement in 1988.

Over the years of their marriage, Ma kept every card he ever gave her, and a letter he sent her from Texas when he was sent there occasionally for work (she probably fainted when she got it, he rarely wrote letters). She also cut out and kept paper clippings related to his successes at work, as he worked his way up to more and more interesting positions. In the USA working world, it was not always easy for Dad, being "the foreigner," even though his accent was only very slight. Sometimes, even some of Mom's own relatives "didn't seem to take too kindly to foreigners," he said.

At some point in the early 1960s, Dad took a trip back to Norway. Farmor and Farfar gathered everyone together and a family portrait was taken in Trondheim. Tante Gerd said Dad was trying to find out if he could buy a small farm somewhere in Norway, to move the family back to the Old Country. But it was not to be, he could not afford it, so we stayed where we were and Dad kept working in an office setting, not on a farm.

Dad worked very hard. Ma was there beside him, supporting him along the way as best she could. She may not have been the typical "Suzie Homemaker" type (Dad said, "She always had her nose in a book"), but she managed to keep our home together through the ups and downs of marriage. She did laundry, fixed warm meals and filled the house with her songs and anecdotes – Dad's hard work and his calm manner projected a stability that

Last Hoff Family Portrait in Trondheim Photograph by Skjold Hilfling-Rasmussen

gave us a sense of security. For this, I continue to thank God Who gave us such good parents.

My Early Childhood Memories of Daddy

I cherish the memories of my father from when I was very small...

...His hands are always warm. I often wonder how his big, gentle hands are so faithfully warm. He takes our cold hands and envelopes them in his, rubbing softly, a concerned expression on his face. After a few minutes, he stops and says, "There, how's that?" (If I had had a particularly rough day I would reply, "A little bit more, Daddy." So, he continued until I was satisfied.)

He has a knack for making ordinary things into clever games. He plays tricks with his fingers. Sometimes he steals our noses, other times he snaps his fingers together, making a funny cracky noise by sliding one finger off the next onto his other hand, the way only he could. Another game we play is "Squeeze-Daddy's Hand-'til-He-Winces." I take his hand firmly in mine and squeeze with all my scrawny might. His face instantly screws up into a grimace of pain, until he can stand it no longer—at least I think so.

When we were babies, Daddy would make funny faces at us to make us smile and google. Ma says that's why people always said her little ones were so expressive. Daddy is always ready to tease us kids, or our friends that come over to play. Ma has to tell them, "Never mind Ernie, he's just teasin' you." She says she's never met anyone like Daddy, "who laughs so hard at his own jokes." Sometimes when my big sisters are listening to the radio, he comes to make fun, and wiggles his rump like a silly to make them laugh. If they are getting all dolled up to go out, he pretends he's doing his hair too, with a ridiculous face and his nearly bald head, making fun of them until they can't help but giggle.

I don't mind working in the yard with Daddy, picking up sticks or raking leaves. I'd much rather do that then help my sisters clean up the kitchen – YUCK. Daddy made a vegetable garden, full of potatoes, strawberries, corn, tomatoes, and green beans, even with rhubarb for Ma (how can she eat that stuff?!) I found an Indian arrowhead when I was working there once. Dad

Heidi, Kjer, Celia, Me, Beau & Ma, Julie & Dad

picks out the weeds or together we pick up stones and toss them in the wheelbarrow, like basketball, and I imagine we are trying to make the most baskets. When it starts to feel too heavy, he wheels it down to the riverbank to dump out the stones, with me traipsing along next to him in anticipation. Climbing up into the empty chariot, I hardly notice all the dirt beside me, for I ride in grandeur. The coachman is a superb fellow, very friendly and he drives the carriage with such skill I can enjoy all the bumps!

He's always mowing the lawn, and sometimes lets me ride beside him on the red Wheelhorse riding tractor. When I'm eleven, I'll learn to mow the field like my sisters and Beau do. One time, Daddy was mowing down by the barn, close to our neighbor Corabelle's house. Her beagle dog, tied up in their back yard, was also named Ernie. He started barking his head off just then. Corabelle, who was usually a very gentle, quiet lady, stuck her head out the back door and shouted loudly, "SHUT UP, ERNIE!" At just that moment Daddy looked up from the mower, and then her face turned bright red. Dad had a good laugh telling that one to Ma.

In the winter, Dad uses his tractor as a snow blower to clean out the driveway. He doesn't like winter because of the snow - he can't go golfin'. I like winter because once in a while we get so much that we have snow days so there's no school and also because Dad takes us skiing sometimes. He taught us all how to ski when we were really little, like four, Ma says but I can't remember when I learned since I was too little. We have all kinds of sizes of old Norwegian wooden skis. Dad took us each down River Road individually to ski with him in the woods up behind Stuart Wilson's property. (He's a rich guy Dad knows. He's got so much money that even the gutters around his house are made of copper). Up there in the wilderness, Daddy showed us all the little animals foot prints in the snow. It was so quiet up there you could hear yourself breathin'. We took a backpack with sandwiches and hot chocolate and ate them sitting on a big ole' rock when I got hungry. That was a really special day. I bet it reminded him of ski trips in Norway with his family.

In the Autumn, when the trees shower their bright leaves on the ground, we rake up huge mountains of color. If it's not too wet, he lets me bury myself. I love the musty smell of all those leaves on my face.

Sometimes he gets mad at us kids when we're naughty. He says, "You kids quit your arguing or I'll come in there and knock your heads together." There's a variation on that theme: "You kids cut it out or I'll come and knock some sense into ya." Or if someone is whining, "Quit your whinebaggin' or I'll give you something to really cry about." Me and Kjer got a big spankin' once when she kept naggin' and naggin' me to go upstairs and get her sneakers for her so we could go out and play. I went and got them but I was mad, so I threw them down the stairs to her on the side of the living room and broke one of Ma's antique vases. I hightailed it out of there but it was too late, we were caught and both Kjer and I got a major spankin' from Dad. How I *hated* it when Ma would say, "Wait until your father gets home…"

My gentle neighbor and younger friend Lynette Carlson, who lost her own Dad way too early, when she was just a little thing, comes over to play a lot. Lynette likes playing baseball or kickball with me and Daddy. Daddy plays softball with us, too. He gets her to be pitcher, even though at first she didn't feel too sure. He teases her and calls her a regular "Catfish Hunter", who was a big important baseball pitcher ages ago.

His lap is always ready to hold a person, especially when that person is a small one. When all my sisters and brother were in the playroom watching television, it was sometimes hard to find a place to sit. I had been upstairs reading a book when I heard laughter from downstairs. I went down and walked into the room to join the fun. The couch and all the chairs were full, so I sat down on the floor. Everywhere I moved to, people complained that I was in the way. Soon I was close to tears, but Dad came to my rescue and said, "Maggie, come sit on Daddy's lap." I ended up with the best seat in the house!

In the middle of one dark night, I came back from a trip to the bathroom and I saw an evil banana man (a banana with legs) creeping up the stairs. (I hated bananas by the way). I was a kid that had a fair amount of nightmares and night terrors. My bedroom was right by the folks' room and when I cried out in fear after a particularly scary repeating dream, it was "Daddy!!" I called for, who came in and calmed down my racing heart. "It was just a dream, you're OK, go back to sleep."

His arms are all encompassing. Whenever I am upset, I walk down the hallway and stand in my parents' bedroom doorway. He glances up, takes one look at me, and immediately perceives that something is wrong. He puts his arms around me and hugs me for a good long while, then he wipes my tears with the cotton handkerchief he always keeps in his pocket. He does not say a word, just hugs, and suddenly the world is all right again.

In the winter, I am out in the snow after school. I like sliding down the small hill behind our house, on a round saucer. I climb and slide and climb and slide until it starts to get dark and Daddy's car pulls into the driveway. The car's headlights shine on the old faded yellow barn where he parks inside. I run to meet him in the dusky light as he walks toward the house with his briefcase, which I imagine contains *very* important computer papers. He smiles as I reach up to hold his hand and we walk to the house. The only sound is the crunching of the snow beneath our feet. Life is safe and all is well – Daddy is home.

MOM: FUN, FRIENDS, and FAITH

In the early summer morning, I heard the promise of another hot day in the cicada's high-pitched call. Lying in bed, I opened my eyes and listened to that wonderful sound. Anticipation swelled up in my heart like a fat balloon as I thought of today's plans. It pushed me out of bed and I ran to the window.

The gauzy white curtains moved gently in the summer breeze. I tried to push the old white paned window further up but it stubbornly stuck half-way. Only a few cottony clouds spotted the bright blue sky: it was a *perfect* day for a picnic. I threw on a t-shirt and shorts which I'd grabbed out of my chest of drawers. I ran a brush through my stringy long blonde hair. The blue eyes of the "Sweet Honesty" cat perfume bottle, a gift from my neighbor and friend Lynette, seemed to wink at me. "Hurry up, silly girl, or you might miss something!"

I skipped down the red-carpeted stairs, and went out the front screen door onto the porch. Hopping over to the pillar, I checked out the mercury thermometer there in the shade. I smiled when I saw that it was already 80 degrees Fahrenheit – today was going to be a real scorcher! Just the kind of day for a trip with Aunt Lil and Uncle Mel Roy.

Friends were very important to my folks, and especially to Ma. "Aunt" Lil and "Uncle" Mel Roy were my parents' dear friends up visiting us from Maryland.

Lil had been Ma's colleague in the early years after Ma and Daddy moved to Washington, D.C. when Ma and Lil were *ung og dum og deglig* (young and dumb and delightful). Their friendship spanned the years and Lil became dear to us all, along with her husband Mel and their daughters Jan and Kathy. Although Mom and Dad moved many times, they always kept in contact with Lil and Mel.

Lil and Mel always planned lots of fun for us kids during their visits to our home. Even mundane things were made amusing. Uncle Mel, always the handyman, once built some concrete steps for Dad leading up to the side porch. He had each of us pick a step on which to write our initials on the corner. Another time they prepared a magnificent treasure hunt, with clues leading us all around the house until finally we found a grand treasure chest full of toys, specially chosen for each one of us. Mine was an adorable doll: just right for me. Today's pleasure was to be a grand picnic, to be held up at the Cannonsville Reservoir, just outside of Deposit. Cannonsville had been a quaint village in a valley until it and four neighboring towns were flooded in the early 1960s to make a reservoir for New York City.[156]

The day before, Ma and Lil had been busy preparing enough food for an army. Uncle Mel asked us, "Are you kids ready for some action?"

"YES!" we girls shouted.

"Where's your brother?" he asked us.

"Oh, he's up in his room, pro'ly lookin' at his comic book collection," someone said. "Or else pickin' his toes!" someone else added, laughing. (It wasn't easy being an only boy with five sisters.)

After Mel had rounded us all up, he pulled out a huge bag of balloons and filled them up with water. We had an all-out water balloon war with fun-loving Uncle Mel. We ran around the house screaming with delight, chucking water bombs and trying to be the one to get Uncle Mel the most drenched. What started with balloons ended up with buckets of water launched from hidden corners of the old house. After our battle plans were exhausted, we got into dry clothes and sat in the backyard eating cold watermelon. I sat on the middle stone of the back steps, melon juice dripping down between my spread boney knees, as my sisters and I spat out the seeds to see who could make theirs go farthest.

How lucky for us that my parents' friends loved us kids, and were not overwhelmed by the headcount of six Hoff children.

Through the years, Mom kept in touch with many of her

childhood and high school friends. Whenever Ma went into town, she stopped to take the time to visit with whichever acquaintance or friend she met. She loved to attend the Hancock High School reunions each year to catch up on the latest with those friends. She also sent lots of Christmas letters to her old friends in the USA and Norway over the years. I had to laugh one time, when in a letter dated April 1989 she wrote, "I still haven't finished our Christmas letters."

Edith Wheelock remained an important friend of Ma's from childhood on. I remember many wonderful summer trips to Starlight Lake for visits with Edie. Her cottage was the quaintest place. The coolest thing was the way they kept the Coca-Cola cans in the tiny brook running in the shade beside the cottage. It kept them delightfully cold, especially nice after sunbathing in the hot sun, down on the dock. We also enjoyed going out on the lake in a canoe or small rowboat. Heidi, Kjersti, Julie and I rowed about, getting oars caught in lily-pads, those botanical wonders I found somewhat eerie. While we played, Ma and Edie would gab non-stop, "catching up" as Ma said.

Edie told me about one of the last times she was together with Ma at the lake. It was just the two of them, both in their mid-70s, and they had decided to row across the lake to the Inn for lunch. That summer the lake was very low, and the canoe ran aground just before they arrived. So, they took off their shoes and waded to shore, dragging the canoe with them. Ma gleefully remarked to Edie, "We still can get ourselves into a scrape, even at our age!"

Edie had other memories of Ma as a child which she shared with me. As a little girl, Ma would hold her collection of bears and make up conversations between them using different voices, talking out of the side of her mouth, fascinating her friends. (We still have her dear "Growler Bear," an authentic Steiff teddy bear which by now is an antique). Edie asked Ma if she could still do a teddy bear voice. She laughed, took a deep breath, and replied in the old bear voice. "Of course, she always was good at languages!" Edie said with a laugh, "Jeanne anecdotes continually run through my mind. Humor and lively wit were characteristic of your mother."

My mom had another dear old friend, Birdie, with whom she also shared many childhood adventures. Birdie was the daughter of John and Marguerite Lee. Once Birdie and Ma rode the old horse all day around the fields at Roods Creek. The next day the horse died. But Ma claimed their actions had nothing to do with it. "He just got the blind staggers, and fell down a hill," she said. As they lived in the same small town of Deposit, Ma kept in close touch with Birdie. In later years, they would play scrabble and enjoy a cup of coffee and some homemade cake or pie together. When Birdie's husband became senile, Ma felt so sorry for her. Ma wrote once in a letter:

> We (Dad and I) try to do all we can to help her keep her spirits up. It's so nice to have such a good friend to be with. Think! We've known each other since we were babies. She had a much harder and sadder life than I did, but she still has her sense of humor and always was 'sharp' as a tack.

Even Mom's hairdresser, Judy Finch, was a good friend. Ma had beautiful dark brown hair, with occasional glimmers of red. She sometimes got a permanent at "Judy's Beauty Parlor" in town, to keep it a little curly. Judy and Mom would talk and visit the whole time, as friends do. Many times, Ma would wash her hair and put it up in curlers – the old hard, prickly kind. I don't know how she slept on them! But what I remember more often was when she'd wash it and put it up in Bobby pins to curl it. She was the Bobby pin Queen. You could find Bobby pins all over the house. She found uses for Bobby pins you wouldn't want to know about. She didn't have any grey hairs until she was well into her 50s. She used to get us to brush her hair for her. She'd sit on the couch watching the news or something, and I'd sit behind her up on the back of the couch and brush her hair. She'd give me a quarter sometimes. She also brushed her Aunt Esther's hair for her sometimes when she was young. I used to get my Lucia, when she was small, to brush my hair for me, too. It's so relaxing!

Ma was always ready to meet someone for tea or whatever to have a little visit. Clearly, Ma *loved* to socialize. She could start up a conversation with anyone in the vicinity and find something of common interest: Dad used to say he pitied the poor soul seated next to her on the long flights back and forth to Europe. Ma's letters to me over the years are full of her social events. Here is an example, three events in one letter:

Can't think of any big news.

(1) I have to be in Book Circle program on the 21st – Environmental Responsibilities. Maybe I told you before I took excerpts from a speech Robert J. Waller (yes, the Waller) made… then I'm going to tell about my experiences, etc…

(2) Birdie and I still play scrabble real often. Then we have goodies and coffee with Dad. I made a chocolate loaf cake that Granny used to make, it turned out great.

[I have that loaf cake recipe still. It's in a very old, small recipe book, "Baker's Best Chocolate Recipes," copyright 1932, which Ma gave me in 1983. On the inside cover she wrote, "To Maggie, Who loves chocolate. Love, Mom."]

(3) Auntie Helen invited me to a pinochle party for lunch, etc. on Sunday. So, Dad dropped me off in Hancock: went back home and came later to pick me up. He seems much more protective of me this past year… We have lots of fun - - although I really prefer Bridge. Bridge you have to use strategy. Six-handed pinochle, you don't have to think. But we gossip and have a lot of fun and jokes.

Auntie Helen had such a hearty boisterous laugh, it was infectious. Ma enjoyed Auntie Helen's pinochle gang (they were several widows from the Hancock area).

Faith in God was important to both my parents. They attended church quite often and occasionally an evening Bible study. Ma used to say she "came from a long line of Christians." She and Daddy would take us to Sunday school and church quite regularly when we were little, until we were teens, old enough to decide for ourselves whether we wanted to attend or not. Some did, and some didn't.

One of us kids once put a sticker up on the outside of my sister Celia's bedroom door, on the side of the hallway which led to Beau's room. The sticker said, "God has the Answer." My brother, at the time a typical teenager, wrote underneath, "But

He ain't talkin'!" My mother later erased what he had written and wisely wrote: "But are you ready to listen?"

Ma wrote me once in a letter:

> I was such a small tot when I was taken to church and Sunday school that I never had any question about our Lord and Jesus. It always was a natural part of my life. My father and mother and Grandparents were brought up the same way. The older folks especially (Great Aunts and Uncles, too were always using remarks pertaining to the Bible). I must have been about 10 or 11 when Uncle 'Hub' Fransisco (my great aunt Ellen's husband) was talking about somebody coming down the hill 'faster than Jehu.' I didn't realize until years later in a Bible study where that expression came from (*see II Kings 9:20*). If I hadn't had my faith and strong convictions of assurance, I never could have done all I did and set out for Norway, etc.

There was even some great-great relative (a woman as I recall) who was what they called "A Shoutin' Methodist" preacher. We went for a while to the Methodist church in town when I was quite little, until my teenage sister and brother came home and told Ma that the pastor said that Jesus didn't *really* do any miracles. We stopped going to that church after that. Mom and Dad returned there years later, when a different pastor appeared.

Then we attended the Christian Missionary Alliance church. The dear Christian saints in that place had a huge impact on me: Pastors Don and Elaine Propert, Bruce and Becky Dyke, Sunday school teachers such as gentle, stick-thin Mr. Lovejoy, who eventually slowly died of cancer, but all during his illness continued to teach us about the enduring love of Jesus which sustained him daily. There was kindhearted Mr. Clift, and German-born Mr. Janssen, the gifted violinist who played hymns with a beauty that moved me to tears. There was Joan Holland, who played piano and sang with all her heart. There was Evelyn Azalia Campbell, who had been important in my mother's life and who always called me "her little sister" in Christ and never forgot my birthday. During prayer meeting, all the saints would be on their knees, in the first few rows of the church, praying for all the folks we knew who had any kind of trouble. Then they got up and did what they could to help whoever needed it, in all kinds of practical ways. God was real to them and it came across to me so clearly.

Ma especially liked it when they had missionaries come and tell their adventures. In a letter written November 3, 1983 Ma wrote:

> We've had Missionary Convention this week: Rev. Robert Stern and Miss Ann McEwen. She's from Guinea, W Africa and he's from Argentina. They are both dynamic speakers and interesting to listen to. He is so humble and spiritual but very forceful – a terrific personality. She is excellent – very intelligent, invincible and a great speaker. I think they are 2 of the most interesting we've had.

Ma enjoyed it when her church had special Bible study sessions. Once the topic was "Healing" and once the book of Revelation. "It's a very good setup," she wrote, "We read about 2 chapters a week, then read them aloud in class. Then discuss a few things at the time they're being read." Once a video they watched used the Revised Standard Version of the Bible, which Ma said, "… I never cared for it (*the RSV*) – having cut my teeth, literally, on the King James Version which to me is more profound."

I think the saint Ma appreciated most was dear Mrs. Gertrude Luck, or "The Candy Lady" as we called her, since every Sunday she had a bag of goodies for us to choose from. She was a tiny little thing, but she could open up the Word of God with a passion rarely seen in our small town. I remember my Mother dabbing the corner of her eyes when she heard Mrs. Luck expounding on "The Two on the Road to Emmaus" from Luke's Gospel. The story starts just after the devastating event of Jesus' death. The two followers did not recognize the risen Jesus at first, while he explained to them from the Old Testament Scriptures why the Christ had to suffer and how it was part of a greater, overarching Plan since the beginning of time. They shared a meal with Him, and He disappeared from their sight, just as He broke the bread. Then they knew it had been Jesus Himself. Mrs. Luck always emphasized the part where they said "Did not our hearts *burn* within us as we talked with Him on the way?" Then she described the wonder of knowing Jesus yourself. Both my parents enjoyed Mrs. Luck's Bible studies. Mom wrote about her years later,

"I think of Mrs. Luck often - - some little thing will remind me of her - - or I'll hear a hymn or a song or a sermon on WPEL (radio). Then I'll think of all the times she and Mr. Luck sang - - or some verse in a sermon which she emphasized."

Ma's faith was something personal, not talked about often, but very real. It was the same for my father, who sometimes gently reminded us in the stormy parts of life, "Where is your faith?" His mother, too, had a humble faith, for when I was in Norway, she gave me her 1912 Bible, and wrote to me in it, *"Jeg siger såm din oldemor – bruk din bibel ofte så vil de gå deg gåt i livet. Farmor"* ("I say the same as your great-grandmother – use your Bible often so it will go well in your life. Farmor.")

If ever you went into Ma and Daddy's bedroom at bedtime (when we were small, we had to go to bed at 8 pm whether it was broad daylight in the middle of summer or not), there they'd be, each one with their nose in a book, often as not the Bible or a devotional. They'd look up with a smile and say, "What's the matter Mags?" First thing on Saturday morning, one or another of us would run down the hallway to their bedroom, and climb up into their huge bed for a little morning chat. Those chats were like vitamins for growing up with a healthy spirit.

Ma kept the habit of listening to the radio her whole life. Very often I heard my mother's radio playing on the table next to her bed, as she listened to some Christian program. She especially enjoyed the gentle, reassuring voice of Dr. Robert A. Cook, who closed each lesson with "Walk with the King today, and be a blessing!" from Kings' College.

In one of her little notebooks Mom wrote out the following in Norwegian, something she wanted to remember from one of her trips to Norway:

Psalm 103: 2 "Bless the Lord, O my soul, and forget not all His benefits.."

Og finner du Ham, da finner du alt
hva hjertet kan evig begjaere.
Da reiser seg atter hvert håp som falt,
og blekner så aldri mere.
- W. A. Wexels

(In finding Him, you find everything that the heart can eternally desire, then every hope that dies will rise again and fade no more.)

Ma knew that there is more to life than just this "seen" world. She wanted us to be soul-healthy. She herself grabbed any moment possible to be quiet and think on deeper things. But finding quiet was not easy with six lively kids!

For sure, poor Ma sometimes got frustrated with the six of us being "rambunctious" as she said. If a few of us started fighting, and someone complained that they'd been hit, she'd call out, "You kids keep yer hands to home!" Under her breath, you'd hear her say, "I can take the noise, it's the fighting I can't stand".

Sometimes we were terribly noisy when she was trying to talk on the telephone. Needless to say, we got on her nerves at times. She might be in the middle of an interesting phone call when we'd come around looking for this or that, clamoring for her attention. "I gotta' go,' she'd say into the receiver, 'I got the kids breathin' down my neck."

One time, she had a call from an elderly Norwegian friend Astrid, who lived in Pennsylvania (she made a *mean* chicken dinner. The skeletal remains she called "the BOONES." In that telltale Norwegian accent her sing-songy voice would say, "Vi can put de boones here on this plate"). We kids were still at the dining room table, laughing and carrying on as usual, while Ma tried to discuss with Astrid on the nearby kitchen phone. "*Ja,* **sier** *du*"… she'd say. «*ja så….sier du det… ja så…*". She became more and more exasperated with us, and kept covering the phone with one hand and saying, "SHUSH in there, I'm on long-distance!" Finally, she got up and strained against the short length of the telephone cord, her face stormy, motioning at us threateningly with the telephone book she picked up off the kitchen table. We didn't pay any attention, until her fiery Rood temper exploded and she threw the heavy telephone book at us with deadly aim from the kitchen. That was the end of it, we were dead on the floor, cracking up hysterically. Naughty kids!

In fact, Ma was notorious for her long phone calls. She truly had the "gift of gab." Sometimes, she'd be in the middle of doing something and the phone would ring and she'd forget what she'd been doing. One time, she was running water for some reason and had to go upstairs for something when the phone rang. She answered the phone upstairs and a major gab session ensued. By the time she got off the phone, the kitchen floor was covered with water. She quickly mopped it up as she heard the school bus arriving. When Julie came in, she sat down at the kitchen table in the captain's chair (Dad's chair). A strange squishy sound came from below. She looked under the table and then up at Ma.

"Shoot!" said Ma, "I must have missed some."

After that, Julie drew Ma a picture of Ziggy which said, "These days walking on water wouldn't be much of a miracle." Ma framed it and hung it up in the kitchen over the sink, perhaps to remind her of the good laugh she had shared with Julie that day, besides her environmental work to keep the neighborhood air unpolluted by the factory across the river.

When Ma was 50-something she decided she was finally going to get her driver's license. She took lessons from the high school shop teacher. "'Commander Randal' tells us to 'keep two hands on the steering wheel at all times,'" she'd tell me. He used just the right teaching methods with Ma, and she was highly appreciative. She was very careful to follow all the driving rules, and she reminded me all the while how important it was "to drive defensively," etc. [She would have fainted if she saw me driving to work putting on makeup at the same time when I was young and silly.] Ma was so proud to have gotten her license. It took some gumption to make the effort at that later stage in life, but the independence it gave her brought joy.

It was also a blessing for Ma to earn a little money by babysitting in these years. She took care of Andrew, who was the son of our music teacher, Mrs. Phyllis Baker. Andrew was just a few weeks old when Ma began to babysit him. He always kept a special place in her heart, for she raised him like one of her own children. Later, she also had his brother, too. They both were special to her.

The year my mother turned 54, 1977, ended up being a very tough year for her. Her mom, our Grannie, passed away in February, and with the funeral and division of antiques, etc., there was some kind of fall-out between my Aunt Julie and Mom. They were not in close contact much at all after that, although they were never as close to one another as Ma had been with her brother Duane.

Then in late 1977, not long after my parents had taken Kjersti to King's College, Briarcliff Manor, NY, Ma became seriously ill with a terrible autoimmune sickness which affected her the rest of her life. Three years later, on November 11, 1980, Armistice Day, Mom described this turning point in her health:

> Armistice Day to-day. I sit here in the Bay Window of our bedroom, listening to the wind howling outside and watching the wet snowflakes whirling down the valley. It's warm and cozy here by the radiator. It's a time for remembering things-both good and bad.
>
> The time has come to recall one of the most gruesome experiences of my life: It was October 1977 on a Monday night-damp and cold. Ernie and I had gone to Bible Club at Mrs. Luck's. When we got seated in the car to return home at 10 o'clock, an excruciating pain gripped the large muscle of my left arm, proceeded on down my arm and straight to the tips of my fingers. It was like a vice grabbing me. I mentioned the severe pain to Ernie as it faded. When we arrived home my arm ached so I took aspirin and went to bed with the heating pad. I slept O.K. but the next morning when I tried to get dressed, I couldn't raise my arm without severe pain. When Ernie left for work, he said he would call at noon to see how I was and would come home and take me to the doctor. I spent the morning sitting on the couch reading to Andrew and looking at TV. I thought, this is silly if it's rheumatism it's probably better to exercise. So, I tried raising my arms and they were quite O.K., so I went out in the kitchen, did the dishes and straightened up. When Ernie called, I told him I was much better and didn't need to go to the doctor.

Ma was never one to go to the Doctor's unless she was nearly on death's door - for one thing, for lack of funds. This time, her situation was truly terrible.

> At 2:30 the same severe pain grabbed my arm in the same manner-only this time it was both arms. And this time the pain did not let up. It got worse and worse—like someone screwing a vice tighter and tighter.

When I finally decided I would have to go to the doctor, office hours would be over by the time I could get a taxi. I called the nurse but the last patient was ready to leave. She said come in at 5:45.

So when Heidi came from school I was sitting in the chair with my arms hanging down resting in my lap and tears were rolling down my cheeks—the pain was so severe. She took over Andrew and preparations for dinner and got our neighbor Shirley Davis to drive us to the doctor.

The Doctor took one look at me and my arms. "Jeanne, this is very serious. You don't get sick often but when you do, you're really sick." He gave me a shot and a prescription and told me to go home to bed and come back at noon the next day, adding, "If you aren't 80 percent better by then, you're going in the hospital."

I went home and to bed and slept quite well altho' when I awoke in the morning I could feel my leg muscles grab now and then. It was going into my legs. I said no one needed to stay with me. Ernie was going to come home at noon to eat lunch and take me to the doctor. I did ask him to give me my mother's medical book as I wanted to read about muscular rheumatism so I would know what to expect. As usual, always wanting to know everything! I read about the various stages and saw some illustration of rashes and noticed a sentence which said, "It has to get worse before it gets better." As I stayed in bed, I felt a twitch in my stomach muscles. I thought I better get up and take a bath as I'll surely will have to go to the hospital. The mailman had come, so I put a coat over my robe and went out to the mailbox. Then I thought, I better switch the valve on the oil tank so the furnace would keep running. So, I went down cellar and did that.

So, I started running bath water. Through the years if I had aches and pains, a good hot bath eases pains.

I didn't realize I already had a fever so the extremely hot bath I took was the wrong thing to do. By the time I got partially dressed and fell back on the bed; I was exhausted, extremely weak and in pain.

I kept telling myself, I had to get up and go downstairs as Ernie was coming for lunch. Well, I said to myself, I just want to lie here a little longer. Then it would be a little longer and little longer. Before I knew it, the back doorbell rang.

Ernie had forgotten his key. I tried to get out of bed. The minute I put any weight on my feet, tensing the muscles, I had excruciating pain in my legs. My arms ached and if I leaned on my hands on a chair to take the weight off my legs, my arms hurt even worse. I managed to force myself to get through the door to the hallway. I braced my back against the wall and slowly edged my body along until I got to the stairway. It was extremely painful. In the meantime, Ernie had come around to the front door and pounded on the door. I called to him and said I was having a very hard time and would be there as soon as I could.

I was so proud of myself that I had gotten to the stairway. Little did I realize what a problem it would be to get down the stairs. I thought I could sit down and slide right down.

She pulled herself into a sitting position, and tried to descend the stairs one by one, with each bump, crying out from the pain of the movement. Dad, standing outside the door from the outside, kept trying to break down the door to get to her. It was horrendous.

It was, in fact, polymyositis, an autoimmune attack which results in extreme inflammation and degeneration of the muscles. (It is thought to be an autoimmune reaction or a viral infection of the skeletal muscle.) Ma always used to say it may have been related to rheumatic fever, which she had had as a child. Dr. Dosseff put her in the hospital immediately on cortisone, and some strong painkillers. She remained in the hospital from October 19th until the 31st. The bill was $1,340 – an astronomical sum to us, but fortunately, it was mostly covered by the insurance company. Doctor Dosseff was close to my mother, since she always discussed with him about Bulgaria, and other topics like Europe, etc. He was originally from Bulgaria. She held a special place in his heart and he visited her several times a day to keep a close eye on her and to be sure she was improving. It was a terribly discouraging time for my mother. The pain was so intense, and it was such a long recovery. She had moments of despair, I'm sure, when she wondered if she would survive the illness.

Kjersti came up from college the following weekend to see Ma in the hospital. Beforehand, she went to Bassin's, the Deposit department store, and she bought Ma a necklace with a flower of all different colors, in a circle shape. When Kjer walked in the room, Ma said, "When you came in the room there was a light shining in you, just like Mrs. Luck's but Mrs. Luck's was bigger." When Kjersti gave her the necklace,

Ma exclaimed, ""OH! Those are the <u>exact</u> colors I've been seeing!!!" and she seemed strangely comforted. She told Kjer that at one point, the hospital ceiling dissolved above her, and she saw Grannie, Duane, and others family members who had passed away, smiling down on her, as if to encourage her in the moments most difficult. Some people, of course, thought it was the pain killer drugs she was on. Who knows? I believe God gave her this encouragement to keep going.

As she lay in her hospital bed in terrible pain, she heard a song over the radio, the dentist's office version of "Do you hear what I hear...a Child, a Child, way off in the night, He will bring us Goodness and Light" (a Christmas song in October?). In that instant, a special message of encouragement and Hope resonated deep within Ma in a very dark moment of her life and her eyes filled with tears. Years later, when she heard that song, it reminded her of the profoundly important Light it brought to her, and she mentioned it to me more than once. "He will bring us Goodness and Light."

When Heidi went to see Ma in the hospital, Ma would tell her what food to buy and how to cook dinners, to keep the family going in her absence. Heidi, who was a Senior in high school and just 17 years old, had a full plate keeping up with the housework and her own school work. The school librarian, Mrs. Potter, who was usually very strict about what people did in the library, would let Heidi sleep in peace, her head resting on the table on top of her books. After Ma's hospital stay, when she finally came home, Ma could not even lift her arms to feed herself. Heidi, who was the oldest home at the time, and ever a capable care giver, cared for Ma until she was able to function independently. It was a long road to recovery.

Ma needed help at lunchtime, too, so Heidi's friend Scott Bowen would let her borrow his car, or he would drive her home each day at noon so she could make lunch and feed it to Ma. Once, my mother, frustrated with her lack of independence, said to Heidi, "Let me try now by myself." Heidi gently put the fork in her hand, which she managed to hold, but with the added weight of one single pea, it was too much, and the fork dropped to the plate. It was difficult for my mother to be so weakened, when she was such a strong and independent character. And poor Heidi carried a heavy load in those days. One day, Heidi felt so overwhelmed, in a moment of loneliness, she sat down on the playroom couch and cried her eyes out. She missed Grannie, who would have been an enormous help, but sadly, she had passed away back in February. The tears were flowing, as Heidi cried out a prayer for help. Suddenly, she felt a presence come along beside her, as if sitting on the couch there with her and she was filled with a sense of peace and comfort. What a wonderful, persevering caregiver Heidi was! (Later, she became an excellent nurse.)

While the Lord helped us through that difficult time and things gradually returned to normal, my mother was plagued for the rest of her life by intense pain, especially in her arm muscles, any time she overdid it cleaning or gardening, etc. But the only medicine she ever took was Bayer Aspirin, which she swore by. She also used "Fastum gel" on her muscles, which I always sent from Luxembourg, because at the time it was not available in the USA. But, these two things were certainly inadequate to deal with pain of that level.

Years later, in 1996, she wrote:

All the furniture needs polishing. Usually, I do a little each day but my polymyositis has bothered me so I didn't accomplish much. I was dumb and lifted a storm window to put it in the side porch door.. It takes a certain knack and I went ahead and did it standing on a stool...Anyway, that lamed me up more than usual.

I cannot imagine living with that illness every day, especially with Ma being such an active soul.

However, she never let the fear of being in pain stop her from doing things like playing cards with us.

One of our pastimes was listening to the radio and playing cards together. Our favorite was "Group Solitaire," playing out on each other's aces. It was total chaos, with cards flying and one screaming at the other, "CHEATER, you used two hands!"... or, after being beaten by someone playing the same card, "FATHEAD!" Even after Ma had her polymyositis, she always insisted on playing with us, and often won (unless Heidi was in on the game). Her arms would ache for days afterwards, but the fun of playing made it worthwhile to her.

We played other games together in the living room after dinner. Ma was fantastic at playing Trivial Pursuit. She'd win every time. Her memory was incredible. Whether it was history, politics, films, you name it, she was awesome. The only one coming close was Beau. Another game she loved was Dictionary, where you would look up a word, and everyone would make up what they thought it meant, or some totally absurd but official-sounding definition (such as, "A South African piss-ant"). Then, all the invented definitions were read aloud by one person and you'd guess which was the true definition, etc. Sometimes, when the bunch was grown, we'd come home for holiday weekends and play charades in the living room. Ma would gesture and act out her thought wordlessly, and sometimes laugh until she'd wet her pants. She'd say, "I'm gonna' bust a gusset in a minute," the tears rolling down her face, as she rushed to the bathroom. We really had a lot of fun together.

Another game Ma liked was the Ball game, a homemade wooden cross-shaped game with big marbles and dice. She often played it with John and Marguerite Lee, Birdie's parents who lived not so far from us in Roods Creek. She'd laugh as she said to old John, "I'm sendin' ya home, John," when she landed in the right spot. As they'd begin a new game she'd call out, "Suckers to the Hub," which meant who knows what, maybe losers get to go first? And speaking of games, how could I forget! Ma loved Scrabble and was a fierce competitor. You *were* allowed to look up words in the dictionary, too, so the game was educational. With the waiting for others to play, it also taught patience.

Ma loved Nature and she loved flowers and birds. She was thrilled when I gave her a small bird book from my ornithology class at college, as she enjoyed watching the birds so much. In a letter she wrote, "All the birds except the orioles are back. They come in May along with the scarlet tanagers, etc. We've had a lot of cardinals this year."

Earlier the same year she wrote, "I sure enjoy the birds. Have had scads of birds. Had to get extra bird feed. I think maybe I'll get a bird bath some time to put in the yard summers. Grandma Rood had one near her beautiful English style flower gardens. She had a sidewalk down the center and 2 more sidewalks down each half. On each side of the walkways were thick flowerbeds. The paths led to a little pond with fish. The Methodist church women used to ask her for flowers for the altar. She had all kinds of lilies, gladiolas, phlox, daisies, peonies, poppies, lilacs, pansies, forget-me-nots."

Ma's Grandma Rood was a "frail, slight little thing" who loved flower gardening. Ma did too. She had absolutely loved picking flowers of all colors and types as a child. She kept a beautiful bleeding-heart plant in her garden by our house, which grew to an incredible size.

My bleeding heart bushes were terrific this year… so big and full of blossoms, she wrote, "In Norwegian, they call them *Løytnantshjerter*" which means "Lieutenant's Hearts" probably because of soldiers separated from their wives or girlfriends. I've always liked bleeding hearts. When I was a little girl and went with Grandma to visit an elderly lady way up Rood's Creek, I was fascinated by her bush with the little hearts on it. Had never seen one before. I was probably about 5 or 6 years old. Although both my grandmothers had flowers (Grandma Rood had a huge, English style garden with all kinds of flowers and other bushes on the property line) neither of them had bleeding hearts.

The flowers Kjersti planted are still in full bloom - they keep repeating and regrowing, impatients, etc.

I think all of us girls are like Mom, we love planting flowers. She always had crocuses, daffodils, honeysuckle, and she loved brown-eyed Susan's and Japanese lanterns. She ran out of the kitchen at break neck speed when Dad would mow the lawn over by the burn barrel, where the Japanese lanterns spread out. "He's worse than a bull in a China closet," she'd mutter in disgust, as she walked back to the house, glad to have saved her flowers once more from the deadly mower and its oblivious driver.

Besides gardening, Ma kept a lot of plants in the house, often the flowering kind. She had a huge green fern in the living room, up on a pedestal stand. I think it had been Grannie's, but I'm not quite sure. As a kid, I was somewhat in awe yet tempted by that inhumanly large fern hanging its arms down to the floor. Ma instructed us *never* to touch it. To me, it already looked sickly with skinny long arms of green pallor. I always wondered, *if I touch it, will it really die?!* Or would *I?*

When I left for university, she always kept me informed about the state of my flowerbed by the side porch, looking down to the valley. She gently cared for the daffodils I loved too. She wrote, "Some of the daffodils grew up right through the leaves so I had to carefully pull the leaves up or tear them off to remove them so I wouldn't ruin the blossoms." Gentleness of heart graced her care of family and friends, too, and flowed from a soul formed by a loving Father from Above, through both the darkest and brightest of days.

HOMEMAKING, HAZARDS, AND HAPPINESS

What was it like to be a homemaker in the 1970s? Mom wrote the following letter for the "Ladies Home Journal." It must have been requested that ladies send in a composition with the title, "I am a Homemaker." At that time, Ma still had 3 teenagers at home, plus Julie, who was seven. She writes well and I just love her humor and insights about raising children.

R.D. 1, Box 7
Deposit, N.Y. 13754
August 3, 1976
Dear Editor:

Homemaking is perhaps the most important career of all. To be a homemaker you have to be lover, cook, charwoman, nurse, doctor, economist, chauffeur, mediator, guidance counselor, diplomat and interior decorator - - sometimes carpenter, plumber and gardener. It can be fun, challenging, rewarding, boring, strenuous and frustrating. The rewards far outweigh the disadvantages.

I was a career girl with an unusually interesting life working at an embassy, experiencing the excitement of wartime Washington and attending receptions studded with diplomats and royalty. It was exciting to shake hands with a future King but nothing compared to the thrill of hearing the cry of my first baby when she was born years later.

Housekeeping doesn't have to be just dishes, diapers and drudgery. Life is what you make it by your attitudes and actions. While performing boring tasks, memories of enriching past experiences can soften discouragement when things seem hopeless. There can be long periods of childhood illnesses with sleepless nights when bills mount higher and higher and the whole house seems a mess. But one vital aspect of homemaking is being there when needed.

Teenagers need their parents as much as small children do. It is important to encourage or reprimand at the right moment. - - discipline not for discipline's sake but to teach endurance to cope with future situations. If the moment is lost, the significance of their complaints or enthusiasm is lost. I had a happy childhood but I still remember how cold and empty our house felt on days my Mother was substitute teacher and we children arrived home ahead of her.

To me the most difficult part of homemaking is trying to figure out how to get enough groceries and still have money left for doctor bills and other necessities. One has to be frugal and economical to the point of austerity.

Although many things must be done on schedule, a homemaker can adjust her work for periods of reading and relaxation. A housewife can do much for family, friends, and community. When local officials and service organizations neglect to act on air pollution or other public interest problems, she can find time to write letters, make phone calls, instigate petitions and contact proper authorities to accomplish some good for the area. While waiting for the washer to finish, she can take five minutes to call a lonely, elderly person for a chat.

By making your home a place where strength and faith can be renewed you render a valuable service.

A contented husband and children with a pleasant home atmosphere will have better attitudes toward work, school and the world in general than someone who has an unstable existence.

How wonderful to have the opportunity to be of service to family, friends and community - - to make life more pleasant for others, sharing their problems and griefs but rejoicing in their happinesses and triumphs. It's like living more than one life. Homemakers of America are truly making a contribution to the integrity and destiny of our nation.

Sincerely, (Mrs. Ernie) Jeanne R. Hoff

My mother truly had a servant-heart: she cared for us in so many ways: in times of trouble, accident or illness.

When children get sick, it can be awfully hard on the parents. How many hours did my mother spend sponging off foreheads, measuring temperatures, spooning out anti-fever medication, and worrying about convulsions? It is terribly scary for parents, wondering how things will turn out and seeing your kids suffer. You don't even think about it until you have kids of your own. Whenever you're sick, it's your mother you want. At night, when I occasionally had nightmares, I wanted the security associated with my father, but when I wasn't well, it was Ma I wanted, she was the great comforter. She would spoil me when I was sick at home with a seriously bad cold. Even though it was nothing more dramatic than a runny nose and a cough with a fever, she showed a lot of sympathy and tenderness, which was better than any medicine. She'd make delicious chicken noodle soup (heated up from a can) and carry it up to my room on a tray with a tall glass of cold milk and saltine crackers.

One time, I must have been in quite a bad way, and when she came home from a trip to town, she brought me an adorable little stuffed red bulldog which I cherished. Maybe that was when I had the mumps, and my face swelled up like a globe of the world. My sisters and brother came in to laugh at the sight, and Ma shooed them all away like flies being a nuisance. (I was *surely* marked for life by my siblings, but then again, who isn't? Ask my brother about the time Celia tied him up, dressed him in Ma's bra and underclothes and then threw him downstairs, looking like a lingerie model, in front of all the ladies my mother had invited over for afternoon tea. It's a wonder he survived five sisters.)

I have to say, neither Celia nor I were so much trouble in terms of illnesses or accidents. The worst case I had was a "misunderstanding" about an appendix (they actually did take it out. Dr. Dosseff said it was the strangest thing, only one small tip of the appendix was slightly inflamed. But that is another story.) Well, come to think of it, I did have a few biking accidents, too. I once got lightly hit by a car while riding my bike. I was trying hard to keep up with Heidi and the neighbor boy, Brad Davis, as they turned left to go up the ramp which led into Uncle Al's barn. I didn't look behind me to see that Mrs. Mills' blue station wagon was just passing by. She was driving slowly, and I wasn't hurt at all, just shook up a bit (maybe not as much as Mrs. Mills, who felt terrible.) There was no blood, and Ma didn't see it happen, so I don't think she was too upset.

Oh yes, and I had another bike accident one summer, which was a bit messier. My sister Heidi, friend Deb Feehan, and I were riding our bikes back home from town. When we got to the top of the big hill to turn left to descend River Road, I insisted to switch bikes and ride down the hill on Deb Feehan's new "banana" seat bike. It was OH SO COOL! Its seat was the shape of an exclamation point without the dot, and the handlebars were tall, curving things of wonder. Riding down the steep hill, my exhilaration turned to horror as I felt the bike beginning to wobble, and before I knew it, I had flipped over the top. I cried uncontrollably, as I fumbled on the ground, groping for my glasses. (I was blind as a bat without them).

Heidi and Deb were quickly by my side, and asked me if I was badly hurt. All I could answer between sobs was, "My glasses! My glasses! Ma's gonna' kill me!" Being somewhat of a tomboy, I went through a lot of glasses, having worn them from the age of 6. They were not cheap in those days either, especially for a family without a lot of money. However, when Ma saw my bloodied arms and knees, the last thing on her mind was my silly glasses. I remember clearly her pained expression as I lay on the couch in the playroom and she poured mercurochrome on my raw wounds to avoid infection. It stung like the devil. She said, "I'm awfully sorry Mags, but I have to do this." Poor Ma.

Keeping a large family from falling into chaos took a lot of energy and endurance. She faced it all like a mature soldier in battle. Ma was by no means a "squeamish" person: she never seemed to mind cleaning up babies' diapers, or the messes from our stomach viruses. It was like falling dominoes in our big family: the "puking bug" would pass from one kid to the next, until the entire household had succumbed, running to the bathroom with the speed of star athletes.

There were other more humorous events which took place in that bathroom: I'll never forget the time when Julie was small, like one year old, and she and one of my sisters were taking a bath together. I walked into the bathroom when all of a sudden, a series of small, round brown floaties appeared on the water's surface. "What the...." I started to say and before I finished, she shrieked and leapt from the bath like a young gazelle, while Julie looked up at us from the bathtub smiling benignly. Of course, it was Ma to the rescue to clean things up, and it was the last time anyone bathed with the little darlin' Julie.

Between the lot of us kids, Ma had plenty of scares from mishaps and illnesses over the years. Once Harald (we call him Beau) had a terrible collision with another boy playing football during school lunch: he was covered with blood and had a bad concussion. (He was so badly injured, my sister did not recognize him as they went past her in the hall, carrying him to the nurse's office.)

One sister had dreadful migraine headaches. She had to stay in bed in a darkened room, motionless, all curtains drawn. Then she was once terribly ill with cerebral meningitis. It was so bad, Ma brought in each of us kids to her hospital bed, as if to say goodbye, in case our sister didn't make it. Our family Doctor Dosseff, a somewhat eccentric but capable physician, was away, so Ma had been obliged to take her to another Doctor, who had diagnosed German measles or something. Thank the Lord Dr. Dosseff got back and immediately recognized her illness. As Ma said, he saved my sister's life.

Later, there were lots of doctor and hospital visits with another sister, who had kidney stones. One time she came draggin' herself up the hallway and dropped in front of two of us sisters, fainting away. It was like something out of a movie, kind of in slow motion, and we thought she was acting, for we were always rather dramatic and playing games of the like.

(For example, Kjer used to pretend she had a bar in the backroom by the upstairs bathroom. She served her customers, Heidi and I, colored water "drinks" and stood up on the table, garishly clad singing, "Fev-uh, fev-uh in the middle of the night ya give me feeeeevuh" or "Brandy, you're a fine girl, what a gooood wife, you would be, but alas my love and my lady, it's the s-e-e-a!).

So, with our tendancy towards drama, we thought this girl was playing: we nudged her somewhat roughly with our feet and said, "Get up, we know you're fakin' it," but when she didn't move, our hearts filled with dread and we ran for Ma. In fact, she had probably just passed a kidney stone, poor thing.

Another sister got hepatitis as a child. After that diagnosis, Celia remembers that Ma rounded us all up to go to Dr. Muia for shots. All us kids trooped in the office behind Dad. Since Celia hated needles, she was very nervous. Dr. Muia said, "We'll do your Dad, first. See," he said, leaving the needle *hanging* in Dad's arm, "it doesn't hurt a bit!" Celia was appalled.

Besides doctor visits, there were *rare* visits to the dentist in the nearby town of Walton. The eight of us packed into the car, many a heart trembling with fear and trepidation. Time for the "come-up'ins" of not brushing your teeth as often as you should have. Once, Daddy had to stop the car on the twenty-minute drive home, so I could vomit from all the blood that filled my mouth after one such dental visit. Afterwards, Ma would pat my hand gently and say, "You'll be alright, Mags."

Ma must've thought the worse was over when just one child remained. Julie lived at home while taking classes at Oneonta State University of New York when she got a terrible illness. At first it wasn't recognized but turned out to be viral meningitis. She was extremely ill and spent several days in the hospital in Binghamton. My mother was so distraught, she spent the first night with her at the hospital. Celia, who was already married and living in New Jersey, took time off to be there to support my parents. Poor Ma and Daddy went through a lot with us.

She truly was a good mom, taking care of us physically, "in sickness and in health." Like all mothers, she never had "time off." She didn't seem to catch colds or viruses often, or if she did, I suppose we didn't notice. We definitely *did* notice her sneezing spells however. She would start with one or two powerful "ACHOOO"'s, and sometimes they just kept on coming. She'd say it was "the Sixteen Sneezes" and called it hereditary, she'd inherited it from one of her relatives (I don't remember which one. I suppose it skips generations: my daughter had it in her early years, and it always made us laugh, we both ended up in giggles.)

Besides illnesses and accidents: mothers deal with chaos and disorder. There were *plenty* of messes to clean up with all of us under one roof. The house was enormous, but Ma managed to keep things under control, at least most of the time. Keeping up with all the housework, minding several kids, a dog, a cat and a husband, was not easy. Think of the laundry she had to manage: 14 loads per week, and for years without a clothes dryer! We hung the wet clothes outside on the clothesline, pinning them up with wooden clothespins. There were times when the water from the well become progressively full of iron, making it impossible to keep clothes white. At that time, she had to take all the white clothes in to the town laundromat to clean them there. Often, she took one of us with her, more for company than to help.

Julie remembers a time she came home from school and Ma was making up beds. Julie sat on one of the big double beds, which had only the bottom sheet on it, and she was overwhelmed with the strong smell of perfume. "Ma, what are you up to now?!" she asked. The coy look on Ma's face was enough of an answer. Ma had washed sheets at home but it had rained, so she didn't manage to get them all hung up outside in time to dry promptly. Some sheets had turned slightly "sour" waiting to be hung outside (we still had no clothes dryer then). She figured the perfume would help her avoid re-washing them. "Necessity's the mother of invention," she said with a laugh.

There is a memory of my mother Julie cherishes from when she was small, but longed desperately to be "big." Julie had wanted to help Ma put things away after a meal. There was a big container of something on the table, and Julie asked if she could carry it into the pantry, to put in the refrigerator. "I'm a big girl, Mommy, I can carry it," she said with confidence. Ma said, "Thank you, Honey, but I don't think so, that's too big for you." When Ma's back was turned, Julie picked it up and went around into the pantry, promptly dropping it on the floor. Nothing broke, but the stuff spilled all over the place. When Ma came around the corner, she saw the look of horror on Julie's face, and instead of being angry, got down on the floor, and began writing letters in the mess! Julie's chagrin was transformed to joy, in the fun of writing nearly the whole alphabet together on the floor before Ma cleaned up the mess.

Despite all the effort required to manage a large family, Ma was also active in local environmental issues. There was a factory (at the time called Celotex Corporation), across the river from our house, which often contaminated the air at night with small particulates. We'd wake up in the morning to see something like a fine white snow covering the car in the middle of summer. Ma, and friends like Bev Zandt, (my best school friend Julie's mother, who also lived near the factory and experienced the particulates problem) fought for many years to reduce the pollution. Ma took daily notes about air conditions, wrote letters, got signatures, contacted government officials and never gave up until things really did improve. The factory management knew her voice by heart. "They try sweet-talking me sometimes," she said, "But it never works with me!" The mother of Ma's friend Edie used to say that Ma was "just like Knubby, her father, who used to really give it his all, when working for a cause." Mom's work with the factory really did reduce pollution, different filtering systems were put in place and afterwards, a gift of 2,000$ was "presented as a gift for the new microfilm machine in the Deposit Free Library" from Norbord Industries (they took over after Celotex). Mom, representing the library board, had her picture taken in the Deposit Courier newspaper.

Besides teaching us to respect and to take care of the planet, Ma always tried to get us to keep our rooms neat and tidy, to put things away. "Everything has its place" she would say. From time to time, she'd get fed up with my messy room and order me to go and clean it up. "If you'd quit slattin' your things around, it wouldn't get into that mess," she'd say in a slightly exasperated voice. She also taught us to take care of our possessions and to appreciate all that we had. One time, Ma scolded Julie for "abusing her toys." Julie had been playing in the sandy dirt with her Barbie dolls and left them there, going inside for some reason. When Ma came home from the grocery store, she nearly dropped the bags of food she was carrying, when she looked down and saw the smiling faces of several Barbie heads sticking up from the dirt, the rest of their bodies buried beneath.

Mom used to send us outside to play when the weather allowed. This was good for our souls as well as her sanity. We didn't have the massive number of toys that kids have today, so we used to invent a lot of games to play. "Binoculars," my brother Beau's creation, involved whoever was "it" sitting in a lawn chair up in the field far from the woods, and using binoculars to identify a sibling down below. We were down at the edge of the woods, and had to pass through a certain clearing without being recognized. You would slither along in the dirt to get to the other side trying to remain unseen. How my heart pounded as I writhed my way across, hoping not to hear Beau's voice call out from up in the field, "I see Maggie going across!" Our clothes were filthy after that game: that meant more laundry for Mom.

Another game called "Moles" which we played inevitably got us into trouble ironically due to the noise. Ma and Daddy always watched the news in the playroom after dinner "to know what's going on in the world" she said. It also gave them a moment of peace. But sometimes, we kids would turn off the lights in the nearby dining room and get down on our hands and knees. We would crawl around wordlessly in the dark, in and around the enormous dining room table legs, feigning blindness and weaving between the chairs playing "Moles" in complete silence, aside from an occasional escaping giggle. Somebody would inevitably bang into the table or knock over a chair with a loud crack just as Walter Cronkite said, "And that's the way it is," and Ma yelled out, "What in the Sam Hill are you kids *doin'* in there?! You kids quit your mucksin'!!"

We truly played a lot of games amongst ourselves. I do not remember games Ma played with us during our younger childhood years; she had all she could do to keep up with housework and caring for us. But Kjersti remembers her playing Duck-Duck-Goose with them when we lived in Endwell (I was too small to remember). She can still picture Ma's smiling face as she ran around the circle in her summer shorts. When we were older, she taught us lots of wonderful and exciting games to play, like Old Grey Wolf, Kick the Can, etc. When we were older, she loved to get us into a game of Trivial Pursuit, Dictionary, or Charades.

In winter, the river occasionally partially froze. But in the winter of 1968, when I was 5 years old, it was extremely cold and the river froze over entirely. We ice skated nearly every day that winter, and sometimes even Ma and Daddy joined us.

We all remember one brilliant winter day Ma came out to enjoy a miraculous event with us. There had been lots of snow, and then it warmed up suddenly and briefly rained, followed by an abrupt drop in temperature. The surface of the snow froze solid. The entire yard was like a huge skating rink. Most of us kids put on our skates and went everywhere over the fields surrounding the house. Ma bundled up Julie who was real little, about 3 or 4 years old, and put her on the old sled. She pulled it up to the top of the driveway, and then sat down on the sled holding Julie in front of her. They rode all the way down the driveway, curving right down by the old apple tree, passed in front of the little red cottage, down the field, all the way down to the neighbor's back yard, not far from the Delaware river which flowed behind the houses on that side of River Road. Ma and Julie laughed loudly all the way and Vesla, our sweet Saint Bernard, ran alongside, barking her encouragement. It was an unforgettable day of our childhood and quite the adventure for us all.

I wonder if this kind of "adventure" seemed boring to Ma after the interesting career days she had experienced in the nation's capital city, Washington, D.C., New York City or in Norway. Did she regret having given all of that up? I know that she certainly did *not* find housekeeping in itself to be fulfilling, but who does!? Ma would rather have been reading or visiting with a friend, or playing a game with us than cooking. She worked so hard to keep things in order, but sometimes things did not get done as she would have liked. She wisely kept it in perspective, for as she once said, "...As my Dad used to say, 'Nobody will know the difference 100 years from now'." Amen to that.

Now that I'm older, I think about how it must have been for her, in those years of her life. The frustration of having to cook and then clean and clean again and find all you'd done had to be done all over again! I hardly noticed all the times she'd bring me my clean, folded clothes, passing from room to room to hand them to each of us. We simply took it for granted, like children

264

do. How many times did she help resolve our crisis moments, which children often have as they grow? It must have been so draining at times.

As mentioned earlier, Mom's faith in God grounded her life. In moments of difficulty, she found comfort in the faith of her youth, and sang hymns that she never forgot, like "Sing them over again to me, wonderful words of Life, let me more of their beauty see, wonderful words of Life…."

MEMORIES & MOTHERHOOD

Family life is not all wonderful: indeed, everyone has moments of feeling down or disappointed. Living with pain as Mom did after 1977 surely multiplied the moments of seeing the world all in grey. Plus, when Grannie died that February, it was a terrible loss for us all but especially for my mother, who had been so very close with her.

So, how did she keep such a positive attitude so often? She was always singing or telling a story about something. Sure, she'd lose her temper occasionally, that fiery Rood temper, and you could see the passionate person she was. Did she ever wish she had not fallen for my father, did she ever long for those carefree days of dating and courting? (She had countless men after her in her glory days in Washington and in Norway.)

I also wonder, had Ma struggled with the whole issue of aging? When she was a few months from 40 and had me, did it make her feel "young" again? (I *seriously* doubt that!) What about when Julie appeared on the scene when Ma was almost 46? The struggle to make ends meet also put such a strain on her. The added mouths to feed were surely a source of additional worry. Certainly, she loved all her children, and always loved us as we were, guiding us by and to Christian values without forcing us into something we were not willing to choose for ourselves. But did she feel love from us all to help lift her from the inevitable moments of sadness? What did she do when she felt the desperate need for solitude or when she felt exhausted from giving and giving to her family?

In January 1980, Ma wrote a short essay in one of her notebooks which illustrates some of how she coped by grabbing a moment of quiet when she could, looking back on good memories, and finding peace, knowing she would see her loved ones again:

> For some reason, all week I had been thinking about Grandma Travis's fried cakes. I hadn't made them for several years. Friday I bought some buttermilk and decided to make them on Saturday morning when everyone would be gone and it would be peaceful and quiet. Bo was only one home and he was upstairs sleeping.
>
> I got out the recipe I had gotten from Grandma years ago (42 years ago to be exact) and it all went fine. The dough seemed to be the right consistency. It was almost as if Grandma was standing by my elbow urging me on. As the grease became hot enough, all the memories flooded back. How you slide the doughnuts carefully down the side of the kettle so as not to splash the hot grease and how they'll first sink to the bottom and how you turn them over quickly as soon as they rise to the top. Then you have to turn them once again.
>
> The secret of Gram's fried cakes is thickness - - good and thick - - almost double those you buy in the store.
>
> What a pleasant hour I had. It was almost like being in Gram's kitchen.
>
> Later that night I kept wondering. Why was I so obsessed with Gran's fried cakes right now. Why not last month or next week? Then it dawned on me as I glanced at the calendar.
>
> It was Saturday January 19th - - Gram's Birthday!! Then I thought how there has to be a hereafter where I'll meet my dear Gram again. She was one of the dearest persons in my life - - my friend, my pal, my comforter, my disciplinarian, but most of all my loving, understanding Gram.

Ma wrote down the following thoughts a few years after her mom, our Grannie, had passed away. She was still missing her mother and her Grandma Kate. (Grief lasts for years, when you've been truly loved.) The questions she wished she could ask her beloved Grandma were perhaps echoes of questions she was asking of her own life.

Gram's Bed July 17, 1980
> I wish I could dial ME 7–2517 and find Grannie at the end of the line - or 503F 21 and hear Gram's cheerful "Hello." But that would be magic. I miss my Gram Travis - Grandma Kate - Aunt Kate to so many in the surrounding area. There's so much I would like to talk with her about.

I wonder how she felt when she sat home alone with Gramp and (her son) Nelson in that 17-room house - - after all the years of activity and hard work raising eight kids. I wonder whether she thought it was worth it. Did the joys outweigh the disappointments and struggles? When she sat with meager means after the early and middle years of plenty- -with sable fur stole and muff and the best of marble bathroom fixtures, etc. and trips here and there. Was she glad she had married Gramp? What did she think about as she designed and sewed her quilt blocks by the picture window?

How much I learned from Gram! So many times I can remember her saying "When you're my age you'll understand," or "When you have children of your own, you'll understand!"

A couple of weeks ago, Ernie, Julie and I went to visit Astrid. When Ernie and I went to bed the first night, I thought perhaps I couldn't sleep too well in a strange bed. Since I have been afflicted with muscular rheumatism it seems my nerves are near the surface and I can feel everything twice as intensely. Therefore, I have to find the right degree of softness or hardness on which to lie.

The minute I got in bed, it all felt so familiar. The certain characteristics of a mattress and old-fashioned coil springs, the thick fluffy pillow, slightly stiff and then the slant of the bed when Ernie got settled. I kept rolling into his back as the mattress slanted with his weight. I felt right at home. What was it!? And then I closed my eyes and there it was! I remembered the times I stayed with Gram and slept with her. I was sleight of build and only 8 - 10 years old and her weight used to make the bed slant. How many memories of Gram & Gramp and the days at the Homestead flooded back. I hadn't thought of Gram's bed in all these years - - and the cozy, secure, all's well with the world feeling I used to know at those times.

(Oh! I know *just* what she meant, for I, too, remember that feeling at my own Grannies' apartment: waking up on a Saturday morning in her bed, feeling so utterly content and safe. I still miss Grannie, too.)

Ma ruminated on her happiest memories from time to time, and expressed her important thoughts by writing them down – possibly a therapeutic action. Most of the time, she kept a grateful heart for both past and present with all she learned along the way. Like all of us, she had moments of bitterness. Yet she found a certain peace in living for the moment and its goodness while remembering and being grateful for the past. Mom had to bear some great difficulties, but she didn't bury herself in them; instead, she cherished the joyful moments of family life, too.

Consider also this essay about being a mother, which Ma wrote when she was 61 years old. I don't know what the occasion was, but it gives wonderful insight into the approach and methods she used in raising us, as well as the challenges she faced. There *was* a satisfaction that came from the importance of raising kids to be worthy human beings.

There's an old saying that says: "A son is your son until he takes him a wife but a daughter's a daughter all of your life."

There is and can be very special feeling between Mother and Daughter. When you happen to be the mother of five daughters, you soon learn that each one is different. They may have some of the same characteristics, but each is a personality all her own. I always treated my girls the way my Mother treated me and in turn, she had learned from her mother.

The developing relationship between mother and daughter depends on how you treat your child. First, it's necessary to shower a lot of love and affection on the small child. Little children need to feel secure. At the same time, it is necessary to have a code of ethics and morals which in turn includes discipline. If you don't discipline your children from the time they are very small, you can run into problems. By discipline I don't mean spanking or brute force (although in the very early years spanking may be necessary in order to make them understand) but you should show them firm but kind discipline. It's all in the way you administer it or in the tone of your voice. It's very good training because when the children are grown and go out in to the world on their own, a disciplined person can cope much easier with the world and people in general.

To raise a large family can be very hectic, strenuous and exhausting but it also can be fun, exhilarating, rewarding and educational.

Raising a large family requires a great deal of innovation. One example: at breakfast time there was constant bickering about the cereal. They would accuse one another of taking too much so there wasn't enough left for someone else. I finally put a halt to that. I asked each child to tell me what kind of cereal she wanted and then I bought each one their own individual box and put their name on. That way no one could accuse anyone of taking too much.

One needs a lot of patience and understanding. I remember when we lived in Endwell, there was something that happened in the neighborhood. Cecilia had not reacted to the situation the way I would have reacted. Not that she did anything wrong, but she hadn't been as kind as I thought she should have been. My friend and neighbor, Marge Caddick said: "Jeanne, you've got to realize that Cecilia is a person in herself. She's part of you, but she isn't you!" I've always remembered that.

I personally feel that it is very important for a child early on to be exposed to good religious training. If you practice your religion and it permeates your home, it will give a certain atmosphere which will seem a natural thing and will be another source of security for the child in later years. It's a joy to me to see Cecilia's little girl Mishawn being trained the same way (Vacation Bible School).

From an early age, children coy or ape their parents. A small child is usually very observant of the mother's actions or way of life.

Almost before the children could walk, we introduced them to books and music. When they were through the cloth book stage, I bought 15 cents hard cover books. They would sit in the playpen and turn the pages. We read to them a great deal and as each child learned to read, she would often read to the younger ones. The girls loved to sing and harmonize. Music became an important part of their life. They learned to play various musical instruments and participated in band and orchestra. Kjersti, Heidi and Maggie belonged to 4H. One year they won the Golden Music award for harmonizing hymns at old folks Home in Delhi (Ages 13, 11, and 9).

We taught our children our way of life. We had certain rules and regulations but each child was handled according to her personality. An approach that worked with one didn't work with another but you soon learned how best to handle each one. I remember when we lived in Endwell, my little red head Kjersti was 3 years old - - very sweet, thoughtful child but with quite a strong temper. One day she threw herself down on the floor at the top of the stairs and threw a tantrum kicking and screaming. I didn't say a word, I just walked into the bathroom and got a large glass of cold water and poured it on her face. I don't know if this would work with others but she never threw a tantrum after that. I learned that trick from Granma Travis. She raised 5 boys and 3 girls. All but 2 of them had red hair!!

I used to say I could understand why there were so many spoiled children or permissive parents. The parents just got tired and worn out and said the heck with it. It's strenuous to be persevering but it does have its rewards.

Our children had various pets through the years, everything from a cat named Johan to a St. Bernard who liked to look at TV with them.

We always gathered in the dining room for dinner. This became our forum where the school aged children voiced their opinion or discussed happenings of the day. It was the girls' job to do the supper dishes. We would all clear the table. I would put the food away and they would take turns washing and drying. It was during these kitchen sessions that we had some of our most interesting discussions. As the years went by and times changed, and the outside world became a tougher place, it was necessary to adjust to a different method of handling the girls. During one of these kitchen sessions, when the subject came up of a Senior High girl who was pregnant, I said how sad it was for her but I made the somewhat unexpected comment that "she who indulges, bulges!" You'd have thought I had dropped a bomb. So even though Maggie was only 5 at the time she was getting her education. This would have been inappropriate when I was growing up but in the ever-growing permissiveness, etc., and the world as it is, I found it was the best way to get a point across. Cecilia used to say, "Mom preaches a sermon at the drop of a hat!"

As my girls got older, they had certain chores they had to do. Sometimes it was spring or fall or we were expecting company, I would get my crew working - - dusting, washing windows, and tidying up. They each had an equal amount. Then I would say, there are some volunteer jobs which I'll pay you for. You don't have to volunteer. Heidi, although she was only 7 or 8 at the time was the one who volunteered the most and did the best job of washing woodwork or scrubbing the bathroom sinks, etc.

It was during and after some of these work sessions that the girls composed a song which they used to sing – and still do when they get to-gether:

We are Mother's slaves
We live in cold caves
We keep the house as neat as a pin
Or else we get our heads bashed in!'
(to the tune of "We are Santa's Elves")

But it was all in fun. We had lots of fun. We played all kinds of games with the children depending on their ages. We still enjoy playing cards, Masterpiece, Clue, Trivial Pursuit and many other games.

However, it wasn't all fun and games. It was a lot of hard work. Some of the children were growing up but we still had a child in diapers and I had to average 14 loads of laundry every week, not counting curtains and bedspreads. There were long stretches of illness like one winter when twice for 3 weeks at a time my sleep was interrupted every night giving medicine or sponging off a feverish child. There were times of serious illness like cerebral meningitis and pneumonia. Sometimes the whole house was a mess and ironing and bills were piled sky high. There were days when I wondered what I was doing in this situation. I had been a career girl for 9 ½ years, 4 of which I lived in Norway.

I had known the excitement of wartime Washington. During my years in the Diplomatic Corps, I experienced the thrill of attending receptions and parties studded with diplomats. It was exciting to shake hands with a future King and to see royalty close at hand - - but nothing could compare to the thrill of hearing my first baby's cry as she made her arrival known years later.

I often thought of cousin Libby as she had admonished us girls in the whirl of dates in Washington. "Don't just get married and bury yourselves in diapers and tedious housework!" Well, life is what you make it. Babies or no babies, I read books, I played Bridge and whenever the Norwegian newspapers arrived from overseas, I dropped my mop and caught up on happenings in my favorite corner of Europe.

Eventually, I was a spokesman and secretary for an anti-pollution group and was soon known as either that wonderful Environmental lady or the kookie anti-industry radical. My youngest daughter was in diapers at that time.

This is a different world today. I think it's more difficult to raise a family now - - especially teenagers. Also, some mothers find it absolutely necessary to work. Although working mothers were not unheard-of years ago, they made up a very small percentage of the work force.

My mother was a school teacher. When I was very small my Grandmother Travis kept me during the day so I was very content. The first 3 years I attended school, my mother was my teacher. I had to call her Mrs. Rood and she was extremely strict with me - - more so than with the other pupils. A few years later when my mother didn't work full time, it was a different story. I can still remember how cold and empty our house felt on the days she was substitute teacher at school and we children arrived home ahead of her. I feel so sorry for those latch key children in the cities who don't have a kind baby sitter to come home to these days.

My girls now range in age from 29 to 15. Three of them are married. Two are still working. One is an Army Officer; one is a practical nurse and dental technician. The 3rd has a degree and could teach high school science and English but has chosen to stay home with her 2 small sons until they are of school age. The 4th will graduate from Houghton College on May 13th. The 5th is here with me and is a sophomore in high school.

As I reflect on my years of raising 5 girls and one son, I believe more than ever "to everything there is a season*". Every aspect of life has a charm if we can but comprehend it at the time, especially how important it is to have a sense of humor.

I never cared for Rock music but I was a great Jitterbug in my younger days. My youngest daughter, Julie, taught me a rock routine one day not too long ago. Last December Ernie and I attended a dinner dance with Heidi and her husband and some Norwegian friends their age. About half-way through the evening, the band started playing "We're Gonna Rock This Town." One of the younger Norwegians asked me to dance. I didn't hesitate as it was the rock song to Julie's routine. When we sat down, Heidi said: "Mom, are you all right?" "Yes," I said, "I'm just a little winded." The husband of one of Heidi's friends just stared at me with his mouth open. I guess he didn't think a 61-year-old grandmother could dance rock!

*Ecclesiastes 3:1 "To every thing there is a season, and a time to every purpose under the heaven." KJV

MOM'S LOVE AFFAIR

From the moment Ma arrived in Norway that first time, a lifetime love affair began. Even twenty years later, her longing to return was unquenched. Finally, by July 1978, Ma had recovered enough from the illness which struck the previous October. A trip to Norway was now conceivable. The long-awaited return to her beloved land was made possible financially through the help of close friends she had kept in touch with in Norway.

It was a wonderful trip, on her own, full of friends, family and good food, playing cards and catching up. Despite all the visiting, she still found time to read several books - in Norwegian, of course.

In the space of one month, she would visit Oslo, Trondheim, the delightful island of Hitra near Trondheim, Røros, Kristiansund, and Larvik. (The last time she had been in Norway was when Beau and Celia were little – in the late 1950s. There appears to be no journal from that trip, which could be explained by the fact she was running after two little ones: not just *any* two little ones, but Celia and Beau!) In her 1978 notebook she wrote:

> Arrived in Bergen at 8:15 Norwegian time. Walked around 40 minutes. As I got off the plane, I realized I was humming a tune, "I'll be seeing you" - some coincidence.
> *I'll be seeing you*
> *In all the old familiar places*
> *That this heart of mine embraces*
> *All day through*

(This 1938 Song became a WW2 hit when Bing Crosby recorded it in 1944.)

From Bergen she took a plane to Gardermoen airport near Oslo. "The Tranøys met me, then we drove to Irene's. Dear, sweet Irene looked so thin and fragile but wonderful." Ma had shared an apartment with Irene (Smith) years ago in Oslo. Irene had been an operetta concert soprano and graduated from the Norwegian Music and Acting Academy. She also played concert piano. This was the friend that had helped Ma years ago with her special Elektrokemist banquet speech, Irene helped "with the 'declamation' – in other words delivery – what words to emphasize, etc. What a sweet wonderful person she was," Ma wrote.

In a three-day whirlwind, Mom visited with as many of her old friends as she could: the Tranøys, Ragna Hansen, Irene, Marit Gudmundsen Algror, Oddvar and Annik Augland, Annette Bellinger Tanderø, Kay and Arne Michalsen, who had been in Ma's wedding party, Ragnhild Kirkhorn and Astrid's brother Haakon Holt and his wife!

She flew up to Trondheim on July 11 and was met by Dad's sister Kari, Kari's husband JP and Farmor, who, she wrote, was "as peppy as ever!" Ma and Farmor stayed up until midnight talking. Over the next few days, they went into the city and shopped, and Mom bought herself "a beautiful red wool jacket and some material for slip covers for the playroom couch and Maggie's spoon." Best of all, she bought herself a beautiful national costume (*bunad*) which she had always longed for.

She and Farmor went to put flowers on Farfar's grave at Lademoen cemetery. He had passed away a few years earlier, in May 1976.

Then Mom went to the cabin (*hytte*) on Hitra, the largest island nearby to Trondheim where uncle JP was born. After, she went to Røros, where Dad's cousins, Ruth and Pella, had a *hytte* (nearly every family in Norway has a *hytte* to escape from the world – the more remote the better.) They played bridge and drank Irish coffee. They stopped at Kongensgrube (the King's Mine in Røros) on the way home. Near Røros, she would have passed by Reitan station, and thinking of Dad's escape to Sweden, wrote in her notebook "Reitan below Røros where Ørnulf went on ski during the war."

Back in Trondheim, she ate reindeer meat at a 1739 Tavern restaurant. Being a lover of antiques, she greatly appreciated the Louis XIV style furniture there. JP and Kari also took her to the fancy "Palmen" restaurant in Trondheim and they ate and danced until 1 AM.

> Diary entry Monday, July 17, 1978: "I woke up early as usual. 5 o'clock. Felt much better. Finished the Liv Ullman book. *Jeg tenker på familien hjemme. Jeg håper det går bra med dem.* "(I am thinking of the family back home. I hope they're all doing well).
>
> July 27, 1978 Julie's birthday. Hope she's OK and has a good time.

Ma and Farmor took the train south to Larvik. "Gerd had a nice dinner ready for us at Helgeroa. They have a lovely place *hytte* with a beautiful view. We visited until nearly midnight."

With Gerd and her family there were more good talks, raspberry picking and playing Bridge and she "played Hearts with Ingar and Kjell Erik," her nephews. One day, "Grethe, Kjell Erik, Ingar, Niels and I went on a wonderful boat trip to Kragerø and back, past Jomfruland, Langesund, etc. We anchored offshore and ate knekkebrød and coffee. Beautiful weather." Tante Gerd remembers so many lovely, "koselig" times there at Helgeroa, also with Mom.

From Larvik, it was back to Oslo and I can't even begin to write all the friends she visited. They picked her up and took her to their homes. Once she was invited to a fancy restaurant on top of the Grand Hotel.

All the while Ma was "whoopin' it up" she remembered us, too. She wrote all kinds of letters and postcards during this trip and bought many gifts for those back home. She was always thoughtful of friends and family that way, writing down addresses and lists in her little notebook so no one was forgotten. We were so glad when she got back home in early August together with her Norwegian friend Irene, who came to NY for a visit, staying with us.

Land of the Vikings

Wherever there were Norwegians in the vicinity, Ma could sniff them out like a bloodhound and quickly make friends, usually finding someone they had met in common. Mom and Dad enjoyed the "flavor" of Norway in the USA by participating in the "Sons of Norway," the largest Norwegian organization outside of Norway. They were active locally, for the "Sons of Norway" group had bought a recreational center just down the road from us in Sherman, Pennsylvania. It was called "Land of the Vikings" (LOV). (I enjoyed waitressing there in the summer. It was full of fun-loving American Norwegians and Norwegian Americans who drove from all over New York and Connecticut, etc. I also enjoyed many a ski trip there.)

Daddy helped LOV with accounting stuff, and Mom fixed up Heidi's old room into an office for him. "That way," she said, "He doesn't have his Sons of Norway accounting work strung all over our bedroom."

The folks were very much involved, even participating on the Board. In April 1983 Ma wrote, "Friday night our Sons of Norway Lodge Board is meeting here so I have to make wienerbrød for 10 people."

Mom enjoyed their company and did some typing for this group. Another time she wrote, "I have to type up some Sons of Norway stuff. It's a nice group of people."

Dad even helped at LOV when there was a cross-country ski event set up for the blind. As I recall, it was connected with "Ski for Light," a non-profit organization started by Norwegian Americans which paired a visually impaired person with a guide. Dad took his old Norwegian custom-made wooden skis down there and participated in helping folks learn to ski.

In another letter Ma wrote, "Went to LOV for a party. They played "Stump the Musician" – their accordion player. Walter Gabrielsen and I wrote down Norwegian ballads and stumped him. Result was, I had to sing 2 verses over the microphone. Had a great time. We square danced. Walter sang a song popular in Norway after the war, "En Liten Gylden Ring," it's about a wedding ring. They both grew up in Oslo and own an apartment

Mom in her bunad and Dad at LOV

there – I know right where it is. We had fun reminiscing about Oslo, etc."

Ma kept in touch with her Norwegian friends all her life. When I went to Norway in 1982, after my first year of university, she gave me phone numbers and had written to her friends so that I could connect with them. Johan R. Lindstrøm (who gave her away at the wedding), Ragnhild Kirkhorn, "Mor" Gudmundsen's daughter, Marit, and good friends from her days working at F.K, Berit Tranoy and Ragna Hansen and of course, Astrid, a friend who she had met later in life in the USA who moved back to Norway after her American husband died. Mom cherished her Norwegian friends and I enjoyed seeing them in Oslo; they were so kind to me. I am glad my parents were totally in agreement when I asked if I might take some of my hard-earned university savings money to go spend a summer in Norway to experience Norway, to get to know our family and to learn Norwegian.

Years later, on June 30, 1986, Mom, Dad and our youngest sister, Julie, went to Norway – it was her high school graduation gift. She was fortunate to have had Mom and Dad to herself for six wonderful years. By then, Mom and Dad were "as comfortable together as an old, worn-in pair of shoes," as Ma said. Finances had improved with only one kid instead of six, and Dad was close to retirement. They flew to Trondheim where Tante Kari and Onkel JP set up a big family party, with the Hoffs, Strøms and Soknes families. How wonderful for Dad to see his mother, sisters and cousins again and enjoy staying in the family home on 37, Statsing. Dahls Street. One day, he managed to meet up with an old childhood boys' choir friend who still lived nearby.

Ma, of course, kept a journal of her trip. She described Trondheim as being clean, cozy and "still remains (at the moment) a charming, medium-sized city." They shopped a lot all over delightful Trondheim.

They also enjoyed a "beautiful ride and scenery" out to the island of Hitra with Kari and JP. Ma wrote, "Love Hitra. Beautiful view of the Fjord." They visited "Thorbjorn Strøm's salmon fish canning – freezing factory. Very interesting…" and had a "great salmon dinner." Some late nights Mom described that special summer evening sun this way, "The night light has a certain cast to it that gives a different look to the landscape. It is indescribable." Norway, Land of the midnight sun: "2 a.m. These night lights are beautiful. Nothing like them."

Mom loved looking for shells along the beach, and "teasing the seagulls" and walking on the island. She visited, played cards, and read books (in Norwegian e.g., by Haakon Lie, Trygve Brattelli, Dagny Tande Led, and Sissel Lange Nielsen).

Mom went out on the fjord fishing with her niece, Heidi (Kari and JP's second daughter), Dad, JP and Julie. The fishing on Hitra was stupendous. "I caught a 10 kilo (20 pound) cod right away. Later caught 2 small ones we threw back. No one else even got a bite! Julie took pictures." Julie remembers that fishing trip like this: "Uncle JP had bought these expensive, fancy new fishing poles. Dad and JP had the fancy poles and Ma picked up a random string from the bottom of the boat with two miserable looking hooks on it, 'I'll use this,' Ma said, (and Dad and JP were kind of laughing at Ma)… Ma suddenly gets a bite, and Dad says 'It's probably gotten stuck in some seaweed'… so Dad takes the string to help her, and with Ma and Dad pulling, one more big tug, and in comes this *huge fish*! Ma was *grinning* from ear to ear," Julie laughed heartily as she recalled the story. "'How'd the poles work out for ya?' Ma laughed and they all laughed, it was just so funny. We cooked and ate that fish," Julie said, "It was delicious."

On another day, our cousin Heidi, Ma, Julie and Dad rowed out to fish "…way out in the fjord: Heidi found the *sei* (pollock fish) bank, she caught 6 at once, Julie caught 5 at once, and I caught 10-12, one at a time. It was lots of fun." Ingunn, another niece (Kari and JP's third daughter) and her husband Terje came out by motorcycle to visit with them too. There were ten wonderful days on Hitra and every minute was treasured.

After, cousin Odd Soknes took them all out to cousins Ruth

Hitra

and Pelle's cabin near Røros, where they stayed in little cabins - with an outhouse. They visited lovely Røros, the old copper mining town with its quaint wooden buildings and classic church. (It well deserves its UNESCO World Heritage Site designation.) They all went for a hike up in the hills. When they crossed a mountain creek, they stopped to drink the cold, *"pure water,"* before heading further up to a *seter* (a mountain farm, used in summer - an integral part of Norwegian farming from ancient times).

Back in Trondheim, there were more family visits with the Strøm family, "lots of laughs." They met up with Bente, the eldest niece, and her husband Ivar. "Very nice, we had a good time," Ma wrote. She always had interesting conversations with Ivar, who is into history, like Ma. One day, Bente picked the gals up to go to see Prince Andrew's wedding on TV, while Daddy walked to Lademoen cemetery instead, to visit the grave of his father, his brother Rolf and his grandma.

Julie recalled a visit to a railroad museum which had WW2 resistance information and a plaque honoring Farfar and others from Trondheim. "Farmor took Dad, Mom and me. We didn't say who we were until after the historian gave his talk, then we told him we were Hoffs, and he wanted a photo with Dad and me by the picture of Farfar. Even after all those years, Farmor could not bring herself to go inside with us, she sat out on a bench while we went inside, it was just too many emotions for her," Julie said. When Julie was looking at photos of family around Farmor's apartment, she asked Farmor about each one. When Julie asked about Farmor's father (there was no photo of Jakob) Farmor seemed a bit agitated, as she spoke rapidly in Norwegian. Daddy explained to Julie that he thought Jakob had affiliated with the NS to guarantee the safety of his family, to protect them. But for Farmor, especially with her family involved in the resistance, this felt like a betrayal and she did not necessarily agree with Dad's gracious point of view. Neither did Gerd.

One day of their visit, Ma and Daddy walked downtown to get the bus for Stikklestad for a reenactment of the 1030 historic battle, the "St Olav Drama," where King Olav II was slain. This play has been staged every year since 1954. Judith (JP's sister) and husband Harald came too. Ma wrote:

> A beautiful sunshiny day. What wonderful countryside all along the fjord, (fjord on left – lots of farms on the right.) Went over the bridge to Hell, ('Luck') Norway. Got wonderful seats. What a terrific outdoor play. Felt like we were back in ancient Norway. What an experience. Loved every minute of it.

At the end of the month, they flew down to Oslo, staying at our old friend Astrid's apartment, and Dad flew back to NY to work. After having lived in Oslo in the late 1940s and early 1950s, Oslo was quite a shock to Ma: it had lost its quaint feel and was "dirty, polluted and full of too many people." Ma and Julie met up with many of mom's old friends which was a delight ("…just like the old days"). They did lots of sightseeing in Oslo: the old fortress, the Home Front Resistance Museum, and at Bygdøy, several ship museums: the Kon-Tiki, Fram, Ra-II and Viking ships, an Embassy visit, and Julie went to an "A-Ha" concert.

They got home on August 9th, more than a month later, and Ma wrote, "Arrived home at Chestnut Grove at noon. So happy to be home. Praise the Lord for a wonderfully, super vacation but also for bringing us safely home! A-men!"

There were other visits to see Norwegian friends within the USA. Mom and Dad drove the long trip down to North Carolina in 1993 to visit their close friends, Erik and Åse Aune-Iversen, who had moved there from New York, and were soon moving back to Norway. Ma wrote, "It will be great to see Åse and Erik. We've been friends for over twenty years. Julie was a just a baby when we met them. Am anxious to hear all their plans. Of course, they have to sell their house first." I remember visiting with the Aune-Iversen family over near Binghamton. We also went on a summer vacation with them down at North Myrtle Beach. They had two children, Lisbeth, who was close in age to Heidi and me, and Petter, a younger son – we always had fun with them as our parents babbled away in Norwegian talk and laughter.

Mom's Memories of Working with Norwegians

Mom had a scrap book full of memories and photos of her days at the Norwegian Embassy. Over the decades, she wrote on the side of the pages, updating it as she followed the careers of her Norwegian friends and former bosses from the Embassy through information in Norwegian newspapers and magazines. She had truly worked with an exceptional caliber of people. She was not however, someone to 'brag' about who she knew, she just told us she had worked with "some very interesting people." I did not really know about this until writing this book and my brother kindly took the time to scan and send us all copies of the pages of Ma's Embassy scrapbook.

For example: Arne Haugland was Mom's boss and Press Attaché, "our press expert on everything," Mom wrote. He had the role of liaising with the media. He became Norwegian Consul General in Liverpool, England, among other things.

Another boss and "good friend" of Mom's was Tor Myklebost, a journalist who was also Press Attaché and who became Press Officer of the Norwegian Foreign Office and eventually, Ambassador to Iceland. He had written a book in 1943, *They Came as Friends*, an account of the first few years of occupied Norway, including the Norwegian home front resistance, translated into English by Trygve Ager*.

One of Mom's bosses, Arne Skouen, was a journalist, writer and film maker who was active in resistance work in Oslo during the early war years. In 1942 he wrote depictions of everyday life in occupied Norway, published in 1943 as *66 leather letters from Oslo* under the pseudonym Bjørn Stallare. He directed many films, including the internationally acclaimed film, "Ni Liv" (Nine Lives), the incredible survival story of Jan Baalsrud, a resistance commando in World War 2.

Mom also knew Arne Skaug, who worked for the Norwegian government in both New York City and Washington DC

---

*Trygve Ager was an American journalist who studied in Norway, author and translator of books dealing with Norwegian culture. He was a co-founder of "News of Norway" at the Norwegian embassy in Washington. In 1943 he co-authored a book with Bjarne Höye, "The Fight of the Norwegian Church Against Nazism" and translated "They Came as Friends" by Tor Myklebost.

Pictures from Ma's Scrapbook:

Arne Haugland   *Tor Myklebost*   *Arne Skouen*

(1942-1946). He was a Norwegian economist, civil servant, and diplomat who became director of Statistics Norway, Norwegian Minister of Trade and Shipping and later ambassador.

She interacted as well with Per Høst, zoologist and documentary film maker, who was affiliated with the Norwegian information service in the US, and made films about Norwegians in the war and military instructional films for the Allied Forces.

Ma wrote a letter which sums up many of her feelings about Norway and Norwegians. She was responding to an article sometime in the 1980s which must have 'raised her hackles' because of its stereotypical portrayal of Norwegians. I love how she looks back on her experiences and uses them to illustrate her point. How clearly she cherished this land and its people!

> I feel the article in the September Viking (magazine) gives a strange impression of Norway and the Norwegian people as a whole. It may describe some of the immigrants of years ago but it doesn't compare with the Norway and Norwegians I've known during the last 41 years. The article describes just one small section of Norway. You can't compare Båtsfjord (of the very far north) with Larvik (of the very far south of the country).
>
> True, most Norwegians don't "gush." They view things more realistically. But it hasn't dampened their humor or their love of song and laughter or their feeling.
>
> In early 1943, when I started working at the Norwegian Embassy in Washington D.C., I knew very little about Norway and Norwegians. Since I was in the Press and Information Section, my knowledge increased rapidly. I learned a great deal during a very

exciting time. I soon learned that Norwegians had very deep feelings and weren't ashamed to show it. I remember the day the cable came that told of the execution of Dr. Gerda Evang's brother-in-law back in Nazi occupied Norway.

I also remember the day in 1945 when Arne Skouen, with great gusto, colored Norway red on the wall map that Trygve Ager had been gradually coloring red as each country was liberated.

When I went to Norway in 1947, who could have been more caring and loving than the first Norwegian family I lived with in Oslo who had offered me a couch in their living room until I could find a better place to stay. Fru Gudmundsen, her husband and daughter were as loving and affectionate as my own family in the USA. Although Fru Gudmendsen didn't speak English, we got along famously with my limited Norwegian and a dictionary.

The staff at Elektrokemisk A/S (now ELKEM) where I worked in Oslo were very outgoing and showed the same concern for me as my other Norwegian friends. How interesting and educational it was to eat at Tante Olva Oevergaard's eating place on Tullins gate (a short street in Oslo center) where "hybelboerer" from all parts of Norway ate dinner. It was fascinating to observe the various types and to hear the many dialects spoken.

Much of their humor, joy and sentimentality is shown in Norwegian songs. What they lack in conversation they made up for in song. Whenever there was a private - - or even impromptu party - - the music started. I can remember Arne Skaug relaxing to "Chickery Chick" *[a silly, peppy song sung by the Andrews Sisters in 1946]*.

I always knew when Per Høst had arrived as the strains of "One Meat Ball" *[Josh White 1944]* would come wafting up from the dark room directly under my office.

The first Norwegian song I had learned was "Ja, Vi Elsker Dette Landet" *[the national anthem]* as it was always sung at the beginning of most receptions whether just the Embassy staff was present or the Norwegian Colony around the Washington area. Just listen to the words:

Yes, we love with fond devotion
This our land that looms
Rugged, storm-scarred o'er the ocean
With her thousand homes.
Love her, in our love recalling
Those who gave us birth.
And old tales which night, in falling,
Brings like dreams to earth.

Gerd Wold*, who later christened the Kon Tiki raft in Peru, worked for the Military Department (at the Norwegian Embassy). Since the Press Department had all the duplicating machines on their 3rd floor, we press secretaries would assist the other gals if they needed it. One time Gerd came with a 40-page legal size stenciled report. I helped her collate all 100 copies (4,000 pages). To make the idiot arbeid (idiot work) go faster, she started to sing and that's how I learned 'Det var en god gammel bondemann.'"

[The song is a kind of classic drinking song, quite silly, with many verses:
« Det var en god gammel bondemann, som skulle gå ut etter øl... etter øl etter HOPP-sa-sa, tra-la-la-la, som skulle ut etter øl »
(There was a good old farmer who was going to go out to get beer... After beer after HOPP-sa-sa, tra-la-la-la, who went to go out for beer).]

Norwegians always write songs to fit the occasion. When the occupation of Norway ended they sang, "Seieren er Vår, Quisling Kom På Grini Igår" ["Victory is ours, Quisling came to Grini yesterday" a song that spoke of how Nazi-government collaboration had ended and would be brought to justice]:
    I learned this from a Fredrikstad gal who was sent over to Washington after the war ended. She told me how that song reverberated throughout the country as freedom had come.
    In 1946, the guitar-playing Student Attaché arrived and there were more songs. Guitar music had been popular for several generations. My Trønder husband's maternal grandmother (Juliania Sekander Oetnes) gave guitar lessons in Setesdal a long, long time ago.
    Anyone listening to Edvard Grieg's music can close one's eyes and just see Norway. As I stood at Videseter [between Geiranger and Loen] and looked down the valley at the huge mountains, they were majestic and awesome but not cold and overwhelming. They appeared almost to be covered with soft velvet. All I could think of

*Gerd Vold Hurum was active in the resistance during World War II with illegal newspapers, including "We Want a Country," later as liaison for couriers and intelligence agents. In 1942, she had to flee to Sweden. She got to London and worked for the Norwegian Armed Forces headquarters. I wonder if Dad met her too? After the war, she got a job at the embassy in Washington DC as a cipher chief. In 1946 she met Thor Heyerdahl, who asked her to become the Kon-Tiki expedition's secretary and contact person on land.

was Grieg's "In the Hall of the Mountain King." Who could be in Ulvik and Granvin in Hardanger without feeling Grieg's "Spring" and "Morning"?! The whole of Norway is Grieg's Concerto.

I never considered the trolls ugly. I thought they were homely little guys who sometimes were mischievous and full of pranks. If I had met one on top of Dalsnibba mountain above Geiranger Fjord, I would have sat down and asked him to tell me about his way of life. (By the way, Norwegian men in America didn't shake hands with American women as they had been taught that it wasn't the custom here.) In Norway, they always shook hands with me as it was the custom there. "When in Rome, etc…"

After a fairy tale wedding in the Nidaros Domkirke in 1952, my Trønder and I returned to Washington. Through the years, many a long letter, magazines and packages flowed back and forth between Norway and the USA. We have always kept à jour of developments in Norway through an Oslo Newspaper received 3 times a week.

Many of the dear Norwegian friends and people I worked with both in Washington and Oslo are gone but I haven't forgotten them and I am still in contact with those who are left.

Norway and the Norwegian people taught me many things and made me one of them. Maybe that's why people at the American Embassy in Norway used to call me, 'The American Norwegian.'"

Jeanne Rood Hoff

This was indeed *one* love affair that never came to an end.

MOM: THE LATER YEARS

In September 1981, I left home to begin my education at Houghton University in western NY State. It was a three-and-a-half-hour drive away, and I had neither car nor driver's license so I didn't get home often. I spoke to my folks weekly, keeping them up to date on classes, friendships, etc. Ma faithfully wrote letters to me with encouraging words like, "Am so glad you did so great in Biology. Keep it up Mags. My Grandpa Travis used to say 'Always do a little more than is required, as those that excel are the ones who get ahead.' I have all the letters he wrote me when I left to go to Washington. Over the years, he wrote quite a few letters."

During those years I was away, Ma wrote many letters to me, for she realized how homesick I was. How those letters encouraged me! She wrote about the many activities that filled her life and it gave me a feeling of "home," besides showing me how much she cared. She worked with Dad in the vegetable garden, she sewed, cooked, cleaned and babysat little Andrew Baker, and visited with friends. She certainly kept very busy.

Julie was now the only child living at home, and later, she attended classes at a nearby college. You can see in the letter below, that Ma also cherished time alone to herself - well earned after so many years of a houseful of children.

(Written on small red paper marked, "jotting from Jeanne Hoff")

September 9, 1981
Dear Maggie,
    Will just scribble a note. It was good to talk to you last night. Sounds like you are busy.
    I talked to Cecilia this morning. The only class she thought

might give her trouble was calculus—mainly due to the instructor's attitude. However, he may turn out to be better than she thinks. Heidi got the highest mark ever in N.Y. State for her recruiting test.

It's wonderful to be more or less alone. I've been sewing and repairing. Fixed a new ruffle for the swivel chair in the bay window.

Julie and I have switched the playroom furniture around a bit to make it more cozy.

I'm also going to make a cover for the studio couch in Bo's room. I bought a pair of drapes at the "A to Z" shop for $2 that I'm going to use for the material.

I just made 4 quarts of pickles for Daddy. I've got to get more sugar to do my kind. Marguerite gave me a lot of big cucumbers. I have some from our garden too. It poured rain yesterday. We needed the rain but could use some dry days now to dig potatoes.

We went up to see Burt about the new furnace. Guess they'll start soon. Hope Daddy makes out all right at the bank for the loan.

I've been down to John and Marguerite Lee's visiting Birdie twice. Then Labor Day weekend, believe it or not, Daddy went down with me. They had stopped by with the cucumbers and we talked about it. Julie had to babysit and couldn't go.

To-day is Mishawn's Birthday and Margeurite's too.

The 50th anniversary party for Vene and Walt Boyer was one of the nicest I've been too. Lots of fun and the music was so nice. There were 112 people there.

Have had Andrew a few times.

Julie has straightened up her room some – switched her two bureaus so she could put the little cupboard from the playroom on the bureau to put all her knickknacks in. Seems much better. Don't know how long the new found neatness will last!

She bought herself some beautiful pants and so she went off to school looking pretty jazzy. Wonder what tales she'll have to tell when she comes home to-night.

Julie and her friends Tammy, Lynne and others would have "girls' night out" once or twice a month. One time Ma said she'd like to join them, and so they all went together to Johnson's Inn. When Ma ordered a "pink lady" the bartender laughed but managed to make the drink for her, and more than one! Ma was dancing around with Julie and her friends, and they laughed so hard at her stories about working in Washington and Norway, etc. They had such a good time, that Julie and her friends would sometimes ask Ma to join them and she did without any hesitation!

Haven't heard from Bo.

I talked to Bev (Zandt), no news there either.

I haven't heard from anyone except this morning we finally got a letter from Farmor. She sent the sock (knitting) directions and a paper from Trondheim. She thanked everyone for a good time here. Her trip home went fine. She sounded good. You should write to her if you get a chance.

Marie is supposed to drop by this afternoon and take me into town and I'll get this mailed.

Love, Mom

P.S. Write soon

It was always a challenge, finding rides into town to shop and run other errands, since they only had one car and Daddy had it at work.

October 31, 1981

Dear Maggie,

I've been thinking about you every day but have been busy with Julie and the new furnace. Julie was really quite sick. I was up nights quite a bit with her and I was quite worried. She thinned right down & looked wan and peaked with dark circles under her eyes. But now I think she'll be O.K. She coughs some. I think she must have had bronchial pneumonia but I'm not sure.

Mr. Rumola got the furnace hooked up. What a difference it makes. It's so warm all over. However, for the first 2 weeks it will take a lot of wood to make a bed of ashes so the wood won't burn so fast and it won't have to be filled so often. So, I am busy checking on it every once in a while. It has a huge inside so you can put lots of wood in at once. It should only have to be filled 3 times a day after it gets going good. I'm sure you'll feel the difference in warmth when you come home. We get our hot water from the furnace boiler now so you have to be careful not to burn yourself. So much for that.

[How did she ever manage filling that furnace with wood with her troubled muscles!?]

Kjer and Miguel are still expecting to hear about an apartment. Miguel got a very bad cold so they couldn't come up this weekend. Kjer weighs 140 pounds now. (She was 8 months pregnant). I didn't know she was Rh negative. With the first child it should pose no problem but the Dr is keeping a close check on her blood. She has to go every 2 weeks now.

[Ma's sister Julia never had her own children due to this Rh factor which was not well understood back then. RhoGAM was not available until the late 1960s.]

Heidi passed her physical, I bet she's happy.

Cecilia and "co." may come up next weekend so whether Heidi comes home to stay or not I don't know. She was trying to find a temporary job on the base in Brooklyn but hasn't yet.

Daddy and I had to go to a Sons of Norway meeting last Tuesday but he stayed home with Julie as we didn't dare leave her alone. Since I'm secretary I had to go. It was warm and poured rain. It wasn't too bad going over but coming back at 10:30 pm it was very bad – pitch dark and pouring rain. I had to drive so slowly.

Elderly Olea Bautz from Blueberry Lake came down on Monday morning for a visit - - of course everything was a mess except dining room and playroom. She brought us a Norwegian pea soup dinner - it's yellow peas more like bean soup. Boy was it good!

We were supposed to go to the Norwegian Folk Dance thing at Land of the Vikings resort next weekend but if Celia comes, we probably won't go. Anyway, we can't afford the dinner price. I babysat Andrew last night.

[Ma is working hard to make ends meet – not an easy task with 2 children in college at once, but she always tried to keep a positive outlook regardless.]

I finally got the laundry floor scrubbed and a lot of mess cleaned up there but I'm not finished and have a lot to do in the kitchen.

Mom had some inventive ways to do housework. One time, in her late 60s, she told me about the time she'd recently climbed out my bedroom window onto a side roof to wash the bathroom and my windows. They were dirtier than she'd thought, and her cleaning rags were all used up and black. On the last window, she needed one last wipe to finish, and seeing as her dirty rags would've only made it more dirty, she took off her big cotton underpants and used the outside of *them* to finish off the window, as she giggled to herself. "Necessity is the mother of invention," Ma said.

Mom also helped her kids with their housework when the need arose. One summer when she was 68, she was down in Brooklyn at Celia's house, watching grandkids Mishawn and Jack for a few days, while their dad was getting his spleen out and Celia was working.

> ...I have washed Cece's windows and curtains. This morning early before we left, I climbed out on the roof by hallway bathroom to do those side windows, much to Julie's horror, but it's good exercise, and I've been used to climbing all sorts of trees, etc., it all comes naturally...I've been climbing trees and up and down ladders and hiking up small mountains since I was a little kid, 5 & over.
>
> I wish I could get new curtains but guess I'll have to use the same old ones. Oh well, such things aren't as important as being warm, etc.
>
> I had to go to town the other day but I was lucky. Mrs. Maloy picked me up just beyond Curt's house and Dick Davis picked me up just outside of town on the way back. I 've got to get my sewing schedule going or I won't get my Christmas tablecloth done again this year. I don't know what I'm going to do about Christmas presents. We are so broke it's terrible – but better days are coming.
>
> We certainly enjoyed the weekend at Houghton. I was so sorry that we didn't get to the chapel on Sunday but there will be other times. What a nice group of girls you have up there. We just loved Meg's family and all the other parents we met. I know you are very busy and working hard. However, when you come home Christmas you should have a long rest.
>
> We haven't heard from Bo for some time. Well, Daddy's in a hurry to get into town so I'll stop.
>
> Love, Mom

On a sub-zero February eve in 1982, in the second semester of my first year at Houghton University, I called home and a fireman answered me! There was an electrical fire at my folks' home. At first, when I asked if they all had gotten out, he said, "I think so." Then another fireman said, from the background, that the family was all safe, they were up at the Scotts' house (neighbors) and the fire was under control. Still, it was very upsetting and my dear roommate Meg remembered hearing someone crying, closed in a bathroom stall, on our dormitory floor, and that was me. She helped to calm me down and hand it all over to the Lord's care. I then called back again, and that time got ahold of Ma. The following are excerpts from a letter Ma sent me which describes the awful event.

Dear Maggie,
    Finally I find a time to write to you. You're on my mind all the time but this place has been like a whirlpool the past few days. I can't wait for the builder to get started but it all has to go through the insurance company. We hope he'll start by the end of next week but the adjuster has questioned the total cost.

[ASIDE: They should have questioned some other things… when the assessor came and checked out all the fire and water damage, he then turned to Ma and said, "Is that all of it?" Julie, who was in 7th grade at the time said, "Ma you forgot one room." She led them down the hallway to the way back room by the upstairs bathroom. This room was an old storage room, which seemed to Ma untouched by the water leakage (but perhaps she was wrong.) Over the years, there had been leaks and it indeed looked somewhat of a disaster. "AH yes" he said, and began writing. The money received was used to renovate the room and it, of course, became Julie's new bedroom. *Typical* Julie, the little rascal.]

Maybe they'll approve sections at a time, i.e., roof and attic, etc. I feel like I'm living in a pawn shop. Everything is all jammed in together. However, we can now start moving things temporarily back into your room as the water stopped dripping several days ago. That section of the attic was sprayed with water so the insulation in that part of the attic was soaking wet.
    You'll have a new ceiling. My closet burnt in several places. I lost some summer clothes. The crèche got slightly scorched but is o.k.
    The end of Kjer's room is a mess.

[It was in one of those walls the fire began – a mouse or squirrel chewing on old wiring.]

We were very lucky not to lose any furniture or antiques (*Ma treasured her family heirlooms*). The insurance will pay to have our bed refinished.

I have had to write down a list of stuff we lost, date bought, cost and what it would cost now. If you don't think that's a job!

[She should have enlisted Julie's help for the creative influence.]

Kjer lost some paperbacks and her owl plate, but her stuffed owl's o.k. (*Kjer was majorly into owls*). The firemen moved the table and all into Ce's room. They even moved Grannie's old green sofa into Bo's room.

[Aside: They should have left it there to burn, already back then the cushions were leaking disintegrated stuffing. In 2003, when I started this book, it was still in Kjer's room, slowly rotting to oblivion.]

We had to send all of Daddy's suits to the dry cleaner with my stuff. My Bunad is O.K.

The bedspread is stained so they'll give me something towards a new one. We'll also have a new springs and mattress.

You know I lost my glasses for a few days. Typical Mom, huh?

[It was an ever-repeating event, Ma's losing and finding of her glasses. We bought her a chain to keep them around her neck but the weight bugged her neck muscles. Little grandson Seth even got her a "nose stand" to set them on in the living room, which helped a little in the later years. She loved that thing and would always say, "Sethie gave that to me, now wasn't that thoughtful?"]

I knew I had (my glasses) in my hand when Daddy called me to come up to see what smelled hot. I was getting ready to go to John and Marguerites'. Well, anyway it wasn't until a couple of hours later that it dawned on me that my glasses were in Kjersti's room. So, when I came back down from Scott's to put Tara in, as the firemen announced on the intercom that the dog was shivering, I thought I would go up to Kjer's room and find my glasses.

[In the middle of a fire, men working hard to save the house, she decides she's got to go up to the room where it was happening, to get her blessed glasses. By the way, Tara was a timorous, short-lived Afghan hound which Kjersti inherited from two guys which were Astrid's neighbors in Pennsylvania.]

That's how come I was there when you called back the 2nd time. Searching for John Kaare's phone number to thank him for offering us to stay at the facilities of Land of the Vikings, I opened a drawer of Kjer's desk. There were my glasses. The fireman had put all the things which were on top of the bureau into the drawer—even the runner which I treasure that was Grandma Rood's! Those firemen were something! What dolls!

I've had a steady stream of estimators, adjusters, etc., here – plus people. When the rug men came to get the rugs I had to help them and supervise a little.

[I can imagine that Ma's "little" meant major hovering and overseeing, knowing how Ma treasured her family possessions.]

I didn't want anything else ruined. They should have brought 3 men but brought only 2. Will have to tell you all the funny details when I see you. Need to keep your sense of humor. I told them they should put me on the payroll.

Of all the strange things that happened, the owner of the rug cleaning company has a Norwegian grandmother and he also graduated from St Olaf College.

[As mentioned, Ma was always running into someone who knew someone she had known in Norway, or who was in some way related to a Norskie. She found the point about St Olaf College interesting since Beau attended there, too.]

Poor Dad was quite shook up for a few days. I think the strain was bad on him. I was just exhausted at the end of each day. Not that I was so shook up but it is a traumatic experience, to try to get some semblance of order out of the mess. I don't like messes. They make me tired and I can't relax when there are messes around.

The Bard-Parker people (*where Daddy worked*) took up a collection – we got $181, so Julie, Dad and I went to Binghamton Saturday. Dad got a new suit, & I got a good pair of leather walking shoes. Julie got sneakers and a duffel bag.

[Despite the hassle and work of dealing with the aftermath of the fire, Ma finds plenty of time for socializing.]

On Friday, Billie B and I spent the day at Vene and Walt's. John and Marguerite have been wonderful. She came right up on Friday and washed dishes, etc. Saturday, she sent up a pie.

We had a wonderful day at Olea's last Sunday. Delicious dinner and lots of fun. She's a riot.

Andrew has been here a few times. He's as cute as ever. He loves playing office with Julie; usually ropes me in on some games too.

Well, I must hurry and get breakfast or we won't get to Sunday School. Daddy wants sausage. I've probably forgotten half of what I wanted to tell you.

Love Mom.

P.S. Your prayers helped, I'm sure.

In the second year of my studies, I got a letter in winter which showed a side of Ma I rarely saw – she had been sick and was somewhat down in the dumps, from the cold and the lack of money. She had also just taken down the Christmas tree and decorations, which is always sad for us Christmas-lovers.

Tues. Jan. 18, 1983
Dear Maggie,
This is just a dumb note to send some mail that came for you. I haven't been to the store to get any tea yet but hope too soon. It has been cold. Just can't get the dining room-kitchen warm. It's 62° in here right now. It's warm upstairs though. Even the 2 front living rooms feel warmer than this. We did get some fuel oil but Daddy won't turn the indicator up to make the fuel oil furnace run more. Hope this cold spell will end soon.

Am still dragging around. Have been spending about ½ day in bed. I get so tired by lunch time. I hope I soon get that medicine out of my system. Nothing tastes good but at least I don't feel nauseated all the time like I did.

Things are as usual. Bo has taken most care of the furnace. He is busy with his music etc. Don't know what his plans are. Kjer and Miguel are coming up sometime in Feb.

I haven't written to anyone. I've been so discouraged. Haven't got my stove fixed yet as we haven't been to Binghamton.

We took out the Christmas tree on Sunday. It didn't shed as much as I thought it would. Have to get the rooms in some kind of shape before the weekend as Amy and Kjell hope to come and play Bridge on Sat. There's an operating group meeting at noon on Saturday at Land of the Vikings.

I lie in bed and listen to the Christian radio station, WPEL and quite often fall asleep in the middle of something. I tried to embroider a little to-day but just got started when Martha called. I love to talk with her. If I could only get my enthusiasm back. I don't seem to have any.

I'm glad you like your classes. I'm very proud of you and your work. I'm so glad you could go to Houghton College. It was so nice having you home. I'm sorry you had to do so much work.

Heidi has a drill this weekend. Cece called. Mishawn called Grandpa. Cece is so busy. When I get some money and can leave, I'm going to spend some time with Cece. But it will be quite a while yet, several weeks, I guess.

Let us know if you need anything. I'll write more another time,
Love, Mom

When Ma and Daddy had their first grandchild, Mishawn, they were thrilled. I could hear the joy in Ma's voice when she called me to tell me the big news. I only found a napkin to write down all the particulars: when she was born, how much she weighed, etc., (I still have that napkin somewhere!). Mishawn was the first of many grandkids, and Ma and Daddy adored each one in a special way. She loved the things they made for her or gave her, like the red bird house Jack made, or the wooden spice cabinet Mishawn made her, or the "Nose" for holding her glasses from Seth.

Ma used to spoil her grandkids at breakfast time. "We want PANCAKES, Gramma!" they would shout. So Ma prepared her famous pancake batter, and then created every shape imaginable, at the request of the grandkids. She could make Mickey Mouse heads, dog or cat heads, and even a dinosaur! Perhaps her love of pancakes came from her father, Cecil, who ate them quite often even for dinner, Daddy told me. Ma used to eat them almost burnt, that's the way she liked them best.

She was strict with the grandkids, as she had been with us, about keeping out of the living room, or at least no "mucksin" in there, as she wanted to keep it nice and protect her heritage (antique furniture and other wonders, such as a sugar bowl, which was once belonged to the granddaughter of the founder of Rhode Island, Roger Williams). There were other historical items which you held your breath to look at, where they lay within the great glass doors of the huge bureau thingy…there was even an off-white hand carved ring made of *bone*, no less, which some relative, I believe George Rood, had made while in prison.

[ASIDE: We are related to a criminal – but he was pardoned. George Washington Rood (born 1830) was imprisoned in Yuma Arizona for killing a lawyer who cheated him out of his gold mine. He lived in Tombstone Arizona at the same time the Earp and the Clanton's had their big shoot out. My cousin Lana went to Tombstone and found his voting record. He had a son Landon who was killed in a hunting accident at age 14, Lana went looking for his grave at Boot Hill cemetery where the Clanton's of the shootout at the O.K. corral were buried.]

On this topic, Lana wrote:

> The lady giving the tours sent me across town where the upstanding citizens were buried and sure enough, I found Landon's grave. I have copies of letters George wrote about his son's funeral and how it was the worst hurt he could ever feel. From there I went to Yuma prison where George was incarcerated for the shooting, I looked up his record, He was pardoned by the governor of AZ and later given a job by the governor in the territory. He made onyx rings and walking sticks and onyx card boxes. Yuma prison is a museum now and a great sight to visit. If I find where I put the letter copies that I have I will mail them to you. I have a gold piece that your mom gave me from George Rood's gold mine, the one the lawyer cheated him out of and my daughter has a ring that he made in Yuma prison, Grannie had a black onyx ring that he made that I think your mom had. If I think of anything else I will let you know. Love, Lana

Perhaps because of her love of history, Ma kept stuff and was great about keeping travel diaries and writing letters which recorded her own life. She sent us letters as well as birthday cards. Even when living it up in Norway in her 20s, she always wrote to her aunt Esther and remembered her birthday (June 24th). I have kept all the cards Ma sent me, they are so lovely, carefully chosen for my birthdays over the years. She would write, "We think of you all the time" and other sweet thoughts.

In my 3rd year at university, I got a letter which I truly cherish. As I am now at the very same age Ma was when she wrote it, I appreciate her thoughts more than ever. By then, three of my sisters were married. Every family has its squabbles and misunderstandings. Something had happened amongst some family members which Ma inadvertently got dragged into (as I was away, I do not know the odorous details.) One called another and got mad and heard something another had said, someone else thought it should have been handled differently, etc., blah, blah, ad nauseam: the typical family garbage which happens to us all, unfortunately. It doesn't matter who it was, for we all fall into stupid behavior at times, when we are stressed. Ma wrote:

> …now it's all over and I don't care. There must have been a reason for it all happening as it was just a series of strange happenings. Maybe some good will come of it. I've lived through so much in my lifetime that I can't be bothered with such petty things. I did feel very bad about (*Family member X*) being lashed out at when X shouldn't have been. Altho' I can understand (*Family member Y's*) anger, too. But I can't be bothered with hassles and touchy people. There are so much more important things in life.
>
> I'm tired now and I only want to be with kind, pleasant people who don't take offense and quibble.

[Ma tried to never hold a grudge and she simply "kicked it to the curb" (as my dear mother-in-law Kay has taught me) and moved on, treating all with kindness and living peaceably as far as was possible on her side – but, perhaps, avoiding drama where she could. We see how grateful Ma always was later in the same letter.]

> It was so delightful to be with Kjer and Miguel. We took the Christmas presents. The little sweater you gave Mikael looks so cute on him. Kjer and Miguel gave us a set of white ironstone dishes for the kitchen. Boy, was I glad.

Bo and I are going to Binghamton to get a clothes drier… Bo got his refund… Can't wait to get the drier. Bo is so thoughtful and kind. Keep praying that good things will happen for him.

Hope all is OK with you. Say Hi to Meg and all the others.

Love, Mom

Ma once told me about an adventure she had driving. She took her eldest grandchild, Mishawn, to Binghamton to shop. On the way back to Deposit, a policeman pulled her over!

"What seems to be the matter, officer?" she asked politely.

"Well, ma'am," he answered respectfully, "You were speeding, going 80 miles per hour."

"That's just not possible, sir, I always drive the speed limit," Ma responded. And Mishawn leaned over from the passenger seat and pitched in adamantly, "My Grandma NEVER speeds!" As it turned out, the car had just been in the garage for service and there was apparently a problem with the speedometer. She did not get a ticket either.

Ma wrote me another newsy letter later that year, which describes her busy social life:

Thursday November 3, 1983
Dear Maggie,

You've been on my mind all week. I hope your cold is better, Daddy said you had a bad cold.

Julie's been sick, but went back to school Monday. Bo got a sore throat but couldn't get a Dr's appointment so he's trying to cure himself (sounds like Ma herself, she only went to Dr's if she was on death's door).

We had a cookie bash at church on Sunday night, but I was too tired to make *Gorokaker* on Saturday so I got up early Sunday morning to mix up Wienerbrød (*a Danish pastry*) only to find there wasn't enough milk. So, I had to wait until Evelyn Campbell and I went to church and stopped at the country store to pick up milk.

I had mixed it up and had it raising when Martha called, saying she and Stan wanted to go to the mall for a quick trip and they wanted me to go to LOV to answer the phone. So, I said I'll bring my dough down there and bake it. SO, while I was waiting for Stan to pick me up, I greased the tins, mixed up the filling, and put it in a jar. Measured out some flour, took some butter and confectionary sugar along plus nuts for the top. Felt like a peddler with his pack. Julie and

I went down and played cards until the dough was ready. I was to be at church at 7:00, Also had to cook dinner of a sort for Dad. Julie, me, Martha and Stan were to be back by 6, but they didn't get back until 6:30. So I rushed home, threw a steak in the oven, told Daddy he would have to eat bread instead of potatoes and finally took off for church 10 minutes late, but didn't miss anything as they sang so many hymns, the main program hadn't started. Evelyn and I went every night for missionary week. Finally, Daddy went the last night.

I can't get used to Standard Time, I wake up at 5 o'clock instead of 6 all the time.

Your prayers seem to be working for Bo. He and Dennis will start playing on Sat. nites in a very nice restaurant near Sidney.

I hope you'll pray about my muscles and tissues, as I've had a lot of trouble during past 3 weeks. Partly due to moving too much furniture around.

Hope you and Meg are O.K. Rest when you can. I'll write again when there's any news.

Love, Mom

Mom and Dad were a great support to me through all my life in various ways. Ma wrote me *so* many letters to help me through my homesickness. My parents were there in May 1985, with my sister Julie, to see me receive my diploma when I graduated. Afterwards, I lived for 5 years in Akron, Ohio, an 8 ½ hour drive from home. Ma and Dad would come out to visit, we spoke on the phone and Ma continued to send letters. At the time of the following letter, it was finally just Mom and Daddy living at home yet things were tight financially.

Thursday January 29, 1987
Deposit, N.Y. 13754
Dear Maggie,

Well, it's trying to snow again. It's too bad I couldn't take a picture of all the snow. It melts a little during the day when the sun comes out. We've had very cold weather—even 20 below one night.

I've been trying to get things put away from Christmas and clean up some. Didn't go anywhere during the very cold days. I was beginning to get stir crazy so yesterday when Daddy had a dental appointment at 9 o'clock so he didn't go to work until after 10, I had him drop me at Marguerite's (*Birdie's mother, whose husband John had passed away recently.*)

When I had checked with her and knew I was going, I made

her some cinnamon buns on Tuesday night. Made me think of the days when Cecilia and Bo were little, when I used to bake and wash clothes lots of evenings.

Had a letter from Celia. Wish you were here to play games. I'm not in the mood for working. Talked to Kjer but no news. Heidi and Brent are waiting to hear from Univ. of Minn. They're good. Am anxious to see little Brent.

Dad and I hole up in the bedroom after supper. I can't go anyplace in this snow. I read and do crossword puzzles. Dad reads his library books.

We haven't eaten at "Mae and John's" restaurant in ages as we didn't have the money, but to-morrow is pay day so we're going.

I've been writing letters to friends that I didn't get done at Christmas time and can't mail them until payday. We just had to get more fuel oil. Things will be better when we get our taxes paid and the weather warms up.

Well, take care of yourself, and let us know what's going on.

Love, Mom

After living in Ohio five years, I found myself faced with some bad decisions in my personal life. The excuses I made sounded pale and one-dimensional, even to myself. Still, I felt only my parents' acceptance and care – never once a word of judgment. I always felt Ma and Daddy were proud of me, through all the small successes of my life. I must say this, my parents did the most important things right: making a home full of love and laughter, and helping me feel unconditionally accepted.

Even when I moved to Luxembourg, continuing to work for Goodyear Tire and Rubber Co., I never heard a word of discouragement, although they would miss me sorely, being an ocean away. Mom swallowed her own feelings of sadness and gave me nothing but encouragement. "You're just like your mother," she told me, "...exploring foreign lands." I sometimes felt I'd dropped off the map, in the small forgotten rich Grand Duchy of Luxembourg (a place many Americans think is part of Germany), where many people speak French but the main language is Luxembourgish, a sort of German dialect with French and Dutch thrown in for good measure. From the time I left home until the last years when she could no longer write, Ma would send wonderful letters, which almost always included a line such as, "We think of you every day." For example:

Monday, January 14, 1991
Dear Maggie,

I have been thinking of you every day and wondering how you are doing. We have had such a busy, hectic but fun time here all during the holidays. I still haven't written my Christmas letter to Norway but hope to do so soon.

What were you doing on Sunday, January 13th at 4:30 in the afternoon? In other words, 10:30 our time? I was taking down the decorations in the dining room and thinking suddenly very strongly of you!

Can't remember what I told you on the phone... Heidi's boys were very good while they were here. Of course, Seth is the bouncing whirlwind but he wasn't too bad. Little Brent has gotten so much more mature now. Baby Ian was as good as gold. We helped her what we could but I was really tired.

We loved the little Santa & especially the Christmas mat you sent. Julie put it under the little basket with the nativity scene on it (Grannie's). It sure glittered with the lights off and just Grannie's Xmas lights on. Julie got me a teddy bear ornament, it's like an angel with a halo. I got a black and white cow with gold colored bell for the tree at the Methodist Bazaar. Jan got me a soft toy cow which walks. I put it up on the large bookcase peeping out from the booklet, "Christmas Around the Farm."

I wish you'd write and tell me what you did at Christmas.

We had a really nice time with Cecilia, Jim and the kids. Those little angels, etc., looked good on tree."

The USA / Iraq war - Operation Desert Shield was going on:

Celia was afraid Jim would be sent over to Germany or Arabia but right now he's to be in charge of informing next of kin. I think the whole situation is terrible and badly handled. I just feel sick about it. But anyway, God's still in heaven so everything will be as it shall be. I think President Bush has been very undiplomatic and stupid in his choice of words and expressions. You can be firm and determined in a nice way and quietly build up all your forces. In Norwegian they would say it was so "*uappetitlig*" method of speaking.

Evelyn Campbell was asking about you. She wasn't surprised you did what you did. She understood thoroughly your feelings and thinks it was right for you. When things calm down, I'll get to see her more often and bring her down here again. I did that once. Picked her up and brought her down.

I told you about getting Norbord (old MDF) to donate $2000 to the Deposit Library for a new microfilm machine.

I keep thinking of all the French songs I know. (*Ma was thrilled that I had learned French*). It brings back a knowledge of the language. When I started speaking Norwegian, I kept thinking of the French word when I got stuck—but that was over 40 years ago!

Bo always hates to leave home when he goes back. He loves the dog and the dog thinks he's special. I think Bo longs for a family group in a way. He like his work and his music, computer, etc., seem to take up his leisure time. It isn't that he's unhappy but I think he's a little lonely. He seemed so relaxed, calm and down to earth.

Ma always liked baseball and sometimes watched the Baseball Championship Playoffs.

"I've been rooting for the Blue Jays ever since Little Brent was born. It was quite exciting...Thank goodness it was on CBS Station so we got it on TV. Made me think of my father. He had wanted so much to play in the Major Leagues... He was a wonderful father. He used to tell us kids Teddy Bear stories. I wish he had them written down. I can remember some parts of them. He made them up as he went along. He did go to the World Series once or twice in New York. Once he brought me back a Mickey Mouse watch. Enough of that. How did I get on that subject – I guess because of the Blue Jays.

In the early days of my transitioning to life far away from my folks, in another country, there were difficult times. Even the time difference of six hours complicated things, I couldn't just call when I wanted, they might be sleeping. I once drove the wrong way over a bridge on a road only for taxis and got yelled at by the police in a language I did not yet speak. There were cultural adjustments to make, languages to learn. I missed my folks a lot in those early days.

Dad took care of some business / banking stuff for me, and wrote me this letter (his spelling):

January 14, 1991
Kjære Maggie!
    We received your letter the other day with the enclosed checks.

I closed your account in Akron and opened one here in your and my name.

In your letter you said you felt that colleague is working against you? He is probably a sore loser anyhow but you can do it. Send him back to USA. It is good however that you work as a team.

How is things going in Luxembourg? Met any new friend, Norwegian or Americans? Have you found a good Lutheran church yet? (*You*) better get going.

How is the weather? We have had a mild winter so far with a total accumulated snow of about 6 inches. Ok with me, the warmer the better.

Nothing new here, same old bash. Julie is busy with her new fiancé. She is now certified school teacher and we are awaiting eagerly thousands of phone calls offering her a job. So far, she has substituted in the famous Deposit school system. Well, the hiring of teachers does not occur that much before the new school year. Hope she finds something soon. Is there any American or other skools that are looking for a bright teacher as Julie, around Luxembourg?

Kjersti is slowly getting over her nauseated feeling due to her pregnancy, which is good. She also scored straight A's in her subjects at Newark. We will be going down to visit with them in about 2 weeks for about 4-5 days.

Love, Daddy

Mom wrote me an amazing, encouraging letter a few months later. Although I did not always share about my troubles, Ma knew. This letter speaks of her own way of viewing disappointments.

April 24, 1991
Deposit, NY 13754
Dear Maggie,

You sounded good on the phone.... We all have our ups and downs. That's the way life is. Doesn't seem to stop but I think as you get to be a senior citizen or at least by the time you are 60 you stop worrying and realize that if you do your best, there's nothing more you can do, so why worry? I don't mean you change your way of living and do rash things, you just don't get upset by disappointments, etc., when things don't work out the way you want or thought they ought to.

Every once in a while through the years I used to wonder why God didn't grant one of my most wanted desires. Although I always felt you couldn't question God because He did what was best for you.

Then one Sunday Bruce Dyke *(at the Christian Missionary Alliance)* preached a sermon and said it was all right to question "why."

I guess I never really understood until I got past 60. Then, in reflecting on all kinds of events in my life, goals I strived for and things I tried to do, and things that actually happened, I realized that although I am not a fatalist, that God grants you a life that is best for you. If one had been allowed to take "another road", it could have been disastrous for one – in other words we ourselves couldn't conceive what the long run results would be but <u>God knew</u>. And as that little sign in Kjer's room says, "When God closes one door, He opens another." I really believe that. I really had a more interesting life than if I had gone to Syracuse and become a librarian! I used to get upset and hurt and worried about a lot of things but as so many times, you have to take things in your stride and make the best of it.

You have to take things as they come and make the best of it – rise to the occasion. I don't get too upset about things anymore. I get discouraged sometimes mostly over expenses.

In another letter full of musings, Ma expressed her sense of Providence, reflecting back on her own life, "..to think that we eventually ended up in the house I had always admired as a kid!... So you see, certain things are planned out for you. Of course, you get results from your choices but some small voice inside tells you what choices to make. But (I) do think some choices are already made for you!" She always said there's no point in worrying over things you can't change and might not even happen anyhow: "*Den tid, den sorg.*" (Literally, "that time, that sorrow" or "Cross that bridge when you come to it.") Another saying we heard often was, "If it's meant to happen, it will, if it's not meant to be, it won't happen, so relax." The song, "Que sera, sera" always reminds me of Mom: "whatever will be, will be."

I tried to get back home to New York each year after I moved. It comforted me to be back home where I grew up, where my parents still lived. Everything stayed the same, giving an impression of stability, which we all need, don't we? Ma, Daddy and I would sit at the kitchen table in the late afternoon for a cup of tea, black tea or "Constant Comment" with cake, and "visit" together, in that cozy familiar place, as I told them about my new life. Ma would've made something chocolate for me, and something else for Dad, since he was not so hot on chocolate unlike the rest of the clan. Ma would serve me a piece of cake, and then offer Dad another piece of apple pie. In jest, she sometimes still referred to him as *gullgutten*. This time, as she handed it to him, she said, "*Vaer saa god, Fatty Dad*" (there you are). She put her arm around him where he sat in the captain's chair and said, "My grandfather used to say, 'Apple pie without cheese is like a hug without a squeeze'". She had so many different sayings from her relatives that she passed on to us. She'd then ask me for more "news" and she would eat up every detail. She was always so interested in new places and people. She was such a good listener. If she hadn't finished her coffee before her pie, she'd take another little slice saying, "I have to come out even" with her coffee.

Ma kept in touch with her nieces and nephews quite a bit. She wrote in January 1993:

> Lana will graduate as an LPN in June. She has been going to nursing school and working a full-time job. Her last child is in college now: I admire Lana. She's got the old Travis-Rood get up and go. She sends me "Daily Word" subscription every Christmas. She was such a beautiful little girl and still is: her daughter who is in the US Navy is stationed in Wales...and expecting next August so can't imagine Lana as a Grandmother. She seems so young & is still pretty. But she was born in 1946 so she's going to be 47 in August! I don't know where the years go.

Ma seemed young, too, in her thinking, even in her later years. The year I turned thirty she wrote:

> Congratulations on your birthday. Think nothing of it. I'll be 70 in October. Don't feel that old – I'm still thinking 30-35. Guess it's because all my parents and Grandparents were always peppy and not old acting.
>
> Well, the world is in a mess all over. How sad. I guess I'll belong to the "old" generation in October but I don't feel any different – just have a few things that bug you once in a while. But if you pace yourself you can do most anything within reason.

When I married an older Italian man named Mario, my mother gave us the most precious wedding gifts: six Pillivuyt demi-tasse cups, multicolored and gold edged which she had bought more than 50 years earlier in a little antique shop in Washington. She also gave me the six tiny enameled multi-colored spoons in their original small blue box, marked "David Andersen, Oslo-Norway" which she had bought years before. For various reasons, Dad grumbled but Ma adored Mario, the charmer, from the start. Mom wrote, "We think of Mario all the time - - especially if we have a glass of wine with dinner. Isn't his birthday in October? Let us know when it is. What a wonderful person he is. I'm so glad for you." She and Daddy lovingly "adopted" Mario's daughter, Sara, into their hearts and always asked about her and sent birthday cards and gifts for her, which pleased me to no end.

Ma and Daddy would come over to Luxembourg at least every other year and we took them around to see different parts of Europe. Just before their first visit, Julie, who was still living at home, wrote me a letter.

> "I'm sure Ma and Dad will have a blast, I had fun picking out your stuff: measuring cups and all. They are so excited about this trip. Really like two little kids. Daddy is finishing up packing. It was so funny because he left the suitcase open and Babs the cat climbed right in! Boy, Daddy would've had a fit if he knew. Mom rescued her in time. *Jeg elsker deg!* (I love you!)
> Love ya loads, Julie-Bubley
> P.S. Chocolate is the root of all evil so send all yours to me."

Ma kept a diary of that first trip, as she often did for almost all of her big trips. It was September 1991 and they drove first to Ossining, NY to have lunch with Kjersti and the kids. "The baby (Matthew) is so cute but so small (*Ma was used to her own Viking-sized sprogs*). He has Miguel's big feet." Kjersti had started writing and publishing books, and Ma was so proud – she mentioned her books in several letters to me in the early 1990s: "She got some rave book reviews – especially from another author."

From Kjer's they drove down to Fort Hamilton, Brooklyn, where Celia lived. "We went over the Tapanzee Bridge and via our old NJ Parkway route. Cece looks great. The kids are fine. Mishawn is beautiful. Jack has grown an inch since he was up home. Enjoyed the family. Played cards with Mishawn." Dad had forgotten to pack any socks so Celia took them to the PX (Army Post exchange store) and saved the day. She drove them to the airport, too. While waiting for their Icelandic Air flight, "a young Norwegian couple sat by us." She seemed to draw Norwegians like magnets.

She was so happy to visit Brussels, and Brugge, where she bought a lovely lace tablecloth. I'll never forget how thrilled Ma was, visiting Paris and especially having her picture taken in front of the famous Moulin Rouge that she had learned about years ago in school. She was so happy to have been to see this place that she always loved reading about. Afterwards she wrote, "Hope all is well with you and Mario. We love you both so much. I'll never forget our trip to Paris which he had all planned out perfectly. I never thought I would get to see all the places there that I studied about over 55 years ago! It was great."

In 1993, the folks landed in Luxembourg on May 13 and the next day the three of us flew to Dad's hometown. Dear Tante Kari and Onkel JP picked us up at the airport. That night we stayed up until 1 a.m. visiting. How especially wonderful to see Farmor again, and I know it meant a lot to her to see us all. We ate like royalty and laughed a lot. Our celebration of the 17 of May was another huge party with superb parades and food and fun, Ma loved it. Truly, it is the best day ever to be in Norway, as everyone is so happy. Farmor was all dressed up in a lovely red dress, as classy-looking as ever.

Breakfast at Tante Kari's was magnificent – she always made the best herring – either pickled or in tomato sauce besides a variety of other delightful options. Tante Gerd came up to Trondheim, too, and the photos I took of the Hoff family were the last of them together as later that year in December Farmor passed away. Farfar had passed on years before in May 1976. One of the last things Farmor said before she died, was, "I want to go Home to *Far*."

One visit in July 1994, Tante Kari and Uncle JP came to Luxembourg when the folks were with us – it was a great surprise, we had a great time together.

After they left to return to the USA, I found a note from Ma:

Dear Maggie,
Thanks for a wonderful time. Fantastic. You and Mario are the most wonderful host and hostess.
We love you,
Mom & Dad

Whenever they came back, we would always go around Luxembourg city in the pedestrian zone, and stop for coffee and pastries. Ma and Daddy came over in October 1995 and "just we gals" went to the movies to watch, *The Bridges of Madison County*. She had been wanting to see it, as she was a big fan of Robert James Waller. She kept the enthusiasm of a young teenage girl! She loved that film. It was so fun to share such moments.

The lovely thing about Ma was her enthusiasm: her face would light up in delight at the things she would see or experience the first time no matter where we went. I loved that about her. Occasionally we got all "dolled up," as Ma used to say, and went out to a fancy restaurant. Ma would put on one of her new dresses, some nice clip earrings (she never pierced her ears, like me) and her classic, bright red lipstick. She enjoyed such times and those special meals in Luxembourg city.

Once Ma and Daddy got to take the train down from

Ma, Daddy and me in Luxembourg

Luxembourg to where Heidi and Brent lived in Italy. What a lovely trip they had! They especially loved traveling through the Alps and had a wonderful time with the Johnsons.

In 1997, Dad "went on-line" and got set up to send emails – so high tech. He and Ma would write an email occasionally and mostly let me know how everyone was doing but Ma didn't care much for computers. In March, after I had called after a downhill skiing trip, Dad answered by email:

> Dear Maggie: Thanks for the call today and a happy easter to all of you. Glad the skiing went well although the beginners trail aint so cool for an old-timer like you...Over here in the old USA everything is going just fine, between the Omaha bombing and the California cult suicides the other day, we are doing fine. So watch out for the computer wizard and the local nuts involved in cults, they are crazy.
>
> Heidi is currently in Florida, visiting Brents' grandparents... they return today since she has to go to Nursing classes on Monday. I am trying to use the touch system on the keyboard so you must excuse me if I miss a few letters here and there.
>
> All Kjersti's boys are OK and finished with winter colds. We haven't heard from Cecilia lately but when we talked to her last, everybody was doing fine, she was busy with a report for the army, justifying the personnel on her payroll. Good luck.
>
> Julie and the girls are doing fine and Roger, I call him TOP-GUN because he is busy playing a game called combat pilots.
>
> I have done some raking outside, hoping it will warm up pretty soon. Here comes my wishlist: *Tyttebær, Multer*, winter underwear, T shirts made of cotton, Barber Cost, *Barber hovle*, the old-fashioned kind, you know, and don't forget to bring one of Mario's old bottle of fine red vine, from the cellar, ha,ha. If I can think of something else before you come I will send additional requests.
>
> *Hilsen*, (Greetings)
> Daddy"

Ma wrote after one of their trips south:

> Dear Maggie, It's Monday last day of March. They had a wonderful, beautiful service in church yesterday with extra music...It's so good to be home. I've been cleaning and polishing furniture but it is hard because normally I do a little each day so being gone so long, things got stacked up. I host study club in April. Am looking forward to seeing you...I have 2 books ready for you and will see about some

more that might interest you. Hope you are feeling OK. I cannot tell you how much I love that photo of Sara. She looks so pretty and happy in that picture. Love, Mom

Later, just when I was having blood tests to prepare for a laproscopy, to investigate the reason for my 3-year infertility, they discovered I was pregnant. My parents were thrilled. When they came over in mid-June 1996, I was 3 months pregnant. That time we stayed in Luxembourg, but how we talked and laughed. I would sit on the blue chair stretched out on the veranda, knitting a blanket for the baby. Ma told me of her pregnancies and deliveries, saying how she would get "as big as a barn" with those Viking babies (remember, Julie weighed 12 lbs 9 ounces). She also said that every single pregnancy was unique and unlike the others.

Then, while they were still visiting, I started to feel sick. Mom wrote in her notebook:

July 1st Maggie didn't feel so good. She talked to Dr and is taking it easy. Dad & I did all the work. She may have to see the doctor tomorrow. Her friend (Nina) from church did some shopping for her.

July 3 Maggie having problems.

I started spotting and ended up losing the tiny baby that I had waited so many years for.

July 5 Maggie had to go to the hospital at 6:30 a.m.

July 6 Maggie is home. Feel sorry for her. Dad and I waited on her all we could.

July 10 Went with Maggie to the Dr. She's doing OK but has a low pulse. He gave her some medicine. She and I played solitaire. We leave Thursday to go home. Sorry to leave Maggie but guess she'll do OK.

I could not even begin to say how much Ma and Daddy helped me through those days. I thought my heart would truly break, the disappointment was crushing. Ma and Daddy were such a comfort, so gentle and kind, hugging me all the time. Ma shared that she, too, had lost her first baby at about the same time, something I had never known. How grateful I was, that God arranged for my folks to be there with me at that dreadful time in my life. My sisters and Tante Gerd sent kind emails, cards, or letters. The letters Ma sent, as I went through the months that followed, are treasures to me. If I had not had this sad event, would Mom have poured out her heart as she did? Even Daddy clipped out an article from *Reader's Digest* entitled "New Hope for Preventing Miscarriage" to send with Ma's letter. Their concern was palpable, their love like the sweetest, pure water. Looking back on this period of my life, I can see how much closer I became with Mom and Dad because of the difficulty and loss, and I am so grateful.

July 16, 1996
Dear Maggie,

I came upstairs early and am propped up in bed to write. I always go upstairs early 8 – 9 o'clock at night so I can stretch out and read or do crossword puzzles, get off my feet.

Babben (*the cat*) is trying to get on my lap but I had to shoo her away.

First, I want to thank you for all the good times and the opportunity to come. I'm glad we were there to be with you during your difficult times.

I always have interesting times on airplanes. The student who sat next to me was from Trier and thought it was great that you had taken us to Trier before...

We do hope you are feeling better.

Kjer and Miguel were at the airport to pick us up so we zipped out to their home in Ossining in good time. They were all well. Lots of activity going on.

Dad has started to play golf. He is fixing the roof over the play room bay window.

Am enclosing an article. Daddy just found it and read it and came in and said to send it to you. I think it will be of interest to you. Don't get discouraged. Time will tell. Whatever will be, will be...

Sept 20, 1996
Dear Maggie,

I've been going to write for a long time. It's almost 7:30 a.m. I always wake up 6-6:30, read my daily devotional readings and then do crossword puzzles. Dad is sleeping away. He sleeps a lot and always has.

I think of you all the time. Every time I wear those nice long-sleeved cotton nightgowns. I even wear them in the summer as I have to keep my arms warm…my arms ache if I don't keep them warm. It's funny because even when my arm muscles are inflamed, they still need to have a sweater on them.

I think of Dr. Dossef and what a wonderful Doctor he was. He sure pulled you kids through a lot of serious illnesses.

[And he sure helped to pull Ma through in 1977. What a tough thing to live with: the illness that plagued Ma the rest of her life, meant she dealt every day with chronic muscle pain because any time she did any kind of work, she paid for it afterwards.]

Dad raised up on his elbows and wanted to know what all the scratchy noise was. 'It's me writing to Maggie,' I said. Oh, 'I should write too,' he said. We enjoyed your long letter.

Well, I hope all is well… Sara must be getting more grown up now. Have you talked to Tante Kari or Gerd? I should write to Gerd. I think of her a lot. This is the first letter I've written in ages.

We love you, Maggie. Think of you all the time. Take care. Thanks for everything.

Love, Mom

During the early years after I had moved away to Luxembourg, and especially in these years of infertility, I was writing to my folks very often and called them every week: it brought me so close to them and they deeply appreciated it, and let me know often. "You are far away from us, but yet with your close contact by letter and phone, you are much closer to us. Keep up the good works," Dad wrote.

For over a year I went to specialists to try to get pregnant again. After a whole series of tests, the specialist said the only way would possibly be via artificial insemination, and finally, I gave up. Mom sent a letter sharing with me thoughts about her own disappointments and God's Providence.

Saturday, September 20, 1997

Dear Maggie,

We think of you every day...I know that you are disappointed that you don't have a child of your own. But Sara is such a sweet girl and I know she thinks the world of you. Perhaps with a visit to a new doctor, something new may be available to correct the problem... but you must be thankful for what you have.

As I reflect once in a while about my disappointments in life, I see how when the Lord closes one door, He opens another. Some things are meant to be. If I had been able to use the scholarship at American University, I never would have ended up at the Norwegian Embassy in Washington. And as I look back at different situations, I can see that it is true about "opening a new door."

I have always felt the presence of God ever since I was a tiny little girl and as I look back on both good things and disappointments, I know it was best what I got or was given instead. I had the most wonderful early years close to nature and outdoors and among my dear family including Grandparents, Aunts, Uncles, cousins, and Great Aunts and Uncles. It was so wonderful to wander over the hills, the pastures, the fields of my Rood and Travis ancestors. They were all so loving, kind but morally strict. Very religious but not stuffy.

I come from a long line of "bookworms" and became one myself at an early age. My Grandma Travis took care of me when I was 2,3, 4 (years old) as Mom taught school up Rood's Creek. Grandma & Grandpa had had a very rich Business. They still had bookcases full of books. My Great Grandma Travis was a teacher. They had all kinds of history books, 1st editions of Fenimore Cooper books. Redpath history with thick leather bindings and covers. All kinds of books in built in book cases and other bookcases and shelves in the upstairs closets. It was so sad that so many or most of those were ruined during the fire when Kjersti was about to be born.

It was such a wonderful life to be able to wander in the woods and pasture land to pick wild flowers, watch the wild animals and to see the Indian Burying Grounds that Grandpa carefully protected.

Now all that whole area up Rood's Creek and down Route 17 to Hancock is grown up to trees, bushes, weeds – big mess. The forest on top of pasture hill has grown dense all the way down to what was the fruit orchard on level with the residence. It's sad. Nothing but bushes, trees and highway where once beautiful farms had been.

Guess I've rambled on a lot but some things just aren't meant to be, I guess. Anyway don't give up on your condition. See the new doctor. Life is full of surprises both good and bad but no matter what, God is there.

I never thought much about it before but it was some thing that I ended up being married in the Trondheim Cathedral - - pictures of which were always included in general selections of and about Norway sent to libraries, clubs or individual groups that requested information and pictures, which was part of my job.

People often wonder how I dared travel on an old freighter to a foreign country, etc. But after 4 years with the press section of the Norwegian Embassy I was thoroughly indoctrinated. Years later when I worked at the American Embassy in Oslo, they used to call me "The American Norwegian!"

Ernie told me later that the personnel manager at the US Embassy nearly flipped when he read my references - - they were all very well-known Norwegians – diplomats, business owners, authors, journalists, movie makers, etc. Of course, after my first stay in Norway, I went back to Washington Norwegian Embassy for 2 more years – then when I went to Norway the 2nd time instead of staying 2 months, I stayed 2 years.

Enough of that, you know the rest of it.

But isn't it something that I ended up in the house I had always loved as a little girl living at Roods Creek... we always took the back road to Hale Eddy on our way back from Deposit. Grandpa used to say he had attended political meetings at Mr. Devereux's house. Think of that.

Enough rambling...Mishawn is here. She is doing well...Dad is doing OK but he has worried a lot about all the things that went flooey at once...the vacuum cleaner, his tractor, the water softener. I didn't think about it until Mishawn complained that her blonde hair was getting red. Then I noticed my hair was getting browner. Well, that's all fixed (iron in the water).

Never a dull moment.

[That paragraph made me laugh right out loud when I read it.]

Well, Maggie, I must stop. My writing is getting worse and my arm muscle hurts. I hope you get something out of this letter if you can read my writing. Give Sara a hug from me and our love and best wishes to Mario.

Love,
Mom

In October 1996 the folks were visiting at Julie's house in Ohio. Julie and Dad sat together to send a joint email:

Hi Maggie, Hi Nosey, Hi Killer Toes,

Guess who's here? Dad is sitting next to me and I'm typing for him. They had a nice trip out. I made a great dinner and chocolate chip cookies. Dad and ma are HERE hahahahahahaha

Trip is getting longer every year. Never seen so many trailer trucks in his life. (Got any arab juice?) The worst part of the trip was the stupid Goodyear tires that has about 36,000 miles on them and already going bald and one has a flat spot. Send me a new set directly from factory for Christmas. Next time I'm buying Michelin.

End of Dad talking. Ma hates computers and says she will just write you another letter she thinks this is a waste of time. Talk to ya later.

Julie

In May 1997, a bunch of the family gathered in Ohio including Auntie Helen. Beau took Mom and Dad out to the Carousel Dinner theater in Akron to celebrate their 45th wedding anniversary on May 24. Mom so appreciated it. She wrote an email (with no capital letters):

dear maggie, hope you have a nice second birthday. well we arrived here all o.k. quite a gang here. Bo was over yesterday a while. poor cecilia could not come the last minute she had to go to a camp lee virginia because the commander's wife had an emergency operation and Cecilia was the one person who was qualified. she felt terrible she wanted to come so badly. boy you should be here with all the gang. The kids are something else. we are all enjoying being together...

After we all left home, it was so rare that we got back together, so Ma was very blessed by it.

Shortly after, at the end of 1997, a miracle happened. On December 5, 1997 I did a home pregnancy test and it was positive! JOY!!! Ma and Daddy were thrilled. After a delightfully splendid pregnancy, my daughter Lucia was born in August. The pastor at Ma's church put a special white rose on the alter on Sunday to give thanks for the birth of Lucia, our little miracle. Ma was nearly crying as she told me, it meant so much to her. How happy both my parents were, and how precious that was to me, sharing my joy with them after so many hard, long years of waiting.

When Lucia was 2 months old, the folks came over to Luxembourg, in October 1998. They were delighted to meet

Dad and Baby Lucia October 1998

her. They brought her the cutest pink frilly girly dress with white lace. She was not a great sleeper and I was exhausted. Dad was wonderful at taking her and helping get her to sleep. "I've never seen a little one fight against sleep the way she does," he said with a grin, "She doesn't want to miss anything."

Dad went nuts for *all* the grandbabies. He would walk slowly around the rooms, patting Lucia's small back, as he held her gently on his shoulder. He set her down on the dining room table and held her hands, her bright eyes fixed on him as he made faces and smiled at her. When Dad would give her up, Ma would hold her, rock her, and sing to her. Dad was a huge help besides burping and carrying Lucia, he set and cleared the table, did dishes and took out the trash and other household chores. It meant so much to me.

We celebrated my mother's 75th birthday during that visit. I made the usual "Double Chocolate Delight" cake as Ma had taught us, and decorated it specially. Mom enjoyed it immensely. That cake is awesome. It was in Grannie's recipe book and we made it ours. By that time, I had lived in Europe for quite a while and tried many other cake recipes: Australian, Belgian, French, German, and Italian recipes, but *that* one is truly the best.

After they left that time, I found a little note in the kitchen, printed carefully in capital letters exactly like this:

MAGGIE,
THANKS FOR EVERYTHING.

318

HUGG THE LITTLE ONE FOR ME.
I MISS YOU BOTH.
LOVE,
DADDY

I sent the folks a long letter plus a bunch of pictures from their visit. Daddy wrote back by email:

Dear Maggi Dooty and Lucia Dooty!
We have received the email and regular letters with photos. I like the one with the little Boppies glancing over my shoulder saying, 'Best ride in town.'
Thanks for the lovely pictures of her. I hope you have finished her passport papers and figured out your vacation schedule for next summer. We have advertised your two-somes arrival next summer and they can't wait to see you, so hurry up. Glad to see Mario spends more time with the little one, if he doesn't, I will be over there to spend the time for him, ha, ha.
Hope you get some good sleep with her, the little boppies. How much (*child*) allowance (*does Lux government give*) for her, a little angel like that should be worth a fortune.
Just to send you a little note, and thank you for the lovely time we had with you all. Greetings to Sara.
Love,
Daddy

In the birthday card the following May 1999 Ma wrote, "We are so glad you now have little Lucia, She is so cute. We are

Grandma sings to Lucia "She'll Be Coming Around the Mountain" in the kitchen, home in Deposit, NY

319

looking forward to seeing you this summer. Wish Mario could have come too......Love and hugs, Mom P.S. Special hello to Mario and Sara.

In the summers Lucia and I flew over and spent two weeks at home with my parents in NY. Ma was always calling Lucia, "G'amma's good girl!" Lucia would play in the yard and proudly bring my mother haphazardly-shaped bouquets of dandelions and daisies. Ma's face lit up with heartfelt appreciation when presented with each one, and she'd say, "Why Lucia! That's LOVELY, thank you Honey!" The number of such gifts she received was countless, but each one was valuable to her and the genuine way she showed it made your heart swell up with love and affection.

Becoming a mother myself helped me to appreciate my mom more than ever and helped me to see her in a new light. I had never realized the sacrifices she made for us, how she took the time for us and thoughtfully raised us well, teaching us to live a good life by her own example.

Alzheimer's

Now begins the part of Mom's story which saddens me to write, but it must be told to complete the picture. In her early 70s, we began to notice short-term memory problems. It was more than just misplacing her glasses, which was a regular event for Ma ever since I can remember. No, this was something else, clearly, something was not right when she would ask the same questions over and over, like trying to figure out which day it was. She also became more short-tempered and seemed easily annoyed by active little children, for example - unlike before.

Already in October 1998, when the folks came over to see Lucia for the first time, I could see that her short-term memory was worse. She asked what day it was a thousand times a day. "Every morning," Dad told me, "She asks me where we are." Dad answered her, with a smile, "We're in PARADISE, Mrs. Hoff." She elbowed him in the side, laughing, and said, "We are NOT!" I could see that she was very dependent on Dad and more affectionate than ever towards him, as he was so patient and kind with her.

Her dementia progressed as the years passed, and although she was sometimes frustrated at her lack of memory (she said with a laugh, "I sure am gettin' stupid!"), it was those around her that suffered most. My Dad was so good, taking care of her as long as he could manage. He displayed a patience and gentleness which amazed us all.

In a note dated May 15, 2000 my sister Kjer wrote after visiting the folks' house, "We had fun at Mom's but I don't know how Dad does it. Mom is constantly asking the same questions over and over. She can't remember what happened 1 minute ago. She asked me who I was only once. Once she gets your name, it's pretty good. I hate this disease."

In June 2000, Lucia and I went on vacation to NY. Kjer and Miguel picked us up at the airport and there was the usual laughter to tears in the van as we caught up on life and carried on with our typical nutty humor. A few days later, Mom and Dad came down to Ossining for an overnight. Then Lucia and I drove back to Deposit with the folks. Dad took us around for a fun ride in the wagon behind his tractor, and we all went shopping at Ma's favorite store: Boscov's. The folks bought Lucia some magical sneakers that lit up when she walked and other clothes "for the buppie" – what a treat for the grandparents to spoil the little one they rarely saw. One night, Grandma read storybooks to Lucia - a big hit. Grandpa introduced her to Mowgli of *The Jungle Book* and the two of them laughed together like old comrades, with him teasing her and making her giggle all through the movie, as they sat side by side.

One night at bedtime, as I was putting Lucia down, I finished reading and was just about to pull up the covers around her, when suddenly she got up from the bed. "Where are you going, Lucia?" I asked. "See Granpa," replied the little not-yet-two-year-old. "But it's time for *bed* now," I pointed out. She turned to look at me with a serious face, and gestured with her small, half-Italian hands to emphasize, "I NEED Granpa!" He was to remain a key person for her the rest of his life.

On that trip several of my siblings with their kids came for 4th of July and we had a grand time, with much silliness, and played Password evenings in the living room. Ma got many right answers, surprisingly, and Dad kept us all laughing. During our times together, I think we all observed Dad being so patient with Ma and her fading mind. He turned a sad and weary situation into something bearable by his humor. We played and gabbed late into the evening. Often, Dad was the first one to end the night, (he always needed a lot of sleep) saying to the gang, "Well, folks, I'm going to bed. Goodnight," as he headed to the front door to lock up.

The last Sunday of our visit, Dad, Lucia and I went to church. Lucia couldn't resist all the toys in nursery and was happy to be with the other kids. At the end of the service, everyone held hands in a circle and they sang a closing song. When we came to the line, "…as we go our separate ways…" looking at Dad, holding his hand, both our eyes filled with tears. It was such a hard thing he was going through and it was a hard thing to live an ocean away from my folks, but it made our times together all the more precious.

After we arrived back in Luxembourg, and I was putting Lucia to bed, she asked me, with hope in her eyes, "Granpa come?" Another day, I heard her pick up her toy telephone and say, "Hello, Granpa? How are you? I fine. You watchin' Mowgli? Bye bye." We did keep in touch with my folks, calling and writing letters and sending photos frequently.

In October, 2000 Mom turned 77. When I called her to wish her a happy birthday, she was her old self in most ways, yet kept repeating the same question throughout the conversation, "So, when are you coming to visit?"

She sent me one of the last letters she would ever write to me. The handwriting is different, a bit messy, she repeats herself of course, and her writing is somewhat unusual, you'll see why. She reminisces a bit over her youth, and other life experiences, as if summing up her life for me and, of course, includes something Norwegian.

Dear Maggie, Mario, Sara and Lucia,
    Thank you so much for my Birthday present. What a beautiful card. I am going to hang it up someplace. I love the front page. Of

course, I went out and bought some more crosswords and will use the rest to get something when I see what I want. Probably a book. I hope you can read my writing. The cat is half on my lap and half on the sofa.

We think of you folks all the time. I'm so glad you are all so happy. We are very thankful for your prayers. My muscular pains bother me but I have learned to cope with and the medicine does help. However, I don't overdo it taking too much. Just what I feel I need. Sometimes it is worse than others. Oh well, I can't complain. I've had a wonderful and fantastic life.

What a great time we had at the family homestead. Grandpa had several acres of land (about 100) but he didn't farm it for a living. He was in the bluestone business along with generations of his father. It was used for curbing and sidewalks in New York City, etc. But when concrete was invented, the bottom fell out of the bluestone business.

Then at one point the banks failed so both my Grandpa Travis and Grandpa Rood families lost a lot of money. That era was called the Depression Era.

But everyone did their best to keep things going. That was in the days of what was called the Depression. I was a young child then so didn't understand what was going on.

Many men out of work would travel on the freight trains to get to someplace. They weren't supposed to but they did. It wasn't like the travel trains. Didn't have rows of seats like the regular trains. There were so many people out of work that they would stop at a house and ask if they could chop wood to earn lunch or dinner. I was often at my Grandpa and Grandma Travis's. He was in the bluestone business. It was usually shipped by train. So when a train stopped to unload stuff, the tramps would hop off and go to the main road or roads where they could ask for lunch or food and they wanted to chop wood or do something in exchange for lunch or dinner. It was a sad time. But when President Roosevelt (Franklin) became in office he started the CCC program which worked to preserve the forests and countryside's. Many young families that were out of work ended up doing that. It saved a lot of people from starving. (Conservation program)

Of course, when I graduated from business college and ended up at the Norwegian Embassy in Washington, D.C., I started a whole new life. I had had 3 years of French and 2 years of Latin so it was great that I could learn Norwegian. We sent out news releases to the American papers and news and information about Norway to the Norwegian newspapers (in Brooklyn, the Midwest, etc.) Of course, I heard Norwegian spoken all during the day so that helped. Then a Norwegian gal that came to work at the Embassy after the war, gave me advanced lessons.

So, Maggie, I guess you know the rest. I feel like I have lived 9 lives.

I hope all is well with you all. We think of you folks all the time.

Thanks for all the wonderful times we've had with you folks in Europe. We love and appreciate the two of you very much and especially love Sara and Lucia.

Love, Jeanne (& Ernie)

P.S. Maggie where did you find that cow sticker?!!

In 2001, one of my sisters wrote me a note which describes so well the terrible effects of Ma's dementia. She wrote:

Dear Maggie,

The visit with the folks went well. Ma is very attached to Dad. That makes it hard for Dad as he is so burnt out. He looked OK to me but tired. I tried as hard as I could to keep Mom occupied and out of his hair. Sadly, the things that used to entertain Mom don't work anymore. She doesn't want to watch the news much anymore because she cannot keep track of what she has heard or seen. She will play Scrabble but forgets how to spell words or what word she had thought to make. If she plays Solitaire, it can only be with one person -Julie and I tried playing with her and she got too flustered. She also was forgetting the game rules and the suits of the cards. It is really depressing. She does still do her crossword puzzles although she looks up most of the answers in the back and she will read the paper several times throughout the day. The absolute hardest part is the repetitive questions. Every day for a week she asked me the same questions over and over again. We would go through this cycle of questions: where do you live, how long have you been here, where is your husband, etc., plus many more and when we finished this cycle of questions, literally within 10 seconds it would start all over again. I can understand how Dad would be tired of it. They were here a week and I was ready to pull my hair out!! Another indicator of the progression of the disease is that she is beginning to be confused with reality. She has a favorite pink sweater and she told me that her Grandpa Travis gave her money to buy it. She had said this to Julie too. Alzheimer's is a horrible disease!"

It seemed incredible, almost ironic, that my brilliant Mom, Norwegian translator and interpreter, woman of impeccable memory, Trivial Pursuit wizard and history buff should be losing vast portions of her brain as the merciless illness progressed. And the ones that loved her could only stand by helplessly.

My parents' neighbors, Kurt and Sherry Vandermark, were an enormous help during this time. They were always such great neighbors, both parents said several times over the years. Sherry would hop over to the house to visit from time to time, sitting with Ma on the side porch for a friendly chat. They both did many things to support my Dad as he tried to keep going under the weight of this burden. Once Kurt was driving into town and saw Ma, in her bathrobe, looking confused walking along the roadside. She was lost, did not know where she was, or where she was going. He kindly helped her into his truck and brought her back home.

For us, her children, we lost an invaluable part of our mother. You could no longer talk with her about your problems, or ask her opinion about a given situation in your life. She simply could not follow a conversation. She would forget what you started to tell her. It was immeasurably sad, losing this side of her, as *confidante*. This was especially true because she had a way of talking with you, which made you feel so very "believed in," as well as listened to. It is difficult to describe this loss.

Dad would drive the two of them down to Texas almost every winter to stay with Ma's eldest nieces, Kat Rood Ray and Lana Rood Farthing. The "Texas gals" Ma used to call them. They were so good to my parents and enjoyed having them around. Kat and Lana would take Ma around all different places shopping. They went to the mall, to all kinds of clothes stores, where Ma would be thrilled to buy a skirt or dress at a great bargain. They went to the furniture store once and Ma helped Lana pick out her favourite desk. After that, they went to a junk store, and Ma surprised Lana by buying a beautiful ceramic pencil holder decorated with birds for Lana's desk.

They also went out to "exotic" restaurants, like Mexican style and sometimes Ma would accompany Lana on some of her home nursing visits. Lana's kids which lived in Texas, like Rhonda, Diana, and David, spent time with Ma and Daddy too, and all loved them a great deal.

On Jan 4, 2001 cousin Kat wrote,

Dear Maggie, It was nice to hear from you. Your Mom is doing OK but she is quite forgetful. Sometimes it's like I'm being interrogated in a police room but I tolerate it quite well - although sometimes I wonder if I'm giving her the correct answers. After a while, I forget how many kids I have and how old they are. We have a lot of fun though and she laughs a lot. I listen attentively to all the stories. Sometimes she tells me one I haven't heard. One day I went over to see her and your Dad and she had just gotten out of the shower and was standing in the kitchen in her underwear so I said, "Aunt Jeanne, I never saw you in your underwear before". With that she laughed and started doing a little jig. She is still quite agile. She looks great.

There was always a humorous side to this sad period of Ma's life. Lana and Kat both told of the time Ma was visiting their mother Auntie Helen, and the two of them got to looking for some missing item and then during the search, realized that they couldn't remember what is was they were looking for, and they both burst into laughter.

In June 2001, Ma and Dad made their last trip together over to Luxembourg to visit. I took two weeks of vacation. The weather was fabulous that whole June. We had, as usual, a wonderful time together. Ma enjoyed so much going around the city, eating pastries and drinking coffee outside on the pedestrian part of Luxembourg, La Grand Rue. Ma was often pushing Lucia's stroller. It was the summer of the life-sized cow statues, placed all over the city, brightly painted in various ways. We stood by one painted a patchwork blue and another leopard brown and white: Ma loved the cows! How appropriate that her last trip over was graced with all those colorful cows!

She and Daddy always loved watching the different people walking by. Wherever we went, she was interested in everything she'd see, and her lips, clad in the usual bright red lipstick, were ever turned up in a happy smile, or pursed to express an "*Ooooob*" or an "*Ahhhhhhh*". She was always the most appreciative and interested tourist. She'd take my arm as we walked around, the other hand clutching her purse tightly in the characteristic Ma pose. Daddy said her pocketbook was a kind of security blanket for her.

We drove to Remich to take a boat ride on the Moselle River. Ma, Sara and Lucia loved the swans, geese, and ducks. That night, up in their room, Daddy was telling us about three campers he saw from the boat as we pulled back into dock. A rather large, hefty woman had fallen into the river right by the shore and the two others were unsuccessfully trying with all their might to pull her up with interesting facial expressions and girations, according to Dad. When they got her up, you could see her rump was all black with mud, and Dad recounted the event with great mirth, as usual. He had a way of telling stories that could always make Ma laugh.

I knew Ma's memory was disappearing, so during this trip I asked the folks about things from their youth. Both Ma and Daddy enjoyed sharing stories from their lives: for Ma, that was normal, for Dad, not so much. (I don't think I'd ever heard about his childhood, and I suppose, I'd never asked.) Ma told how her Grampa Travis took her to Sunday school. How he and Grandma Kate helped the roaming gypsies that would come looking to cut wood for a meal (during the Depression). How Grampa Travis would always help neighbors, etc., who were out of work or into any kind of trouble. She spoke of the games she played with her sister and brother, and of how their father invented so many bear cub stories for them. She also spoke several times about how "*All* the girls at the American Embassy in Oslo were after Daddy" and about the first time he called her up to go on a date.

Dad said he'd had a wonderful childhood, how every summer they went to the countryside outside Trondheim and stayed on a farm right near the fjord (Vikhammer). All the railroad kids got to know one another and would have a grand time all summer. He mentioned his friend Gunnar that sang all the time they walked the streets of Trondheim. "That all ended with the war years and I had to grow up fast," he said. He spoke of his time in the Norwegian Airforce and how he had wanted to be a pilot but was refused, and how, after the war, he signed up on a ship, "to see the world: India, Brazil, Portugal..." Much of what Dad said I had never heard before.

We prepared a lot of Italian food and Ma ate and ate to her

heart's desire. The problem was, she couldn't remember how much she'd eaten, or how long ago. She seemed to be a bottomless pit. And the amount of chocolate she ate! Immeasurable quantities. I loved spoiling them, and did everything possible to give Dad a degree of freedom while they were here. Dad would take walks by himself, when Lucia would let him out of her sight. He went to buy a coffee, his newspaper, a soccer ball for Lucia, etc., and enjoyed a bit of freedom. He started to look less haggard. He needed the space, since it was exhausting caring for Ma by himself, bathing her, helping her dress, helping her get from room to room, answering the innumerable questions. At the end of just 2 ½ weeks I was dead tired. But even though she couldn't manage to bathe or dress herself on her own, it really struck me how she kept her good sense of humor. One day, as I helped her dress, she said to me with a laugh, "Would you look at me, European traveler, translator and career gal, not even able to dress myself!" I did her nails, finger and toes, and said to her as I clipped, "You know Ma, my Lucia has inherited your 2 big toes." Ma had two slightly disproportionately large big toes. "That's good," she said, "You know those big toes help me keep my balance."

Dad and I went for one last walk before they returned to the States, down to the shopping center "Match Espace" in Beggen. Lucia slept nearly the whole time in the baby jogger. I bought Dad a long-handled orange shoe horn, and we had treats and coffee. I felt so sorry as I understood how overwhelmed Dad felt taking care of Ma. He had simply had enough and was exhausted, it was so emotionally and physically draining.

They flew back to NY on July 5th, and how sad it was returning to the house and unmaking their bed, seeing their room so empty. A week later, we called them and Lucia was thrilled to hear their voices again. When Dad said to her, "How's my little sack o' potatoes?" she burst out laughing.

Back home in Deposit, Ma, ever the Early Bird riser, became a person that slept and slept. This kind of change was also so strange to see. Even when they were at home, every day when they woke up in the morning, Ma would ask Dad where they were. He would alternate replies saying one time, PARIS, and the next ROME, or some other exotic place. Again, I think it was his strong sense of humor that helped him through a very sad situation for so long.

Dad encouraged Mom to keep up her little routines. She still did her crossword puzzles, watched the news, and would go up the front sidewalk to get the mail after breakfast. He would help her to "cook" by telling her where the pans were, how to fill it with water, boil vegetables etc. It took more time than doing it himself, but he told me, "I think it helps her to at least do things she used to be able to do before." One time Dad said really scared him, when she stood in front of the refrigerator and pointed to it and said, "Now, what is that thing?" Even everyday common objects became unrecognizable.

As time went by, her illness continued to progress until Daddy simply could not carry on by himself. He was getting "caregiver burn out," and he had one illness after the other (including bladder surgery), and became terribly worn-out. So, they moved to Wadsworth, Ohio to stay with Julie and her family. They renovated the house a bit to accommodate the folks. God bless Julie, who took this on, as a busy young mother who already had her hands full. Our wonderful brother-in-law Roger, Julie's husband, loved Ma like his own, and he was an enormous support for Julie, who carried the weight of Ma's care, besides home schooling and caring for their 3 small children. Of course, Beau, who lived nearby, and Daddy helped, too.

After just a few months, the relentless illness progressed to a point where Ma had to be put into a home called Altercare (in April 2002). All our hearts were broken, I think Julie's most of all. None of us ever would have dreamed of placing our mother in "an institution" but all of us agreed it had to be done. It was against everything Ma ever stood for. How could this be happening to us, we all thought, *How can it be possible, that it comes to this?* But, there was simply no other option.

Living an ocean away was also frustrating for me. All this going on and I could not help in any way. The guilt is even worse, and the helplessness, when you live so far away. Sure, you can analyse logically, thinking, even if I was there, it wouldn't help much. But it's your emotions that win, and you end up with this sinking feeling in the pit of your stomach. Your mind returns there, over and over again, and there is no resolution. I tried to put this energy into praying for Mom and all the family, which helped to some degree.

Ma was placed in the Alzheimer's wing, since she had the tendency to wander, besides many of the other symptoms of that awful disease. Still, the Lord was gracious to us: Altercare was a wonderful place, only 2 minutes' drive from Julie's house. The nurses and caregivers loved Ma and were so good to her, and Daddy, Beau and Julie were nearby. They would take turns visiting so someone was there every day at least for a short visit. The consistent routines were good for Ma.

She had rare moments of clarity, which were both painful and comforting for them. She also wanted to know when she would get out, which pierced their hearts; but then, at least she recognized them, if only for a short while. In fact, strangely enough, all through her illness the one person she always recognized was my brother Beau. It's true, who *could* forget a face like that?

There was some comfort in knowing that Ma didn't really know what was happening to her most of the time. I think she suffered less emotionally than the rest of the family. While our hearts were ripped apart by her descent into dementia, she seemed to have no idea what was happening to her. Kjersti said that in a way it was like she returned to childhood, and she did look very childlike, in the photos of her in activities at Altercare.

In the beginning of her time at Altercare, I called and spoke to Ma every week. Even then, she always knew my voice, strangely enough. She would even ask about "my little girl" and about Mario sometimes. It was so wonderful just to hear her voice, so full of warmth and concern. Of course, the conversations were very limited and repetitive, but at least I could tell her I loved her, and hear that voice I loved. I wrote her many letters, and Julie would read them to her over and over. When she got our letters, it was clear that she understood they were from her daughters, and she loved getting mail.

In October 2002, Mom moved into the next stage of her illness. She would have fits of yelling and anger, extremely frustrated. Sometimes she'd go into an anger fit, and they would call Julie, who managed to calm her down over the telephone. One time one of my sisters called, and Ma vented her anger, saying that Dad was helping "that woman with all the children all the time," instead of spending time with her. That association came from the fact that when Dad visited her, as he left, he'd tell Ma, "I have to go now." Then he'd say something about Julie and/or the kids, so she associated his leaving with Julie. When I would call her, as soon as she got off the phone, she would start yelling and got mad because "Dad is with that woman in Europe". Of course, they couldn't reason with her. Then it got so any time she'd go into her anger fit, they would have to call Julie over to calm her down. They tried giving her different medication but it didn't help much. Altercare asked us all to stop calling, at least temporarily, since they were worried about the fits.

In November 2002, Ma had what seemed to be a mini-stroke. One of my sisters wrote me on November 7, 2002:

> Mom woke up yesterday with the following symptoms: unable to understand/follow directions (Julie had to show her how to use the toilet), unable to identify everyday items (not able to feed herself or drink), extremely difficult to arouse from sleep, and altered speech (spoke slowly). She was stuck in the 1940s living in her Norway era. Initially, she thought Julie was her sister and Dad was her father. (At one point, Julie told me, when Dad left the room, Ma started carrying on about "how strict our father is with us, never letting us go out," etc! Julie was cracking up.)

Throughout November, Ma had a few of these mini-strokes. On Monday, November 25, 2002 Julie sent me a note. She knew I'd been feeling bad about not being able to call Ma. She wrote:

> Sorry about the Mom thing, but it is very important not to call and talk to her. She'll have an episode (fit) and then usually I have to go over to Altercare and calm her down. She has what they call a

mini (kind of a mini-stroke) then it takes a couple days of sleep and working with her to help her to learn how to feed her self-again go to the bathroom etc., that's why it's so important not to have extra stress for her. (Anything outside the normal routine throws her off now). It's hard enough at this stage, because she still has awareness that she can't remember, so it's hard for her.

She seems to like it there at Altercare and they are very good to her. I have had to go every day for a while then went back to normal and then she freaked because of a visit from somebody and the 2 phone calls, so we are back to everyday. As you can see, the last thing I need is more stuff, so get the word out, no more phone calls. But letters are great, she loves them and reads them over and over. Phone calls to the nurse to check on Ma are also fine, just refrain from talking to her. I think it might be the confusion of not seeing the person she's talking to, I don't know, it's weird. I used to be able to calm her down on the phone but now I have to go in person. So tomorrow we go there for Thanksgiving dinner and hopefully Thursday I have Ma here. Well, I gotta go so I can get all the home school done before the library and Altercare visit. Cya later. Julie

Julie was simply amazing in her care of Mom through this ordeal. She has a real gift dealing with the elderly (as well as kids!).

The first weekend in December, Julie and Roger went to get Ma for a Saturday so she could decorate the Christmas tree with the family. Ma always loved Christmas, and really enjoyed the activity, although she wasn't really sure where she was. The surprising thing was, the next day at Altercare, Ma told the nurses to guess what she had done the day before. When they asked her what she did, she said that she had decorated a lovely Christmas tree. She actually remembered! This shows how very much family traditions meant to Ma. The fact that she remembered meant a lot to Julie, too, that I know.

In December she somehow broke her hip and had to have an operation. Either she fell, and it broke, or it broke from the osteoporosis and she fell. This was an excruciating time for Ma, during which she suffered terrible physical pain. This was of course, awfully distressing for Julie, Daddy and Beau especially, who saw her suffering so much firsthand.

After the hip operation, she began physical therapy. One time, when the physical therapist was trying to ask Ma questions in an evaluation, she only answered in Norwegian, as if she had forgotten how to speak in English. They had to call in Daddy to translate Mommy's answers! It made Daddy laugh, and they were all wondering about this behaviour, but it did not last long, it was just a phase. How odd yet amazing the human brain is.

The Valley of the Shadow

In January 2003 she had another stroke. This time she was paralysed - she could no longer swallow, etc., and it was clear she was approaching the end. We were all called to Ohio to see her for the last time. How terrible that long trip was for me – I did not know if I would get there in time to hold her hand and kiss her once more. As it turned out, we all got to see her before her death. We stayed in her room, doing everything possible to express our love, and keeping the place filled with laughter, reminiscing, and talking as if she could join in the conversation. When one was overcome with sorrow, they would leave the room and another one would go and comfort them – that way Ma didn't see our pain of losing her and was surrounded only with love. Once Kjersti left the room and went down the hallway sobbing. Big Jack, Celia's 6-foot-plus son, went and put his arms around her and they cried together. Even the nurses, who were so strong, had to break down in tears at the sight.

The nurses and aids were wonderful. They brought us things to eat, and coffee to keep us going.

When I stayed one overnight at Altercare to be with Ma, and during the next day, the various nurses would tell me stories about Ma. She would sometimes speak to them in Norwegian with a twinkle in her eye. Often, she'd be singing some old song that made them smile. They all spoke of her in such affectionate terms, it was easy to see that she had won their hearts in the short time she was there.

Someone was always holding Ma's hand, and rubbing her head, and talking to her during those last days. When Daddy held her hand, he'd say to her, "I gotcha Mommy, I gotcha." It moved us to tears. We sang her old hymns and other old songs she liked. She rarely opened her eyes, but somehow, you had the feeling she could hear us. My cousin Lana, a nurse, had seen a lot of people die. She always tried to be there holding their hand or making sure a relative is there, if possible. My sister Julie who now works in a nursing home and hospital does the same. Lana swears that "they all know, if someone is with them even if they appear to be in a coma. At the last moment they may open their eyes, so they do know."

When the end came, on January 24th, Dad, Julie, Beau and Heidi were there. Julie's terrific pastor, Roger Loomis, led by the Spirit, had come to visit. He had just been there to visit, and was supposed to leave for a conference in Cincinnati. But he felt so strongly that he should go again to Ma in Altercare. When he got there, he asked them if they wanted to pray together for Ma. They held hands, and formed a semi-circle around Ma's bed. At the end of the prayer, Ma opened her eyes, looked up, and it seemed she saw beyond them. A look of joy and peace lit up her face, as a rosy color filled her previously death-white cheeks. Over the years I learned that Ma, whenever full of emotion, be it from joy or love, would get choked up, and a few tears of intense motion would escape. At that moment, tears came from her eyes, rolling slowly down her face, and in a moment, she was gone. How kind the Lord is. It was as if Jesus Himself came to take her, and in His kind and generous way, let us know that indeed, Ma is with Him in Glory.

Mom was cremated, as she wanted, and the beautiful urn which Julie had selected was placed in Hale Eddy Cemetery in New York. There, in Hale Eddy, are also the tombstones of several relatives, the Clappers, Travis's, Roods and Surines. Her plot is in line with and less than 8 feet from Uncle Duane's and Aunt Helen's plot, which Celia thought was fitting when she picked out the plot (she wrote, "They can play bridge together.") One plot holds 8 cremation urns. Celia went to Bainbridge to pick out the headstone, which is a double stand up headstone of grey polished granite. The stone is from a quarry in NY State, which Celia thought Ma would like. Unfortunately, they could not use bluestone. We know, because Celia asked. What a woman.)

On the stone, at the top center, is the name Hoff (between 2 crosses – they didn't have cows, Celia said) and at the bottom left below the Hoff name is Dad's name and birth date, on the same line to the right is Ma's name (Jeanne Rood, no Dorothy since she hated it) and dates of her birth and death.

Celia was one of the first to go back to Deposit after Mom's death (Dad was still in Ohio with Julie). She wrote:

> It was especially difficult to be in the house at Chestnut Grove with her cows and all her things. I still cannot bring myself to enter her room, her smell is still in the house. I never know when I am going to see something that hits me with a strong memory of her, and my eyes well with tears. On the other hand, I feel so much closer to her when I am home. I close my eyes as I sit on the living room couch, I hear her steps and I hear her say "Whatcha doin', Cee?" I think so much about the times we had when we were kids and how she was ALWAYS there. I pray for strength and give thanks for the blessing of having her as my mother and I feel better. But I still miss her so much, guess that is something we will all be living with. I still miss Grannie. Time heals all wounds, but does not totally stop the ache.

Mom's nieces and nephews would miss her too. Lana wrote in an email shortly after Ma's death:

> Hi Maggie,
> She was a wonderful aunt. We laugh at the time Aunt Jeanne and our mom were looking for something and they both forgot what it was. We were blessed with a great aunt and a wonderful friend, Rhonda and Diana speak of her a lot too, here in Texas she will be missed, Just to let you know we loved her a great deal,
> Love Lana

How to describe the feeling you have after losing a mother of such calibre? I somehow felt infinitely uncovered, terribly exposed. Losing a parent also makes you feel loaded down with a weighty feeling of the uncontrollable passing of time, a sense of aging, for me, previously unknown. If that is what it feels like to be truly grown up, then I'd rather not.

The Memorial service for Ma was held on May 31st, in the First United Methodist Church on 2nd Street in Deposit. Julie's Pastor Loomis, who was Ma's pastor at the end of her life, made the trip out from Wadsworth, Ohio and did the service together with the local pastor, Craig Gommer. During the service grandsons Mikael and Seth read poems in memory of their grandma. After the service there was a Committal Service at the graveside at the Hale Eddy Cemetery, where her ashes were placed.

Almost a year after Ma had passed away, on January 11, 2004, I had been missing Ma a lot, and thinking about Grannie, too, who was born on January 10th. I had made it a habit every year to call Ma on Jan.10th. I had been feeling kind of down, thinking that this month it will be already one year since Ma passed away. All day I had been at the edge of tears. That night I remembered a pack of old letters which I had asked Daddy to bring me on his last visit in June. They were a bunch of letters Ma had given me years ago, which I kept under my sink at home in Deposit. They are mostly letters from Grannie to her mother, Kate, written during college, and other letters Grandma Kate had kept from her various children and friends. I started reading them, and those from Ma's Uncle Vern, and Uncle Ralph, etc., and I felt so happy; it seemed I could hear their gentle voices from the past. The family ties, as well as their humor, blessed me and I went to bed contented.

In the early morning hours, I began to dream: I was at home, in New York, in the house at Chestnut Grove. Heidi and Daddy were there, and Ma was there, but we knew that it was Ma, her spirit, although she looked like her normal self. She was unable to communicate with us, and seemed at a lost to where she was and what she was supposed to do. She sat on the couch in the living room, and followed us around. At one point she tried to walk through a wall, as if to check if she wasn't a ghost or something. Finally, the others were not around, and Ma and I were in the kitchen. It was night time, and I saw her standing by the kitchen sink, looking up through the window. It was as if she yearned for something. I asked her, "Are you going up to Heaven now, Ma?" And I too looked up into the sky. Suddenly, I saw a very bright light: it was as if the heavens were rearranging, the stars where swirling around into an elliptical shape, and I saw such brilliance and beauty as I've never seen, light of an indescribable intensity.

There was a kind of rare and lovely music which was somehow physical, I do not know how to describe it. Then Ma went up into Glory and everything became dark. I ran upstairs to tell Heidi, who was sleeping in Kjer's bed, in my dream. As I described what I saw, the beauty of it overwhelmed me, and the kindness of the Lord, and I began to cry. I woke myself up crying for joy. Mario had been trying to wake me, and he asked me what I was dreaming. When I said that I saw my mother going up to Heaven, he said, "Then why are you crying?" But all I could answer was that the extreme and indescribable beauty made me cry.

I am sure that God sometimes speaks through dreams, although it is rare. I'm so grateful for His gentle ways of reassuring us. In the church service I attended that very same morning, we sang the hymn, "Immortal Invisible, God Only Wise." This verse came alive to me:

> *Great Father of Glory, pure Author of Light,*
> *Thine angels adore Thee, all veiling their sight.*
> *All praise we would render: Oh, help us to see,*
> *'Tis only **the splendour of Light** hideth Thee.*

I miss her warm voice, her smile, her laughter, her songs, her funny expressions and sayings, but what a blessing it is to know I will see her again someday. I carry a picture in my mind of the last time I saw Mom; we were in the Brussels airport bathroom (of all places) and she wiggled her hips in the usual Jeanne Dorothy fun-loving fashion, a smile on her face. She was so full of life. How precious is this gift of life, to be treasured daily, as are the loved ones around us.

My Memories Of Ma: A Poem

Little Lightening in a big straw hat,
Chasin' round the farm,
Big Toes stubbed and feet so flat,
Big eyes brown and warm.

The village queen, from old Rood's Creek,
Left for Oslo town,
She laid a kiss on Ørnulf's cheek,
He finally settled down.

Edna's daughter, but Norway's girl,
Adventures sought and found,
6 kids born, life's still a whirl,
And Jeanne keeps dancin' round.

Memories and thoughts of you,
Each one holds them dear,
A Mother's love is always true,
Her presence ever near.

I hopped and skipped down the sidewalk squares,
And through the front screen door,
Bakin' or cleaning: you were always there,
And Life felt safe and sure.

A ready smile, a warm embrace,
Songs from long-gone years,
Missing spec's she'd lost some place,
Laughter to the point of tears.

Cows and cats and clarinets,
Pinochle, "Go Fish",
Chocolate, Scrabble, "Now who plays next?"
Offers for lickin' the dish.

Memories and thoughts of you,
Each one holds them dear,
A Mother's love is always true,
Her presence ever near.

Flossy, Esther, and Grandma Kate,
Family stories told,
Politics and long debates,
Respect for young and old.

The Shepherd's love revealed once more,
As loved ones watch and wait,
He gently closed the earthly door,
And opened Heaven's gate.

Chocolate cake and a cup of tea,
Wish I could share with you,
And though you are not far from me,
Still, sorrow stabs me through.

Memories and thoughts of you,
Each one holds them dear,
A Mother's love is always true,
Her presence ever near.

- Margrethe Hoff, January 2003

DAD: THE LATER YEARS

When Dad was sixty-two, in 1987, he retired and eventually decided to take up oil painting. Beau, who had studied art at St. Olav College in Minnesota, gave him a book on mixing colors and VHS tapes of Bob Ross episodes he had recorded for Dad. Dad truly enjoyed Bob Ross, with his gentle, teaching manner. He practiced in the bay window of the living room, "where the light was good." Norway was stamped on his memory, and he covered the canvases with mountains, strong and majestic.

By 1995 his skills had greatly improved, and Ma wrote, "You should see some more of Dad's painting. He's really into it. Has tapes and got some more instruction books from the library." Landscapes were his thing. (Once we went to Paris to the Louvre

Painting by Dad

together and went to all the wings of the museum with the most landscapes. Sometimes we sat down for quite a while, in the middle of the room, in silence, taking it all in. He really enjoyed Jean-Baptiste Camille Corot's work there.) I recall the wonder in Dad's voice as he mentioned how amazing it was, the many, varying shades of green in the world, there were so many, and he had never realized it until he took up painting.

Dad always loved soccer, too. When I came home from my studies for breaks we played impromptu games of soccer with folks in the area: Lackners, Lobdells, Jeff Hempstead, Julie, me and Dad, who played goalie. I was impressed with Dad's soccer skills, and thought, *Wow, that's crazy, for someone his age.* (He was only in his *fifties* and I thought that was old – that is hysterical to me now). Jeff had organized 'rogue' soccer games for years. Surprisingly enough in little Deposit, that group included, at times, someone from Holland, from France, from Germany and of course, one older Norwegian. In fact, Jeff took Dad to the 1994 World Cup in a huge stadium to see Norway vs. Mexico. There were smoke bombs and balloons, and "Sons of Norway" fans who sang. It was quite a moving experience, Jeff said, having Dad be there to see players from "the Old Country" kicking the ball around and especially, winning the game, 1 – 0.

Above all else, golf was probably Dad's greatest passion and he took his clubs everywhere he travelled, even playing once in Luxembourg when he came to visit. He often golfed with "Mr. Jones" at Afton ("best course around") and with the "over the hill" gang almost every Tuesday. Occasionally, the group all played at Senior Citizens golf contests in the area. "They keep at it until the snow flurries start. Talk about maniacs!" Ma wrote once. In the later years, Dad and his elderly friends would laugh and joke as they commiserated about being "old" with all their common aches and pains and having to run to the bathroom all the time ("...the only thing it's good for!" and "...you old pisser, you!" They teased one another as they continued to golf, not walking but riding in the golf carts by then.) Some of the golf buddies were gardeners and gave Dad lovely fat, homegrown tomatoes, which he appreciated.

Dad and his friends often helped each other out. Dad drove his friend Olin Hart to see the eye doctor in Sayre, Pennsylvania (about an hour away). He took him to the Veterans Hospital in Syracuse occasionally, too. He also drove our family friend (and our violin teacher) Mrs. Phyllis Baker up to the hospital in Syracuse a few times when she had eye troubles. He said Mrs. Baker was so thoughtful of them when they had the house fire. He also drove Ma around to her activities, quite often, and gave rides to Ma's good friend Birdie when needed. The free time of retirement was spent in many useful ways.

Both parents adored their grandchildren, as mentioned earlier. Ma would buy books for the little ones just as soon as they could hold a book. She'd sing songs for them, too. Dad would take a baby and carry it around on his shoulder, walking slowly around the room, patting the little love-bundle on the back ever so gently. Mom wrote in January 1994, after Julie and Roger's visit with little Esther: "That baby is something. She's very alert and 'wise.' Of course, Daddy spoiled her carrying her around." He truly adored the babies, every single one. When they were a bit bigger, he'd sling them over his shoulder, both of their arms hanging down his back and he'd say, "I got a sack o' potatoes here," and the toddler would laugh. "Grampa, I'm not a sack o' potatoes, you silly!"

Dad with baby Esther

Dad once told about watching one of Joshua's soccer games, when he was quite little. "Yesterday we went to Kjersti's to see little Joshua play soccer. What fun that was. Those little buggers was out in the field, bunched together like a bee-hive, kicking and shoving at the ball, their little feet and arms a swinging. What a circus, I laughed till I almost fell down. Then the parents were screaming and hollering at the kids, it was hysterical." Dad attended many a soccer game of his grandkids over the years when possible.

The grandchildren had an impact on Dad for the better, in many ways. When Brent Jr was a toddler, he adored his grandpa, who he called, "Paw-Paw." The little guy was absolutely the sweetest kid, and always told him, "I LOVE you, Paw-Paw!" It was after this that Dad began to say the same words to us and his grandkids, words he had had not verbalized but expressed in actions.

Dad was always very active, but like his mother before him, he suffered with arthritis, his knuckles were knobby and his ankles pained him, he got stiff after sitting too long, but he never complained. There were a few years he took vinegar mixed with honey in the morning to help reduce pain but I doubt it worked because he stopped. In a letter from Ma (Sept. 1996) she wrote, "Dad's fingers bother him some - - worst some days than others. We've had so much rain."

The rain made the lawns around the house a deep and vibrant green and Dad loved being outside, mowing on his tractor. He also had many tasks to maintain the big house, scraping and painting railings and trim, etc. Different family members came home and helped, Beau, Roger (and Julie), Miguel (and Kjer), but none of us kids lived close to the folks so the bulk of the upkeep fell on Dad. Besides raking up all the leaves, the trees surrounding the house were getting old and branches would fall and needed attention. Our neighbor Kurt would help Dad often and he remembered with a laugh how Ma, who loved the trees, would come running out of the house with a concerned look on her face saying to Dad, "Don't cut anything down!!"

Old houses need roof work at times. Once, in his 70s, Dad was working on the highest roof and fell down onto the lower roof, then to the ground! When he saw the doctor, all was ok, just some bruises. "*How* did you ever fall from such a height and not break something?" the doctor asked, incredulous. "Well, I just rolled the way we learned in ski jumping in Norway, it came right back to me, the most natural thing," Dad said.

Dad never liked the cold and snow. Towards the end of winter, he was always looking for that first robin, harbinger of spring. In winter, he was plagued with sinus troubles. He usually wanted to sleep with the window open so he could breathe better. One February he wrote, "Here in the good ole USA, we have had quite a winter, cold and lots of snow. Accumulation so far 2 ½ feet. You can keep it." He was always hoping someone in the family would buy a place down south so he could stay there in the winters.

This created a bit of dilemma, because Ma wanted to stay home in Deposit and Dad wanted to have winters in the south. In 1992, Dad even rented a small place in Florida, as an experiment, and Ma decided she wasn't going to go with him so she stayed in Deposit where Julie still lived. I spoke to them both that February, Ma up north and Dad down south, and felt the distance, like the misunderstanding, between them. I could hear in Dad's voice that he felt badly and missed Ma and Julie but had felt the need to make the trip – he was feeling *old* and like he could not stand another cold winter. I told Ma that this was not done *against* her, and that I could see, with every passing year, she meant more to him. Ma said we "have to take the bad with the good and no one's perfect." But that was the last year they spent a winter apart for any length of time.

Eventually, he and Ma would drive down to Texas for winter which took a little over 30 hours. The first trip was in January 1995. Dad wrote a letter (a miracle in and of itself. The spelling is his. Notice his love of mountains.):

Dear Maggie,
    I thought to give you a detailed description of our trip here to Texas…our driveway was full of ice, but I got out the salt and cinder, and soaked the drive-way with it and it worked. We got out and was on our way. The first part of the journey was thru Penns. on route

81. The roads was bare and the sun was shining, temp in the 40s. We had nice weather all the way to Texas...continued thru Virginia, including the beautiful Virginia mountain range...picked up Route 40 near Knoxville, Tennessee. I have never been in Tenn before but it is a beautiful state, different from any other state because it is splattered with little knolls rather than hills or mountains with small pine trees all over the place. It does not look like a big state on the map but when you drive thru it, it's quite long...we entered the state of Arkansas where our industrius Bill Clinton was born. We went to a little town called "Hope" and the sign said that this is where Bill Clinton was born. We didn't stop to visit.

[Do I detect a hint of sarcasm? Dad was a staunch Republican while Ma was a Democrat.]

We went tru Memphis and Little Rock before we turned north to Jonesboro where Mamy's friend lives...stayed a couple of days and had a good time. Had a good visit. They are getting old. From Jonesboro we went thru the state of Arkansas, quite a long trip and entered the state of Texas.

Texas is a big state, you do not realize this til you start driving tru it. Texas is a nice state, but lack one thing, and that is the mountains. It has however a nice climate, temperatures in the high 60s and the most important thing is that I can breathe normal again. What a relief.

As mentioned earlier, they stayed in Lana's ranch style house with her husband Bill, "who is a very nice and quiet fellow. I do like him." It had "lots of room" and was located "near Lake Livingston which is 12 miles across and over 50 miles long. A very big lake with lots of good fishing. Bill has a big boat which he takes down to the lake." Mom and Dad enjoyed their nieces, Kat and Lana, and Lana's kids who lived nearby or came to visit in Texas (Rhonda, Andy, etc.)

Well, here we are in Texas, waking up every morning with blue skies and warm temperatures, and I think that Mrs. Hoff is enjoying herself immensely. When we see the forecast up north, with snow and sleet, we are fortunate that we can be here where it is warm.

So much for Texas, Maggi, how is things in good old Lux? How is Mario doing, is he monitoring his blood pressure, we are not getting any younger. Say hello to Sara from me, hope she is doing OK.

We have talked with Julie and Bo over the phone and they are doing OK. Julie will phone as soon as she is expecting the new baby so we can plan to travel to Ohio. We haven't heard from anybody else so we assume everything and everybody is doing well.

I am sitting here at the kitchen table to write this letter to you, so don't fall off the chair when you get this letter.

I sure miss you Maggi, and hope to hear from you soon. We are both doing fine and enjoy this fine weather.

Med mange tusen klemmer to you,

Love, Daddy

The trips to Texas to the "Texas" gals became an annual event – with Dad wanting to stay for months and Ma wanting to stay for weeks for she loved being in her own home and didn't seem to mind Northern winter weather. Dad found a Lutheran church in Texas which he attended, and said how much he enjoyed singing the hymns, which were "just like the ones he sang back in the old country."

There were also so many wonderful trips to Luxembourg for Mom and Dad, as mentioned earlier. Dad was always trying to help in some way: he learned how to do a load of wash, cut the grass, cleaned out my garden and loaded and unloaded the dishwasher. Ma fed the cats and watered my plants. They were such a blessing. I took them shopping and got Ma long-sleeved, cotton nightgowns to help keep her arms nice and warm and a bright yellow rain coat. Dad got a bright red Izod golf shirt and some T-shirts – how I loved spoiling them. I was so grateful that I could have them nearby.

Once, I roped Dad into recording music with me on my four-track Tascam. I had recorded the piano part to "Ingrid Sletten av Sillejord" before the folks came over. Dad and I sang the vocals and I mixed it together. I cherish that recording! After we were done, I played it back over the speakers, and Dad sat on the steps above my room, with Ma in front of him, his arms around her, as we all listened. What a special moment! They were both delighted.

In the 1996 trip to visit us in Luxembourg, Daddy went up to Norway, and Heidi went, too. Tante Gerd went up to Trondheim to visit with them as well. Gerd said that "Kari and

JP did everything so that we could have a great time." How rare it was for the American and Norwegian sides of the family to be able to meet up.

In the summer after my mother's death in 2003, Daddy came over by himself to visit us in Luxembourg. My dear friend Nina and I drove to the airport in Brussels, Belgium to pick him up. We were chatting away together, as we always had so much to talk about. We did not see him come out the doors, and he walked up and tapped on my shoulder. How we all laughed and Dad just shook his head, smiling, "Ya' dumb bunnies."

Dad seemed pretty good, yet his sorrow hovered in the background. I was so glad to spend time with him, but how awful it felt with Ma missing! He talked about her often during the visit, or said famous Ma quotes like "Ain't that just *ducky*?!" I always had a small vegetable garden and when I said how much I enjoyed it he said, "Your mother comes from a family of farmers so that's no surprize," referring to her in the present tense.

I was happy that he wanted to talk about her, it felt healthy.

In the evening, I'd pop my head in Dad's room to say goodnight after Lucia was in bed. He would be reading his Bible before he slept. We had some chats about spiritual things, and he wondered about how it says, "Absent from the body, present with the Lord" and yet another place says when Christ returns, the dead in Christ shall rise first (maybe, the first refers to the soul, and the second, to the resurrection of the body.) I suppose he was thinking about Mom's passing and wondering about these things. "Well," he said, acknowledging all we do not understand, "The most important thing is to try 'to love the Lord your God with all your heart and with all your soul and with all your strength and with all your mind and your neighbor as yourself,' - that's the heart of it all."

From the start, Lucia had her Grandpa wrapped around her little pinkie finger. They played all the sorts of games you play with a nearly five-year-old: "Go Fish," ball games, and make-believe telephone calls where Lucia, dressed as Princess, conversed with her Prince, Grandpa. Lucia would also "cook" in her little kitchen and bring Grandpa poisoned food (oh, the drama!) At his request, she would "taste" it first, and then throw herself down dead in his lap. He didn't get much of a break as Lucia would barely let him out of her sight, but occasionally he took walks on his own, which he always enjoyed. One day we drove to the coast, Knokke-Heist, Belgium, and went biking on the boardwalk there along the sea 4 miles to the Zwin bird reserve. It was probably the last time Dad biked – not bad for 78 years old.

Despite the pain of Mom's absence, we had a wonderful time with Dad that July. He was his usual calm, laid back self and we laughed a lot, as we always did. Dad was great for shopping: if I had a couple of outfits I was trying on he'd say, "Yeah, get them both, ya' look *great!*" We had so many goodies that he loved, Mille Feuilles (*Napoleons kake*), *sill* (herring), kaviar, fish, Norwegian waffles with *gjetost* (caramelized goat cheese), and *multer* (cloudberries). We went to the Scandinavian shop by the airport and bought goodies and had lunch. At home, we often ate outside on the terrace in the warm summer breeze. Each time we did something that we always used to do together with Ma underlined the gaping hole Ma left, but we talked about her so it felt somehow like she was with us, just a breath away.

Dad went to Texas again after Mom had passed for his annual visit, staying with Lana and Bill. The whole gang, Lana, her daughters Denise and Diane, some of Lana's grandkids, and Dad flew out to California for Lana's son, Andy's wedding. There was

Dad with "Sara-Bella" in Paris

a Chinese wedding and a church wedding, which Dad enjoyed greatly. I remember him telling me afterwards the fun he had with the family. He also said, "there's one thing you have GOT to see, out there in California, it's those huge red trees: absolutely incredible!" The sequoias truly impressed him.

In the summer of 2004 Dad came back to Luxembourg and we took him, with Lucia and Sara, to Disneyland near Paris and to visit the city itself. He enjoyed teasing Sara, who he called, "Sara Bella," rolling his r's like an Italian. Lucia stuck close to Grandpa. We all had fun in Disneyland, and Dad got a kick out of the Wild West-themed "Silver Spur Steak House." We saw all the usual Parisian sights: l'Arc de Triomphe, Notre Dame Cathedral and we took the boat ride to see all the intricately designed bridges. We also went to the foot of the Eifel Tower (Dad was afraid of heights and didn't want to go up.) I think what he enjoyed most was sitting at a café on the Champs Elysees, looking so American in his GMC truck baseball cap, with Lucia on his lap, making comments about the people walking by, which caused her giggles to keep bubbling over and teenage Sara to break into sweet smiles.

When Dad had turned 70, the family gathered at the homestead in Deposit to celebrate. Julie and I could not make it but quite a gang showed up. Even Tante Gerd managed to get over from Norway to bless Dad on his big day.

Ten years later, in August 2005, the whole family managed to meet in Deposit to celebrate Dad's 80th birthday, complete with live band: Harold and his buddies. All Dad's grandchildren had a blast together playing kick the can, old grey wolf, flashlight hide and seek, card games (like UNO) and occasionally "Talking Chess" with Aunt Celia. There were big tents set up and the neighbors and some cousins came, too. Daddy sat on the porch and opened presents, looking out over all the activities with a smile. Grandson Josh filmed the event and it was a party that went down in Hoff history. I believe it was the last time we were all together but, of course, without Ma.

In May 2006, Daddy came back to Luxembourg for another visit. Nina and I picked him up from the Brussels airport but this time we were more careful to watch for him as he came out from the flight. How odd it was to see him without any glasses – he had had cataract surgery and no longer needed them for distance. There was lots of laughter in the car ride back, and Nina said, "Your dad is a *stitch*." He was always teasing and kidding with people. When we got home, Lucia and Sara were so happy to see him. He asked Sara about her boyfriend, Nicolas, and gave her some advice – it was too cute. Everywhere we went, Lucia would tell people, "This is my Grandpa!" all full of pride.

One Sunday, I led worship at church and the theme was the Names of God. Our international church, All Nations, was quite new and we met at the Catholic parish hall, so it felt warm and informal. Dad and I sang an old Norwegian song together, "Navnet Jesus" (The Name of Jesus) and Dad read the English translation in a gentle voice. After, he added, "Whenever you need help, or when you get up and go to work, and if you think sometime, 'I just *can't* do this or that,' then you call on the Name of Jesus and somehow, everything is all right again." It was such a special moment, and all the people just loved him. I could not believe he agreed to do that with me.

One day, at breakfast, we were talking about buying Dad some slippers in Luxembourg city. "What about that store on the Grand Rue," Sara proposed. "Oh, it's too expensive, forget it," I said. So, Dad pipes up and says with a smirk, "What about the Salvation Army second-hand store?" And Sara, Lucia and I all cracked up laughing.

Dad and I went to the Scandinavian shop and got the usual goodies he loved. I was wearing a long shirt with a short jeans jacket and leggings. Dad said to me with a smile, "You look like a Polish refugee." We both laughed. (Why Polish? I have no idea. I'm just telling you what he said. That was Dad.)

Rob, an American friend of Mario's, took us to the Hackenberg fortification of the *Ligne Maginot* (Maginot Line), a World War I museum in North Eastern France with an underground train, etc. The guide was good, but his English was horrific. He kept saying something about "in zee foressss," and Dad finally leaned over and whispered to me, "Which forest is he talking about?" And I said, "He's saying 'in the Fortress.'" We couldn't stop giggling and it was made worst by the fact we were so few on the long tour.

That was the thing with Dad, the way he laughed so heartily, it made *you* laugh. With Lucia, they would get to messing around and he kept going and going until she laughed so hard she wet her pants sometimes (just like good ole J.D. – Jeanne Dorothy).

One night, after Lucia was in bed, it was cold and I lit a fire in the fireplace. It reminded me of when we kids were small and Dad would make a fire back in Deposit in the "chimney" (fireplace) in the dining room, in the good ole days. We sat on the couch and watched the flames dance and the embers glow, and I dared asked him about the war. He began to speak of the year he was a political refugee in Sweden. He laughed remembering how they would "sip the goods" at the place where he and his refugee friends worked on a farm and made beer that one summer, "Might as well, we said," and he laughed as he took off his reading glasses to wipe his eyes, remembering the fun of his youth. His tone changed when he remembered the challenges of being an unwanted refugee and he spoke of Anna, his Swedish girlfriend, with whom he lost contact. He tried to find her after the war on two different occasions, unsuccessfully. "Funny, how life turns out," he said.

It was a unique moment, having a quiet evening with Dad, hearing him reminisce like that – it was so very rare.

In 2008, Dad came to visit again and we went down to Aprilia, near Rome, Italy to visit good friends, Carla and Ermes Gabanella. (Dad knew Carla and Ermes already because we had enjoyed a mini-trip together to a lake in France, years earlier, in 2003.) Ermes used to work at Goodyear in Luxembourg in the same department with me and spoke decent English. His fun-loving wife, Carla, had babysat for Lucia years before, teaching her Italian nursery rhymes. They spoiled us in a million ways, with great food and laughter. On our visit, Ermes took us around to sightsee Rome and other places nearby. The weather was great, but very hot. Ermes and Dad would have a cold beer together at the end of every day and laugh over who knows what. Dad taught him the Norwegian way to say "Cheers!" (*SKOL!*)

We visited Sermoneta, an ancient, beautiful village with well-preserved walls up on a hill. As we walked the narrow streets, Dad often held Lucia's hand and made funny comments so she would giggle. After visiting the main sites, we all sat down on a bench and looked out from up above and enjoyed the panoramic view below.

In July 2010, Daddy came to visit Lucia and me at our duplex in Steinsel. He was almost 85 and in great shape. The next day, we drove the 1.5 hours to Hahn Airport, Germany to pick up Tante Gerd, 81, who flew down from Norway. Brother and sister were so glad to see one another, and talked about the old times in Norway and their youth. They prattled away in Norwegian - there were so many laughs. They shared a common sense of humor, teasing and somewhat sarcastic "but never in a mean way," as Gerd said.

I prepared a kind of meat for dinner one night which turned out tough as leather. "But it's *good*," Tante Gerd insisted kindly. "*Kor du LYG!*" Dad said ("How you *lie!*") and we all laughed. We had our apéritif out on the balcony each night. As Dad sat out enjoying the evening, I tried to open a bottle of 1990 St. Julien Cabernet Sauvignon in the kitchen and the cork broke into pieces. The wine's quality was uncompromised, thankfully, so Tante Gerd and I improvised a filtering system and Dad never knew the difference. She winked at me when we touched our glasses together and said "*Skål*" (Cheers) and Dad said, "*Skål* now folkens!"

After that meal there was one serious talk, when they spoke of the war years. Gerd told about the strongest memory she had; coming home, seeing their father, crying bitterly, after the assassination of two of his friends. It was terribly hard to get food then, they both remembered. They told of the time *Mor* went to trade on the black market some things for sugar, meat and eggs and when she came back, and stepped off the boat, there were the Nazi soldiers: they took everything she had just gotten. "She wept bitterly," Gerd said. It was a serious moment in our otherwise happy discussions, taking them both back in time, highlighting the experiences held in common from the early 1940s when they were children. How grateful I am, to have been there; it felt like going back in time with them.

Those short days together were otherwise filled with light-hearted conversation. One day Lucia, eleven years old, told us all about her school choir that had just sung at an old folks' home. "So," I asked, "How were the elderly people?" Lucia, with the candour typical of children, said with a neutral face, "They were half dead." We three adults tried not to laugh. "And," she continued, "their jaws were wiggling up and down, like this…" she moved her own jaw up and down. We supressed laughter. "Ooooo," said her Grandpa, "Maybe they were tryin' to *sing* with you!" He then made a series of funny faces and we could not hold it in any longer – truly inappropriate laughter, but that was Daddy – never any filters.

Our time with Gerd came to an end and we drove her back to the airport and they hugged each other goodbye.

Dad stayed another week and helped me by doing work in the back yard, cutting up branches for my fireplace. We also hid some cables in white tubes around the door frame and other useful things. We shopped at IKEA just over the border in Belgium, for things for the apartment, both of us attracted by the Scandinavian designs.

In July 2011, Tante Gerd flew back to Luxembourg for about 4 days to keep an eye on Lucia while I was working. (She was a great help during those years of being a single mom, cheering me on in many phone calls and coming over for Lucia's confirmation.) Lucia and I would be leaving in a few days for our USA summer vacation. The morning after Gerd arrived, we were in the kitchen visiting and sleepyhead Lucia came in, all snuggly warm and bright cheeked, and she said, "I dreamt I was with my cousins in America. But on the plane going over, Tante Gerd was with us!" And I looked at Gerd, and she at me, and we both said, "Why *not*?!" So, we got ourselves in action and it turned out there was a seat free on our flight over. We went to the Scandinavian shop and she bought goodies for her brother, who would be so surprised.

It was a great trip - first we spent time at Kjer and Miguel's in

Dad and Gerd laughing in Wadsworth, Ohio

Clinton Corners, NY where Lucia and her cousin Hannah were creating film videos, as they often did together. At one point they asked Tante Gerd to hold the camera and film as Kjer and I were also in their movie. Gerd, whose vision was already poor then, struggled and squinted and soon Kjer and I were down on the ground laughing to the point of almost wetting our pants (again). Gerd and the girls giggled with us, too. We then drove out to Ohio and Dad was so happy to see us, especially his sister. One day, we went to the Wadsworth Library in town, as Dad often went there. A rather strange, unusual-looking person passed in between Dad and Gerd as we left the library. Dad turned to Gerd with a big smile on his face and said in Norwegian, "Did you get a good look at Klem Hansen back there?" Klem Hansen was this made-up person of Dad's imagination used in various contexts to warrant a good laugh. Gerd said it was another of her brother's unusual forms of humor. Those days of our visit, Gerd and Dad sat outside in the shade at Julie's house and carried out their usual shenanigans. You could hear their laughter from inside the house. Sadly, this was the last time they saw one another.

After Ma had passed away, Dad continued living for several years with Julie and the King family in Ohio. Julie had a very special relationship with Dad. He continued to go to Texas in the winter, golfed when he could wherever he was, went to the library and read a lot. At one point, a lady from the library asked him out on a date, according to Ruth and Esther. After the date, everyone was dying to know how it went. "She just talked and talked. Too much," Grandpa said and that was the end of that.

Dad was Grandfather to the King children as well as all the kids that passed through that very active home, including the little ones that Julie babysat or home schooled. He would listen and give advice when asked and generally kept the laughter going.

One of Esther's favorite memories was at dinner one day there was only instant mashed potatoes instead of the usual real mashed potatoes. Esther, Julie's eldest, hates instant mashed potatoes so she said, "Yuck, Ma!" And Julie said, "They're not that bad, right Dad?" She was looking for confirmation from Dad. He took a spoonful of the instant mashed potatoes, paused for a moment as he tasted them and replied in the hip jargon of the youth, "Epic fail," and walked away from the table. They all cracked up and it went down in the King family history.

Dad took the time he needed for himself, as he had his own space at Julie's, but he also helped where he could in various ways. For example, he drove his granddaughter Ruth for her guitar lessons in his beloved big red truck and stayed at the diner across the street until she was done. They all knew him there at the diner, Ruth said. He attended the grandkids' soccer games, which started when they were quite small and he heartily laughed at the way the little ones clumped up on the field around the ball like a swarm of bees on honey.

"All my friends loved Grandpa," Esther said of those years. "With Grandpa's sarcasm and humor and ridiculous faces, you never quite knew if he was laughing at you or with you, and even my friend that was the most insecure loved being around Grandpa - he somehow set her at ease." Grandpa's laughter was something the grandchildren would always remember. Brent Jr said that was his favorite memory, laughing with Grandpa and hearing his hearty laughter.

My gentle husband James also liked being around Dad and Dad enjoyed talking with him. James and I had reconnected from our days at University and married in 2014. James learned things about my Dad which I never knew at all. They both had worked on ships in their younger years, so they shared ship stories. Dad told James about his favorite moments on the ship. James described their talk this way: "I remember very well one of the first conversations I had with your father in 2014. We were talking about how we both had spent time working at sea on ships at about the same age. He mentioned how he loved to go out on the deck of his ship alone on clear nights and in the dark silence to see the countless bright stars that seemed just arm's length away, filling the sky from horizon to horizon. I, too, had enjoyed doing exactly the same thing when at sea on the ship I worked on, and I immediately felt a connection with Dad and thought, how blessed I was for God to have given me your Dad as my Father-in-Law, a kindred spirit."

Solitude and quiet. Under the stars. One must slow down to experience such stillness. Dad was not a soul to be constantly meeting with people and talking. He was more of a quiet soul, in general. Dad began to really slow down, physically, in his late 80s. At around 88 years old, he stopped driving his beloved red pickup truck and really started to decelerate and finally, grew perceptibly old.

Early on January 6, 2015 tragedy struck: Cecilia's husband Harold, 69 years old, passed away in his sleep. He had truly loved and cherished my sister, so this sudden loss was profound. My sister Julie decided not to let Dad sleep in late (as he usually did), but went in to his room early to wake him and tell him the sad news. What she found was almost as shocking, there was Dad on the floor, unconscious! The ambulance took him to the hospital, he had pneumonia and congestive heart failure (CHF). He was on a ventilator to keep him alive. The timing of Harold's passing probably saved Dad's life.

James, Lucia and I took a flight two days later out of Luxembourg for Newark Airport, rented a car and drove through a blizzard in Pennsylvania to get to Ohio to see Dad, not knowing if he would still be alive or not. Upon arrival, we went to see him in ICU. He was there all weekend, but got better each day and wanted to get out! A few times we were visiting him there at Barberton Hospital, one of his doctors, Dr. Ola A. Thuestad, who was a Norwegian, came in to check on him. They spoke Norwegian together and almost seemed like old friends. We thought, this is crazy, how did Dad end up with a Norwegian doctor in a small city in the state of Ohio? God's Providence.

Close to the end of our stay, when we saw Dad's feisty ex-sailor behaviour (he gave a nurse the finger at one point when he'd had just about enough of hospital interruptions), we started to think he *would* survive! However, his heart had been damaged by the CHF and he was so very weak. It was so hard to leave him, but we had to get to New York to join the rest of the family to stand by Cecilia and say goodbye to Harold at his funeral.

Julie did an amazing job helping Dad through the months that followed: doctor visits, meds, etc. Every week that followed, every month, we thought perhaps we would get a call that Dad was gone, but he hung in there. In June he had another kind of attack and was in the hospital again related to the heart troubles. At the end of July, we returned to Ohio and stayed for two weeks. By then Dad was out of the hospital, and was so glad to see us again. It was unsettling to see him so weak. He did not talk much. Tucking him into bed one night, this man, my strong father, who used to tuck me in bed, was so fragile. Climbing slowing into his bed, curling up a bit, I helped him with his covers and he said to me, "Thank you for watching over me today."

It was also alarming the way he hardly spoke and answered questions with a short, "yes," or "no." He was never a man of many words anyhow, but clearly he was still not well. He sat in his bedroom, staring out the window, covered in a blanket, doing nothing. He was wearing a cream-colored Izod golf sweater, a cowboy hat and his glasses, with the sunglasses clips up in the air. To try to cheer him up, to pull him out of the slump he was in, I began to play songs he loved on the little cheap electric piano in his room. When I played an all-time favourite, "Ingrid Sletten av Sillejord," a song with a melancholic melody with especially moving lyrics about a girl and her cherished gift, his face brightened and he came to life again, so to speak.

He began to tell Lucia, James and I a story which the song had obviously triggered in his memory, a story from the war years, which I had never heard before.

"I saw these big guys, crying..." his voice trailed off. He spoke slowly, with phrases punctuated by pauses. He went on, describing the song itself. "She had a cap. It was a knitted cap... it was the *only* thing she had, and it was given to her by her mother, and she wore it out," his voice trembled with emotion. "She had it for so many years that she wore it out...and... I saw...soldiers...at...the Isle of Man, in England... crying...when this song was shared...But the one that sang it, at that time, I don't remember who it was...So, these big guys," he lifted his shoulders as if remembering great men with broad shoulders, "... who had been through battles...the *tears*," he lifted his hand, tracing remembered tears down his face. "It was unforgettable."

He was quiet again. I said, "At the end of the song, she goes to get the cap and nothing is left but threads."

"Yes, something like that," Dad said. "That's SAD!" Lucia said.

"It's a tremendous story. It was amazing," he said, shaking his head and smiling. "That was an island where all refugees came... before they were admitted into the Kingdom. You know the royalty was influential in that because the Prince and the King... the royal houses of England and Norway were related."

"Those were Norwegians on the Isle?" I asked.

"Yes - well, actually it was a political camp, because no one could come into the UK itself before they had went through this center on the Isle for background checks and all that stuff."

"You were like 18 or 19, right?" I asked.

"I was just a kid! And coming from where I had lived and to be right in the *middle* of all this stuff, it was emotionally, something you'd never forget, it was really something. And that was through *music*," he emphasized. There were men present at the event he recalled that did not speak Norwegian, yet they wept at the song. "Music doesn't have any language, it's international," he said.

I asked him, if he thought music might have come from heaven.

"I wouldn't be surprised," he said, "Music, everyone can

understand whether it's a Hungarian rhapsody or (something else)…and it's amazing what it can do…If you could capture those kinds of moments! It was great. One thing that doesn't need letters, or words - music: everyone can understand."

I then played another of his favorites, "Edelweiss," a song written in English from the *Sound of Music* which I knew he loved. He tried to sing along but, oddly, all that came out were words in German. He seemed lost for a few moments, he stopped, and his chin trembled as he tried to control the depths of his emotions. I do not know where he was in that moment, but it was clear that music had once more quickened his soul.

Those moments with Dad were priceless to us. Just having him "come back" to us and share an important moment in his life, one he'd never shared before, was a treasure. It was made even more important because at the time we felt we were close to losing him and were trying to adjust to the idea of his departure from this world.

Other days we sat with him out on the porch when he was able, and once drove him to Bidinger's for ice cream (he insisted to treat us). After that, James drove us to the park and we sat there in the car a while, looking out over the small pond and all the green lushness which Dad thoroughly enjoyed, being near nature and seeing something different.

The next day, I called Tante Gerd via Skype. Dad and Gerd were so glad to hear one another. His face lit up as he spoke with her. "*Når jeg blir frisk, så skal jeg hjem på besøk*," he said (When I am healthy again, then I will come home to visit). Hearing this desire that he had sent a pang to my heart, for we all knew that it was not to be.

One afternoon, during that visit, James was helping Julie by fixing a few boards on the garage. Dad joined us and sat by the house. James was sawing manually a long piece of wooden board, which wobbled and wobbled. Dad got up and slowly walked over with his cane. Then he stopped and put his cane up on the wood to stabilize it and facilitate the sawing. James looked up and smiled. Dad stopped at the tomato plant on his way back to his chair, to nip off the outer leaves to give more strength to the small, growing tomatoes as he had learned years ago in Norway. Even in his weakened state, he did what he could to live and participate in life.

He turned 90 years on August 11, 2015 and I made a *bløtkake* for him and sitting around the table at Julie's house, we asked him if he had any words of wisdom. He said only, "Socrates. Socrates said it all." To know thyself is the beginning of wisdom. Realize you do not know all that much. Be humble. If anyone thinks they know something, they still have a lot to learn. The older we get, the more this truth resonates.

Julie asked Dad about a "bucket list," were there still things he wanted do before the end of his life? His biggest wish was to return home to Deposit for the end of his days. He had a random list of other things which Julie arranged over a several month period before she drove him from Ohio to New York State: picking apples at an orchard and making an apple pie, going to the movie theatre, picking out the perfect piece of salmon (his favorite) and grilling it outside, a dinner at Red Lobster, and finally, one last time at the golf course – so there he was, ninety years old, swinging the golf club one last time. (Julie recounted to me the story of the "bucket list" in 2024, and added, "I miss him every day.")

Under the care of excellent doctors and with Julie's oversight, by the grace of God, Dad was given more time on this earth and on March 1, 2016 he moved back home to Deposit. Kjer, Beau and Julie were there a few days, leaving on March 3rd. Then it was Celia's turn to care for him. She also had a very good understanding with Dad, and spoiled him rotten. Dad was happy to be home. He sorted through his painting books and got his paint stuff organized. He remarked on how nice and quiet it was. He rearranged the living room "to be able to have better light for painting." Heidi had bought Dad a portable stereo so he could easily listen to his music there in the living room. Celia watched documentaries and Western films to all hours of the night, while Dad ate ice cream with chocolate syrup and peanuts.

It was so good for him to be back home in the familiar place where he had lived for decades with Ma and raised us kids, and it was good for Celia to have company. Her son Jack came to stay, to help take care of his grandpa. Mishawn had come back earlier to live there too, with her children, Cecilia and Stiel, so it was not an empty house by any means. In Norwegian, Great-Grandfather is *Oldefar*, which to the children, sounded like "Oldflower," so that's what they called him.

Sometime that March a mouse was caught in the living room. Mice are a normal but obnoxious part of life in the country. Dad decided at that point that they should get a cat as they were "infested with mice, and rats are right around the corner." So, they got a cat in April, which was surprising as Dad was definitely *not* a cat kind of guy, he loved dogs. The creature was given various names but most included Dad's favorite word: *bæsj* (sounds like 'bosh,' and means, 'poop').

In an email, Celia wrote to us on April 3, 2016:

> We have a cat.
> We have a litter box.
> We have a cat carer (me)
> It's name is Athena.
> Dad calls it Boshibelli.
> Steil calls it Boshie.
> Cece calls it Bosh.
> Great........a cat named shit. Save me."

In May, Celia texted us:

Dad is doing fine. He has good days and bad, mostly good. He seems to swing with the weather, when it is gray and rainy, hard to get him motivated. And of course, April is nonstop rain here. However, he has been reading the manual to Harold's lawn mower (Cub Cadet, zero turn) which is in the shop being serviced) as he thinks he is going to be out there cutting grass. God save me. He enjoys getting his email but he rarely replies. Mishawn and kids doing well...The other day while G'pa was sleeping and her mother told her it was nap time, she crawled into G'pa's bed. Mishawn went to get her and unbeknownst to all of us, she tucked a toy (stuffed bulldog) under the blankets so Oldflower could have a toy to sleep with when he went to bed. Hysterical. He and I were dying laughing when it came time for him to go to bed in the evening and we found it.

On the 17th of May, Dad's thoughts returned to Norway and the family there. At 6:30 a.m. that day, he was up, "bright eyed and bushy-tailed." He asked Cecilia to be sure to get a special message out straight away to all his family in Norway, because of the 6-hour difference and wanting the entire family over there to get the message "in time." "Ørnulf sends Greetings and Happy *Syttende Mai* (17th of May). He wishes to extend greetings to all the Hoff family in Norway from the Ørnulf Hoff family in the USA on this joyous day." Sometime in July, Grethe Findahl, Dad's niece from Oslo, stopped by, out of the blue, with two Norwegian friends. They had no idea she was in the States, she just appeared, knocking at the back door. Everyone was delighted. Cecilia said she looked fabulous. "Dad was floored and *so* happy," Celia texted us. It was an unexpected blessing.

We sent texts and photos to Dad often, and tried to keep in touch. One crazy photo of Lucia and her lifetime friend Aurora

Dad with great-granddaughter Cecilia on a tractor.

making silly faces, looking cross-eyed made Dad "laugh out loud," Celia responded. Hearing back about these small things were important to us; it gave us an ongoing connection.

Later that year, in August, James, Lucia and I came back to the States from Luxembourg, to visit family and drop Lucia at university in western NY state. Dad was doing quite well. His study of the zero-turn mower paid off: there he was, mowing the lawn dressed in his shorts and cowboy boots. He took his great-granddaughter, little Cecilia, on his lap and drove around, making sure she had on earmuffs to protect her hearing.

Dad seemed to be mostly his old self, sharp as a tack. We ate together as a family and laughed a lot. My nephew Matt was there, too, and we enjoyed his company. James, Lucia and I sat up with Dad at night, watching Westerns (I kept falling asleep) and eating ice cream (to give Celia a break – she swears she still knows the lines to all those movies.) As we left to return to Luxembourg, Dad teased us about leaving Lucia in NY, "*You* will be far away but that just means that *we* can spoil her rotten!"

In late November, after a snowstorm, Dad asked Celia where his Norwegian wooden skis and boots were – I suppose he was thinking of trying to get outside to ski! No one had seen them for decades. Celia texted us with her usual humor:

I did this to myself because I was sitting with him as he was eating breakfast this morning. We had gotten SO MUCH snow. I told him that I was thinking about getting skis for Stiel and Cece for Xmas. The minute I said this I realized how dumb a comment this was to make in front of Dad (STOP LAUGHING). Then he asks where his skis were and he thought his boots were in his closet. I said I would look for them but I hadn't seen them in years. He was very indignant about how these skis were custom made for him and explained in detail how. He then said he used to ski to work. I asked him well how long ago was that (I do remember him skiing to work, as we all do) He said not that long ago so they should still be around. Mentally I did the math. Over 35 years ago. I said this to him and told him I would look. He then reminded me they were custom made, etc…

James and I spent some time in Norway late in 2016 and took photos of many places Dad loved: Nidaros Cathedral,

Ravnkloa and more. It was Lucia's idea to create a Norway video for her grandpa since we all knew he would not return to 'the Old Country.' We met with Dad's sisters, Kari (in Trondheim) and Gerd (in Larvik) and recorded a video message from them individually. I had taken with me a CD with the song Dad and I had recorded in Luxembourg, "Ingrid Sletten av Sillejord." Kari had just listened to it, when we recorded her message. She said:

Hello big brother! Here is your little sister! I wish so much that you were here to have a good chat and to hear you speak Tronder, (*Trøndheim dialect*) for I know you still remember it.

We've had the nicest time with Maggie and James, "my honey," and it's been so *hyggelig*. We ate *fårikål* and then you *know* that we spoke about you and your (*love of) fårikål* (*Dad's favorite Norwegian traditional lamb meal*).

Your little sister had to wipe away the tears, when I heard that song, exactly the song Far always loved so much... the lovely feeling, when it was sung. When I heard you and Maggie sing it together, then I started to cry.

Thank you for the lovely times we've had... Ørnulf, I would have *so very much* wanted to see you here now... I send you a good, warm hug and wish that you may still have pleasant, good years, which we all hope for, but, we are starting to be old...

I hope we will see one another, either here or There...Enjoy your whole family and greet them from me and J-P..."

Gerd's message included funny memories of her mischievous brother and, like Kari, ended with affection, "I wish that we could all be together...I miss you, I love you." Lucia took these messages from Dad's sisters, all the photos and videos of Norway and created a lovely film for her grandpa, including the music of Grieg and the song Dad and I had recorded years earlier in Luxembourg, "Ingrid Sletten av Sillejord."

In early 2017, I accepted a job with my company back in the USA with plans to move in June so we could be closer to Lucia and Dad instead of an ocean away. It felt like the right thing to do although it was extremely hard to leave Luxembourg, my beloved home for 27 years. We got back to New York the following Easter and picked up Lucia from university before heading to Dad in New York. He was delighted to see us all again. Lucia showed him the video she had pulled together for him. He loved it and greatly appreciated seeing his sisters again, and all the old joys of Norway. It meant so much to hear his sisters' messages.

I loaned him a painting Tante Gerd had given me of Trondheim's Old City Bridge, painted by Dad's cousin, Pelle (Per) Ystad, leaning it up directly in his sight of vision. Dad thought Pelle and Ruth were still alive (but they had passed years and years before). We showed him a lot of photos of Norway which we had taken from boats, fjords and mountains, and he just loved it and said he'd like to live back in *Norge* as he missed his friends.

Dad seemed fairly good but one could see that he was failing. He got around mostly with his cane and moved slowly. He had several moments of what he called continuous *Déjà vu* which frustrated him. He would read the newspaper and his brain told him he had already read it, when he had not. He got confused once looking out the upstairs window and thought our white rental car was someone there to spy on us, as if back in Nazi occupied Norway. When I gently said "It's OK, Dad, it's just our rental car," he snapped out of it. Celia really knew how to handle him, too, in the tricky moments. She was gentle and kind and a total diplomat.

We had several good conversations, Lucia, James, Dad and I. Dad was so interested in hearing about Lucia's college classes, and delighted in her interest in the medical field (she eventually became a labor and delivery nurse). Most of all, he was thrilled that we were moving back to the USA, although he, too, had loved Luxembourg, and the many visits there.

Many an afternoon during our visit, Dad sat peacefully outside on the side porch that looked down the field which was still too wet to mow. He loved to observe the birds and the deer. It felt good to help a bit with cooking and caring for Dad: taking up his breakfast, cleaning up little accidents on the carpet, sitting with him to watch westerns or *Dances with Wolves* and eating ice cream together. He enjoyed a glass of wine in the evening and got a kick out of the two great-grandchildren, teasing them and making faces so they would laugh.

In June 2017, we moved to Akron, Ohio where I worked at corporate headquarters. I'd called Daddy from time to time. On July 4th, we spoke by phone and he was "so happy to be able to mow the lawn again." It had rained a lot and he said he could "barely keep up with it" for the grass was growing so quickly. Heidi and kids were there in Deposit for a visit which made him glad. "They're all having a good time," he said, "and what a good cook Heidi is!"

In August, we went home to celebrate Dad's 92nd birthday. Upon arrival, we went straight up to Dad's room and had a lovely chat. He said, "I'm so glad you're here," and looking at Lucia with a laugh, "You'll keep things under control." Dad seemed increasingly at peace. He did pretty much as he pleased. For the birthday meal, Celia and her son Jack made an amazing BBQ dinner. Celia made Dad a delicious *bløtkake*, his favorite. Little Cecilia put her arms around Dad, and hugged him saying, "Happy Birthday, Oldflower!" Grandsons Matt and Ben were there too, along with Jack, Mishawn and kids, Celia, James and Lucia and me. Dad's good Italian friend, Alex Conte, came too and Dad was glad to see him. Alex said what a solid, calm man Dad was, a good influence on him. Alex said to his old friend with a smile, "You're pretty important. It's nice to be important but it's more important to be nice." Their strong friendship was important to them both.

I thought to myself, *How blessed Dad is, having reached such a full age, celebrating this birthday late in life, surrounded by*

Word Cloud about Dad based on his grandchildren and great-grandchildren's descriptions

loved ones: a few of his children, grandchildren and even two great-grandchildren plus a good friend…

Dad laughed quite often during this visit but at the same time he was more quiet, tired and did not talk all that much. At one point I was alone with him and he mentioned his cousin Odd, who had also escaped to Sweden from Norway in WWII. "Odd's wife, was her name Siri? She had a brother that ran off to Peru or somewhere in the Americas. I guess he was looking for something he never really found…" His voice trailed off and I wondered what other random memories were filling his thoughts. Was he looking back on his own life, his own adventures as a sailor?

At the end of October, James and I travelled back to NY from Ohio, wanting to get as much time with Dad as we could. (We visited and stayed with James' folks in Hancock in their cozy home that always reminds me of Grannie's.) The trees were just gorgeous that year - orange, red and yellow, splashes of luxuriant, excessive color for the sheer joy of it - God's generous good heart so visible in the autumn abundance.

When we arrived in Deposit, there were grandly designed Jack-o-Lanterns literally done by Jack with his niece and nephew, Stiel and Cece, and his sister Mishawn. I mean they were carved *professionally*. It was great to see Dad again and we asked how he felt. "Physically, I got no complaints," he said, "But up here (he tapped on his head)…" He continued to notice problems with his memory, the Déjà vu anomaly. Still, he asked James if he'd been singing at all, following up on a conversation they had had back in August! "I see you still got your shorts on," he commented to James with a smile, noticing his attire.

It was lovely to be next to him, to hold his hand and give him a hug. He told us about his *"forest friends."* He was always keeping an eye out for the deer and for eagles. Once Dad was mowing out in the field (he could mow for hours in his cowboy hat) and he stopped the tractor. He kept looking up across the way, then over at Celia and back up the hill. She thought maybe he needed something and descended from the side porch to see if something was the matter. Dad said, "I have my friends here." *OK, Dad, fine*, she thought to herself and went back to the porch to watch him, wondering if he might seriously be losing his mind. Then, a minute later, she saw six deer including a buck running down across the field in front of Dad, heading down to the river, Dad sitting there, perfectly still. "*My forest friends.*" He named the buck "Henry."

Thanksgiving on November 23rd was spent together in Deposit. Dad was withdrawing more, sleeping more. He didn't want to come down for the big meal. He sat in the big comfy recliner in the walkway area near the bathroom, wearing his old orange Texas baseball cap. We visited with him there, cozy, *koselig*, covered with his blankets, smiling at us. Little Cece and Stiel were there, and Lucia, James and I. Dad seemed happy, and teased the little ones. His eyes were bright, he seemed so "with it," and he was looking at us all with affection, but goofy-looking with a recently missing front tooth. He was sure, peaceful and calm as usual, but very tired. He again asked James with a smile, "Are you singing still?" Little Cecilia hid under the foot of his blanket, then popped out, and he pretended to be so surprised, smiling at her, enjoying her sweet face. Tender moments.

The last day we went up to say goodbye and Dad was sleeping peacefully in his big bed. When we came in, he heard Lucia's voice and woke up. His face was nearly glowing, his cheeks rosy and he looked at us all with such love – it seemed as if he had been dreaming something incredibly beautiful before he awoke. The warmth and peace in his face, the kindness in his voice was unforgettable. "James, did you get some property? You will get your farm, it'll come." (James and I were debating about building a homestead out in the country in upstate New York on family farm land– which we later did).

To Lucia, he said, with his eyes sparkling, "Lucia, I *love* your jacket," (it was brand new and he noticed it). He held on to her arm and spoke of his animal friends which he loved to observe. "You know, that eagle comes around and flies nearby. He could land right on your arm, with his great claws that look terrible but really he is a gentle creature and he'd never harm you." He told her she was going to be enjoying soccer, and I thought, *Oh, he's confusing her with me* as I used to love playing soccer. (The next month, Lucia was in Africa with her university and they all played soccer every day, Lucia loved it.)

Dad truly seemed almost Other-worldly and brimming with the light of an infinite Love as he spoke with us in a level of warmth unparalleled. (Heidi had experienced something similar, she told me, when she was home helping care for him. He mentioned angelic singing to her, when he awoke from a dream.) We kissed him goodbye, wondering if it might be the last time. The three of us had been praying for quite a while that God would bless the sunset weeks and months of his life and give him a peaceful ending to his days, all in God's timing, in God's way, according to His Will.

As we walked to the car to drive Lucia back to University, Lucia said, "You know, if Grandpa would be taken Home to heaven now, that would be OK with me." That was the first time she ever spoke in that manner, for she often said, "What would I do without Grandpa!?" her loving, calm and dependable Grandpa – since her birth, he had been an important, stable male figure in her life, always believing in her, encouraging her. James and I felt the same way about Dad's coming departure without verbalizing it - we were at peace – it was God's preparation, His kindness.

An Eagle's Passing

Three days later, on Tuesday November 28, Dad suddenly could not talk or walk - he couldn't get up and when he spoke, it was only a few Norwegian words. At the hospital in Binghamton, they saw no signs of a stroke but by the next day, his organs were simply shutting down, his breathing was labored and his heart beat irregular. Celia let us all know and began the somewhat complicated process of having Dad discharged and bringing him home where he wanted to pass away. Early on Thursday, Beau, James and I left Ohio, driving first to pick up Lucia in western NY. We arrived at Wilson hospital by 4 p.m. and entered Dad's room: he was awake! He nodded his head and smiled at us. Beau and I spoke to him in Norwegian mostly. He made funny faces at all of us, the usual grimaces, to make us laugh and let us know he was still himself. His chest gurgled but he wasn't in pain. He slept. When he woke at 6 pm I asked if he was comfortable and he answered with a very clear "Yes," in English.

Lucia refreshed his mouth with a special swab she dipped in water and her grandpa made his funny faces at her. His hands were all swollen and bruised from all the needle pokes. *How odd it is*, I thought, *seeing him so fragile, and how precious, to see Lucia's gentle care.* The other sisters sent me texts so that I would give Dad kisses from them all the while. Jack came to see his dear Grandpa and was overwhelmed with tears at first, but then he and Beau made Dad laugh, I mean belly laughter, which made him start coughing. Beau stayed at the hospital and slept in the recliner by Dad that night. Early in the morning, when a nurse came in to fluff Dad's pillows, he pointed to her and said in a distinct whisper, "Thank you."

On Friday we told Dad today would be the day we were "breaking him outa' there." Celia, the great organizer, had worked it all out for later that day. Dad said, clearly, with a big grin, "*Excellent.*" Gerd called me from Norway and wanted me to put the phone up to her brother's ear. She spoke gentle words and then sang to him, "Ingrid Sletten av Sillejord," and he smiled. It was the last time she spoke with him and it involved song – so appropriate for them both, and it moved me so, witnessing their goodbye. Tante Kari also called me and asked about Dad and wanted to be remembered to him. *Takk for alt.* (Thanks for everything.) Dad tried to take my hand, his movements jerky, but gentle. I kept writing to my other sisters in Ohio and Indiana to keep them updated. Several times Dad asked, "Heidi? Kjersti? Indiana?" He pronounced Heidi's name the Norwegian way which he never did (Hay-dee not High-dee).

Around noon, they said Dad was cleared to leave and Beau said, "*Vi gaar hjem*" and Dad repeated it (we go home) in Norwegian.

The service people got Dad home around 13:00 and he was temporarily in a single bed in the living room which had been his art and music corner. His niece, our cousin and nurse Kat Rood, came to help, too. She is a real gem. Lucia and I sat in chairs next to Dad's bed. Lucia asked if she could adjust his pillow, and he nodded. Afterwards, he looked at her with loving eyes and whispered, "So nice." He became so gentle in these last years.

Mishawn, knowing her grandpa's love of music put on a CD of Pavarotti, "Santa Lucia." Mishawn and Lucia pretended they were singing as the male opera voice booms, and Dad mimicked, too. Seeing their antics, Dad laughed a big belly laugh (and promptly began to cough and gurgle) but it was another moment of connection which we all cherished.

He slept off and on during the day. At one point he was looking up towards the ceiling with wide eyes, appearing to see things, moving his head a bit as if watching something. I asked him, "Dad, what are you seeing?" "What am I seeing?... WOW!" he said, in wonder of something *good* (Angels? Loved ones in heaven? Life memories? I do not pretend to know, but it filled me with thanksgiving, to see the way he was leaving us; there was no fear).

Later, the firemen came and carried Dad upstairs, so by Friday night he was back in his own bed. Kjersti and Heidi arrived, Julie had just had surgery so could not be there. Grandson Mikael drove up, too. We were altogether sixteen family members surrounding Dad. Occasionally, neighbors Kurt and Sherry stopped by and friend Alex, too. When Dad was awake, it was clear he was happy to see each one as we said our goodbyes in different ways.

Even through those difficult days, it seemed like Dad was taking care of *us* through his humor and his few words. He screwed up all the strength he had to do these things. Once he took hold of Beau's hand and pulled it to his chest and said, "I appreciate." Beau continued to sleep beside Dad each night so he was not alone.

On Saturday night, Dad's breathing slowed considerably and one of my sisters called us all in. Everyone surrounded his bed and said goodbyes, kissed Dad, etc. My niece Mishawn was dramatically sobbing on the floor, kneeling by the bed, hands folded in prayer and her daughter, little Cecilia, was kneeling and praying on the other side of the bed. Mishawn asked if she wanted to come over by her and the little one looked up from her folded hands, opened one eye and snapped back, "MOM! I'm trying to *pray* here!" I tried not to laugh out loud.

It was then quiet in the room, hushed, as we hoped for some precious, parting words from my father's lips. Then, he opened his eyes, and said, "*Well*, folks…" He always used to say "*Well* folks" when he was on his way to go to bed. He clearly was giving us a message of 'can you all please get out of here as I'm going to sleep now.' I found it to be *hysterical.* I went over to Heidi who sat in a recliner as people filed out of the room behind me. I put my head on her shoulder, giggling and trying not to laugh out loud. Someone patted my back, thinking I was sobbing, which only made me laugh harder. It was just too funny. Dad was not going to go out that way in the middle of drama with a million people around. He never wanted to be the center of attention. As Matt walked by, Dad made a final funny face at him, like his usual self. It was almost like he was saying to us, "*fooled you!*" Yet it was good, for each person indeed said a kind of formal goodbye.

By Sunday, December 3rd, Dad's breathing was even more irregular and he no longer spoke a word. Lucia had to go back to Houghton University, and when she said "Goodbye" to her grandpa it was the hardest moment of all for me. She held his hand for a long while, caressing his fingers quietly, looking into his face with such love, as if she were memorizing it. Lucia kissed her grandpa goodbye and said gently, "I love you Grandpa," and turned to walk away for the last time. Heidi, sitting in the recliner cried silently, as did I.

Heidi and I sang a few songs on Sunday morning and read a few Scriptures to Dad. James read from his Psalter a few times, his deep voice soothing and calm, words refreshing like cool water, accompanying Dad through the valley of the shadow of death.

There were many other things that happened in those few days, but I only record a few of the things I had written in my journal. Grandson Mikael sat by the side of the bed and spoke his goodbyes. People had their own ways of grieving and we tried to respect one another in those precious days of his parting. How grateful we all were, that Dad could be leaving this world in his home, in his own bed, in such peace, accompanied by many family members - such a gift!

Kjer and I went outside for a breath of fresh air on that Sunday afternoon. The cool, early December air felt good. As we walked down the field Dad had mowed hundreds of times, by the river, a majestic bald eagle soared overhead, silently riding up high, on the arms of the wind. Others had seen it that day, too, and it seemed appropriate, for Dad's name Ørnulf means "eagle-wolf" – strong and fearless as an eagle, smart as a wolf.

Later that day, I was alone in Dad's room, sitting in the recliner, watching him. His breathing was so slow. I counted each breath, precious sign of life...one...two...three. God breathed life into the first man, and he became a living soul. Breath of Life...four...five... Suddenly, Dad's face took on such a glowing, youthful appearance it startled me – he looked so young! I jumped up from the chair and knelt beside his bed, taking his hand in my two hands. I spoke his name, "Dad," and then, as quickly as it happened, the rosy color left his face and he turned a lifeless, ashen grey. His jaw moved up and down a few times but he did not breath again.

His soul had departed peacefully.

An Eagle had passed.

AN AMERICAN-NORWEGIAN CHRISTMAS WITH THE HOFFS

It was a cold, crisp Saturday morning in early December at Chestnut Grove in upstate New York. I was about 7 years old. I woke up, hopped out of bed and ran over to look out the window. It looked out over a small roof, facing down towards the old red cottage which hovered precariously above the Delaware River. I could not believe our luck: it had actually snowed again during the night. "PERFECT!" I shouted as I quickly dressed and whipped my long, thin hair up into haphazard pigtails shooting out at different angles from my head.

I ran down the long hallway and popped my head around the corner into my parents' room. Nope, they were not still in bed, so it was not as early as I thought. Leaving their empty room, I headed back down the hall to the top of the stairs. I briefly considered sliding down the railing and decided against it for 2 reasons: 1) I might get caught and 2) it was faster to run. I ran and hopped down the red-carpeted stairs, two at a time, left hand on the wooden railing, at the bottom turning the corner to head for the kitchen.

Ma was there in the corner, to the left of the kitchen sink at the old mixer, whipping up pancakes for breakfast. "Good mornin' Mags," she said, "What kind of pancake would you like today?" She was a world-class pancake shaper and I asked for Mickey Mouse. My little sister Julie was in the old white wooden highchair, fashioned by a great-great grandparent. We had *all* sat in it as babies. She was flicking Cheerios off onto the floor one at a time, Tiddlywinks fashion.

I sat down in Daddy's wooden chair, "The Captain's Chair," and waited for my pancake to be ready. "*Vær så god,*" (Here you go) Mom said, handing me the plate. I smothered Mickey in butter and maple syrup. Ma made herself a pancake which she burned slightly – that's how she liked them.

One of my older sisters straggled in, her eyes bleary with sleep, in contrast to my barely contained excitement. "You know we're gettin' the tree today," I said. "You'd better eat and get ready fast."

After we had all eaten, and Ma had cleaned up Julie's mess, we all began to get dressed to face the winter weather. "Bundle up good," Ma said, as she cleared the dishes from the kitchen table. It was a mad struggle to find all the needed accessories in your own size. "Ma, have you seen my red mittens that Farmor knitted me?" my brother Beau asked, milling through the "miscellaneous" wooden drawer in the pantry, odd gloves and socks flying. Vesla, our big Saint Bernard, was right there in the middle of all the chaos, tail wagging in hope of an adventure.

Daddy, who had been clearing the snow from the driveway, came in through the back door, a smile on his face, the bald center of his head covered with a Norwegian hat with a snowflake motif and a wiggling pom-pom on top. He made one of his silly faces to make us giggle and said, "Come on, you *bæsj*-hounds, let's go!"

The big sky-blue station wagon was warming up in the driveway, the white exhaust billowing out from behind. "I get the way-way back," called one of my sisters in a singsong voice, claiming the most desired of seats, which faced backwards out of the rear window. Kjer and I climbed in after her and the rest of the family piled in.

We drove into town and out to Loomis Hill to Kulesza's Christmas Tree farm *en masse*. We tumbled out of the car and began the seasonal search. Their tree farm covered many acres: a whole mountain of trees to choose from. We would select the biggest one (it had to be at least 8 feet tall). "What about this one?" Celia called out and we all traipsed over to see. "Well, it's kinda' scraggly on this side," another sister's voice came from the

*Margrethe,
Heidi, Kjersti
Julie*

back of the tree. We searched up and down the hill, running around the many trees, our laughter cutting through the cold air. When we finally found the perfect tree which we all could agree on, Dad and Beau would cut it down with a hand saw and drag it back to the car to tie on top.

The tradition of the Christmas tree hunt was repeated every year. One year we went for the tree on Kjersti's 16th birthday (December 14th), and she was the one to find the perfect tree that day. Daddy and Beau cut it down and she went to look at the remaining stump. I can still see her looking up from counting the tree stump's growth rings, her cheeks rosy-red, her eyes bright and green. "It's 16 years old!" she told us, "Just like me!"

Then there was one time the clever men cut off too many of the lower branches to get the tree to fit into the living room and into the tree holder. The result was a Charlie-Brown Christmas tree look-alike. The ever-ingenious Beau saved the day, however, by drilling holes and re-inserting branches. We called it "the Bionic Christmas tree" that year.

Ma struggled each year to get the timeless, seemingly antique, strings of lights to all shine. Back in the day, when one bulb went, they all went. I'd hear her gently cussing under her breath as she tried to untangle them and find the dead bulb. Finally, she'd get them sorted and handed them to Dad who would put them up on the tree. We'd stand in line as Ma handed out ornaments, us kids arguing over who'd get to hang the cool Norwegian elves on skis or an elf stirring a pot of *Julegrøtt* (Christmas porridge). We each had our own Christmas angel to hang. Mom always strung the Norwegian flags on the tree from top to bottom, in the old Norwegian tradition. The tree was also graced with metal clip things holding real candles, usually white, but Ma never lit them (she told of a tree once in her youth that went up in flames).

Ma kept the various homemade Christmas ornaments we had created over the years, like Beau's paper chimney Santa made from an old cigarette box or the classic, colored paper chains. These and others were faithfully put up on the tree until they fell apart.

The tree stood like a giant in the middle of the largest living room, which was kept cool in winter. When you opened up the white door to go in there, the unforgettable perfume of fresh pine would overwhelm your senses with delight, and to this day that smell floods my mind with precious memories of Christmases past.

Behind the tree was the door leading out to the side porch, which looks down on the valley. On that door, Ma always hung the Three Kings picture which she had made. It had pieces of various brightly colored cloth, cut out in the shapes of the three wise men bearing gifts of gold, frankincense and myrrh, carefully sewn onto a large black burlap material. The first King's robe was shiny, rich yellow, Ma's favorite color, followed by a robe of deep blue and one of bright red. These were all adorned with sequins and golden threads giving the feel of royalty. The "sand" below was swirls of glitter on glue, and a gold-colored metal rod held it up in place.

Ma would always decorate in the dining room too, especially the bureau below the big mirror. The mirror itself was framed in garland of shining red, silver and green. The bureau had angels holding candles, at least one small nativity scene, and always there were some of the things we had made as kids, regardless of the shape they were in with the passing of years (in the middle of the mirror she hung a wreath made of transparent plastic bags from the '70s which I think Kjer had made. I'd wager it's still in a box in the playroom closet somewhere, along with the grey dress-up wig, leftover Hoover vacuum cleaner parts from the 1950s, and a disheveled collection of baseball gloves.)

Above the ledge of the mantel was an old clock, next to which she placed my old plastic mouse, with his nose up in the air. There was a Norwegian pig, and some small Santas. From that ledge of the fireplace all the stockings were hung. Even Vesla had one. Daddy's was a tiny green sock but all the others were the usual red with white trim with our names written. Ma filled them mostly with chocolate and candies, and often a clementine, too.

The front hallway was decorated as well. On top of the yellow china closet standing on the right wall, if you faced the front door, was a sleigh led by three reindeer bearing elves. Nearby was my piggybank marked "Merry Christmas," shaped like Santa's sack full of toys. This was just to the left of an old, tall, handmade Norwegian *Julenisse,* or Christmas elf, with a mischievous smile who carried a sack over his right shoulder and held a brown walking stick in his left hand. At his feet were fluffs of white cottony snow. All this was framed with a border of green shining garland carefully arranged by Mom.

The handrail leading from the hallway to the upstairs was wrapped in more garland, and a Christmas ball ornament hung from red ribbon in between each of the rails.

We had the coolest old Nativity scene. Ma would carefully unwrap each piece and hand it out to us to set up one by one. I wonder how she managed to keep us all in line under such excitement. There was a bit of jostling over who got the boy with the lamb on his shoulders, and other choice characters. The Nativity scene was setup in the old wooden creche which was placed on the wooden bookshelf which could be swiveled around. One could lie on the green couch and look up at the precious scene of Jesus' birth, God become man, alongside the Christmas tree.

It wasn't like there was a lot of extra money for gifts, but somehow the tree was always overflowing with brightly wrapped packages. (Cecilia once snuck downstairs before Christmas Eve and unwrapped, then re-wrapped a present addressed to her as she couldn't wait to see what it was!)

I loved the way Ma would wrap the gifts. She always took the time to wrap each gift with such care. She would take tissue paper of one color, find a lovely Christmas card from previous years and cut it out and stick it onto the package, framed on both sides with golden cord, and written in her clear, straight printed handwriting.

My mother always made Christmas the most special of times in our family. She genuinely cherished the season and enjoyed it with a childlike delight which she has passed down to all 5 of us her daughters. To this day, each one of us, celebrates Christmas with passion. There was always Christmas music playing; Perry Como, Bing Crosby, or a Norwegian boys' choir singing "*Du Grønne, Glitrende Tre, God-Dag*" from an ancient 78 record. I imagined it was a recording of Daddy as a child singing in the Trondheim Nidaros Cathedral boys' choir. He had told us how he and his choir friends used to sing from a hidden spot, way up high above the congregation. That record sounded like angels singing.

Ma would help us to decorate the whole downstairs, and she baked and decorated all kinds of cookies, including Norwegian *krumkaker* and *gorokaker*. She was wonderfully gifted at creating Christmas spirit, and seeing as Daddy was Norwegian and Ma had lived and worked in her beloved Norway where they met, there were lots of traditions kept in honor of our heritage. This included circling the Christmas tree and singing Norwegian carols, some of which were complete with motions and clapping. My favorite was "*O Jul med din Glede.*" We also opened the gifts on Christmas *Eve* as they did in Norway.

(Eat your hearts out, poor American suckers: kids waking you up at ungodly hours on the morning of the 25th as we slept blissfully – gifts already opened and enjoyed).

On the 24th, the anticipation began in earnest when we would all sit down at the dining room table which was decked out it its fanciest garb, including the best china and the cute little *Julegris* (Christmas pig). For the lovely Christmas meal, we all sat in our usual places, Mom and Dad at the ends of the table, Grannie strategically placed between the two kids who had had the foresight to "call it" in advance. That was the one night we girls cleaned up the dishes so fast (I tried to hide out in the bathroom on occasion to avoid the labor – they called it "dishwater colic" – but it didn't work). Mom would count out each fork, spoon and knife from her Norwegian silverware after it was dried by hand, to be sure nothing was lost.

After the dishes, we would be sent upstairs to Beau's room to wait for Santa's arrival. One was *not* allowed to see Santa, after all. Celia, the eldest, herded us up there and closed the door as the excitement mounted. These were magical moments never to be forgotten. We listened for the familiar sounds of footsteps and reindeer on the front porch, the ringing of jingle bells, and finally, what we waited to hear, the front door opening and Daddy yelling out into the night, "Goodnight, Santa, goodbye!" At that cue, the door was opened, and all six raced down the hall, down the stairs and into the living room where, lo and behold, gifts awaited each one. There on the side, Grannie sat on the green couch, quietly watching the grand entrance, with her kind and knowing smile. Her attention to each of our desires and her generosity made much of this experience possible.

When all were in place, Daddy would stretch out on the floor, reach under the tree and read out a Christmas tag, "To Grannie, from Kjersti" and one after the other the goods were distributed and unwrapped.

Often, after all the gifts were opened and it was late, everyone might be up in bed but Ma would wait until there was "peace and quiet" so she could savor a few moments of solitude. She sat in the yellowish rocker, listening to Christmas music and looking at the tree. I sometimes caught her sitting there, watching the brightly lit tree, smiling, with a happy faraway look on her face. Perhaps she thought of the wonderful family and friends who had impacted her life over the years, or maybe she was just giving thanks for the chance to snatch a few moments to herself.

In her bedroom dresser she kept an old Christmas poem called, "The Road of Time" which said:

> "The Road of Time is a winding road
> But at Christmas corner we still look back,
> At Christmas corner we pause and gaze
> Through memories' mist at the dear old days…"

There were many a Christmas Eve when Ma's favorite nephew Tony would come for a late-night visit, bringing Daddy a big bottle of whiskey. When Tony was a teenager, Mom's dear brother Duane had passed away suddenly, and Dad had taken Tony under his wing as much as he could. One adventure they shared, Tony and Dad had been waiting for some train, laughing and talking, and they got to drinking in that train station and had missed the train altogether. You knew Tony had arrived at our huge old house, no matter what room you were in, his big booming voice was full of laughter and good cheer. Ma would lean up on her tiptoes to kiss her brother's eldest and only son. "Oh Tony, you *doll,* you, Merry Christmas!" she'd say with much happiness cracking in her voice. (We thought Tony was super cool: he was huge, and he always asked us girls to walk around on his vast back.)

Years past by too quickly, and we grew up and moved away but always held Christmas, and especially Christmas at home, as a treasure.

After my youngest sister Julie had married there was a Christmas when she and her husband couldn't make it home to New York from Ohio for the holiday, when her first child Esther was small. Their visit was postponed until the 2nd week of January. So that Julie wouldn't feel so bad about missing the important holiday at home, Ma told her, "I'll keep all the

Dad and Mom, who both loved Christmas

381

decorations up so you can see them when you come." When Julie and her family arrived, they all went into the living room to see the tree. Ma reached up to an old ornament which Julie had made as a child. "Do you remember this one, Julie?" she said. As she touched the ornament, it seemed every single pine needle on the tree simultaneously dropped from the branches to the floor, and the tree was transformed into a pitiful "Charlie Brown" style tree before their very eyes. Julie cracked up laughing, as Ma said, "*Well!* Will you *look* at that, has it been so dry in here?!"

With a smile on her face, off she went in search of the vacuum cleaner.

AFTERWORD – "Vi Holder Sammen"

I never expected this book to take over 20 years to write but my life took many curves and unexpected left-turns and other priorities won. Then, at the start of 2023, the year Mom would have turned 100, a great longing to complete the project intensified and I began to work on it with focused energy until its completion. With the years of writing, the book's content was modified and expanded, becoming fuller. And I changed, too.

What began as a gift for others became a journey enriching *me*. Looking through my old journals (I guess I am like my Ma!) has been richly rewarding, looking back through the good and the bad, the happy and the sad: there is always so much to be thankful for and somehow, it all fits together as it should, even the mysteries, like Mom's Alzheimer's.

Studying my parents' lives brought me closer than ever to them. Researching and reflecting led to a deeper understanding of who my parents were, of how they were shaped, of their disappointments, *their* unexpected left-turns as well as their successes and joys all of which led to us becoming a family.

The origins of the Norwegian side of our family, the Hoffs in Trondheim, were hardly more than a shadow before I began. Hearing Tante Gerd's stories brought me closer to Dad, my grandparents, and my aunts. Spending more time with my cousins and talking with them about what I had discovered in researching this book, further deepened the Norwegian family connections and brought it all into full living color.

I remember the day when Tante Gerd told us how one of the

Norwegians' rebellious actions against the Nazis was "wearing paperclips on our jackets."

"Paperclips!? Whatever for?" I asked her.

"Paper clips keep papers stuck together - these paper clips symbolized that the Norwegian people would stick together against the Nazis. *Vi holder sammen!* (We stick together)," she said.

My parents' journey led them from two countries to form a family which, in many ways, integrated two cultures. They stuck together through hard times and maybe their love for Norway played a part in holding them together, too, against the stresses of life and the harsh reality of one another's imperfections after "Norway" met "America."

Meeting with so many Norwegians in October 2023 knit my heart further to my roots. I will never forget the weekend that started in Røros with Dina and Putte picking us up and taking us to meet their Uncle Magnus. And then the ride up through windy heights, stopping the car and standing in the biting wind

Tante Gerd shows how they wore the paper clip during the war

so they could point out the way Dad and his friends had come from, and the way they would have taken, skiing further on towards Langen Farm, over the open, snowy terrain. All the way in the car, we talked and shared our thoughts about that time, with a mounting excitement as we learned more and pieced together the events. Then we came to Stugudalen and met Odd and Kristin and heard the sad and moving Morset family saga. (See Appendix L for excerpts from Peder Morset's letter to his family before his execution by the Nazis.) Losing his grandpa and others, and the sorrow of those losses impacted the entire family, even down to following generations. As Odd said, life is so fragile and easily destroyed, yet we find something to build strength upon. "Perhaps, for me, it has resulted in a better understanding of other people," he later wrote.

We sat around the table and looked at maps and talked, comparing pieces of information and figuring out the escape route based on all the information gathered.

Then the next afternoon we met Roar, Toralf and Rita, grandchildren of Ole from Langen Farm, who shared their families' stories with us as we sat companionably, and I told them my Dad's story which led us together so many decades later.

Indeed, we were gathered together with these new friends as I had been gathered together with my family and all of the other lovely people who had befriended us and helped make this book what it is during the course of the last year and a half.

We experienced again and again the true Norwegian spirit of hospitality and kindness and willingness to help; just as Mom and Dad had both known throughout their own lives. It is still true, "*Vi holder sammen.*"

I wish I could sit down today and tell my parents about this journey. I would also express how grateful I am for the many ways they have positively impacted my life. And I would ask so many questions!

"...the hand of the Mighty One...the God of your father... God has helped you and blessed you with a blessing from heaven above and with a blessing of the earth... He made the blessing of your father and mother stronger than the blessings of stable mountains and everlasting hills." (Genesis 49:24-26)

Indeed, my parents have made me rich, rich in the ways that really count, blessed with blessings that truly last. They gave us a foundation to build upon. Their marriage was far from perfect, and I do not mean to imply we had an ideal family life, but they gave us what they could, and it was truly very good, in the blending of American and Norwegian cultures, in their own humanity and imperfections, in forgiveness, grace and love and laughter.

I am ever so grateful. Truly, even until Eternity, "*Vi holder sammen.*"

"...a book of remembrance was written before Him..." (Malachi 3:16b)

ACKNOWLEDGEMENTS

The night after I broke my wrist in January 2023, I dreamt I held a newborn baby on my cast-bearing arm. When I awoke, I knew it was *this* book I was giving birth to, having determined that year to "set my face like a flint" for as long as it took to complete it. ("For with God, nothing shall be impossible," as it was said about another baby, centuries ago.) I would not have been able to "deliver" without the help of the following people:

Mom's dear old friends:

Aunt Lil Roy, with her gentle, warm voice, answering questions and sending letters.

Edith Wheelock Martin, "Edie," who spent time on the phone, too, listening patiently as I read Ma's diary from 1936, enlightening the entries with her shared experience.

Rest in peace, you two.

My older American cousins, Lana, Tony and Kat who sent me emails and articles and spent time on the phone, answering questions and making me laugh with the memories they shared.

Brian and Carol Nearing, James' brother and wife (and our good friends) listened for hours and shared our excitement about this book. In-laws, Mom and Pop Nearing and Den and Sandy Elliott have always been interested and encouraged me along the development of this "baby."

My brother, Harald Rikard Hoff, "Beau," took the time to make high quality scans of slides, old photos and Ma's albums which was invaluable. He also listened with interest and encouraged me every time I'd call with the latest breakthrough of information from Norway, Sweden or the Isle of Man.

My Norwegian cousins, Ingunn and Terje, Benthe and Ivar,

Grethe, and Ingar who shared their homes and listened with such focused attention and interest, fed us great meals and laughed with us. Your enthusiasm for this book encouraged me more than you know. Special thanks to generous Ivar, who gave me souvenirs of the war: a tiny box of homemade cigarettes, probably like the one Farfar shared with his Russian prison mate, coins and other treasures. He also looked up information in Norwegian books and sent me screen shots – so helpful!

Friends like Meg and Bruce Sawyer, Mark and Debbie Pearlmutter and Barb and Greg Jensen, who listened, asked questions and encouraged me. Barb kindly helped with corrections on early chapters, giving some helpful suggestions, too.

Linda Hegge, my Norwegian friend from when we lived in Luxembourg, who helped with a few tricky translations and listened to the early Dad chapter with interest and excitement.

Blake and Nicole Arensen, who helped with the formatting and final proofread of this book, in Kenya, Africa. You two rock.

For all those that prayed for me, family and friends, I thank you.

A special thank you to the writers' club, "Scribblers" in New Berlin, NY: you all encouraged and inspired me greatly.

Lars Hansson, retired professor from the University of Göteborg, who, from his doctoral studies, had the names of refugees in 6 of the 7 districts bordering Norway, but not Jämtland where Dad passed through. Lars looked up information about Dad and kindly directed me to the Swedish National Archives to obtain more, even providing me with phone numbers and website addresses.

People from the Swedish National Archive who answered many questions and sent me documents about Dad's year in Sweden. You were so patient with me.

How thankful I am for museums and their helpful staff! Bjørg Eva Aasen of the Norwegian Railroad Museum in Hamar answered many questions, Arne Langås from The Falstad Centre took the time to send me information about my grandfather's imprisonment and Per Kristian Sebak from Museum Vest of

Bergens Sjøfartsmuseum kindly sent me information which clarified Dad's seafaring experience.

Elin Johanne Jacobsen at Arkivsenteret Dora in Trondheim, who helped us find books and documents and shared pertinent memories her mother had told her about the war. Also, others there at the Arkivsenteret Dora, who stood nearby, listened and ran for books to help us. What a clever way Trondheim has repurposed the old German concrete U-boot bunker, renovating it into a space for archives, a library, etc.!

The people from the National Archives Services of Norway, Grethe Flood, Gunn Løwe, for your patience and sending me so many useful documents without even charging me! Each day more information came into my email, I was jumping for joy – what a blessing that Norway took the time to digitalize so many old records, without which there would have remained so much mystery about my Dad's journey during the war.

It has been absolutely unbelievable the number of people on the other side of the ocean that have come into our lives and assisted in various ways for this book's development. They have become friends, demonstrating a kindness and generosity that still amazes me: *TUSEN HJERTELIG TAKK* (a thousand thanks)

To Dina Margrethe Aspèn and her father Idar Oliver Putte Aspèn of Tydal who responded to that first email and were pulled into the story with us. We connected immediately. Over several months, they interviewed two elderly family members, step-dad Jørgen and Uncle Magnus, who had been border guides for refugees and Dina researched and wrote and spoke with me many times as we gathered and shared more information. Dina and Putte picked us up in Røros in October 2023, arranging and driving us to meetings with "Uncle" Magnus and Odd and Kristin in Stugudalen.

Dina and Putte showed us the way Dad traveled over to Sweden and somehow "arranged" a herd of reindeer to block the road on a bitterly cold, windy day so we felt a kinship with the Sámi that helped Dad on the last leg of his journey.

We brainstormed about Dad's journey, and Dina made maps showing the route, looked up weather reports for the days Dad traveled and spent hours helping as we discussed and exchanged ideas. The two of you have become friends and we cannot thank you enough for your support.

"Uncle" Magnus (Jon Magnus Rotvold), who took the time to talk about the years he and his family helped refugees over to Sweden as a boy despite the danger, although he was reticent to speak of such things and felt it was "only his duty" and nothing exceptional. Your humility humbled me.

Toralf and Roar Øverås, grandchildren of Ole O. Berggård, who led Dad and friends over the border into Sweden. Toralf and his wife, Rita Hilmo and Roar drove to Røros to see us and shared the few stories their mom, Reidun, had told about the war. Rita shared stories about her grandparents Peder and Ella Hilmo who also helped refugees. They brought a big picture of Langen Farm, where you can see how close the buildings were together where Nazi patrols stayed often during the war. We sat for hours, sharing stories in the cramped space of an AirBnB in Røros, drinking tea and eating chocolate and enjoying unique moments, knowing that my Dad and their Grandparents' paths had crossed so long ago, and there *we* were, becoming friends decades later.

Odd Håvard Morset and Kristin Ottesen, welcomed us into their home and spent hours sharing their family stories from the war. Odd opened up great maps and highlighted the path over to Malmagen from Stugudalen. I'll never forget the excitement, maps spread out in front of us, Odd, Dine, Putte, Kristin, James and I around the table, talking about journeys that took place 80 years earlier but changed the course of many lives. The Morset family had so many courageous members who shined a light for freedom at the cost of their lives. It was a privilege to hear your experience and what you learned from your father and grandfather. It was an emotion-filled afternoon. How unusual to find out afterwards that our father's names were just a few lines apart in the Malmagen Customs book of refugees, and to imagine that they may have worked together as lumberjacks in the forest of Sweden in 1943.

Dr. Sue Nicol, retired Lecturer from University College Isle of Man, who shed much light on Camp Onchan where Dad was screened before joining the R.N.A.F. in London. Your insights were invaluable. Thank you for your excitement about this book and spending time in phone calls, and sending me presentations, photos and critical information, and just being a kindred lover-of-all-that-is-Norsk.

Swedish author and journalist Marit Manfredsdotter of Brekken, who shared her thoughts and stories with me, connected me with Bo Lundmark and encouraged me by saying, "if a book is meant to be written, you can be sure that people will come out of the woodwork to help make it happen." So true!

Bo Lundmark, Lutheran priest and author, who spoke with me and kindly sent information about the Sámi of Gröndalen he had worked with, known and written about.

Author Birgit Rimstad, who spent time with me by phone, encouraged me and sent me photos and information about Kjesäter. What an enormous pleasure to receive her amazing book in the mail, *Unge tidsvitner – jødiske barn og unge på flukt fra det norske Holocaust*, about Jews that fled to Sweden from the Norwegian Holocaust. The interviews of refugees, conducted decades later, was incredibly helpful – and one mentioned "our" Uncle Magnus. How kind of you to send it!

Musician and author Per Vollestad who spent time by phone sharing about the importance of music and song during World War 2 in Norway from his book, *De Sang For Livet*, and reviewed some lines from my book, too.

The chapters on Dad's childhood and the war years in Norway would never have been written if not for my Tante Gerd, Dad's sister, "the Oracle." She listened, shared her memories, and kept us laughing. It was amazing the details she recalled, many times sharing something which was afterwards confirmed exactly to the letter, by articles or documents. For example, she said they were evacuated from Trondheim *after* Dad had left for Sweden. Sure enough, looking it up online, Trondheim was bombed July 1943, three months after Dad escaped. She was so careful about her thoughts, coming back on occasion (rarely) saying, "You know, I'm not 100% sure about X, so don't include that." She is one sharp lady, and I'm so proud she is my auntie. She was so very interested in this book, helping me not to give up but to "push" through to the end. How thankful we are for you, and your love for us (*Vi er så glad i deg!*).

The doctor who truly helped me through the worse labor pains of this book, who spent hours editing and cheered me on, was my husband of ten years, Dr. Bradley James Elliott. His insights and talents were invaluable – that PhD sure came in handy. We met in Houghton years ago, reconnected in 2013 and the rest is history. There are no words to say how much you mean to me. Thank you for joining me on this journey, for your patience and for helping me believe that I truly *am* a writer.

"Not that we are competent in ourselves to claim anything for ourselves, but our competence comes from God." - 2 Corinthians 3:5 NIV

NORWEGIAN GLOSSARY

Bløtkake – Norwegian cream cake with strawberries and bananas
Blåbær– Blueberries
Bunad – Colorful, traditional national costumes
Domkirke – Cathedral
Far – Father
Farfar – Father's father (Grandfather)
Farmor – Father's mother (Grandmother)
Fullmektig – District manager
Fyrstekake – Prince's cake, made of almonds
Gate – Street
Grenseloser - Border pilots, those Norwegians living by the border of Sweden who assisted refugees to escape Nazi-occupied Norway in WW2
Gorokake – Thin cardamom cookies made in a press
Gullgutten – *"the golden boy"* what my father jokingly named himself as a young man
Hjemmefronten – the "Home Front" or underground, or resistance movement in WW2
Hytte – cabin
Hønsegården" – the henyard
Høvding – Chief, what people called my grandfather
Jul – Christmas
Koselig – cozy, intimate and pleasant, giving a warm feeling of well-being
Kontorsjef – Office manager
Krumkake – A waffle-like cookie made on a decorative griddle usually shaped into a cone, often filled with cream and fresh fruit.
Lefse – thin, soft pastry made from potatoes, often eaten with

butter, cinnamon and sugar.

Mor – Mother

Multer – cloudberries

Nasjonal Samling (NS) – Norwegian far-right political party that collaborated with the Nazis.

Nortraship – The Norwegian merchant fleet outside German controlled areas in WW2 established by Norwegian authorities in London

Skål – "Cheers" literally means bowl

Sámi – traditionally Sámi-speaking indigenous peoples inhabiting northern regions of Scandinavia

Statspolitiet –the Nazi-run Norwegian police

Stripet - "striped" – what Nazi-sympathizers were called during WW2 in Norway

Styremann – Helmsman on a ship

Tyttebær – a type of berry, lingonberry

Tran – cod liver oil, taken every day by many Norwegians to stay in good health

Vi holder sammen! – We stick together! Common expression of solidarity used in WW2, symbolized by wearing a paperclip

ENDNOTES

1. Morin, Roberta conversation with Margrethe Hoff April 30, 2024. Roberta (Amundsen) Morin was Louise's daughter, granddaughter of Frank Surine.
2. McIntyre, Andrew, February 27, 2024, sent a copy of telegram which his grandmother (Bill's sister) had kept
3. 41-23817 | American Air Museum www.americanairmuseum.com archive/aircraft/41-23817
4. ABMC War Dead Certificate www.abmc.gov/print/certificate/496686
5. Duane T Rood | American Air Museum
6. Internment camps in Sweden during World War II - Wikipedia Jöran Granberg, [Memories of the Framby Internment Camp in Falun Sweden, 1942-1944], 2008
7. www.sonsoflibertymuseum.org/usmarinecorps/1stmarinedivisionww2/ shelby-zorn-lassiter-l707072.cfm
8. www.wnyc.org/story/118150-wnyc-wwii-broadcast-at-the-national-library-of-norway/
9. Rood, Jeanne, Hancock Herald January 8, 1948 "Jeanne Rood Says Don't feed Former Friends of Nazis" letter to the newspaper written from Oslo December 20, 1947
10. Ralph Bunche - Acceptance Speech (nobelprize.org)
11. See **Appendix A** - Ma's completed "Request for Report on Loyalty Data" Civil Service Commission Form 84A
12. Will H. Hays | U.S. Postmaster, Movie Czar & Politician | Britannica
13. https://www.digitalarkivet.no/kb10081104061197 Line 15
14. en.wikipedia.org/wiki/Trøndelag Teater
15. en.wikipedia.org/wiki/Henry Gleditsch
16. See **Appendix B** – Nidaros Boys' Choir Trondheim 1934
17. Köpple, J (2023) Email to Margrethe Hoff, 24 February.
18. Nidaros Cathedral | Nidaros Cathedral (nidarosdomen.no)
19. Köpple, J (2023) Email to Margrethe Hoff, 24 February.
20. Trondheim politikammers arkiv, vaktjournal April 9, 1940. Box 49, Statsarkivet i Trondheim (DORA)
21. Løchster, Jochan Trondheim Police Chamber archive, Box 49, Statsarkivet in Trondheim (DORA)
22. Myklebost, Tor, *They Came as Friends* (Doubleday Doran & Co. 1943 (translated by Trygve M. Ager)) page 12
23. Myklebost, Tor, *They Came as Friends, op cit.* page 79
24. Terdal, Leif, *Our Escape from Nazi-Occupied Norway: Norwegian*

Resistance to Nazism (Trafford Publishing 2008) page 31

25. Höye, Bjarne and Trygve Ager, *The Fight of the Norwegian Church against Nazism* (New York: The Macmillan Co., 1943), page 66
26. Myklebost, Tor *They Came as Friends, op cit.* page 266
27. Norway's Teachers Stand Firm, booklet published by the Royal Norwegian Government Press Representatives, 1942. NTNU.edu Skannet på en flerfunksjonsmaskin fra Xerox001[2].pdf (ntnu.edu)
28. Store Norske Leksikon snl.no/lærerstriden The teacher controversy was the Norwegian teachers' fight against the Nazification of the schools. For more info see Tyranny Could Not Quell Them! By Gene Sharp 1952
29. Myklebost, Tor *They Came as Friends op cit.* page 227
30. Vid gränsen. Mottagningen av flyktingar från Norge 1940 –1945 Dec 13, 2018 Doctoral Thesis by Lars Hansson, PhD University of Gothenburg (At the Border. Sweden's reception of refugees from Norway 1940-1945)
31. Myklebost, Tor *They Came as Friends op cit.* page 228
32. Ibid, pages 229, 233, 234
33. Everyday life - The National Archives of Norway (arkivverket.no) www.arkivverket.no/en/using-the-archives/world-war-ii/everyday-life#!#block-body-3
34. www.arkivverket.no/en/using-the-archives/world-war-ii/everyday-life#!#block-body-5
35. Harald Langhelle – Wikipedia Henry Gleditsch – Wikipedia and web.archive.org/web/20050524190052/http://www.tkb.no/historie/Langhelle.htm
36. Myklebost, Tor *They Came as Friends, op cit.* page 288.
37. Martial law in Trondheim in 1942 - Wikipedia
38. Web.archive.org/web/20050524190052/http://www.tkb.no/historie/Langhelle.htm
39. Web.archive.org/web/20050524190052/http://www.tkb.no/historie/Langhelle.htm
40. Myklebost, Tor *They Came as Friends, op cit.* page 288
41. Ibid, page 287
42. Fosdalens Bergverk – Wikipedia
43. Majavatn-affæren – Store norske leksikon (snl.no) Majavatn-saken (1942) - Norsk digitalt fangearkiv 1940-1945 - Fanger.no
44. Aasen, Bjørg Eva (2023) Director of Train Museum, Hamar - Email to Margrethe Hoff, October 24
45. Rimstad, Birgit conversation April 13, 2024 with Margrethe Hoff. Birgit interviewed some thirty Jews who fled to Sweden during WW2, which was the basis of her Master's degree and later, a book, *Unge tidsvitner – jødiske barn og unge på flukt fra det norske Holocaust*
46. *Røe, Tormod (1982). Merakerbanen 100 år. Historielaga i Stjørdalsføret. ISBN 82-990879-0-2*

47. Rimstad, Birgit conversation April 13, 2024 with Margrethe Hoff.
48. Ottesen, Kristin conversation with Margrethe Hoff October 2023

in Stugudalen. Kristin's grandfather was Einar Stueland – see Bergen Dovesenters Styre 1939 – 1953.
49. Tydalboka.no – See Section "Courier station at Aunefætten"
50. Lundmark, Bo page 4 *In the Shadow of the War* Yearbook Funasdalen
51. Sangen fra en dødsdømt 18-åring: «O kjære mor, kun fire timer har jeg igjen på denne jord» (forskning.no)
52. www.fanger.no/prisoncamps/855
53. Kandahl, Torolv, Norway fights on. May 12, 1942 Radio Interview by Gladys Petch, Royal Norwegian Information Services, NY office
54. no.wikipedia.org/wiki/Liste_over_illegale_aviser_i_Norge_1940–1945 List of Illegal Newspapers in Norway 1940-1945
55. The Illegal press activity in Trondheim www.strindahistorielag.no/wiki/index.php/Den_illegale_pressevirksomheten_i_Trondheim
56. Åke Fen, Radio interview by Gladys Petch Om Norges illegale presse; om produksjon og distribusjon av aviser, innsamling av nyheter [THE UNDERGROUND PRESS IN NORWAY] (nb.no) Nasjonalbiblioteket|Nettbiblioteket Royal Norwegian Information Services, New York office, September 5, 1944
57. Åke Fen Radio interview by Gladys Petch
58. Åke Fen Radio interview by Gladys Petch
59. www.sciencenorway.no/history-second-world-war-war/whats-the-truth-about-the-communist-resistance-in-norway-during-the-second-world-war/2091110 Frode Færøy, a researcher at Norway's Resistance Museum at Akershus Fortress, has investigated WW2 extensive illegal Norwegian press.
60. www.strindahistorielag.no/wiki/index.php/Den_illegale_pressevirksomheten_i_Trondheim The Illegal press activity in Trondheim
61. From the booklet "ALT FOR NORGE! Utgitt til Kong Haakons 70-arsdag 3.August 1942" av den KGL Norske Regjerings Informatsjonskontor London
62. Terdal, Leif *Our Escape from Nazi-Occupied Norway: Norwegian Resistance to Nazism op cit.*, page 65
63. Kersaudy, Francois, *Norway 1940* (Lincoln: University of Nebraska Press, 1987), pages 103-104
64. Radio series Gladys Petch NYC Royal Norwegian Information Services, "Norway does not yield". Mr X (Anker Øgaard, norsk journalist) forteller om den norske motstandsbevegelsen.NRK (the Norwegian Broadcasting Corporation), 21.06.1942
65. Sysselsetting og arbeidsformidling - Arkivverket Våren 1943 blei det etter press frå tyskarane sett i verk tiltak for å mobilisere all tilgjengeleg arbeidskraft. Dette hadde også samanheng med utviklinga av krigen. Lov om alminnelig nasjonal arbeidsinnsats av 22. februar 1943 kom i kjølvatnet av det tyske nederlaget ved Stalingrad. I innleiinga til lova heiter det at det norske folk må sette alle krefter inn i den kampen på liv og død som Europa fører mot bolsjevismen. Sosialdepartementet fekk fullmakt til å skrive ut all arbeidskraft som ikkje var fullt utnytta eller som blei brukt til arbeid som ikkje var nødvendig. Menn i alderen 18 til 55 år og kvinner mellom 21 og 40 år plikta å melde seg til registrering hos arbeidsformidlinga. Dei fleste

som blei innkalla blei sende til Organisation Todt sine anlegg.

66. Forced labour under German rule during World War II - Wikipedia

67. Jacobsen, Elin Johanne Conversation with Margrethe Hoff, October 25, 2023 Arkivsenteret Dora in Trondheim

68. Hansson, Lars, *Vid gränsen. Mottagningen av flyktingar från Norge 1940 –1945*, (At the Border. Sweden's reception of refugees from Norway 1940-1945) in the section, *Escape to the Border,* 2018, University of Gothenburg, PhD dissertation

69. Rimstad, Birgit H., *Jødiske barn og unge som overlevde det norske Holocaust Flukten fra Norge. Det svenske eksilet. Livet etter 1945* Masteroppgave i historie Institutt for arkeologi, konservering og historie, IAKH Universitetet i Oslo, vår 2013 (Masters in History)

70. Store Norske Leksikon - Grenseloser i Nord-Norge under andre verdenskrig

71. Hansson, Lars, *Vid gränsen. Mottagningen av flyktingar från Norge 1940 –1945*, (At the Border. Sweden's reception of refugees from Norway 1940-1945) 2018, University of Gothenburg, PhD dissertation

72. Lundmark, Bo *In the Shadow of the War* (*I Krigets Skugga*) article in Yearbook Funasdalen ämten 2017. Årsbok för Jamtli, Heimbygda och Jämtlands läns konstförening. Årgång 110. Tryck Elanders, Fälth & Hässler 2016

73. See **Appendix E** - Kjesäter Refugee Camp in Sweden - Three Youths' Register cards with interrogations April 1943

74. Tydalsboka.no/index.php/okkupasjonstid-og-etterkrigsar/?highlight=verdens%20krig&hilite=verdens+krig Section: *Tysk nærvær* (German Presence)

75. Tydalsboka 2 (L948.419t in Arkivsenteret Dora in Trondheim), page 268

76. Tydalsboka 2 (L 948.419t in Trondheim Arkivsenteret Dora), page 268

77. Rotvold, Jon Magnus, "Onkel Magnus," conversation with Margrethe Hoff October 21, 2023 in RØROS, Norway

78. Overås, Toralf and Roar (2023) Conversation with Margrethe Hoff October 22 at RØROS, Norway. They are grandchildren of Ole and Berit. Their mother, Reidun, Ole and Berit's daughter, told them this story about Tormod and their grandmother Berit.

79. Rotvold, Jon Magnus (2023) Conversation with Margrethe Hoff October 21, 2023 in RØROS, Norway. Uncle Magnus is relative of Idar Oliver Putte Aspèn of Tydal.

80. Tydalsboka.no page 68 of Tydalsboka 4

81. www.norgeshistorie.no/andre-verdenskrig/1753-flukten-til-sverige.html

82. Uthus, Bodil *Apent Landskap 70 nye og gamle naerbilder fra Selbu og Tydal* page 226. Reidun fra Langen Mai 1991 ("En kveld hadde far med seg to unge gutter heim som han skulle følge videre over grensa neste dag." Reidun was born August 1934).

83. Overås, Toralf and Roar (2023) Conversation with Margrethe Hoff October 22 at RØROS, Norway. They are the grandchildren of Ole and Berit.

84. Rotvold, Jon Magnus (2023) Conversation with Margrethe Hoff October 21, 2023 in RØROS, Norway. Uncle Magnus is relative of Idar Oliver Putte Aspèn of Tydal.
85. Lundmark, Bo Under section "Escape from Feragen" *In the Shadow of the War* (*I Krigets Skugga*) article in Yearbook Funasdalen ämten 2017. Årsbok för Jamtli, Heimbygda och Jämtlands läns konstförening. Årgång 110. Tryck Elanders, Fälth & Hässler 2016
86. Havard, Odd conversation with Margrethe Hoff October 2023. Odd's father, Ola Morset skied the same route Dad did, and his name is just a few names above Dad's in the Malmagen Customs Station log book (March 16 – see Appendix C). Odd's father described to his son the way he had journeyed over the border just weeks before Dad. He described following the Sámi from Gröndalen down to the station.
87. Bygdebok for Tydal, page 322
88. Tydalboka, See Section "Jews and War Prisoners"
89. How Norwegian World War Two refugees shaped Swedish migration policy - The Local Lars Hansson U of Gottenburg article in thelocal.no
90. Rimstad, Birgit *Unge tidsvitner – jødiske barn og unge på flukt fra det norske Holocaust, op.cit.,* page 38
91. Norwegians in Sweden during World War II - History of Norway (norgeshistorie.no) www.norgeshistorie.no/andre-verdenskrig/1754-Nordmenn-i-Sverige-under-andre-verdenskrig.html
92. Tormod and Ola Morset (Odd Morset's uncle and his father) passed this same way. Ola Morset fled from Norway in March 1943 as the Gestapo and the Rinnan Gang pursued the whole family which was deeply involved in resistance work. Ola's name is listed in the Malmagen Border police station log book on the same page as my father. "Ola ..in the moonlight skied… across the border," see page 181 in Per Hansson "*Og Tok De Enn Vårt Liv*" which describes the Morset family saga. They fled to Sweden after a tragic raid on their home in Selbu : one brother was shot and their father, Peder, and another brother were taken and tortured. Eventually Peder was executed in Trondheim in May 1943. See Appendix L to see excerpts from the immensely moving letter Peder wrote to his family from prison before his death.
93. Lundmark, Bo *In the Shadow of the War* (*I Krigets Skugga*) article in Yearbook Funasdalen ämten 2017. Årsbok för Jamtli, Heimbygda och Jämtlands läns konstförening. Årgång 110. Tryck Elanders, Fälth & Hässler 2016
94. Lundmark, Bo *In the Shadow of the War (I Krigets Skugga)* article in Yearbook Funasdalen ämten 2017. Årsbok för Jamtli, Heimbygda och Jämtlands läns konstförening. Årgång 110. Tryck Elanders, Fälth & Hässler 2016
95. Lundmark, Bo Conversation by phone with Margrethe Hoff, April 10, 2024. Bo Lundmark is a Swedish Lutheran priest who worked with the Sámi and wrote about two Sámi brothers who did resistance work, including helping refugees get from Gröndalen to the customs station Malmagen.
96. Lundmark, Bo interviewed by Marit Manfredsdotter in the article

Minnene fra krigen lever fortsatt - nearadio.no
97. See **Appendix C** - Malmagens Border Customs Log Book Sweden 1943
98. Flyktningar i Sverige - Arkivverket (Refuges in Sweden – Archives) Political Refugees can be searched by last name.
99. Manfredsdotter, Marit article Minnene fra krigen lever fortsatt - nearadio.no Interview with Bo Lundmark
100. See **Appendix D** - Tannas landsfiskaldistrikt Sweden April 1943
101. Anne « WWII Norge www.wwiinorge.com/our-stories/Anne Jackson (née Villars-Dahl)
102. Rimstad, Birgit, *Unge tidsvitner – jødiske barn og unge på flukt fra det norske Holocaust* (Norway: Glyndale Norsk Forlag AS, 2016) page 188
103. See **Appendix E** - Kjesäter Refugee Camp in Sweden - Three Youths' Register cards with interrogations April 1943
104. Flyktningar i Sverige - Arkivverket (Refuges in Sweden – Archives) Search by last name
105. See **Appendix E** - Kjesäter Refugee Camp in Sweden - Three Youths' Register cards with interrogations April 1943
106. Hansson, Lars *Vid gränsen. Mottagningen av flyktingar från Norge 1940 –1945* (At the Border. Sweden's reception of refugees from Norway 1940-1945) 2018, University of Gothenburg, PhD dissertation
107. https://foto.digitalarkivet.no/fotoweb/archives/5001-Historiske-foto/Indekserte%20bilder/6995321552.jpg.info
108. Radio.nrk.no/serie/museum/sesong/201712/DOOF01005017 December 16, 2017 *Kjesäter in the Second World War*
109. *Nordmenn i Sverige under krigen | Slekt og Data   Slektogdata.no "Frem til 1944 ble flesteparten av mennene sendt på skogsarbeid i regi av den svenske staten"
110. Norwegians in Sweden during World War II - History of Norway (norgeshistorie.no)
111. See **Appendix F** – Swedish Commission Refugee documents (11 pages in Swedish) for the documents about Dad's jobs and movement around Sweden as a refugee
112. Rimstad, Birgit *Unge Tids-Vitner op cit.*, page 88
113. Ibid, page 87
114. Ibid, page 101
115. Ibid, page 87
116. Flukten til Sverige - Norgeshistorie and The resistance struggle in Norway – Store norske leksikon (snl.no)
117. Anne « WWII Norge www.wwiinorge.com/our-stories/Anne Jackson (née Villars-Dahl)
118. Holocaust Encyclopedia, Norway, German Invasion of Norway, www.encyclopedia.ushmm.org/content/en/article/norway
119. See **Appendix G**- Arkivverket – Forsvarets Overkommando. 2. Kontor.Arkiv 8.1 Mottakersentralen…Flykninger ankommet med fly fra Stockholm som del av transportoperasjonen "Balder," 1944-1945, page 222 (Defense High Command Refugee Reception Center refugees arriving from Stockholm by plane as part of transporation operation "Balder")

120 Norwegian police troops in Sweden during World War II - Wikipedia

121. Elfviks gård – Wikipedia Swedish Defence

122. www.ibiblio.org/hyperwar/AAF/VII/AAF-VII-4.html#fn59 The Army Air Forces in WW2 page 111

123. Balchen, Bernt, *Come North with Me* (E.P. Dutton & Co, 1958), page 195

124. Ibid, page 261

125. Ibid, pages 262-263

126. Ibid, page 268

127. Ibid, pages 257, 258

128. Ibid, pages 263, 264

129. Parnell, Ben, *Carpetbaggers: America's Secret War in Europe* (Eakin Press, 1993) page 212

130. Balchen, Bernt, *Come North with Me* (E.P. Dutton & Co, 1958) page 267

131. Manx Radio programme about Norwegian Second World War internees in the Isle of Man Manx Radio programme about Norwegian Second World War internees in the Isle of Man - Sound Archive - iMuseum

132. (Manx Radio programme about Norwegian Second World War internees in the Isle of Man Manx Radio programme about Norwegian Second World War internees in the Isle of Man - Sound Archive - iMuseum

133. www.arkivverket.no/utforsk-arkivene/andre-verdenskrig/smakebiter-fra-arkivet/varslipp-2021?q="Operasjon%20Balder"#!#block-body-2

134. Nicol, Dr. Sue, conversation with Margrethe Hoff, January 24, 2024

135. Vollestad, Per conversation with Margrethe Hoff May 2, 2024

136. Nicol, Dr. Sue, History & Heritage public lecture at University College Isle of Man, The Isle of Man and Norway during WWII, June 2017

137. Norway in exile - The National Archives of Norway (arkivverket.no) Arkivverket/World War 2/Norway in Exile

138. See **Appendix G** - Dad 1944 Reception into England

139. See **Appendix H** - Dad's RAF Card

140. See **Appendix I** - The Norwegian Enlistment and Discharge Office - RNAF

141. www.Arkivvet.no

142. www.flickr.com/photos/trondheim_byarkiv/4723977893/ Amerikansk bombeterror mot Trondheim lørdag (26 July 1943) American bombing terrorizes Trondheim on Saturday July 26, 1943

143. Hansson, Lars *Vid gränsen. Mottagningen av flyktingar från Norge 1940 –1945* (At the Border. Sweden's reception of refugees from Norway 1940-1945) 2018, University of Gothenburg, PhD dissertation

144. See **Appendix J** – Farfar's Imprisonment Information

145. Arkivet.no/en/history/during-the-war ARKIVET Peace and Human Rights Centre, Kristiansand, Norway

146. Farmor showed the little fork to me and told me its' story the summer I spent with her in 1982.

147. www.sciencenorway.no/forskningno-norway-second-world-war/soviet-prisoners-of-war-in-second-world-war--nameless-until-

now/1446955#:~:text=The%20total%20number%20of%20Norwegian%20
war%20casualties%20is,Soviet%20prisoners%20of%20war%20who%20
lost%20their%20lives."Soviet prisoners of war in Second World War –
nameless, until now" Sciencenorway.no by Isak Ladegaard *30. January 2012*
148. Vollestad, Per phone conversation with Margrethe Hoff, May 2, 2024
Also see Per's book, *De Sang For Livet*, 2023
149. www.forskning.no/andre-verdenskrig-historie-krig-og-fred/sangen-fra-
en-dodsdomt-18-aring-o-kjaere-mor-kun-fire-timer-har-jeg-igjen-pa-denne-
jord/2067207
150. Vollestad, Per *De Sang For Livet* Kagge Forlag AS 2022 page 7
151. www.britannica.com/place/Norway/World-War-II
152. Cousin Grethe Findahl told us when she was at university, she brought
some German friends home with her to Larvik while Farmor was visiting
them. Farmor politely and quickly excused herself and went to her room.
Afterwards she told Grethe she was sorry she had to leave but she simply
could not bear to hear German being spoken.
153. Westfal-Larsen & Co. A/S www.theshipslist.com/ships/lines/
westfallarsen.shtml
154. Ole Severin Belt - Sjøhistorie (sjohistorie.no) www.sjohistorie.no/no/
sjofolk/358720/
155. www.snl.no/matros   Store Norske Leksikon
156 www.dcnyhistory.org/cannonsvilleindex.html   The construction of the
Cannonsville Reservoir in Delaware County, NY was started in 1955 and
placed into service in 1964, it holds 95.7 billion gallons at full capacity.
"When the water filled the valley, it consumed 19,910 acres of Delaware
County; eliminating 94 farms, destroying five settlements - Cannonsville,
Granton, Rock Rift, Rock Royal and Beerston, and displacing 941 people.
158. Luke 1:37 King James Version

APPENDICES

Appendix A - Ma's completed "Request for Report on Loyalty Data" Civil Service Commission Form 84A for working at American Embassy in Oslo

Appendix B – Nidaros Boys' Choir Trondheim 1934

Appendix C - Malmagens Border Customs Log Book Sweden 1943

Appendix D - Tannas landsfiskaldistrikt Sweden April 1943

Appendix E - Kjesäter Refugee Camp in Sweden - Three Youths' Register cards with interrogations April 1943

Appendix F – Swedish Commission Refugee documents – 10 pages

Appendix G - 1944 Reception into England (4 pages): Operation "Balder" index card Defense High Command Refugee Reception Center refugees from Stockholm by plane by operation "Balder" To the New Arrivals – Isle of Man Interrogation Camp Onchan, Isle of Man

Appendix H - London Military RAF card 1944

Appendix I – The Norwegian Enlistment and Discharge Office - RNAF

Appendix J - Farfar's Prison Card Trondheim Kretsfengsel

Appendix K - Dad's Seafaring Registration Cards from the National Insurance Office for foreign affairs (FFU), and the archive of the Norwegian Seafarers' Directorate, showing seagoing service registered in the Central Seamen's Register from 1949.

Appendix L – Excerpts of Peder Morset's letter from prison to his family before he was executed by the Nazis for his family's resistance work.

Appendix A - Ma's completed "Request for Report on Loyalty Data" Civil Service Commission Form 84A for working at American Embassy in Oslo

STANDARD FORM 84A PROMULGATED AUGUST 4, 1947, BY CIVIL SERVICE COMMISSION	**REQUEST FOR REPORT ON LOYALTY DATA** THIS FORM TO BE USED FOR INCUMBENT EMPLOYEES AND EXCEPTED EMPLOYEES WHERE INVESTIGATION IS CONDUCTED BY AGENCY (Part VI—Executive Order 9835)	

To:
The following information is furnished for identification purposes on the person named below. Kindly furnish a report on any derogatory loyalty information contained in your files. (The fingerprints of this person are attached.)

1. FULL NAME (initials and abridg- ments of full name are not acceptable)	(Surname) Rood	(Given name) Jeanne	(Middle or other names) ~~Rood~~ Dorothy

2. ALIASES AND NICKNAMES Legal signature is Jeanne Rood.
In early years sometimes known as D. Jeanne Rood.

3. DATE OF THIS REQUEST

4. SPECIAL NUMBERS KNOWN TO REQUESTING AGENCY (FBI number or FBI file number, passport number, Army or Navy serial number, seamen's certificate of identification, alien registration number, Social Security number, etc. Specify which)
Passport No.1498(FS230999) Social Sec. No. unknown but probably listed under D. Jeanne Rood.

5. PLACE OF BIRTH Deposit, N.Y.	6. DATE OF BIRTH October 4, 1923	7. TITLE OF POSITION, OCCUPATION OR PRO- FESSION secretary

8. SEX ☐ MALE ☒ FEMALE	9. MARITAL STATUS ☒ SINGLE ☐ MARRIED	10. IF MARRIED, GIVE SPOUSE'S FULL NAME, AND DATE AND PLACE OF BIRTH NIL

11. ORGANIZATIONS WITH WHICH AFFILIATED OTHER THAN RELIGIOUS OR POLITICAL ORGANIZATIONS OR THOSE WHICH SHOW RELIGIOUS OR POLITICAL AFFILIATIONS
Daughters of American Revolution, Potomac Chapter, Wash.,D.C.
Sigma Eta Sigma Honor Society, Strayer College, Wash.,D.C.

12. DATES AND PLACES OF RESIDENCE FOR THE LAST 10 YEARS

Date	Street	City	State
9/1/41	1326 Kalmia Road, N.W.	Washington, D.C.	
3/1/46	118nW. 13th Street	New York	N.Y.
4/12-47	Holmenkollveien 48	Oslo	Norway
10/30/48	---	Hancock	N.Y.
12/1-48	1326 Kalmia Road, N.W.	Washington, D.C	
6/10-50	Bjørn Farmannsgt. 4	Oslo	Norway

13. DATES, NAMES AND ADDRESSES OF EMPLOYERS FOR THE LAST 10 YEARS

Date	Employer	Address
Present time to present	Elektrokemisk A/S Rådhusgaten 23, Oslo, Norway	
12/1948-6/50	Norwegian Embassy	3401 Massachusetts Ave., NW Washington, D
6/47 - 10/48	Elektrokemisk A/S Rådhusgaten 23, Oslo, Norway	
3/46 - 3/47	Norwegian Inf. Service, 30 Rockefeller Plaza, New York, N.Y	
2/43 - 3/46	Norwegian Embassy	3401 Massachusetts Ave.,NW, Wash.D.C.
8/42 - 2/43	Bureau of Internal Revenue, Income Tax Div., Wash. DC	

6/1/50 - 8/1/50	Transit N.Y.-Oslo And vacationing in ~~Norway~~ Oslo
10/1/48 - 12/1/48	Living At home. Hancock, N.Y.
3/1/47 - 6/1/47	Transit N.Y.-Oslo- and vacationing in Oslo.

14. THIS AGENCY HAS LOYALTY INFORMATION REPORT(S) FURNISHED BY THE AGENCIES INDICATED BELOW:

AGENCY WHICH MADE THE LOYALTY REPORT	DATE OF REPORT	REMARKS

15. THIS SPACE RESERVED FOR RETURN REPORT TO AGENCY WHERE NO DEROGATORY INFOR- MATION IS DEVELOPED	16. NAME AND ADDRESS OF REQUESTING AGENCY Dept. of State, Washington, D.C. I certify that the foregoing is complete and correct.

SEE REVERSE FOR REPORT ON CASES WHERE DEROGATORY INFORMATION WAS DEVELOPED

404

Appendix B – Nidaros Boys' Choir Trondheim 1934

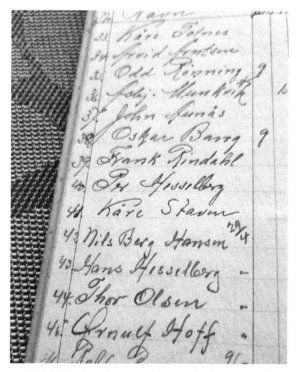

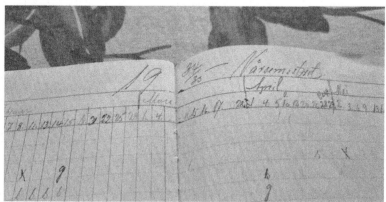

Dear Margrethe,
This is what we have found in our archives: Ørnulf Hoff started on 29.4.1934.
The year 1934/1935 there were 52 sopranos and 40 altos. The member lists and
photos from 1936-1940 were destroyed in the ward, so we don't know how long
he was singing.
Warm regards from Trondheim!
Johannes Köpple

Appendix C - Malmagens Border Customs Log Book, Sweden 1943

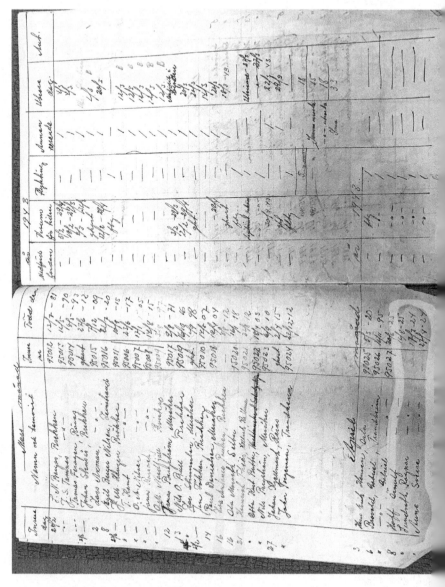

Appendix D - Tannas landsfiskaldistrikt Sweden April 1943

Förteckning
över utbetalda resebidrag för transport av flyktingar från Funäsdalen till flyktingläger:

Utbetalt den:	Utbetalt till:	Belopp:	Diarien:r.
22/11 1942	Jon Olofsson,Funäsdalen	45:-	12/42
2/3 1943	Olav Anker Haugene	24:7o	1/43
" "	John Mange Sjölien	24:7o	2/43
10/3 "	Egil Berger Nilsen	17:2o	4/43
19/3 "	Ola Morset	19:4o	5/43
" "	Mikal Brattba kk	17:4o	6/43
" "	Irene Jensvoll	17:4o	7/43
" "	Ingvar Jensvoll	17:4o	8/43
30/3 "	John Torgersen	19:2o	9/43
6/4 "	Hans Erik Tangevold Hansen	19:4o	10/43
7/4 "	Gabriel Brovold s:r	16:4o	11/43
" "	Gabriel Brovold j:r	16:4o	12/43
10/4 "	Ragnar Sundseth	17:4o	13/43
" "	Örnulf Hoff	17:4o	14/43
" "	Sverre Aune	17:4o	15/43
15/4 "	Einar Erling Bardosen	15:4o	16/43
" "	Villy Säther	15:4o	17/43
20/4 "	Odd Örjan	17:4o	18/43
24/4 "	Brynjulf Wahl	19:4o	19/43
" "	Wilfred Krogh	19:4o	20/43
" "	Odd Germundshaug	19:4o	21/43
11/5 "	Esbjörn Viken	13:4o	22/43
" "	Kaare Viken	13:4o	23/43
" "	Paul Odden	13:4o	24/43
" "	Kåre Sundt	13:4o	25/43
" "	Arvid Jensås	13:4o	26/43
" "	Arne Bårdstu	13:4o	27:43
16/5 "	Maren Hogna	15:4o	28/43
" "	Olov Hogna	15:4o	29/43
" "	Bjarne Hagen	13:4o	30/43
" "	Ole Helland	13:4o	31/43
" "	Karl Grönning	18:4o	32/43
26/5 "	Per Ek	13:4o	33/43
" "	Knut Lie	13:4o	34/43
28/5 "	Egil Berntsen	13:4o	35/43
31/5 "	Johan Grindvold	13:4o	36/43
10/6 "	Arnt Meyer Lie	13:4o	37/43
16/6 "	Viktor Nyvoll	13:4o	45/43
17/6 "	Peder Löberg	13:4o	46/43

Summa kronor   663:4o

Tännäs distrikts landsfiskalskontor den 25 juni 1943.
e.f.

A.Konow.

Appendix E - Kjesäter Refugee Camp in Sweden - Three Youths'
Register cards with interrogations April 1943

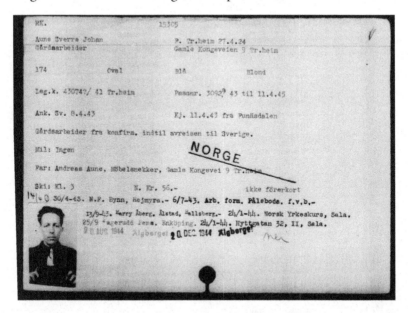

øK.   15306

Sundseth Ragnar   F. Tr.heim 17.3.24
gårdsgutt   Innherdsveien 51 Tr. heim

161   Oval   Blå   Blond

leg.k. 50679/42 Tr.heim   Passnr. 30938/43 til 11.4.45

Ank. Sv. 8.4.43   Wj. 11.4.43 fra Funäsdalen

Visergutt ca. 1 år. fra konfirm. Hotellpiccolo 6 mndr. De siste 2 år
gårdsgutt indtil avreisen til Sverige.

NORGE

Mil, Ingen

Far: Sverre Sundseth, Rørlegger, Innherèdsveien 51 Tr.heim

Ski: Kl. 3   Ingen penger   Ikke førerkort
30/4-43. N.F. Bynn , Rejmgra.31/5.Gillberg gård. Svennevad.
Adr.: 1o.6.43. c/o Bengtson, Björkmäter, Ervalla.

29/6-43. Gillberga, Svennevad, Örebro län. - 12/9-43. Hagen, Ålsta, Gällsberg.-
25/1-44. Norsk Yrkeskurs, Kungsongen 2, Sala.
Iflg. lenstm. i Västermanland 8/6-44; 3/3-44. Hyttgatan 32, sala.
2 0 AUG 1944 Klgberget 2 2 NOV 1944 Förnabruk 2 0 DEC 1944 Förnabruk

R A P P O R T

TIL KGL.NORSK LEGASJON

avgitt av politikonstabel Leif Berg.

12-4-43 avhörtes ved Kjesäter

Ragnar Sundseth,f.17-3.1924,i Trondheim av norske,gifte foreldre,rör-
          legger,Sverre Sundseth,og hustru Pedine, f. Vangberg,
          döpt og konfirmert i Ladesoen kirke,gårdsgutt,bor
          Innherredsvegen 51,Trondheim,ikke förerkort,ikke
          straffet,ikke medlem av politisk parti,eller NS,ingen
          av familien er medlem,hadde ikke penger med seg,
          forklarer
at han de siste to år har arbeidet ved Tyske hus i Trondheim som gård-
gutt. Her har han vært fra april 1941 til han nu rönte over grensen
på grunn av arbeidsmobiliseringgn. Han kom over grensen 8-4-43 sammen
15305 og 7.Begge disse er pålitelige.
          Bjarne Aberg ,Finn Olsen og Erling Gressmann er kommet tidligere
og kjenner avhörte.

Ragnar Sundseth.

RK. 15307

Hoff Ørnulf   F. Tr.heim 11.8.25
Skoleelev   Statsing. Dahlsg: 37 Tr.heim

175   Oval   BlA   Blond

Leg.k. 50961/42 Tr.heim   Passnr. 3094a/43 til 11.4.45

Ank. Sv. 8.4.43   Kj. 11.4.43 fra Funäsdalen

Avbrutt middelskole ca. 1½ md. før eks. grunnet avreisen til Sverige.

Mil: Ingen   Reiste E. 18/6-44 F.

Pmr: Harald Hoff, Fullm. ve N. S. B. Statsing. Dahlsgt 37 Tr.heim.

Ski: Kl. 2   Ingen penger   Ikke førerkort
30/4-43. N.F. Bynn, Kejmyra. 24.8.Herrborum,Söderköping.
18/9-43: Centralhotellet, Norrk.   20/9/43 Norsk Forlegning, Sjögestad.
5/10-43: c/o Nilsson, Lösingegt. 2 A, Norrköping.
6.10.43 Ö.Kyrkogt. 31. Norrköping 22/3-44. Östra Kyrkogt. 31, Norrköping. /2

RAPPORT

til KGL.NORSK LEGASJON

avgitt av politikonstabel Leif Berg.

12-4-43 avhörtes ved Kjesäter
Ørnulf Hoff,f.11-8-1925 i Trondhjem av norske,gifte,foreldre,fullmektig
Harald Hoff og hustru Margrethe ,f.Otnes,döpt og konfir-
mert i Lademoen kirke,skoleelev, bor Statsing.Dahlsgate
nr.37,Trondhjem,ikke medlem av NS eller politisk parti
formant og forklarer
at han har gått tre år ved Trondheim borgerlige realskole og var elev
ved skolen da han nu rømte over grensen på grunn av arbeidsmobilisering
-en. Han kom over grensen 8-4-43 sammen med 15205 og 6.
Han har ikke deltatt i illegalt arbeide eller annet som gjorde
det nödvendig å römme.
    Per Boknes er avhörtes söskendebarn og er kommet hit för.
Egil Alstad er fra hjembygda hans og er ansatt ved legasjon i Stockholm
og kjenner avhörte.

Appendix F – Swedish Commission Refugee documents
10 pages

Hoff, Örnulf   * 11/8 1925
                    norsk

* Trondheim
Skolelev   män

Heml x	Inkom den	Utgick den	Ans. x	Rem. x	Avsändare/adressat — ärende (event.)
		x			
			x		
			x		
				x	

ARBETSFÖRMEDLINGEN
NORRKÖPING
Tel. Namnanrop.
"Arbetsförmedlingen"
D. nr F. 121/44.

Vid besvarandet av denna
skrivelse torde ovanstående
diarienummer åberopas.

E/H.

Kungl. Socialstyrelsen,
Registrator H. Tholander,
Stockholm 2.

Norska medborgarna Örnulf Hoff och Asmund Palmberg
ha hänvänt sig till arbetsförmedlingen i Norrköping i anledning att de från Kungl. Socialstyrelsen erhållit sina
pass i retur men att förändelserna voro belagda med en
lösenavgift av 12 kronor.

Då nämnda personer en längre tid varit utan arbete
och för närvarande uppehålla sig på rekvisition, får arbetsförmedlingen härmed anhålla att passen måtte få till-
ställas dem utan kostnad.

Norrköping den 6 mars 1944.
För: NORRKÖPINGS STADS ARBETSFÖRMEDLING

Stig Billgren.
(Stig Billgren)

411

KUNGL. SOCIALSTYRELSEN
UTLÄNNINGSBYRÅN
BIRGER JARLS TORG 5.
Postadress: Box 2068. Stockholm 2.
Tel. Namnanrop: Socialstyrelsen
Tjänstemännens mottagn. o. tel.-tid
kl. 10—13

0042

Ink. till Soc. styr.
den 8.DEC.1943
D:Nr VI

Till (An — To — A) KUNGL. SOCIALSTYRELSEN

Ansökan om **visering** for (*Ifylles i två exemplar.*) **Visa application** for (*To be completed in duplicate.*)
Gesuch um **Visum** für (*In zwei Exemplaren abzugeben.*) **Demande** de **visa** pour (*A remplir en double.*)

1. tilnamn — Familienname surname — nom de famille	*Hoff*
2. samtliga förnamn — sämtliche Vornamen Christian names in full — tous les prénoms	*Arnulf*
3. födelsedatum — geboren am date of birth — né(e) le	*14/8-1925*
4. födelseort och land — Geburtsort und Staat place of birth and country — lieu de naissance et pays	*Trondheim Norge*
5. nationalitet — Staatsangehörigkeit nationality — nationalité	*Norsk*
6. religion	*Luther Evangelisk*
7. yrke (titel) — Beruf (Titel) Occupation (title) — profession (titre)	*Sjömann*
8. gift med (samtliga namn, födelsedatum) verheiratet mit (sämtliche Namen, Geburtstag) married to (names in full, date of birth) marié(e) avec (tous les noms, date de naissance)	—
9. barn (förnamn, födelsedatum) Kinder (Vornamen, Geburtstag) children (names, date of birth) enfants (prénoms, date de naissance)	—
10. Var vistas f. n. make (maka) och barn? Wo halten sich z. Z. Mann (Frau) und Kinder auf? Where are husband (wife) and children staying now? Séjour actuel du mari (de la femme) et des enfants?	—
11. Referenser i Sverige (namn, adress) Referenzen in Schweden (Name, Adresse) References in Sweden (name, address) Références en Suède (nom, adresse)	
12. Vistats i Sverige sedan den — Eingereist in Schweden am Arrived in Sweden on — Séjourné en Suède depuis le	*8/9 19 45*
13. Passet, som bifogas, är giltigt till den — Der Pass, hier beigefügt, ist gültig bis zum The validity of the enclosed passport expires on — La validité du passeport ci-joint expire le	*30/6 19 45*

Föredragandens anteckningar. — Reserverter Platz. — For official use. — Place reservée   Signum

S. S. nr 632. ²⁰/₆ 1942. 50.000 + ¹⁵/₇ 1942. 50.000 + ¹⁸/₁₁ 1942. 15.000 + ¹⁹/₁₂ 1942. 25.000 + ⁸/₆ 1943. 50.000 + ²⁵/₃ 1943. 50.000 ex.

14. **Uppehållsvisering** sökes för tiden **Aufenthaltsvisum** wird nachgesucht für **Residence visa** is required for **Visa de séjour** est demandé pour	²⁰/₁₀ 19 43 – ²⁰/₁₀ 19 44
15. Syftet med vistelsen Zweck des Aufenthaltes Purpose of stay But du séjour	Fabrikkarbeiter.
16 **Arbetsvisering** sökes för tiden **Arbeitserlaubnis** wird nachgesucht für **Labour permit** is required for **Permis de travail** est demandé pour	/ 19 – / 19
17. för anställning såsom — zur Anstellung als for employment as — pour emploi comme	
18. i (ort) — in (Ort) at (place) — à (lieu)	
19. hos (arbetsgivarens namn och adress) bei (Name und Adresse des Arbeitgebers) at (employer's name and address) chez (nom et adresse de l'employeur)	
20. lönevillkor — Gehalt conditions of employment (salary etc.) appointements	kontant (bar, cash, comptant) Kr. pet (pro, par) in natura (in kind, en nature):

21. Närmare motivering (event. å bilaga). — Nähere Begründung (event. in Anlage).
Further supporting particulars (if necessary in supplement). — Renseignements complémentaires (évent. en supplement)

KONTROLLAVD
9 DEC 1943

Norrköping den (the, le) 22/11 1943

Egenhändig namnteckning:
Eigenhändige Unterschrift:
Applicant's signature:
Signature du demandeur: Arnold Wolff

Bostadsadress och telefon under uppehället i Sverige:
Privatadresse und Telefon während des Aufenthaltes in Schweden:
Privat address and telephon during stay in Sweden:
Domicile privé et téléphone pendant le séjour en Suède: Östra Kyrkogatan 31 I
arbet: AB Firma Norrköping

Obs! Passet kommer att återställas per post under den uppgivna adressen. Under ansökans behandling inträffande adressförändringar torde ofördröjligen anmälas till *Socialstyrelsens Utlänningsbyrå, Box 2068, Stockholm 2.*
Zur Beachtung! Der Pass wird unter der angegebenen Adresse per Post zurückgesandt. Während der Antragszeit eintretende Adressänderungen sind sofort zu melden an *Socialstyrelsens Utlänningsbyrå, Box 2068, Stockholm 2.*
Note! The passport will be returned by mail to the address indicated. While the application is being examined, any change of address has to be reported immediately to *Socialstyrelsens Utlänningsbyrå, Box 2068, Stockholm 2.*
N. b! Le passeport sera retourné par la poste sous l'adresse indiquée. Tout changement d'adresse survenu pendant que la demande sera examinée devra être communiqué à *Socialstyrelsens Utlänningsbyrå, Box 2068, Stockholm 2.*

3

0042

Socialstyrelsen får härmed anhålla, att Länsstyrelsen, efter vederbörande polismyndighets hörande, behagade yttra sig över denna ansökan. *1334* *uppakalls/rättvis*

Stockholm den *15 12* 19

1943

På Socialstyrelsens vägnar:

Nedan reserverat utrymme för yttranden avser även det fall, då ansökan ingivits hos länsstyrelse eller polismyndighet för vidare befordran till Socialstyrelsen

den 2 2. JAN. 1944

Länsstyrelsens yttrande:

Från länsstyrelsens sida finnes intet att erinra emot bifall till ansökningen. Linköpings slott i landskansliet den 20 januari 1944.
RR.

Carl Hamilton

Lennart Almén

Polismyndighetens yttrande:

Poliskammaren får med överlämnande av närslutna polisrapport förklara, att poliskammaren på grund av sökandens arbetsanställning icke vill motsätta sig bifall till ansökningen.

Norrköping i poliskammaren den 19 januari 1944.

(Gillis Kleberg)

(ev. forts. å sid. 4)

Ink. till Krim. Polisavd.
i Norrköping
den *17 12 1943*
D. No *847*

N:o *738 7/0. 19 43/*Ink. till POLISKAMMAREN
i Norrköping den *17/12* 19 *43.*

RESOLUTION
*Överlämnas till poliskammaren
i Norrköping* som anmodas avgiva
yttrande i ärendet samt därmed och närmare
handlingen på lämpligaste sätt i
handläggas av den *16 dec 1943.*

(S. G. Odéen)

414

NORRKÖPINGS POLIS
KRIMINALAVDELNINGEN

P. K. nr 738 U.D. 1943.
H.D. nr 847/1943.

Doss. nr

Utl.disr.   Nr 102/XXII

Rapport.

M å n - dagen den 17 januari   1944 .

Ang.
H o f f, Örnulf,
norsk medborgare.

Ansökan om uppehållsvise-
ring.

Genom resolution av den 16 december 1943 hade
länsstyrelsen i Östergötlands län anmodat polismäs-
taren i Norrköping att avgiva yttrande med anledning av en från Kungl. Socialstyrelsen remitterad
ansökan från **norske medborgaren Örnulf Hoff** om upp-
hållsvisering under tiden 20/10 1943 - 20/10 1944.

Sedan ärendet överlämnats till kriminalavdelning-
en har tf. kriminalkonstapeln Erik Påhlsson verk-
ställt utredning i saken och därvid inhämtat följande:

Enligt härstädes fört utlänningsregister ankom
sökanden till Norrköping den 6/10 1943 från Lunne-
vad, Östergötlands län. Han har sedan ankomsten
till staden varit boende i huset nr 31 vid Östra
Kyrkogatan härstädes samt varit anställd som lap-
pare vid A/B Förenade Yllefabrikerna här i staden
sedan den 7/10 1943, vilken anställning han fort-
farande innehar. Sökanden innehar uppehållsvisering
till den 20/10 1943.

Sökanden har i saken uppgivit följande:

Han, som är av arisk börd och luthersk trosbekän-
nare, är född den 11/8 1925 i Trondheim, Norge,
inom äktenskap mellan norska medborgarna, järnvägs-
tjänstemannen Harald Hoff och dennes hustru, Marga-
reta, född Otnäs, ogift, samt i Norge senast boende och skriven i Trondheim.

Han hade vistats i föräldrahemmet till den 6/4
1943. Därunder hade han i 7 år genomgått vanlig
folkskola samt därefter 3 år i middelskole, varvid

han avlagt examen motsvarande realexamen i Sverige. År 1940
hade han konfirmerats i Trondheim. Någon anställning hade
han inte innehaft i Norge.

Den 6/4 1943 hade han ankommit till Sverige och då om-
händertagits vid flyktingslägret Kjesäter, där han fått
kvarstanna omkring 1 vecka. Därefter hade han förflyttats
till Öreryds förläggning, där han likaledes stannat omkring
1 vecka. Han hade därefter erhållit anställning som skogs-
huggare och blivit förlagd vid ett skogshuggareläger i Reimyre, i vilken anställning han stannat omkring 1 månad. Den
24 maj/hade han erhållit anställning som jordbruksarbetare
vid Herrborums gård, Bottna, inom Östergötlands län, där han
kvarstannat till den 19 september 1943. Han hade därefter
intagits på Lunnevads förläggning, Sjögesta, inom Östergötlands län, där han undergått vaccinering. Den 6/10 1943 hade
han flyttat till Norrköping, där han den 7/10 1943 erhållit
anställning vid A/B Förenade Yllefabrikerna, i vilken anställning han åtnjuter en veckoavlöning av omkring 60 kronor.

Anledningen till att han begivit sig till Sverige hade
varit, att han på grund av patriotiska skäl icke sympatisera-
de med den nya regimen i Norge, varför han fruktat förföl-
jelse från de tyska myndigheternas sida.

Han sade sig icke hava deltagit i någon som helst politisk
verksamhet och icke heller varit för brott eller förseelse
straffad eller tilltalad.

Ingenjören Yngve Möller, boende Norra Plankgatan 46, samt
anställd som avdelningschef vid A/B Förenade Yllefabrikerna i
Norrköping, har vid förfrågan uppgivit, att han, som tjänst-
gjort som förman för sökanden sedan dennes anställning i före-
taget den 7/10 1943, icke haft anledning till någon anmärk-
ning mot honom. Sökanden har en veckoinkomst av mellan 60 och
65 kronor.

Enligt här förda anteckningar är sökanden här i staden icke
tilltalad eller straffad för brott eller förseelse.

Som ovan.

(David Andersson)
kriminalkommissarie

(Erik Påhlsson)

KUNGL. SOCIALSTYRELSEN
UTLÄNNINGSBYRÅN
BIRGER JARLS TORG 5.
Postadress: Box 2068, Stockholm 2.
Tel. Namnanrop: Socialstyrelsen
Tjänstemännens mottagn. o. tel.-tid
kl. 10—13

15307

Ink. till Soc. styr.
den 16. APR 1943
D.Nr VI

Till (An — To — A) KUNGL. SOCIALSTYRELSEN

Ansökan om **visering** for (*Ifylles i två exemplar.*)   **Visa application** for (*To be completed in duplicate.*)
Gesuch um **Visum** für (*In zwei Exemplaren abzugeben.*)   **Demande** de **visa** pour (*A remplir en double.*)

1. tillnamn — Familienname surname — nom de famille	Hoff
2. samtliga förnamn — sämtliche Vornamen Christian names in full — tous les prénoms	Örnulf
3. födelsedatum — geboren am date of birth — né(e) le	11.8.25
4. födelseort (land) — Geburtsort (Staat) place of birth (country) — lieu de naissance (pays)	Norge
5. nationalitet — Staatsangehörigkeit nationality — nationalité	Norsk
6. religion	Luthersk-evangelisk
7. yrke (titel) — Beruf (Titel) Occupation (title) — profession (titre)	Skoleelev
8. gift med (samtliga namn, födelsedatum) verheiratet mit (sämtliche Namen, Geburtstag) married to (names in full, date of birth) marié(e) avec (tous les noms, date de naissance)	/
9. barn (förnamn, födelsedatum) Kinder (Vornamen, Geburtstag) children (names, date of birth) enfants (prénoms, date de naissance)	/
	/
	/
	/
	/
10. Var vistas f. n. make (maka) och barn? Wo halten sich z. Z. Mann (Frau) und Kinder auf? Where are husband (wife) and children staying now? Séjour actuel du mari (de la femme) et des enfants?	
11. Referenser i Sverige (namn, adress) Referenzen in Schweden (Name, Adresse) References in Sweden (name, address) Références en Suède (nom, adresse)	
12. Vistats i Sverige sedan den — Eingereist in Schweden am Arrived in Sweden on — Séjourné en Suède depuis le	8/4 1943
13. Passet, som bifogas, är giltigt till den — Der Pass, hier beigefügt, ist gültig bis zum The validity of the enclosed passport expires on — La validité du passeport ci-joint expire le	11/4 1945 ✓

Föredragandens anteckningar. — Reserverad Platz. — For official use. — Place reservée.	Signum

jril — 20/10-43.

417

14.	Uppehållsvisering sökes för tiden Aufenthaltsvisum wird nachgesucht für Residence visa is required for Visa de séjour est demandé pour	11 / 4 19 43 — 11/10 19 43
15.	Syftet med vistelsen Zweck des Aufenthaltes Purpose of stay But du séjour	Politisk flyktning
16.	Arbetsvisering sökes för tiden Arbeitserlaubnis wird nachgesucht für Labour permit is required for Permis de travail est demandé pour	.../... 19 ... — .../... 19 ...
17.	för anställning såsom — zur Anstellung als for employment as — pour emploi comme	Skogsarbetare.
18.	i (ort) — in (Ort) at (place) — à (lieu)	Tredje viseringsområdet
19.	hos (arbetsgivarens namn och adress) bei (Name und Adresse des Arbeitgebers) at (employer's name and address) chez (nom et adresse de l'employeur)	
20.	lönevillkor — Gehalt conditions of employment (salary etc.) appointements	kontant (bar, cash, comptant) Kr. .... per (pro, par) .... in natura (in kind, en nature):

21. Närmare motivering (event. å bilaga). — Nähere Begründung (event. in Anlage)
Further supporting particulars (if necessary in supplement). — Renseignements complémentaires (évent. en supplement)

KONTROLLAVD.
16 APR 1943

Öreryd ..... den (the, le) 11.4.43

Egenhändig namnteckning:
Eigenhändige Unterschrift:
Applicant's signature:
Signature du demandeur:

Postadress under uppehållet i Sverige:
Postadresse während des Aufenthaltes in Schweden:
Postal address during stay in Sweden:
Adresse postale pendant le séjour en Suède:

Obs! Passet kommer att återställas per post under den uppgivna adressen. Under ansökans behandling inträffande adressförändringar torde oförtröjligen anmälas till *Socialstyrelsens Utlänningsbyrå, Box 2068, Stockholm 2*.
Zur Beachtung! Der Pass wird unter der angegebenen Adresse per Post zurückgesandt. Während der Antragszeit eintretende Adressänderungen sind sofort zu melden an *Socialstyrelsens Utlänningsbyrå, Box 2068, Stockholm 2*.
Note! The passport will be returned by mail to the address indicated. While the application is being examined, any change of address has to be reported immediately to *Socialstyrelsens Utlänningsbyrå, Box 2068, Stockholm 2*.
N. b! Le passeport sera retourné par la poste sous l'adresse indiquée. Tout changement d'adresse survenu pendant que la demande sera examinée devra être communiqué à *Socialstyrelsens Utlänningsbyrå, Box 2068, Stockholm 2*.

Appendix G - 1944 Reception into England (4 pages):

Operation "Balder" index card

Defense High Command Refugee Reception Center refugees from Stockholm by plane by Operation "Balder"

TIL NYANKOMNE.

Meldinger fra Norge gir stadig opplysninger om at våre
landsmenn hjemme utsettes for livsfare ved uforsiktig
snakk utenfor landets grenser.
Forsvarsdepartementet finner det nødvendig å innskjerpe
den største forsiktighet ved omtale av forhold , og av
personer i Norge.
Spesielt framheves at det på det strengeste er forbudt
å gi opplysninger om hvor , ved hjelp av , og på hvilken
måte De har forlatt Norge.
Forbudet omfatter ikke bare offentliggjørelse i presse og
kringkasting , men også opplysninger som framkommer i ,
private samtaler og i private brev , - i det hele alle
meddelelser som kan gi utenforstående kjennskap til Deres
flukt eller til opplevelser i forbindelse med den.
OVERTREDELSE AV FORBUDET VIL KUNNE MEDFØRE ALVORLIG STRAFF
OVERTREDELSE AV FORBUDET VIL KUNNE UTSETTE DERES SLEKT OG
VENNER FOR TORTUR OG PINSLER.

**OBS.Naar De kommer over til England er det paa det strengeste forbudt
aa omtale avreisen fra Sverige til Isle of Man,samt opholdet her.**
Jeg har lest nærværende dokument og bekrefter å ha gjort
meg bekjennt med forbudet mot uforsiktig omtale m. v. av
forhold og personer i Norge., **samt avreisen fra Sverige.**

_____ Leipzig . den   8/ 5 - 44

        Ørnulf HOFF
Fullt navn med trykte bokstaver. _____
                                        Underskrift.

To the New Arrivals

JNR.....................................

SAK NR.....BN.807.....

LONDON

24, CONNAUGHT SQ., W. 2

Reg. nr. 15507 i Sverige.
Se rap. av 12.4.45 fra Leif Berg.

RAPPORT

TIL

RIKSPOLITISJEFEN

AVGITT AV : politikonstabel Rankert T h u l a n d .

    År 1944 den 28.juni fremsto som vitne på R/E i Camp Onchan n:

H o f f , Arnulf; f. den 11.august 1925 i Trondheim;skoleelev; ugift; uten forsørgelsesbyrde;har ingen militærtjeneste;angir seg hverken tiltalt;straffet eller botelagt.Er hjemmehørende i Stadsingeniør Dahls gate 57, Trondheim.
Han reiste til Sverige hvor han ankom den 7.april 1943 og har siden uavbrudt oppholdt seg i Sverige til han reiste til U.K. med fly fra Stockholm den 18.juni 1944. Han ankom til Camp Onchan den 19.juni 1944 oppført på Flyattasjeens liste.
Han er i besittelse av norsk pass nr.3094a/43 fra Stockholm,gyldig til 11.april 1945.
Han er gjort kjent med saken og sitt ansvar som vitne; er villig til å avgi forklaring; formant til sannhet; forklarer:

1.   Vitnet har ikke deltatt i noe slags illegalt arbeide i Norge.

2.   Vitnet har aldri hatt noe å gjøre med tyske militære myndigheter; han har heller ikke hatt noe å gjøre med Gestapo; Statspolitiet eller Grensepolitiet.

3.   Vitnet har aldri vært medlem av N.S. Heller ikke noen i hans familie har vært medlemmer i N.S.

4.   Årsaken til at vitnet reiste til Sverige var at han var trett av å v ære hjemme og fordi han hadde hørt at det var anledning til å komme videre fra Sverige til England og han gjerne vilde komme over til de vepnede norske styrker.

5.   Han reiste hjemme fra sammen med Sverre Aune og Ragnar Sundseth begge kammerater av vitnet fra Trondheim.
    De tok toget til Reitan st. Overnattet der. Men neste dag gikk de videre over fjellet til Kjøli gruber. Derfra fortsatte de til en hytte som de hadde fått anvist. Fra hytten fikk de følge videre til grensen ved Stugudalen.

6.   Han har tilbrakt den lengste tid i Norrkjøping ved en fabrikk.

7.   Vitnet har ikke korrespondert hjem fra Sverige. Han har ikke vært i kontakt med noen som har tilskyndet eller oppfordret vitnet til å reise hjem igjen til Norge.

Isle of Man Interrogation Camp Onchan, Isle of Man

Appendix H - London Military RAF card 1944

NAVN Hoff, Ærnald	Clerk	GRAD Ac 1	NO. 6872
FØDT 12.8.25 STED Trondheim	STATSBORGERSKAP Norsk	BLODTYPE

FOTO No.   IDENTITETSKORT F.P.33205 - 26.7.44   PASS   L.K.T. 59-21027

ADRESSE

GIFT? Nei   BARN UNDER 16 ÅR

NÆRMESTE PÅRØRENDE F: Harald & Margrete Hoff,
            Dahl's gt. 37, Trondheim
    Onkel & Tante: Erling & Ulla Flodland,
            Brooklyn, U S A

CIVIL UTDANNELSE (TEORI)

    Middelskole (3 år) i Trondheim 1943

GRAD

PRAKSIS

    I Tekstilfaget, Norrköping i 1 år 1943/44
        veving, farvning m.m.

CERTIFIKATER
    Ingen

SPROG
    Delvis Engelsk og tysk

MILITÆRUTDANNELSE

KOMP	PLASS	DATO	GRAD
Ingen			

VAR 9. 4. 1940 ANSATT Trondheim

MØTT TIL KRIGSTJENESTE Ikke   HVOR

TJENESTEGJORT I			
	FRA	TIL	GRAD

ANTATT I F.V. 1.7.44   SOM

LEGEUNDERSØKT 27.6.44

KATEGORI Str.A.

SENERE UNDERSÖKELSER

VAKSINASJON

TJENESTE I F.V.
FRA 26.7.44 TIL   VED F.P.K.(Regnskapskontoret)

REFSELSER		
DATO	FORSEELSE	STRAF

AVANCEMENT

DATO	GRAD	ANC

DIMMITERT   GRUND

DEKORASJONER

DATO	NORSKE	ALLIERTE

MERKNADER Rekl.AC2/Clerk wef.1.7.44(Jnr.7460)
Rekl.AC1/Clerk Aoc.wef.1.11.44(Jnr.8667)

DELTAGELSE I KURSER

DATO	KURSUS	STED	RESULTAT

PERMISJONER :

Appendix I – The Norwegian Enlistment and Discharge Office - RNAF

REGISTRATION CARD

Surname HOFF,   85393   Christian Name(s)   Ørnulf.

(IN BLOCK LETTERS)
Born : (year) 1925,   (date) 11.8.   (at) Trondheim.   Position : Skoleelev,

U.K. National
Passport No,   from   Registration No.
Closest Relations : (Name & Address). State "Parents," "Wife" or "Child." Underline those economically dependent on you.
Mor: Margrete f. Otnes. Statsingeniør, Dahlsgt 37. Trondheim.

Far: Harald Hoff.   "   "   "   "

Position   Income   Means in U.K.

Civilian education Folkeskole. Middelskole.   Do you speak English?

Situations during past 5 years

Previous Military or Naval Service

If none give reasons

Any Special Information

Permanent Address   R.N.A.F. V

Place of Issue :
Date   /   194 /

ALTERATIONS RE MOVEMENTS, ADDRESS, RANK OR POSITION TO BE ENTERED BRIEFLY

pm. Stokholt   5.1.49   N.Y   iµ NYK
aum. — ,, —   5.4.49   N.Y   "
pm. Alar   23.4.49   N.Y   "

Appendix J - Farfar's Prison Card Trondheim Kretsfengsel

Hoved-
fengslingsregister

NAVN: Harald H o f f
BOPEL: Stadts.Ing. Dahlsgt. 37, II etg. Trondheim.
TELF:

K r e t s fengsel, c

FØDT: 27,11.93 Trondheim.

Trondheim.

YRKE: Jernbanefullmektig.

Er innsatt i vare-
tektsfengsel i forbindelse med sak, J.nr. 417/44.
siktet for: gissel.
Bemerk:

Etter ordre fra POLITIFULLMEKTIG V o l d s t a d . Kl. 16.45
Trondheim 30.8.44

Fangen er den 4/9-44 i henhold til ordre fra insp. Voldstad
løslatt mot meldeplikt.
overført til
Hans adresse blir: som ovenstående

Appendix K - Dad's Seafaring Registration Cards from the National Insurance Office for foreign affairs (FFU), and the archive of the Norwegian Seafarers' Directorate, showing seagoing service registered in the Central Seamen's Register from 1949.

Nr. 753102   Navn _Hoff, Arnulf_   Født ¹⁹/₈ -23

Ind-tråd	Ut-tråd	Uten. dato	Klasse	§ A A SA	Arbeidsgiverens		Yrke	Y. nr.	Lønn	A Pre-mie uker	Anmerkning
					navn	konto nr.					
					Westfal-Larsen	58,179			721.-		
					B. Møller-Priensen	50,015			421.-		
					Gukowsen & Flakstad	5072			445.-		
									55.-		

Nr. 85223

Ekfefelle   Pikenavn   Født

Kort nr. Fors.pl.

S. nr.	Beh.	Beh. lege	Sykdomsdiagnose	Sykerygd						A trygd				Fys. beh., reise, flytning, yrkesopplæring m. v.
				Beh.	Fra	Til	Uker	Fra	Til	Uker	Fra	Til	Uker	

S. nr.	Hvem sykehusbehandlet Navn og adresse	Beh. dan	Beh. lege	Sykdomsdiagnose	Sykehus				
					Beh.	Fra	Til	Uker

APPENDIX L – Excerpts from Peder Morset's Letter to his wife Marit and sons, smuggled out by a priest before Peder's execution by the Nazis in Trondheim's Kristiansten Fortress.

May 16, 1943
To my dear ones: Marit and the sons which survived, I sit here thirteen days with two death sentences upon me...
There are 12 of us awaiting the same. I am the oldest, the next is 52 until about 20 years old.
There is nothing lacking, we have enough food and reading material.
The reading material which interests me now is The New Testament. The others have their magazines. They are good guys and... good mates – sharing everything with one another.
It comes to me sometimes that I suffer a great injustice. I am convicted of using a weapon with the police – I, who could not bear a weapon against any man – not even in self-defence. And I have prayed to God several times that I might come back to you, to you who I love. It is not because I do not want to die, but because I believe I could still do so much for you.
What befalls you is a hundred times heavier than what I face. I will gladly die, for I believe truly that I will meet Oddmund. I am so glad now that he got to go first.
Now I see clearly that all that which has befallen us, it is still a big blessing for us all. Therefore will I pray you that you must be happy and not grieve.
Dear Marit, try to be happy, I know that you love me with a woman's whole, warm heart. You can still do that afterwards. You are not separated from me if I go away, and God will give you strength...
You were in every way the one that stood nearest to me...a part of myself. Thank you, Marit, for all you have been to me...you are a true woman.
And to my sons, will I say: I love you all just as much...
God will bless you all...
Much has been laid upon you at a young age. But you have all experienced so much that now you are adults. I think often that perhaps Tormod will take this the worst... Dear Tormod, don't do that. None of us are guilty in this. Don't let this darken your future with its shadow...
Translated with permission from Odd Håvard Morset

BIBLIOGRAPHY

Balchen, Bernt, *Come North with Me* (New York: E.P. Dutton & Co, 1958)

Hansson, Lars, Vid gränsen. Mottagningen av flyktingar från Norge 1940 –1945 Doctoral Thesis, University of Gothenburg (At the Border. Sweden's reception of refugees from Norway 1940-1945), (Sweden: 2018)

Hansson, Per, *Og Tok De Enn Vaart Liv* (Norway: Gyldendal Norsk Forlag,1982)

Kersaudy, Francois, *Norway 1940* (Arrow Books Limited,1991)

Lundmark, Bo *In The Shadow of War* from HÄRJEDALENS GRÄNSBYGDER Jämtlands Läns Museum 2017 sent to Margrethe Hoff by email April 17, 2024

Myklebost, Tor, *They Came As Friends* (Garden City, NY: Doubleday Doran& Co, Inc, 1943)

Rimstad, Birgit, *Unge tidsvitner – jødiske barn og unge på flukt fra det norske Holocaust* (Norway: Glyndale Norsk Forlag AS, 2016)

Røe, Tormod, *Merakerbanen 100 år*. Historielaga i Stjørdalsføret. (Norway: ISBN 82-990879-0-2, 1982)

Terdal, Leif, *Our Escape from Nazi-Occupied Norway* (Canada: Trafford Publishing, 2008)

Uthus, Bodil *Apent Landskap 70 nye og gamle naerbilder fra Selbu og Tydal* Chapter: Reidun fra Langen Mai 1991 (Norway: Selbu-Trykk, 2022, second edition)

Vollestad, Per, *De Sang for Livet* (Norway: Kagge Forlag, 2022)

OTHER SOURCES

THE NATIONAL ARCHIVES SERVICES OF SWEDEN
  (Det svenske riksarkivet)

THE NATIONAL ARCHIVES SERVICES OF NORWAY
  (Det norske riksarkivet)

TRONDHEIM ARCHIVE CENTER
  (Arkivsenteret Dora in Trondheim)

THE FALSTAD CENTRE (Falstadsenteret)

THE NORWEGIAN RAILROAD MUSEUM
  (Norsk jernbanemuseum)

BERGENS MARITIME MUSEUM
  (Bergens Sjøfartsmuseum)

ABOUT THE AUTHOR

Margrethe "Maggie" Hoff is an exposure scientist who lived and worked in Europe for 27 years. She returned to her roots in upstate New York in 2019 where she and her husband lived in a solar-powered tiny house for five years. She plays guitar, piano, and loves to sing and write music when she's not reading, gardening, biking or taking walks in the woods.

Made in United States
North Haven, CT
20 January 2025

64544359R00241